Outlaw Masters Of Japanese Film

Dedicated to the memory of my late father, Paul R. Desjardins, 1919–2003, who went through hell his last few years and was consequently unable to finish his own book on his pioneering work in electron microscopy (in the field of plant pathology).

Also to my mother, Rosemary, who has had her own gauntlet to run in the last year and has managed to come out the other side.

Both my parents have always been loyal, loving and there for me, never turning their backs on me during my extended period of raising hell.

To my girl, Lynne Margulies, a truly great soulmate in all things, including the creative process.

And to the memory of late director Kinji Fukasaku, a great inspiration to anyone daring to think of giving up in the face of adversity. I was lucky to get to know him and to consider him as a mentor as well as a friend.

OUTLAW MASTERS OF JAPANESE FILM

CHRIS D.

I.B. TAURIS
LONDON · NEW YORK

Advisory Editor: Sheila Whitaker

Published in 2005 by I.B.Tauris & Co Ltd
6 Salem Road, London W2 4BU
175 Fifth Avenue, New York NY 10010
www.ibtauris.com

In the United States and Canada distributed by Palgrave Macmillan,
a division of St. Martin's Press, 175 Fifth Avenue, New York NY 10010

ISBN   paperback   1 84511 086 2
       hardback   1 84511 090 0
EAN   paperback   978 1 84511 086 4
       hardback   978 1 84511 090 1

A full CIP record for this book is available from the British Library
A full CIP record for this book is available from the Library of Congress
Library of Congress catalog card: available

Publication of this book was aided by a grant from the Japan Foundation

Typeset in Ehrhardt by Dexter Haven Associates Ltd, London
Printed and bound in Great Britain by T J Internatonal, Padstow, Cornwall

CONTENTS

ACKNOWLEDGEMENTS

There are several people without whose help this book would not have been possible and who deserve my thanks right off the top. First, my friend Yoshiki Hayashi, who all through the 1990s faithfully sent me videos of countless vintage Japanese genre films, recorded off Japanese cable that were otherwise unavailable for viewing. He has also showed me enormous hospitality whenever I have visited Japan, setting up several of the interviews here, shepherding me to various obscure movie poster and book shops, introducing me to many wonderful friends, including respected Japanese critics, performers and filmmakers. Second, Dr Akiko Agishi of Creative Enterprises International, who helped me coordinate virtually all the interviews in this book, provided me with affordable translation and basically just helped however and whenever she was able. The late Kinji Fukasaku, who took time from his busy schedule to personally write letters to many of the interview subjects here (and several who weren't able to meet with me) asking them to consider my interview requests, and was also just an all-around encouraging presence whenever I saw him. Isao Tsujimoto, who since 1994 (when he was then Los Angeles director for the Japan Foundation) has helped by encouraging me to apply for the Japan Foundation Fellowship Grant, which was an enormous assistance in my first trip to Japan in 1997 doing the research and interviews for not only this book but my voluminous, yet-to-be-published *Gun And Sword: An Encyclopedia Of Japanese Gangster Films 1956–1980*. Dennis Bartok, head programmer of The American Cinematheque in Los Angeles, who had the good taste, the faith in me and the intuition that I really did know what I was talking about when we first started programming Japanese genre cinema together in the mid-1990s. My girlfriend, Lynne Margulies, who has been extremely supportive, loyal and patient – and even enthusiastic – about all my projects and is truly a kindred spirit when it comes to a mutual taste for offbeat, extreme genre cinema. Toshiko Adilman, lifelong friend and translator for Kinji Fukasaku, who has become close friends with all of us at The American Cinematheque, has helped me immensely in all my writings on Japanese genre cinema and always selflessly offers her assistance when she is able. Philippa Brewster, my editor at I.B. Tauris, who showed me not only enthusiasm but patience. Sheila Whitaker, who after reading my DVD liner notes for *Female Convict, Scorpion-Jailhouse 41*, thought I might have a book in me and brought me to Philippa's attention. Finally, my mother, Rosemary, my late father, Paul, my brother, Vincent, and sister, Mary.

    Also, enormous thanks are in order to Ai Kennedy; Shoko Ishiyama; Kurando Mitsutake; Naoko Watanabe, Rie Takauchi and Masako Miwa of the Japan Foundation; Mr Kazuo Nawada; Mr Toshinobu Mogami; Yoshihiro Ishimatsu;

Stuart Galbraith IV; Quentin Tarantino; Julie McLean; Jerry Martinez; Andres Chavez; Takashi Miike; Akiko Funatsu; Hiromi Aihara; Kenta Fukasaku; Christian Storms; Linda Hoaglund; Kiyoshi Kurosawa; Dave Shultz; Barbara Smith; Gwen Deglise; Margot Gerber; Marc Walkow; Mark Rance; Kyoko Hirano; Eiichi Ito; Daniel Savitt; Patrick Macias; Carl Morano; Mona Nagai; Satoko Ishida and Masaki Koga of Shochiku; Merlin David; Yasue Nobusawa of Nikkatsu; Takayuki Yuhara and Tomoko Suzuki of Kadokawa-Daiei; Anthony and Matthew Timpson; Masaharu Ina, Tetsushi Sudo and Shozo Watanabe of Toho, Hideyuki Baba and Yasuhiko Nakajima of Toei.

GLOSSARY

(There are a number of Japanese words I use in the text, some quite often, and I feel that it's important to provide this glossary. These words are presented in italics in the text. However, there are some words, such as ninja, samurai, kabuki, that have entered into common usage in the English language, and I do not italicize or include them here.)

bosozoku – teenage car and/or motorcycle gangs, often serving as
  apprenticeships for the *yakuza*
chanbara – swordplay cinema, usually samurai
daimyo – samurai lord
eiga – film, movie(s)
gendai – modern
hara-kiri – ritual suicide with sword
ippiki okami – lone wolf
jidai-geki – historical period piece, usually samurai-oriented
jingi – honor and humanity; sometimes used to signify the code of gamblers and
  yakuza
jitsuroku – true account
kaibyo – cat ghost
kaidan – ghost story, strange tale
kempeitai – military police
manga – comic book
matatabi – wandering, gambling swordsman
ninkyo – chivalrous
onnagata – male performer cast in female role; common in nineteenth-century kabuki
theatre as well as early twentieth-century silent era films
oyabun – boss
pink – intense softcore porn, often with ultra-violent content
roman porn – pink films with 'romantic' as well as S&M-styled interludes
ronin – masterless samurai
shorinji kenpo – hand-to-hand fighting and boxing style combining philosophy and*
martial arts
sukeban – delinquent girl gang leader
yakuza – gangster
zankoku - cruel

INTRODUCTION

Originally, *Outlaw Masters Of Japanese Film* was conceived not in book form but as an idea borne out of brainstorming sessions for repertory film programming between Dennis Bartok and myself way back in 1996. I had met Dennis, head programmer of The American Cinematheque in Los Angeles, in 1994, when we discovered we held a mutual interest in Japanese genre film directors from the sixties and seventies. I had then initially worked with him as a volunteer consultant, first co-programming *Days Of Snow And Blood*, a retrospective on the late Hideo Gosha in the summer of 1996. Isao Tsujimoto, who was at the time the Los Angeles director of The Japan Foundation, a worldwide cultural institution devoted to spreading Japanese popular as well as traditional culture outside Japan, was enormously enthusiastic about our ideas and provided significant support as far as grant proposal encouragement, as well as creative input on our programs. The Hideo Gosha series, composed largely of his edgy, hard-boiled samurai films as well as a couple of his *yakuza* pictures, was a success. Since all three of us were anxious to see more of the films ourselves, as well as expose them to a wider audience, we subsequently co-programmed the first Outlaw Masters series in 1997, featuring films directed by Kinji Fukasaku, Kihachi Okamoto, Eiichi Kudo, Koji Wakamatsu, Kenji Misumi, Yasuzo Masumura and Kazuo Mori. A retrospective of the films of Tai Kato followed in 1998. Since 1999, when I came on staff at The Cinematheque, we have had an Outlaw Masters Of Japanese Film series – now known simply as Japanese Outlaw Masters – nearly every year, including additional retrospectives on directors, Kinji Fukasaku and Kiyoshi Kurosawa, and such period action stars as Raizo Ichikawa and Shintaro Katsu.

Before I go any further, I should explain our definition of an 'outlaw master'. This term is a simple way of describing the directors coming out of the Japanese movie production lines of the late fifties, the sixties and the early seventies: genre filmmakers who made genre movies usually labeled as samurai, *yakuza*, horror, *pink*, etc., but who pushed the envelope beyond the usual conventions in some way, either in style or content; or filmmakers who simply, in the tradition of great American pulp directors like Samuel Fuller, Anthony Mann, Don Siegel and Phil Karlson, just made damn fine, fast-moving pictures that could hit you squarely between the eyes and leave you breathless. They did not have to have arthouse movie pretensions. However radical their style of frame composition or editing, however daring or perverse their subject matter, these traits were virtually always borne out of intuition, an innate sense of aesthetics rather than calculation. Instinctive artists who were too often ignored, not only by critics in Japan but by Western critics as well. Although directors like Akira Kurosawa, Masaki Kobayashi,

Kon Ichikawa, Shohei Imamura and Nagisa Oshima have all made great genre
pictures, or films that have brilliantly deconstructed genre, we have very rarely
included their works in our Outlaw Masters series at The American Cinematheque.
You will find none of them included here in this book. All of them have never had
that much trouble being recognized as pantheon directors of world cinema, nor
have they been ignored in print. But there are other truly great directors hailing
from Japan since the fifties, directors who either toiled away or who are still toiling
away in the salt mines of debased genre, who are only now sporadically starting to
get their long-overdue recognition.

All the filmmakers in this volume represent Japanese 'outlaw filmmaking' in one
way or another. Some, like Kinji Fukasaku and Junya Sato, have redefined genre,
especially the *yakuza* film, by unobtrusively creating a tapestry of socio-economic
backstory and thus a political context for their ferocious, ultra-violent studies of
the Japanese underworld. Others, such as Eiichi Kudo and Kazuo Ikehiro, helped
to pioneer a hard-won intelligence and realism in period samurai pictures when the
studios were still too often pushing the tried-and-true formulaic and sentimental.
Kihachi Okamoto, like Seijun Suzuki, brought a bracing irreverence and kinetic
energy to his genre pictures, and was able to swing brilliantly from biting satire in
one film to tragic realism in the next with deceptive ease. Yasuharu Hasebe was an
unpretentious connoisseur of the action picture, adept at turning out tongue-in-
cheek soufflés as well as his more usual hard-boiled crime dramas. Teruo Ishii was
a unique example of an independent director who was able, through some sleight
of hand, to work successfully within the studio system for decades, biding his time
through occasional hack work, but more often bringing his offbeat sensibilities and
visual signature to everything he did. He was also a pioneer of integrating and
updating the erotic/grotesque tradition of nineteenth-century kabuki into a number
of Grand Guignol films in the sixties and seventies. Seijun Suzuki was another
independent director who worked for over a decade in the studio system, but someone
who was ultimately more confrontational and less willing to play the game than Teruo
Ishii. He was devoted to pushing the envelope until it tore, and, when that finally
happened, his studio employers fired him. From his third picture on, his films are
astounding examples of often hackneyed material rehabilitated to the point of being
nearly unrecognizable, all unpretentious genre pieces rendered fresh and supremely
entertaining, faithful to genre expectations but somehow simultaneously mind-
bending deconstructions. Masahiro Shinoda was a borderline case, someone who,
at first glance, seemed to be too much in the 'arthouse' mold. But ultimately his
nihilistic, cosmically existential and complex world-view won out. The fact, too, is
that he has been repeatedly ignored by many film journalists and critics in the last 20
years, writers whose subject is 'serious' Japanese cinema and who should know better.
Although he has made many non-genre pictures, his unusual genre masterpieces
Tears On The Lion's Mane, *Assassination*, *Samurai Spy*, *Under The Cherry Blossoms*,
Demon Pond and – especially – *Pale Flower* have remained comparatively unknown

and unappreciated in the West. I suppose one could also argue that Koji Wakamatsu is another borderline inclusion. At first glance, Wakamatsu would seem to inhabit that shadowy movie underworld that could best be described as Japanese underground cinema, an arena that has seen numerous 'outlaw' geniuses shoot comet-like through its firmament, from the likes of writer/directors Shuji Terayama and Toshio Matsumoto to Masao Adachi and Atsushi Yamatoya. But Wakamatsu, without question, was the most successful, not only in terms of output – well over 100 films – but also in terms of influence. Working in debased and despised forms, from the violent *pink* film to 'true account' serial killer pictures, he has brought a startling, visceral and uncompromising social, psychological and political context to nearly all his films (at least, the large handful that I have seen). He has, over the years, counted controversial, respected directors like Nagisa Oshima and Kinji Fukasaku as friends and associates, as well as more radical artists like Masao Adachi.

I also felt that it was imperative that at least two performers – one male, one female – from the golden age of 'outlaw' genre pictures be included here. Though not filmmakers themselves, Shinichi 'Sonny' Chiba and Meiko Kaji helped to shape and mold nearly all their projects once they found themselves stars, pictures that were largely action genre efforts tailored specifically to their larger-than-life charisma. Both are continuing to grow in reputation as their films receive a wider and wider audience all over the world.

But the 'outlaw' sensibility, despite the economic hard times for the Japanese film industry, did not die and fizzle out at the end of the seventies. The 'outlaw' spirit in genre pictures germinated and grew like some impossible-to-kill virus culture, blossoming again since the late eighties with films shot directly for video as well as the occasional theatrical release. Individuality and independence has flourished in the nineties through to the present with a new generation of Japanese 'outlaw' filmmakers, represented here by Takashi Miike and Kiyoshi Kurosawa. Both, in their own way, are mavericks, with unassuming yet fiercely opinionated ideas about genre filmmaking. Both have turned out films that are astonishing deconstructions and reinterpretations of genre cinema. And yet both still deliver faithfully to those anticipating an exciting genre picture. Like many of their predecessors mentioned above, they deserve inclusion in this book because they are able to simultaneously destroy and rebuild genre expectations within the duration of a single, exhilarating motion picture.

In each chapter that follows, you will find an essay briefly discussing the respective director's sensibilities, descriptions of a number of his films and a filmography as well as an interview with the filmmaker.

I have to report with some sadness and frustration that there are a number of filmmakers I would have liked to include here but who, due to matters of space, had to be omitted. I had especially planned on including an essay and a filmography on each of the four directors who are amongst my favorite Japanese 'outlaw' filmmakers. All four – Hideo Gosha, Kenji Misumi, Yasuzo Masumura and Tai Kato – have been deceased for a number of years and interviews were, of course, unavailable. They more than deserve inclusion here. Perhaps one day I'll be able to devote an entire volume not only to these four but to all the rest who didn't make it in, many others from the 1950s through to the 1970s. Filmmakers such as Nobuo Nakagawa, Kosaku Yamashita, Norifumi Suzuki, Sadao Nakajima, Kimiyoshi Yasuda, Kazuo Mori, Tokuzo Tanaka, Akira Inoue, Toshio Masuda, Keiichi Ozawa, Takumi Furukawa, Hiroshi Noguchi, Takashi Nomura, Shugoro Nishimura, Kaneto Shindo, Buichi Saito, Junji Kurata, Shigehiro Ozawa, Makoto Naito, Kazuhiko Yamaguchi, Ishiro Honda, Jun Fukuda and Motomu 'Tan' Iida, to name a few, as well as such directors from the 1990s and beyond as Shinya Tsukamoto, 'Beat' Takeshi Kitano, Takashi Ishii, Hideo Nakata, Rokuro Mochizuki and Sogo Ishii.

There are also unsung performers from Japanese genre cinema who deserve to be looked at and appreciated for their enormous contributions: such stars as Ken Takakura, Koji Tsuruta, Shintaro Katsu, Raizo Ichikawa, Bunta Sugawara, Noboru Ando, Tomisaburo Wakayama, Tetsuro Tanba, Hiroki Matsukata, Joe Shishido, Tetsuya Watari, Hideki Takahashi, Junko Fuji, Yumiko Nogawa, Michiyo Yasuda, Kyoko Enami, Reiko Ike, Miki Sugimoto, Hiroko Ogi, Junko Miyazono and Reiko Oshida – once again, to name only a few.

1

Kinji Fukasaku

1930–2003

Kinji Fukasaku was still directing the sequel to *Battle Royale*, *Battle Royale 2*, mere days before his death from cancer at the age of 72 in January, 2003. Even though his doctors had recommended that he curtail his workload with the hope of prolonging his life, the director had decided to ignore them and try to get one more movie under his belt before he shuffled off this mortal coil. It must have been especially frustrating for him, as he'd beaten the disease earlier in the decade and had barely slowed down his film career at the time. He'd also been a very active head of the Japanese Director's Guild since 1996.

Fukasaku directed his initial five films in 1961, the first four of which – two *Wandering Detective* and two *Vigilante With The Funky Hat* pictures – were short, barely 60-minute-long programmers designed to fill out the second half of Toei studios' double bills. His fifth film and first at feature length was *High Noon For Gangsters*, an anarchic, pull-out-the-stops gang heist movie filled to the brim with wild ideas and daringly offbeat juxtapositions. One element that is still relevant today shows the cynical, manipulating leader (Tetsuro Tanba) using the racist tension generated by two gang members, a southern cracker (Danny Yuma) who is jealous of his nympho wife's attention to a black GI deserter (Isaac Saxon), to keep the whole gang slightly off-kilter and under his thumb.

It never fails to amaze me that Fukasaku was able to integrate his provocative ideas about social injustice and the oppressive political and economic environment in Japan into many of his earliest films. *The Proud Challenge* is another example, the story of a reporter (Koji Tsuruta), blacklisted for his Communist Party ties, trying to expose a plot between Japanese politicians and the CIA to transfer weapons through Japan into Southeast Asia.

Fukasaku was one of the pioneering *yakuza* film directors trying to introduce a realistic ambience into gangster movies, something that would come to be labeled as *jitsuroku* when the trend really caught on in the early seventies. Fukasaku was at the head of the pack, unleashing such uncompromising films for the time period as *League Of Gangsters* and *Wolves, Pigs And People*. *Wolves* especially is one of the grittiest, angriest *yakuza* films ever made in Japan. It's as potent as any of his later mid-seventies pictures, with a lone wolf (Ken Takakura) plotting with his girlfriend (Sanae Nakahara) and an avaricious thug (Shinjiro Ebara) to trick his kid brother's (Kinya Kitaoji) delinquent gang to help them rip off a money courier at the airport. Things go wrong when Kitaoji's bunch return to the hideout, with the precious briefcase, before Takakura and discover just how much money was *really* involved. The kids hide the loot but get caught by Takakura and Ebara, who imprison them in a ramshackle warehouse, torturing them for the money's whereabouts. Meanwhile, their big brother (Rentaro Mikuni), a member of the gang that's been ripped off, is pressured to find his brothers and get back the cash. What ensues is a grueling contest of wills as all three brothers have to decide what is ultimately important to them. Events spiral out of control as filial ties crumble, ending in bloody, downbeat fashion. Awe-inspiring, topped off with Isao Tomita's amazing hybrid score of lounge jazz, Coltranesque squawk and distorted surf guitar.

Fukasaku continued to insert hot potato issues into his pictures. In *Ceremony Of Disbanding*, freshly unaffiliated gang member Koji Tsuruta becomes disillusioned with an old comrade and neophyte gang boss (Fumio Watanabe) when he decides to bid on the construction of gross-polluting factories in a poor neighborhood that is already surrounded by environmentally unsafe plants. Tsuruta not only identifies with the inhabitants but is upset because his old flame and her son live there. Tsuruta is ready to resort to violence with his estranged pal, but a young, rival gangbanger beats him to it, fatally stabbing Watanabe before his very eyes. Tsuruta realizes the boy is from the opposing mob and heads over to their HQ, where he not only wipes them out before being mortally wounded but also kills two corrupt politicians who'd instigated the bidding war.

The following year, 1968, Fukasaku continued to direct cutting-edge *yakuza* pictures for Toei, but also accepted an offer from Shochiku studios to helm an adaptation of famed mystery writer Edogawa Rampo's *Black Lizard* from a stage play by Yukio Mishima. Isao Kimura portrays shy, stubborn detective Akechi, who plunges down a rabbit hole of psychedelic depravity in his quest for female jewel thief Black Lizard (played by famous drag star Akihiro Maruyama).

Black Lizard was an unqualified success, so Shochiku asked Fukasaku to do another picture with the star, Maruyama, right away, utilizing a similar approach. To his credit, he did not want to jump right into something without adequate preparation. He prudently realized he would need time to make sure the sequel was done correctly. Shochiku already had the rights to another property, a crime scenario, and asked Fukasaku to undertake it in the interim. This became *Blackmail Is My Life*, which follows the exploits of a young up-from-the-slums swinger (Hiroki Matsukata) who will do nearly anything to keep his freewheeling lifestyle intact. His lucky streak of blackmailing unravels in vicious fashion when he and partners (Tomomi Sato et al.) unwisely target business allies of a powerful, behind-the-scenes political boss (Tetsuro Tanba).

Somehow Fukasaku also found time to direct the wild and woolly space opera *The Green Slime* the same year, an American–Japanese co-production starring Robert Horton, Luciana Paluzzi and Richard Jaeckel. It was a film that caused him considerable embarrassment in later years, in spite of the fact that many of his biggest fans, including Quentin Tarantino, have professed their love for the fast-moving, over-the-top monster fest. Personally, it's my favorite of Fukasaku's handful of science fiction movies.

Finally, Fukasaku felt ready to proceed with the second Maruyama project at Shochiku, and returned the next year to lens *Black Rose Mansion*. This time the story concerned a wealthy, introspective businessman (Eitaro Ozawa) who installs chanteuse 'Black Rose' (Akihiro Maruyama) in his elegant private men's club to attract customers, but is alarmed when she also lures scores of homicidal past lovers. Ozawa realizes too late that not only he but his wastrel son (Masakazu Tamura) as well have both fallen for the femme fatale.

Tetsuya Watari in *Graveyard Of Honor*

Fukasaku also directed *Boss* in 1969, the first installment of Toei's new contemporary *yakuza* series, *Japan's Violent Gangs*, a kind of *jitsuroku/ninkyo* hybrid with Koji Tsuruta as a world-weary gang boss returning from prison who finds that the newly allied corporate gangs have left little breathing room. Little by little, his gang is chipped away, with an underboss played by Bunta Sugawara the first to bite the dust. Tsuruta hopes to find common ground with the elder sharks dominating the waters and consults with an old friend (Ryohei Uchida) who is employed by the head godfather (Asao Uchida). But things don't go smoothly for long. Strangely enough, Tsuruta uncovers an ally in the bullying, drug-addicted boss (Tomisaburo Wakayama) of a bunch of rebellious misfits. Still, one by one the dominoes fall until only Tsuruta is left. He meets Ryohei Uchida outside a mob gathering, duels with him, and Uchida gallantly gives up his life to save his friend. He knows his new bosses are scum and wants to leave an unobstructed path for Tsuruta to assassinate them. Which Tsuruta does before being overwhelmed.

Fukasaku returned briefly to Shochiku in 1970 to direct the restless youth fable *If You Were Young – Rage*, tracking a closely-knit crew of hard-up young men who pool their resources to buy a dump truck but are soon torn apart in a chaos of class turmoil and youthful indiscretion. One of the boys perishes in a violent workers' demonstration, another is arrested for robbery, and a third gets married. The remaining two (Tetsuo Ishidate and Gin Maeda) try to persevere, but nightmarish complications set in when their jailed comrade escapes from prison. A vitriolic indictment of post-war Japan's absence of opportunity for young people.

Koji Tsuruta returns in *Gambler – Foreign Opposition* (aka *Sympathy For The Underdog*), one of the few entries in the *Gambler* series not devoted to a pre-WW2 period *ninkyo* saga. Tsuruta is banished by mainland *yakuza* to Okinawa where he ends up getting together with sympathetic friends (Noboru Ando and Asao Koike) and a belligerent youth (Tsunehiko Watase). All too soon, homicidal fireworks with not just the local gang led by scarred, one-armed Tomisaburo Wakayama, but American gangsters, too, suck the wind out of their sails. Even worse, hard-earned gains are threatened when the corporate mainland boss (Asao Uchida) unexpectedly arrives at the climax with his gangster minions. Brutally unrepentant with a subtle sense of humor.

Fukasaku has mentioned in several interviews that he feels 1972 was a turning point in his career, finally giving him almost total control over his projects. In *Under The Fluttering Military Flag*, one of his favorite, most personal pictures, a WW2 widow (Sachiko Hidari) pieces together the Rashomon-style puzzle of her soldier husband's (Tetsuro Tanba) fate through a bureaucratic maze and the contradictory recollections of surviving comrades. What emerges is a catch-22 struggle against madness as she learns Tanba had been executed for killing his insane commanding officer (Shinjiro Ebara), a man guilty of murdering his own men if they failed to follow orders. Fukasaku almost always shared screenwriting credit on his films, and this scathing anti-war indictment was co-written by director Kaneto Shindo.

Street Mobster, the sixth and final entry in Toei's *Modern Yakuza* series, looks at an arrogant wannabe (Bunta Sugawara) who rockets his way up out of the gutter into bigger rackets only to be constantly beaten down by the established gang. The mob boss (Noboru Ando), who remembers what it was like to be down and out, is fond of Sugawara despite his big mouth, but Sugawara's dissolute lifestyle, murderously jealous girl (Mayumi Nagisa, in a bravura performance) and messed-up pals prove his undoing. Nothing can stop the death-dealing that ensues in this classic, what amounts to a dry run for *Graveyard Of Honor*.

In 1973 Fukasaku undertook what was to become one of the most acclaimed *yakuza* films ever made. *Battles Without Honor And Humanity* was adapted from a series of articles by Koichi Iiboshi, a journalist and former *yakuza* recounting the genesis and gang wars of several prominent, post-WW2 Hiroshima *yakuza* families. Working from a scorching script by Kazuo Kasahara, Fukasaku follows a rootless ex-soldier (Bunta Sugawara) as he wanders through the chaos of a destroyed Hiroshima, finally falling in with a *yakuza* gang led by weaselly Nobuo Kaneko. He becomes blood brothers with a member of another gang (Tatsuo Umemiya) while in prison. When again briefly free, we see Sugawara's rise in the ranks, Umemiya's eventual death and another comrade, hot-headed Hiroki Matsukata, splitting off from Kaneko's bunch. When Sugawara is paroled again in the mid-fifties, he finds things changed and is disheartened at the factional infighting that has fragmented his former gang. Kaneko tries to manipulate him into killing Matsukata, who now has his own up-and-coming mob, but Sugawara is non-committal. Kaneko succeeds in getting someone else, and they catch Matsukata at his most vulnerable while he's shopping for a doll for his adopted daughter's birthday. Sugawara goes to his funeral, and the bosses attending, including craven Kaneko, panic as he pulls out his gun. But he shoots up the funeral altar where the hypocritical bosses have paid tribute, effectively rendering meaningless the idea of *jingi* (gang code of ethics).

The film was a huge success, and Toei turned it into a series, with Fukasaku once more at the helm for *Battles 2, Hiroshima Death Match*. Sugawara is something of a tangential character, observing the plight of a young outcast (Kinya Kitaoji) with low self-esteem who is constantly beaten by a sadistic

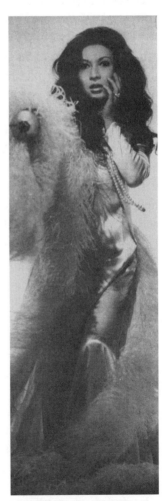

Akihiro Maruyama in
Black Lizard

neighborhood tough (Sonny Chiba). Kitaoji joins the gang of a callous boss (Hiroshi Nawa) and ends up falling in love with his browbeaten daughter (Meiko Kaji). At the climax, trying to ingratiate himself, Kitaoji makes a hit at Nawa's request, then hides in an abandoned restaurant. When the police close in, he blows his brains out.

Fukasaku and Kasahara continued the gritty *jitsuroku* exploration through the fifth entry, *Saga Conclusion*. All are exemplary examples of hard-boiled *yakuza* realism, featuring not only Toei performers like Sugawara, Umemiya and Matsukata but also such former Nikkatsu stars as Akira Kobayashi and Joe Shishido. When Toei wished to do more films in the series, calling it *New Battles Without Honor And Humanity*, Fukasaku and the star, Sugawara, signed on. However, this time a fresh squad of writers joined the ranks, including such veteran *yakuza* film scribes as Fumio Konami, Koji Takada and Susumu Saji. Once the sixth, seventh and eighth (and supposedly final) film had been lensed, Toei decided that they still wanted more. Fukasaku demurred, and Eiichi Kudo was drafted to direct the final installment, *Aftermath Of Battles Without Honor And Humanity*.

All eight of Fukasaku's *Battles* entries, taken either alone or together, are an astounding achievement. But, right in the midst of the series, Fukasaku conjured up another *yakuza* picture that eclipsed them all, a white-hot blast furnace of a movie that left only scorched earth in its wake. Based on a real-life character from Fukasaku's own home district of Mito, *Graveyard Of Honor* tracks the post-WW2 progress of alternately monstrous/bewildered Rikuo Ishikawa (Tetsuya Watari), a sociopathic loser who can't seem to get along with even his misfit *yakuza* pals. A humiliating scolding by his boss (Hajime Hana) leads to Ishikawa returning later with mayhem in mind, but the boss escapes mortal injury. With a contract out on him, Ishikawa takes refuge with a gentle woman (Yumi Takigawa) he'd once raped, and soon they develop as close as Ishikawa will ever come to a 'normal' relationship. He does the pinkie-trimming *yakuza* method of apology for his boss, and it brings an uneasy truce, but Ishikawa remains a shunned outcast. After being introduced to the dubious pleasures of heroin by a junkie whore (Meiko Seri, in a haunting scene), he begins hanging out with a ne'er-do-well addict (Kunie Tanaka). Ishikawa's addiction sinks him deeper into an abyss of self-pity that has him assassinating his best friend (Tatsuo Umemiya) over an imagined slight. At the same time, his girl, Takigawa, has caught tuberculosis from him, and Ishikawa wakes up one morning to find that she's slashed her wrists. Living in a hell largely of his own making, Ishikawa starts to go over the edge. When he begins to eat his girlfriend's bones after her cremation, his former gangmates plot his death. But they have to postpone their plan when Ishikawa and his junkie buddy barricade themselves inside their ramshackle crash pad in a shootout with the cops – something which Ishikawa manages to escape. Miraculously, Fukasaku's non-manipulative direction and Watari's painfully felt performance somehow manage to elicit compassion as well as horror at this inhuman monster. There's a scene near the end where Ishikawa is returning from a tombstone engraver, his impotent attempt to atone for his behavior towards his girl and murdered friend, when he stops in a back alley to fix. Suddenly he's ambushed by his former comrades, knifed repeatedly and left for dead. As he lies bleeding in the mud he looks up at the sky, and we see his point of view of a balloon floating in the azure blue. Accompanied by Toshiaki Tsushima's lyrical score, the viewer experiences one of cinema's most memorably heartbreaking moments. Amazingly, Ishikawa still doesn't die, finally jumping to his death from a prison hospital roof, landing in a literal explosion of blood.

In *State Police Vs. Organized Crime*, a live-and-let-live police detective (Bunta Sugawara) has his friendship with a *yakuza* drinking buddy (Hiroki Matsukata) destroyed by internecine gang warfare and the intervention of his supervisor (Tatsuo Umemiya), an anti-corruption crusader. Sugawara's police detective is one of those unsung anti-heroes, a man who remains true to himself because he believes more in human decency than he does in duty to his predominantly cold-hearted, bureaucratic colleagues. And, for that, he pays the ultimate price. An unsentimental, realistic dissection of the often strange symbiosis of Japan's law enforcement and underworld.

What was explored with a more omniscient viewpoint in *State Police* is looked at from a hot-blooded perspective in *Yakuza Burial*. This was Fukasaku and Tetsuya Watari's follow-up to *Graveyard Of Honor*, and Watari is astonishing as a brooding, maverick cop who doesn't have any patience for the niceties of bureaucratic red tape.

To his chagrin, he gradually realizes he has more in common with his *yakuza* nemesis (Tatsuo Umemiya) and the estranged wife (Meiko Kaji) of Umemiya's imprisoned boss. When Watari's supervisor (Mikio Narita) comes down hard on him, Watari initially thinks it's because he's become Umemiya's drinking buddy and Kaji's lover. But it becomes clear that high-ranking cops have established a tacit alliance with Umemiya's main rival, a politically savvy gang boss (Kei Sato), to help control street crime. When Watari hides Umemiya after he's been wounded in the ensuing gang war, Sato's gang kidnaps Watari and forcibly addicts him to heroin. As a result, Umemiya is ambushed and killed, and Kaji almost shoots drugged-up Watari believing he's the betrayer. We learn that she, herself, has been a closet junkie all along to deal with not just the criminal chaos around her but her own dispossessed Korean heritage. Watari has Kaji drive him to police HQ, goes upstairs to where boss Sato is in conference and empties his gun into him in front of his shocked police superiors. He then calmly leaves. Watari's former partner (Hideo Murota) follows him outside and shoots him in front of Kaji. Watari dies in her arms. A fascinating and emotionally exhausting flip side to the *Dirty Harry* archetype.

Fukasaku also made two very entertaining *yakuza* caper movies in 1975 and 1976, *Gambling Den Heist* and *Violent Panic – The Big Crash*, the latter being one of his wildest action films with the last third a non-stop demolition derby through the city as protagonists Tsunehiko Watase and Miki Sugimoto attempt to escape a lunatic caravan of covetous *yakuza*, police, TV reporters, bikers and independent thieves who are all attempting to get their hands on Watase's huge bank haul.

Hokuriku Proxy War was another *jitsuroku yakuza* blitzkrieg, this time set in a snowy Hokkaido coastal town where a murderously independent *yakuza* boss (Hiroki Matsukata) is bent on gaining tighter control of the territory. Sonny Chiba is slickly venal as an oily, smooth-talking gangster and Ko Nishimura convincing as always, as an elder boss obstinately sticking to his guns. The splendid Yumiko Nogawa unfortunately doesn't have much to do. Filmed on actual Hokkaido locations, the stormy winter atmosphere is savage and palpably chilling, giving the cold-blooded brutality on display a teeth-chattering edge.

Although Fukasaku did not direct many *jidai-geki* films, the ones he *did* do were generally designed as all-star epics. In *Shogun's Samurai*, a fanatical, power-obsessed Lord Yagyu (Kinnosuke Yorozuya Nakamura) will do anything to keep the disfigured, going-mad Shogun (Hiroki Matsukata) in office, including genocide and warring with his own son, one-eyed Jubei (Sonny Chiba). This was the feature-length film version of a phemonenally popular seventies Japanese TV show, *Yagyu Clan Conspiracy*. At Toei's behest, Fukasaku also directed his own version of *The Loyal 47 Ronin* the same year, *The Fall Of Ako Castle*. The all-star cast was headed by Kinnosuke Yorozuya, Sonny Chiba and Mieko Harada, and eschewed much of the sentimental, elegiac elements that helped to capsize many of the other versions of *Chushingura* that have been produced since the silent era.

Message From Space was the big-screen counterpart of another popular Japanese TV series known as *Swords Of The Space Ark*. Vic Morrow, Sonny Chiba and Hiroyuki Sanada lead the cast of interplanetary heroes in response to a distress signal from a planet in trouble in an imaginative, *Star Wars*-inspired sci-fi/fantasy. Be forewarned, though, that the voice dubbing in the English-language version of *Message* is some of the worst the viewer will ever encounter. That, in concert with the only so-so effects and grating-on-the-eyes production design, makes this one of Fukasaku's few hard-to-sit-through films.

Between 1980 and 1983 Fukasaku labored on three productions for the very hands-on producer Haruki Kadokawa, the self-made head of a vast publishing empire that often produced movie versions of their most successful best-sellers. Although Kadokawa films from the nineties have often been good to excellent (the original version of *Ring* directed by Hideo Nakata is a prime example), his efforts in the eighties were a decidedly more mixed bag. *Virus*, *Samurai Reincarnation* and *Legend Of The Eight Samurai* are all epics, and they all suffer from an overly ambitious vision without an adequate-size budget or shooting schedule to properly address that vision. All three have moments of power and patches that are very entertaining. In some ways, *Virus* is the most watchable. It's the chronicle of a germ warfare accident that goes unreported due to the fear of political repercussions, and, as a consequence, only a mere handful of people are left on earth before the last frame unspools. *Samurai Reincarnation* features Sonny Chiba again as Jubei Yagyu, but this time he's up against an executed Christian samurai, Amakusa Shiro Tokisada (Kenji Sawada), who has come back from the dead. Making a pact with the devil, Tokisada has resurrected three of Japan's most famous swordsmen, including Musashi Miyamoto (Ken Ogata in one of the most God-awful wigs you'll ever see in any movie). Collaborating with cinematographer Kiyoshi Hasegawa and art director Tokumichi Igawa, Fukasaku establishes a hypnotic blend of kabuki theatricality, bone-crunching martial arts mayhem, dreamlike erotica and creepy supernatural horror. *Legend Of The Eight Samurai* was the latest version of *Satomi Hakkenden*, a famous samurai legend incorporating sword-and-sorcery-style fantasy. However, not only are some of the production values questionable, the English-language version is almost impossible to sit through.

In 1992 Fukasaku returned to crime action films with *Triple Cross*, a tale of labyrinthine relationships and gruelling violence punctuated with dark humor. A wronged lone wolf (Kenichi Hagiwara), a bleached-blonde pretty-boy conman, his savvy, punk rock girlfriend, a coked-out hitman (Yoshio Harada), a Japanese heavy metal band and a small-time *yakuza* clan all vie for the possession of a treasure trove of cash. The last half-hour is non-stop mayhem, with some out-of-control Hong Kong action influence blended in with old-school, seventies-style brutality.

With *Crest Of Betrayal*, Fukasaku cultivated a hothouse hybrid of two of the most famous Japanese period stories, *Ghost Of Yotsuya* (*Yotsuya Kaidan*) and *The Loyal 47 Ronin* (*Chushingura*). Koichi Sato is Iemon, one of the 47 masterless samurai plotting revenge after their lord is forced to commit *hara-kiri*. He is also being haunted by Oiwa, the wife he murdered to marry an insane rich girl, Oume. Phantasmagorical imagery, swordfights and colorful kabuki production design mingle in this examination of the spiritual microcosm of the feudal psyche.

Battle Royale was Fukasaku's last fully completed picture, and it stands as one of his most uncompromising, an ultra-controversial, action-packed examination of the institutionalization of violence. A fascist teacher (Beat Takeshi Kitano) maniacally leads his high school class on a government-sponsored survival-of-the-fittest experiment on a desert island. Over-the-top carnage escalates into an apocalyptic climax; 40 years after bursting on the Japanese film scene, a testament that the maestro had lost none of his fiery social conscience or subversive dark humor.

KINJI FUKASAKU – COMPLETE FILMOGRAPHY

1961   *WANDERING DETECTIVE – TRAGEDY IN RED VALLEY (FURAIBO TANTEI – AKAI TANI NO SANGEKI)*
WANDERING DETECTIVE – BLACK WIND IN THE HARBOR (FURAIBO TANTEI – MISAKI O WATARU KUROI KAZE)
VIGILANTE WITH A FUNKY HAT (FUNKI HATTO NO KAIDANJI)
VIGILANTE WITH A FUNKY HAT – THE 200,000 YEN ARM (FUNKI HATTO NO KAIDANJI – NISENMAN-EN NO UDE)
HIGH NOON FOR GANGSTERS (HAKUCHU NO BURAIKAN, aka *VILLAINS IN BROAD DAYLIGHT)*

1962   *THE PROUD CHALLENGE (HOKORI TAKAKI CHOSEN)*

         GANG VS. G–MEN (GYANGU TAI G-MEN)

1963   *LEAGUE OF GANGSTERS (GYANGU DOMEI)*

1964   *JAKOMAN AND TETSU (JAKOMAN TO TETSU, aka ONE-EYED CAPTAIN AND TETSU)*

         WOLVES, PIGS AND PEOPLE (OKAMI TO BUTA TO NINGEN)

1966   *THE THREAT (ODOSHI)*

         KAMIKAZE MAN – DUEL AT NOON (KAMIKAZE YARO – MAHIRU NO KETTO)

         RAMPAGING DRAGON OF THE NORTH (HOKKAI NO ABARE RYU)

1967   *CEREMONY OF DISBANDING (KAISANSHIKI)*

1968   *GAMBLERS' CEREMONY OF DISBANDING (BAKUTO KAISANSHIKI)*

         [Note: this is not a mistake; this film is different from the preceding title.]

         BLACK LIZARD (KUROTOKAGE)

         BLACKMAIL IS MY LIFE (KYOKATSU KOSO WAGA JINSEI)

         THE GREEN SLIME (GAMMA DAISAN GO – UCHU DAI SAKUSEN, aka GAMMA #3 – COSMIC WAR)

1969   *BLACK ROSE MANSION (KUROBARA NO YAKATA)*

         JAPAN'S VIOLENT GANGS – BOSS (NIHON BORYOKUDAN – KUMICHO, aka JAPAN'S ORGANIZED CRIME BOSS

1970   *BLOODSTAINED CLAN HONOR (CHIZOME NO DAIMON, aka BLOODSTAINED CREST, aka BLOODY GAMBLES)*

         IF YOU WERE YOUNG – RAGE! (KIMI GA WAKAMONO NARA)

         TORA! TORA! TORA! [Co-directed with Richard Fleischer and Toshio Masuda]

1971   *GAMBLER – FOREIGN OPPOSITION (BAKUTO GAIJIN BUTAI, aka YAKUZA COMBAT FORCES, aka GAMBLERS IN OKINAWA, aka SYMPATHY FOR THE UNDERDOG)*

1972   *UNDER THE FLUTTERING MILITARY FLAG (GUNKI HATAMEKU MOTO NI)*

         STREET MOBSTER (GENDAI YAKUZA – HITOKIRI YOTA, aka MODERN YAKUZA – OUTLAW KILLER)

         OUTLAW KILLER – THREE MADDOG BROTHERS (HITOKIRI YOTA – KYOKEN SAN KYODAI)

1973   *BATTLES WITHOUT HONOR AND HUMANITY (JINGINAKI TATAKAI)*

         BATTLES WITHOUT HONOR AND HUMANITY – HIROSHIMA DEATH MATCH (JINGINAKI TATAKAI – HIROSHIMA SHITO HEN)

         BATTLES WITHOUT HONOR AND HUMANITY – AGENT OF WAR (JINGINAKI TATAKAI – DAIRI SENSO)

1974   *BATTLES WITHOUT HONOR AND HUMANITY – SUMMIT OF OPERATIONS (JINGINAKI TATAKAI – CHOJO SAKUSEN, aka POLICE TACTICS)*

         BATTLES WITHOUT HONOR AND HUMANITY – SAGA CONCLUSION (JINGINAKI TATAKAI – KANKETSU HEN)

         NEW BATTLES WITHOUT HONOR AND HUMANITY (SHIN JINGINAKI TATAKAI)

1975   *GRAVEYARD OF HONOR (JINGI NO HAKABA)*
        STATE POLICE VS. ORGANIZED CRIME (KENKEI TAI SOSHIKI BORYOKU, aka
        COPS VS. THUGS)
        GAMBLING DEN HEIST (SHIKINGEN GODATSU)
        NEW BATTLES WITHOUT HONOR AND HUMANITY – THE BOSS'S HEAD
        (SHIN JINGINAKI TATAKAI – KUMICHO NO KUBI)

1976   *VIOLENT PANIC – THE BIG CRASH (BOSO PANIKKU – DAI GEKITOTSU)*
        NEW BATTLES WITHOUT HONOR AND HUMANITY – THE BOSS'S LAST
        DAYS (SHIN JINGINAKI TATAKAI – KUMICHO SAIGO NO HI)
        YAKUZA BURIAL – JASMINE FLOWER (YAKUZA NO HAKABA – KUCHINASHI
        NO HANA)
        HOKURIKU PROXY WAR (HOKURIKU DAIRI SENSO, aka *HOKURIKU GANG*
        WAR, aka *AGENT OF WAR OF THE NORTH)*

1977   *DOBERMAN DETECTIVE (DOOBERMAN DEKA)*

1978   *SHOGUN'S SAMURAI (YAGYU ICHIZOKU NO INBO,* aka *YAGYU CLAN*
        CONSPIRACY)
        MESSAGE FROM SPACE (UCHU KARA NO MESSEJI)
        THE FALL OF AKO CASTLE (AKO DANZETSU)

1980   *VIRUS (FUKKATSU NO HI)*

1981   *SAMURAI REINCARNATION (MAKAI TENSHO,* aka *RESURRECTION OF EVIL)*
        GATE OF YOUTH (SEISHUN NO MON)

1982   *DOTONBORI RIVER (DOTONBORIGAWA)*
        THE FALL GUY (KAMATA KOSHIN KYOKU)

1983   *THEATER OF LIFE (JINSEI GEKIJO)* [Co-directed with Sadao Nakajima and Junya
        Sato]
        LEGEND OF EIGHT SAMURAI (SATOMI HAKKENDEN, aka *STORY OF EIGHT*
        DOGS – CARDINAL VIRTUES)

1984   *SHANGHAI RHAPSODY (SHANGHAI BANSU KINGU,* aka *SHANGHAI VANCE*
        KING)

1986   *HOUSE ON FIRE (KATAKU NO HITO)*

1987   *SURE DEATH 4 – REVENGE (HISSATSU! 4 – URAMI HARASHIMASU)*

1988   *FLOWER OF CHAOS (HANA NO RAN)*

1992   *TRIPLE CROSS (ITSUKA GIRAGIRA SURU HI,* aka *THE DAY'S TOO BRIGHT)*

1994   *CREST OF BETRAYAL (CHUSHINGURA GAIDEN – YOTSUYA KAIDAN,* aka
        LOYAL 47 RONIN – YOTSUYA GHOST STORY)

1999   *THE GEISHA HOUSE (OMOCHA)*

2000   *BATTLE ROYALE*

2003   *BATTLE ROYALE 2* [Kinji's son, Kenta, who co-wrote the screenplays to both *Battle Royale*
        films with his father, took over the directorial reins when Kinji died early on in the
        production]

KINJI FUKASAKU – INTERVIEWS

The following interview took place in the early summer of 1997 beside the Beverly Hilton's deserted swimming pool (it was overcast and rather cool). Toshiko Adilman, Kinji's long-time friend and translator, visiting from Toronto, did the on-site translation.

CD: Tell me about the first two films you directed, the pair of Wandering Detective *pictures?*

FUKASAKU: The system in place in those days was to let new directors make their first films as relatively short features, 60 or 65 minutes. This was to see if they had any talent. If they felt you had talent after those films, they'd let you direct the longer pictures. So those were shorter second features to the longer first features on a double bill.

CD: Your first entry in the Gang *series,* Gang Vs. G–Men ...

FUKASAKU: ... is the story of an ex-*yakuza* who becomes an undercover policeman. A role played by Koji Tsuruta.

CD: The Gang *series, even though a bit old-fashioned at first, as it progressed it became more true to life, for example your* League Of Gangsters – *a precursor of the* jitsuroku *type of* yakuza *picture that became commonplace in the seventies. Then there were your other early* yakuza *pictures, like* High Noon For Gangsters *and* Wolves, Pigs And People, *which are pretty amazing, considering when you made them.*

FUKASAKU: I think you're correct to say that. But the stories were all fictitious and not based on any real people or events.

CD: Do you feel that you were one of the pioneers of that jitsuroku *style of* yakuza *picture?*

FUKASAKU: Perhaps. The first film of mine that I felt really successfully blended that documentary feel with the fictitious drama was *Street Mobster*. From that film on, I was more aware of the real past and contemporary underworld, characters and events I could draw on to give the films a more reality-based feeling.

CD: You never directed any yakuza *movies that could be termed* ninkyo eiga. *Did you not want to direct any* ninkyo *films?*

FUKASAKU: Back then Toei had two studio branches, one in Kyoto, one in Tokyo. The one in Kyoto made the *jidai-geki* pictures, the samurai *chanbara*, and also, as the sixties progressed, the *ninkyo yakuza* films, which were also set in period – say the late Meiji era, the Taisho era, the early Showa period. I was stationed at the Tokyo branch, and we concentrated on making contemporary films. When we did *yakuza* films, they were set in a relatively contemporary time period. The *ninkyo* stories from Kyoto didn't really fit with our dramaturgy. The pictures directors like Umeji Inoue and I did in the *Gang* series, films like *Gang Vs. G-Men*, were modern-style action films, but at the same time they were not very realistic. The more realistic pictures came in with films like *Street Mobster*. I think that gives you a clear delineation.

CD: In your films Gambler – Ceremony Of Disbanding, Gambler – Foreign Opposition, Japan's Violent Gangs – Boss *you see Koji Tsuruta, a* ninkyo *actor, playing a much more world-weary character –*

FUKASAKU: – World-weary?

CD: Out of place. A more alienated character than you see when he starred in ninkyo yakuza *films.*

FUKASAKU: I always thought that Koji Tsuruta's personality was more in tune with that kind of character, someone who is left behind, frozen in time.

Poster for *Street Mobster* (aka *Modern Yakuza – Outlaw Killer*)

One of the first films that I worked on with him was *The Proud Challenge*, which was not a *yakuza* film. And I felt that then. He was playing a newspaper reporter who'd been sacked because he was an idealistic Communist.

CD: Did Mr Tsuruta ever express any objections to things his character had to do in your films?

FUKASAKU: No, no, I didn't ever have any problems with him.

CD: In Gambler – Foreign Opposition, *Tsuruta's character wears sunglasses through virtually the entire movie, even when he's in bed with his girlfriend. Whose idea was that?*

FUKASAKU: (*laughs*) I had him do that in *The Proud Challenge*, too. He was a journalist in that and a *yakuza* in the *Gambler* film. But it was my idea. You know, sometimes I thought when he was playing these characters his face looked a little too gentle. I wanted to occasionally make him look a little different, tougher.

CD: More sinister.

FUKASAKU: So I had him wear the sunglasses.

CD: In Boss, *Tomisaburo Wakayama plays a wild, drug-addicted gangster and, as it turns out, he has more in common with the strong, quiet gang boss, played by Tsuruta, rather than with the corporate gang bosses, men without honor. Both Tsuruta and Wakayama hold them as a common enemy and almost become friends because of that.*

FUKASAKU: Yes, strange bedfellows.

CD: Can you talk about working with Wakayama?

FUKASAKU: Tsuruta had always been a star and pretty much always played the lead role. The character in *Boss* didn't really suit his tastes, and he wasn't very keen to do it. In comparison to Tsuruta, Wakayama had a quality that was conducive to playing a bad guy. Much like other actors such as Lee Van Cleef or Humphrey Bogart. Wakayama belonged very much to that school of tough guy. In the beginning of the movie Tsuruta's and Wakayama's characters are enemies, but before you know it, when they both face a common adversity, they become close. I thought that that idea was very interesting. And the audience liked it, too.

CD: Ryohei Uchida also appeared in Boss *as Tsuruta's old friend who has joined up with the more corporate gang. You have him dressed in a white suit through the whole picture. Did you have any special reason for that, since he was the only member of the corporate gang to wear white and who had any remnants of decency left?*

FUKASAKU: Well, Tsuruta looked better in black, and, to be honest, Wakayama wasn't too stylish. But Ryohei Uchida had a natural sense of style to him. He looked good in the suit. Also, he wore the white suit to show he was a member of a more prosperous, money-conscious gang. It made him stand out from the rest of his gang, but I wasn't consciously doing it because he was the only honorable one.

CD: In Street Mobster, *Bunta Sugawara is a post-WW2 orphan of the streets with no moral upbringing. Before the prostitute played by Mayumi Nagisa becomes his girlfriend, his only experiences with women are through rape. In fact, he and his friends had raped Nagisa earlier, something that had led her down the path to prostitution. And he also can't get along with other* yakuza. *Sugawara's character is similar to the character played by Tetsuya Watari in your later film,* Graveyard Of Honor.

FUKASAKU: *Graveyard Of Honor* was based on a real character, while *Street Mobster* was completely fictitious. But I had already had the idea for *Graveyard Of Honor* before *Street Mobster*. I was aware of the real-life gangster Rikuo Ishikawa, because he had come from the same area as me down in Mito, and thought his story would make a good film. I decided to incorporate elements of his character in *Street Mobster* to see how it would work. When it turned out well, I made up my mind to do the story in an even more realistic style in *Graveyard Of Honor*.

CD: There seem to be quite a lot of superficial roles for women in yakuza *films in general —*

FUKASAKU: – What about Mayumi Nagisa in *Street Mobster*?

CD: She was going to be part of my question. She's one of the exceptions.

FUKASAKU: And Yumi Takigawa in *Graveyard Of Honor*?

CD: Yes, she was great in that. I'm not talking specifically about your yakuza *films — more in general terms. You don't get many strong females in* yakuza *pictures except for the more mythical* ninkyo *films, such as* Red Peony Gambler *with Junko Fuji. Mayumi Nagisa's character in* Street Mobster *is such an incredibly strong role for a woman in a* jitsuroku-*style* yakuza *picture. She really does seem to be one of the exceptions.*

FUKASAKU: I think if you look at films such as *Street Mobster*, they are exceptional films. They aren't run-of-the-mill.

CD: Why, though, aren't there stronger women's roles in those kinds of yakuza *films? Perhaps it's naive or maybe just too obvious in this day and age to say this, but I also think women in Japan, because of the ingrained culture, have had a harder time than women in Western cultures in asserting their individuality.*

FUKASAKU: Well, I would turn that around then and ask you if there are any strong women's roles in American gangster pictures.

CD: Not really. I suppose you're right. There were some in the forties and the fifties. But they were more in the detective or film noir genres. Movies like Out Of The Past *(1948) with Jane Greer,* Gun Crazy *(1950) with Peggy Cummins,* Crime Of Passion*(1957) with Barbara Stanwyck. But it's true, movies like the* Godfather *trilogy and Martin Scorsese's* Mean Streets *don't really have particularly strong female characters. Perhaps later on when you get to Lorraine Bracco in* Goodfellas *and Sharon Stone in* Casino.

FUKASAKU: Well, when you do a *jitsuroku yakuza* film, just by its nature you're going to be telling a tale about men. And when you have to concentrate on one or two male characters, you just don't have the space to concentrate as much on any female roles. And then, when there's action, at least in the past in Japan, women have not been as physically strong, and they don't traditionally go around killing people. You also want to establish the attractiveness of whatever female characters you do have, so you can see the dilemma.

CD: You see more of the assertive female characters in some ninkyo *films like the* Red Peony Gambler *pictures, movies which are admittedly not connected to any historical reality.*

FUKASAKU: However, characters like Junko Fuji in *Red Peony Gambler* are not necessarily more complex because they are strong characters. In some ways, they are one-dimensional, similar to the characters that Ken Takakura played in those *ninkyo* films. They don't do any bad things. They always remain clean.

CD: There's a more truthful picture of the yakuza *in the* Battles Without Honor And Humanity *series. But you don't see as much of their moneymaking activities as you do in, for instance, some of Junya Sato's* jitsuroku yakuza *pictures. You will actually see the* yakuza *forcing women into prostitution, in collusion with labor unions, extorting money. But in the* Battles Without Honor *films you see more of the gangsters having meetings, devising betrayals, then bloody vendettas and gang wars erupting. Why did you decide to concentrate more on that?*

FUKASAKU: I encompassed the period from 1945 through 1955 in the *Battles Without Honor* movies. Most of Junya Sato's films start around 1965, a time where there was a big crunch for the *yakuza*. They were starting to become more corporate and had to become more ingenious in ferreting out income for their very survival. The *Battles Without Honor* films are also set outside Tokyo, in Hiroshima right after the war. There was a lot more street crime, much more mindless violence and many gang wars in struggles for supremacy.

CD: There was also the black market and drug-dealing which you do show –

FUKASAKU: – I was trying to show the *yakuza*'s race to catch up as Japan's reconstruction took place after the war. Those *yakuza* did not have brains or social status. They were trying to run after the bus, so to speak, so they wouldn't miss the ride to prosperity.

CD: There was also supposedly collusion between the yakuza *and the US occupation forces in the late forties and through the early fifties. Was there some reason you didn't touch on much of that in the series?*

FUKASAKU: That alliance, you could look at that as the *yakuza* riding along with the US occupation. In Tokyo and Osaka, both the Japanese police and the US military entrusted the *yakuza* to keep order in the black market. Some American soldiers also provided the *yakuza* with goods to resell on the black market at a profit. Also, arms were stolen from the military and resold.

CD: There's hints of that in Battles Without Honor And Humanity – Summit Of Operations.

FUKASAKU: The selling of commodities on the black market from the US military, you see that in the beginning of *Graveyard Of Honor*.

CD: The US occupation was nervous about Communist influences in the labor unions and would often employ yakuza *as strike-breakers when there were labor conflicts.*

FUKASAKU: Yes, the *yakuza* definitely helped out the US occupation forces in that regard. I really didn't touch on that in the *Battles Without Honor* series.

But my earlier movie, *The Proud Challenge*, was about that and was meant as an exposé of the CIA's plot to crush the Communist and socialist left in Japan.

CD: All through your Battles Without Honor *series there is incredible violence. Were the gang wars, not only in Hiroshima but also in Osaka and Tokyo, that violent in real life?*

FUKASAKU: Hiroshima was the only city that I'm aware of where even ordinary citizens became victims of the violence. People getting caught in the crossfire.

CD: And the films largely taking place in Hiroshima, it's almost as if the gangsters are mutations from the radioactive fallout …

FUKASAKU: (*laughs*)

CD: … in a metaphorical sense. That this was the nadir of the worst because of its location, where the atom bomb was dropped.

FUKASAKU: I felt that metaphor, too. The genesis of the extreme violence with the gangsters almost appearing right out of the dust and smoke of the mushroom cloud. And that's why we used the stock footage of the bomb going off at the beginning of the film.

CD: There's a scene in Battles Without Honor And Humanity – Saga Conclusion *where a young gangster is in a shootout in front of a Toei movie theater showing a Junko Fuji film and actually dies on top of one of her film posters. Was that a comment that the romanticizing of the* yakuza, *as in the kind of* ninkyo *films that she was in, ultimately had a destructive effect on certain impressionable segments of the audience?*

FUKASAKU: Yes, you could say that. But, more specifically, having him die on her picture was just an ironic comment on the fate of this boy who wanted to achieve the *yakuza* idyll but couldn't quite get there.

CD: One of the writers on Graveyard Of Honor, *Tatsuhiko Kamoi, also wrote several of Tetsuya Watari's pictures while he was still at Nikkatsu studios, including Yukihiro Sawada's* Kanto Society Of Leading Mobsters *(Kanto Kanbukai, 1971), which I think is one of Watari's best films. Did Watari have anything to do with him coming on to the project?*

FUKASAKU: Tatsuo Yoshida, who was the producer, first asked Mr Kamoi to write, but his script didn't end up being used for the most part. So I hired Fumio Konami and Hiro Matsuda to take a crack at it.

CD: Tetsuya Watari's last few yakuza *pictures at Nikkatsu were leaning more towards the* jitsuroku *approach, and his roles seemed to get a bit tougher than his earlier sixties Nikkatsu films. But, in* Graveyard Of Honor, *it was a startling transformation, as if he'd become another person. Did he feel that the part was a challenge? Or maybe an unflattering role for him?*

FUKASAKU: Watari was very excited and felt it was a great challenge. But some of the producers who had worked with Watari at Nikkatsu were rather reluctant to see him take the part.

CD: Was the character his part was based on also a heroin addict in real life?

FUKASAKU: Yes.

CD: Bunta Sugawara plays a police detective in State Police Vs. Organized Crime. *How did he feel about playing a policeman as opposed to the gangster role he usually took on?*

FUKASAKU: Well, he'd played *yakuza* in so many of the previous films we decided he should play a policeman, but a bad policeman.

CD: But his character isn't really bad, is he?

FUKASAKU: (*laughs*) As far as society and morality goes, he's bad. He's compromised. Maybe he doesn't come off as that bad. You could describe him as being humane, even though he's corrupt. And in contrast to the more ordinary, average policemen who all seem a bit inhuman.

CD: Tetsuya Watari plays a similar character in Yakuza Burial *and doesn't really fit in with his fellow cops or with the* yakuza. *Was this something you'd been working on or something the studio proposed as a follow-up to* Graveyard Of Honor?

FUKASAKU: Well, Watari wanted to do another film with me. But we'd exhausted the *Battles Without Honor* story. So we came up with this idea of an immoral cop, much like Sugawara's character in *State Police Vs. Organized Crime*. But we wanted to go even further examining his character, and show that, despite his faults, he really is more ethical and humane than his fellow police detectives.

CD: Watari has made only a few films since Yakuza Burial.

FUKASAKU: He ended up concentrating more on TV work. He's still very popular on television.

CD: Where did the idea come from for Hokuriku Proxy War?

FUKASAKU: That was from a true story in Hokkaido. The character in real life, the one played by Hiroki Matsukata, was killed soon after our film was made.

CD: There's a scene where Matsukata's enemies are buried up to their necks in the snow and then jeeps are aimed to run over their heads. Was that something that really happened?

FUKASAKU: Oh, yes. That was from real events.

CD: I'd like to ask an unrelated question, if you don't mind, about Bunta Sugawara. He had started at Shintoho studios in the fifties and became a leading man there before the studio went bankrupt. But, after that, he had to start again from scratch, playing bit parts at Shochiku, then Toei, before finally becoming a leading man again around 1969. Did he feel any bitterness? Or did he tend to be more philosophical?

FUKASAKU: Well, of course, as an actor he wanted to play bigger roles during that leaner period. I think he was frustrated. Even when he came to Toei there were other popular stars like Koji Tsuruta, and Ken Takakura. He had to wait a long time for his second break. His first starring roles in the *Modern Yakuza* series, and the film I directed, *Street Mobster*, that was the last in that series, were all low-budget films.

CD: And what was it like working with Noboru Ando, who had been a yakuza *in real life?*

FUKASAKU: He had gone to jail after that shooting incident. Then, when he got out, he disbanded his gang and became an actor fairly quickly.

CD: How big was his gang?

FUKASAKU: The biggest they ever were? I think maybe around 500 members. They had control of a fairly large area in Tokyo for a while, the district known as Shibuya.

CD: Junya Sato had done the film series with Ando, True Account Of The Ando Gang. *How much of what was in the films really happened, do you know?*

FUKASAKU: They were based on his memoirs, and when *yakuza* write memoirs quite often they end up justifying their actions. I don't believe that Ando was an exception to the rule. You could probably take about 50% of it as being real. However, I believe an exception to this were the articles written by *Battles Without Honor*'s original writer, Koichi Iiboshi. He had also been a *yakuza* and ended up becoming a reporter. I think his writing you could take 80%, maybe even 90%, of it as the truth. Many of the people from his writings were still alive when they were first published, so if there'd been fabrication involved it would have been exposed.

CD: How was Ando to get along with? He seems a natural actor.

FUKASAKU: In a way, I accept a lot of *yakuza* like that. They tend to be very fun people. Sarcastic, but a lot of fun. One habit that many of them have, though, is that they'll never look into your eyes when you're talking to them.

CD: I've heard rumors that some of the head producers at Toei had originally come up from the ranks of the yakuza. *Is that true?*

FUKASAKU: There was a very big producer there named Koji Shundo who had been in the *yakuza.*

CD: How did real-life yakuza *feel about your* yakuza *films? Especially about seeing* yakuza *portrayed in an unflattering way?*

FUKASAKU: There was the godfather of one gang who was portrayed in one of my films by Tetsuro Tanba. He wanted to check it out before it was released, so he set up a special screening at Toei. He came, sat there and watched the film. Afterwards he remarked that he was a little surprised that his subordinates, some of the men he'd brought with him, were so quiet during the film that they didn't attempt any retaliation in response to what they were seeing on the screen. (*laughs*) That was a bit scary.

CD: How do you feel about the yakuza *genre?*

FUKASAKU: By the time I started making the more realistic *yakuza* films I'd already been a director for over ten years. I felt that with that approach, the more documentary style, I would finally be able to distinguish my films from those of other directors. I felt that strongly for the first time when I made *Street Mobster*. And from then on, especially with *Graveyard Of Honor*, I really like my work.

CD: Do you think that there have been any good yakuza *movies made during the 1990s?*

FUKASAKU: Maybe a few. One of the only great *yakuza* pictures made since the *Battles Without Honor* and *Graveyard Of Honor* films in the seventies is a picture from 1983 called *Ryuji*. It was directed by Toru Kawashima and written by the actor Shoji Kaneko, who played the main role. Sadly, he died of cancer shortly after the film was made.

CD: What do you feel is the difference between Japanese and American or European gangster films?

FUKASAKU: The thing that really makes a gangster film interesting, whether it's a *yakuza* picture or a gangster movie from the West, is if an audience of ordinary people like you and me, non-gangsters, can somehow relate to the characters in the film. When you find a common human thread. There are two French crime films that I think are especially good in that way. One is Clouzot's *Quai Des Orfevres* (1947), with Louis Jouvet, and another, Jacques Becker's *Touchez Pas Au Grisbi* (1953), with Jean Gabin. In contrast, I think many American gangster films are presented more as entertainments. Flamboyant. The *Godfather* films – I think those films were researched and were realistically based. But, at the same time, they have a slightly different attitude, meant more to entertain. An exception would be Scorsese's *Goodfellas*.

CD: Mean Streets, too. Why do you think yakuza *films were so popular in Japan during the 1960s?*

FUKASAKU: During the sixties and early seventies the students were rebelling against the status quo and government policies. There were incidents with The Red Army. But these sentiments weren't only prevalent amongst the students. There was a kind of restless, rebellious energy bubbling under the surface with the general public. There were clashes between students and police on campuses and in other areas of the city. It was a time when students, the general public and women who worked in the water trade would go to late-night movie theaters to see the *yakuza* pictures. It was a kind of emotional release.

CD: It's ironic that the ninkyo yakuza *pictures that were most popular in the sixties have almost left-wing sympathies, with a good gang or lone hero helping the working class, who are being exploited by evil gangs or the government. But in reality, during the early twentieth century, the original period of many of these movies, the real* yakuza *were usually right wing and frequently collaborating with repressive government forces. What do you think accounts for that discrepancy in the* ninkyo *films? Was it because there were many left-wing screenwriters turning out the scripts? Or were there actually some 'chivalrous' gangs?*

FUKASAKU: (*laughs*) There were a lot of leftist writers and directors, but also many in the general audience shared that leftist sentiment. The students and blue-collar workers who made up a good portion of the audience cheered that type of story. The creators of those films really enjoyed that kind of scenario and loved presenting it on the screen.

CD: How did the more conservative yakuza *respond to those films, the stories with the lone wolf hero or heroine fighting for the common man? Because I've gotten the impression that those films were also popular amongst* yakuza.

FUKASAKU: They liked those movies because it made them look good. It was good for their image!

CD: *Do you think it could possibly have had any influence on real* yakuza *behavior?*

FUKASAKU: I don't think so, because it was all relative in a way. Also, they would have ways of justifying whatever they did as right in the context of their group or for the welfare of their comrades. They responded more to the energy in the films. Ideas expressed of how noble it was to die for their beliefs and for the sake of their comrades. Right or left, it didn't particularly matter.

CD: *What are some of your own favorite films?*

FUKASAKU: It's difficult, because it's very hard to compare the films that were well received with the movies that were well made but not well received. They're all like children and all so different. Sometimes you love the children more that are a bit simple-minded. But of course you have affection for the others, too. So, out of the 50 or so films I've made, perhaps if I chose ten as the most loved. Then, again, maybe it would be better if you picked them.

The next interview consists of excerpts from a long question-and-answer session Dennis Bartok and I had with Kinji in March, 2002, as a supplement for the American DVD releases of three of the films he directed at Shochiku studios: Black Rose Mansion, Blackmail Is My Life *and* If You Were Young – Rage. *The interview took place in an empty conference room in Shochiku studios' Tokyo office. Toshiko Adilman did the on-site translation. Ai Kennedy helped on some retranslation and clarification after editing. Dennis Bartok is signified as DB and I am signified as CD.*

DB: *Were you surprised when the first film that you did with Akihiro Maruyama,* Black Lizard, *was such a success?*

FUKASAKU: *Black Lizard* was very popular and successful when it was released. Shochiku offered us the chance to do a second film, one that would also star Maruyama. Something that made its success even sweeter was that it was the first picture I had directed outside of Toei studios.

CD: Black Lizard *was adapted from a play by Yukio Mishima that he, in turn, had adapted from a story by famous Japanese mystery writer Edogawa Rampo. Was Mishima involved with* Black Rose Mansion?

FUKASAKU: Shochiku's offer was to make a film with a similar theme to *Black Lizard*. Maruyama, of course, was a man playing a female role, and this new film was to be based on his *Black Lizard* character. But *Black Rose* wasn't from any original story. We spent a lot of time discussing how to make the new picture. We tried to consult with Mishima, but he was busy leading his political group. So, he wasn't directly involved. It was quite impossible for us to expect any meaningful input from him.

DB: Although Maruyama stars in both films, Black Rose Mansion *is very different from* Black Lizard, *more melodramatic and melancholy. Why did Shochiku agree to do such a different kind of film?*

FUKASAKU: As a studio right then, Shochiku was undergoing dramatic changes, gradually transforming their traditional structure to the modern age of cinema. Nagisa Oshima, who had directed his first pictures there, had just left after creative disputes. They were making a lot of reforms, but they did not want to really abandon their tradition. They felt that, with Oshima having taken the creative lead for a while, the traditional roots of the studio had changed. They wanted to return to their traditional strengths and focus again on a melodrama. The president of Shochiku, Mr Kido, was a movie buff, and he loved Shochiku's traditional films. So, we took his feelings into account in developing the story. And that's how we went from *Black Lizard* to *Black Rose Mansion.*

CD: There had been a long tradition of onnagata *in kabuki theater and in the beginnings of Japanese silent film of men portraying women, but not much at all since the sound era began. What was the reaction of the men in the cast to having to play a romantic love interest with Maruyama?*

FUKASAKU: (*smiles*) Yes, there was quite a reaction. Films were set in the realistic sensibilities of the time, and so the actors wanted the role of the heroine to be played by a woman. There were difficulties, and then, too, Maruyama had people he wanted to work with that didn't always pan out, either.

CD: Though Black Rose Mansion *is much bigger than life than Nikkatsu studios' mood/action films, a lot of the imagery reminds me of their romantic film noir movies from the sixties. Pictures with Yujiro Ishihara and Ruriko Asaoka, like* Sunset Hill *(Yuhi No Oka, 1964), directed by Akinori Matsuo. What do you think of those films? Did they have any influence on* Black Rose Mansion?

FUKASAKU: Although I never made a film at Nikkatsu, I was a big fan of their movies with Yujiro Ishihara and Ruriko Asaoka. Even if I wasn't consciously aware of it, I was definitely influenced by those films. *Black Rose Mansion* probably reflects this. Nikkatsu films were different from any kind of realism. They were trying a lot of different things. Another aspect that certainly had an impact on the romantic mood of both *Black Lizard* and *Black Rose Mansion* were the performers. The actor who played the hero detective, Akechi, in *Black Lizard*, Isao Kimura (who's gone now), was originally a stage actor. He and Maruyama got along and worked well together. Similarly, the young actor Masakazu Tamura, who played Wataru in *Black Rose Mansion* – he's still alive and active, and made a great team with Maruyama, too. I also must mention Eitaro Ozawa, who played Tamura's father. He was originally a stage actor, too, and I'd been looking for an opportunity to work with him. The fact these actors interacted so well with Maruyama, and understood what we were trying to create, helped to create the proper mood for both pictures.

DB: Although you're known predominantly for your yakuza *films, you've also worked in many other genres. What is it in a story that attracts you as a filmmaker?*

FUKASAKU: Well, as far as *Black Lizard*, and especially *Black Rose Mansion*, I wanted to have lots of unique characters interacting. That was one of our intentions right from my initial discussions with the scriptwriter. I wanted to make them ensemble dramas. In my films that followed, including my *yakuza* films, I was also drawn to this multi-character approach.

CD: You see an incredible amount of characters in many films from not just Toei but the other studios too all through the 1950s and 1960s. How much of that was predicated by the huge rosters of studio players on the payroll and how much stems from the dramatic structure of Japanese films? You see familiar faces in movie after movie, depending on the studio.

FUKASAKU: There are two sides to that. In Japan, kabuki theater has a tradition of many characters on-stage, making for a lively and entertaining production. It is a long-standing tradition. The audience looks forward to a complicated web of relationships. Japanese audiences have been accustomed to this going back to the Edo period [nineteenth century]. So that's where we get this showiness, this distinctive mood of kabuki. It's something I've always been interested in and have tried to incorporate into my films, including my *yakuza* pictures. Shochiku, too, had its roots in kabuki. It was historically important to them. But, as you've said, as the number of actors on the payroll increases, the company tries to utilize these resources. All of the studios worked this way, whether at Toei with period dramas and *yakuza* films or at Shochiku, with melodramas. Even up to the mid-seventies, this was the kind of film the studios wanted to make and the audiences were eager to see.

DB: How did Blackmail Is My Life *come about?*

FUKASAKU: It took a long time to determine the approach on *Black Rose Mansion*. But Shochiku wanted another film right away and already had the rights to the *Blackmail Is My Life* story. It was an action film, they knew I was familiar with action filmmaking and they had already brought in Hiroki Matsukata, a young actor from Toei. It was an easier screenplay to coordinate than *Black Rose Mansion*. That's why we made it beforehand.

CD: Of all the films you did at Shochiku, Blackmail *seems the most like a Toei film. Even still, there are differences. What was the approach Shochiku might have had towards* yakuza *action films, as opposed to Toei?*

FUKASAKU: *Blackmail* is about a group of young people who get into trouble by coincidence. It triggers them to start a blackmail business. Its themes involve the main characters' relationships, the shady business negotiations, friendship and the love between a man and a woman. If you take a look at these themes, you can see that the film has more melodramatic elements than the usual Toei action picture. If I could've done it at Toei at the time, I wouldn't have needed to do the same thing at Shochiku. Making this film, I wanted to employ the theme of the friendships of youth. Another element of Toei filmmaking was having the main character or group beat the villains. It was a very common studio request to show this catharsis. The ambivalent main characters can be virtuous for the first time when they defeat evil. But, in Shochiku's case, it was not necessary to beat the villain in an unrealistic ending. It didn't matter if the movie concluded with the lead character's failure as long as the protagonist's life was completely penetrated. It was more important how vividly their lives were presented. Those were the differences between the two companies. Toei's method of drama had to go one of two ways: the hero beats the villain, but he dies, too; or the hero's actions bring about the villain's defeat, and the cops catch him. Endings with a sense of emotional failure were impossible for Toei in the sixties. Even though my colleagues and I would try to make them see, the producers and company heads couldn't appreciate our point of view. Gradually, that changed at Toei in the seventies. The *Battles Without Honor And Humanity* series happened. Those stories almost always end with the hero's sense of frustration. You can see clearly in the resulting films those dramas that had my emotional involvement, the ones that I enjoyed making the most.

DB: How much real corruption was going on in the Japanese political system during the sixties, as it was depicted in Blackmail Is My Life? *Did you take any flak for showing blackmail and murder amongst politicians?*

FUKASAKU: The public began to be acutely aware of this corruption during the sixties. It led to Prime Minister Tanaka's indictment. I think the awareness really started during that decade. I believe the audience liked the film because of its level of reality.

CD: You've used several of the actors in the film before and since in your Toei pictures – Hiroki Matsukata, Tetsuro Tanba; can you tell us about them?

FUKASAKU: This film was my first using Hiroki Matsukata. After this picture I became more closely aligned with Toei than Shochiku, and could work more easily on projects. I think the catalyst was *Blackmail Is My Life*. Many *yakuza* pictures of the time were set right after the turn of the century. *Ninkyo yakuza*, chivalrous heroes. However, I wanted to make *Blackmail* as a contemporary film. I wanted to make it realistic for myself. Hiroki Matsukata and Tetsuro Tanba had done many *ninkyo yakuza* pictures. But, whenever I worked with them, even when I worked with the biggest *ninkyo* stars like Koji Tsuruta and Ken Takakura, I purposely had their characters perform in a modern setting. I was much more perfectly in tune with a contemporary milieu. Hiroki Matsukata had a modern style and was a star who could really act. Toei sensed his importance, and so did audiences. This was a big influence on not only Bunta Sugawara's debut, but many other young actors as well.

DB: You've worked off and on in crime films from the beginning of your career. What attracts you to the genre, why do you think that you're so good at making that type of film?

FUKASAKU: I started to take an interest in movies in 1945, when Japan was defeated in the war. Right then, we were able to see a variety of films, and I was influenced by them, especially American and European pictures. But I found myself surrounded by piles of charred rubble and black markets. I wanted to make films for the young people who were having to live, wounded and bleeding. I think that that's the reason I was so into crime films. There were so many juvenile delinquents in the sixties. It really started even before that, in the fifties. I had a similar question when I made *Battle Royale*. 'Why are you so interested in juvenile delinquents at your age? Why now?' One of the reasons was that, when I was young, I was surrounded by many such incidents. At the time, I was not influenced by any of the happy-ending success stories from America. A boy living in the conditions I was in could not believe in them. That's why I could make films based on emotional failure easier than success stories. I think it's connected, why I started to like movies about crime. If I think about the kind of film I would like to make, it's always a story about emotional failure, even if it's a commercial movie.

CD: Two of your earliest sixties yakuza *pictures,* High Noon For Gangsters *and* Wolves, Pigs and People, *have that quality of emotional failure. Both films had gritty social issues, too. As you've said, that kind of downbeat crime film became easier to make*

Battle Royale

at Toei in the seventies. But, by the same token, movies like High Noon For Gangsters *and* Wolves, Pigs And People *must have been difficult to make in the early sixties.*

FUKASAKU: Toei *yakuza* pictures back then, the main characters fulfill their frustrated emotions, and they end by defeating the enemy, with the consequences of death or incarceration from the police. It keeps a balance in society. It's a very simple involvement of audience and film. And the audience can easily go along with the ending. However, what I wanted to do, what I still want to do, is based on a resistance to society. That feeling is my emotional spring. My desire is not only in defeating evil but how far desire can go. Even if desire doesn't get that far and fails, as long as you stick with an emotion then the main character could be understood. I lived my youth that way. I think I follow the pattern of my own dramas. Companies like happy endings, but in real life, the villain *doesn't* always get caught by the cops and *doesn't* always die, either. However, the audience believes that that just doesn't happen. If the audience thinks that, then the producers think it, too. There's nothing I can do about it. Producers complained to me many times, 'Why do your movies get so dark?' However, if I ask them: 'Do you think it's okay for the main character to get this happy or unrealistic ending?', even the producers cannot say yes. I understand the method of American movies, business-wise, with everything ending happily. Remembering back, American movies were reaching the whole world, and I feel that people have changed a lot. But, still, I've come to the conclusion that it's impossible to have a happy ending today. This is the biggest problem facing mankind now, and I don't have a solution for the future.

DB: What was the origin of the story of If You Were Young – Rage?

FUKASAKU: There was a production company called Shinseisha that had been trying to develop projects to encourage young people. When the TV series *Young People* (*Wakamonotachi*) was on, audiences made it popular and well rated. They asked me if I could make a film like the series. I guess they saw that my films already had this tendency towards youth and crime. The production company was trying to find a different direction, and I guess they wanted to show that side, too.

CD: How would you describe the difference of the youth of today, for instance the youth of your film Battle Royale *with the youth in* If You Were Young?

FUKASAKU: In *If You Were Young*, it was the producer's request to give hope for the future. However, reality is too harsh. There was that sense already in *If You Were Young*. The main characters were struggling in different ways to escape from reality, in this instance to escape mass unemployment. However, they never do get out from under it. Finally, one of the friends in the group commits a crime. The crime drags them all down, and they get lost and stopped in their tracks. In *Battle Royale*, the situation goes much further, the kids are pushed to the edge in a crueller situation. It's impossible to find hope in that kind of future. One of the themes of *Battle Royale* was that every human struggles in their own way and tries to make a stand. The reason *If You Were Young* was less complex is not because the situation was different. It's more that *If You Were Young* was from a generation when you could believe in other people. If you cannot believe in others, how can anyone benefit? So, people back then tried to rebuild trust, even though there was so much crime, and it was a pretty tough generation. You could see the effort of people trying to believe in others. Now, we can't trust anyone. Kids can't trust adults – not other students, not teachers. That's the situation in *Battle Royale*. People used to try hard to reconnect, rebuild friendships. That's the motif of *If You Were Young*. I think those are the differences.

CD: In If You Were Young, *I recognized Choichiro Kawarazaki from some sixties* chanbara *like Tai Kato's* Cruelty Of The Shogunate's Downfall *and other films at Toei. And Ryunosuke Minegishi (now known as Toru Minegishi), who was in a lot of Daiei's delinquent and* yakuza *pictures. But what about the others?*

FUKASAKU: The cast members were all professionals. Some of them were from Bungakuza. They belonged to these drama troupes and studied acting.

DB: You've received a tremendous amount of recognition in the last few years, what with the success of Battle Royale. *You've had retrospectives take place around the world at such places as the Rotterdam Film Festival and The American Cinematheque in Los Angeles. The retrospective series toured many major cities of the United States. How do you feel about this recognition, and what are you planning next?*

FUKASAKU: I throw out the question 'Can you find hope in the future?' to young people with the film *If You Were Young*, and I do the same with *Battle Royale*. How the cast members take that question and perform and how the viewer accepts their performances, that's what I've been seeing. It gives me a sense of satisfaction to receive that much feedback about a film I've made. Especially *Battle Royale*. I got tremendous feedback from England and France as well. People ask me, 'What's next?' However, the situation has become difficult all of a sudden. There was an awful act of terrorism. How can I handle the terrorism problem myself? My frustrations, of all kinds, have been growing since the 1950s. And I have undergone all kinds of emotional failures towards that end. There is the Afghan problem now in this situation, and the terrorism problem, too. Is it possible to lead people towards an effective answer? And how can I present it to the viewer? I know that this is a very tough debate. Confusion – we have this moment, plus the difficult circumstances of filmmaking. Now the facts force us to face things. It's not that different between Japanese audiences and others around the world. I don't feel that I am in the spotlight. I'll sum up the questions of the interview. All kinds of problems in the world keep getting bigger. I would like to truthfully answer how I feel. But I feel it's a little too late for me, it's a little too heavy at my age. Even though I've made assumptions of what you really wanted to ask me, I hope I can make a film next which would answer those questions. That is why I am fighting a hard battle now.

2

Eiichi Kudo

1929–2000

More than any other director I had the pleasure of meeting, including Kinji Fukasaku and Seijun Suzuki, the impression I retain of Mr Kudo is that of a *sensei*, a teacher. There was an aura of serenity and wisdom about him – an unpretentiousness and a delightful sense of humor as well as a sober side, an awareness of the good and bad in life unobstructed by illusions.

It strikes me as ironic that Kudo was initially resistant to making *jidai-geki* films. Nervous about his inexperience in the genre, he had to be pushed into moving to Toei studios' Kyoto branch, where period movies were made, by his then boss. Ironic in that Kudo turned out three of the most gruelling, relevant samurai pictures made in the sixties, films right up there with the best of such directors as Hideo Gosha, Kenji Misumi and Tai Kato.

Toei's *jidai-geki* from the fifties could vacillate between the sublime and the ridiculous, the scale tilting towards the latter, with worthwhile movies outnumbered five to one. But Kudo's earliest *chanbara*, films like the *Bloody Account Of Jirocho* quartet, have hints of the virtues apparent in his later, more mature films. Despite being designed for indiscriminate action lovers, Kudo's *Jirocho* films have an appreciably less sentimentalized, more straightforward approach than many of the other programmers churned out in profusion as the sixties began. Notwithstanding an occasional musical number, you could tell Kudo was intent on dispensing with the corn as much as possible.

Still, it is amazing that Kudo was able to conjure up one of the all-time greatest samurai films, *Thirteen Assassins*, only three years later. A gritty look at the efforts of 13 men given the task by an official (Tetsuro Tanba) of assassinating the malevolent, out-of-control lord (Kantaro Suga) of the province, the ambience and attention to period detail is exemplary, the writing caustic, the performances nuanced. The men are led by an elder samurai (Chiezo Kataoka) possessed of a zen-like calm, and he's evenly matched against the lord's comparatively honorable, justifiably paranoid captain of the guards (a superb Ryohei Uchida). When the 13 men spring their elaborate trap for the lord's cortege as it enters a small village on the river's edge, the carnage erupts and proceeds unabated for the final half-hour of the film's just over two-hour running time. Nearly everyone is slaughtered in the process, including Katoaka and Uchida.

Castle Of Owls, a famous ninja tale just remade in the late nineties by Masahiro Shinoda, is not in quite the same scorched earth league, partly due to its lush color cinematography. However, it *is* another surprisingly intelligent, consistently involving saga full of authentic period flavor. Ryutaro Otomo is the lead ninja intent on eventually assassinating the shogun and overturning the government that has long suppressed his clan. He comes up against several formidable adversaries, amongst them a counter-insurgent samurai (Minoru Oki) and a seductive lady-in-waiting (Hizuru Takachiho) who is actually a ninja, too. To Otomo's dismay, he falls in love with Takachiho, and before the film reaches its halfway point the female assassin is chagrined to find herself reciprocating his feelings. What could easily have come off as awkward and clumsy in lesser hands Kudo manages with ease, developing the love story by degrees in a credible fashion. In fact, Kudo's direction is so good one doesn't mind the comparatively unrealistic, upbeat ending.

Shot in black and white, *The Great Melee* is the second of the three great samurai films I have alluded to, with an even more realistic, down-and-dirty approach than *Thirteen Assassins*. A reform activist (Kotaro Satomi) is pulled inexorably into the fray when an acquaintance being hunted by government troops hides in his house. Samurai police burst in, kill the man and attempt to arrest Satomi. Unfortunately, his wife runs into the street after him and is mercilessly cut down. Rescued by fellow activists who create a diversion, Satomi is sheltered by a good-natured, hard-drinking, apolitical *ronin* (Mikijiro Hira). A wealthy opposition samurai (Toru Abe) begins to organize a disparate group, including Satomi, a female ninja, a sex-obsessed priest (Rinichi Yamamoto) and a samurai family man (Shiro Osaka), in an effort to assassinate the abusive lord. However, the cruel, arrogant lord (Kantaro Suga again) has a conscientious, high-ranking swordsman as his keeper (Ryutaro Otomo). Consequently, *all* the killers bite the dust before reaching their royal target. Previously apathetic *ronin* Hira, traumatized when he sees pal Satomi cut down, and shocked when he hears the lord's resulting callous laughter, snaps, takes up his sword and finishes off the petty tyrant himself. As Kudo mentions in the following interview, the film was a stark allegory of the radical student movement in early sixties Japan, and the movie captures this feeling perfectly without sledgehammer juxtapositions or proselytizing.

Kudo's third loosely-linked *chanbara* gem was *Eleven Samurai*, in 1967, and it, too, is in black and white. A royal official (Kantaro Suga) from Edo on a rural stag hunt shoots an arrow into the back of a farmer too slow to get out of his way, then places another arrow in the eye of the local *daimyo*, who was riding in the area and protested against the murder. The brutal, high-ranking Suga rides off with his samurai retainers as the other lord dies in the arms of his outraged men. The balance of the picture follows the wronged clan members, led by Isao Natsuyagi, as they attempt to find an opening to ambush and assassinate the tyrant. They're joined by an unkempt, slightly unhinged *ronin* (Ko Nishimura) who is a master swordsman and ruthless killer. Once again, the evil lord's loyal commander is played by Ryutaro Otomo, a man nearly taxed to the breaking point in trying to protect his shamefully inhuman superior. Yet again, the film's last 20 minutes are taken up with unrelieved carnage as Natsuyagi's men attack the lord's procession on a country road. Blood mixes with mud in a fierce rainstorm, and Otomo and Natsuyagi skewer each other in combat after the lord is slain. Nishimura, the *ronin*, is the sole survivor, and gleefully lops off the dead tyrant's head as souvenir.

Although all three of these black-and-white *jidai-geki* were written by the same writer (Kaneo Ikegami), have very similar stories and even have the same actor – Kantaro Suga – playing nearly identical tyrants, each picture emerges as a distinct variation on a theme. Kudo brings a gravity, a fearfully intrinsic logic to the proceedings that never becomes leaden, and captures the feudal mindset of fanatical loyalty and pitiless vengeance with an unerring eye that has few equals.

With that in mind, it is a pleasure to report that Kudo brought identical virtues to his handling of the *yakuza* genre. His two films in Noboru Ando's vehicle, *Japan's Underworld History*, are relentless, emotionally complex accounts of gangster life. Kudo expertly steers these early prototypical *jitsuroku* pictures, with *Blood Feud* the most remarkably fascinating in its depiction of a strange surrogate father-and-son relationship between a cop (Junzaburo Ban) and a veteran soldier-turned-gang-boss (Noboru Ando). An insightful textbook case of one driven gangster's morbid psychology.

Industrial Spy is a clever, subtle look at class warfare in the guise of an industrial espionage thriller. Tatsuo Umemiya excels as the morally ruthless blackmailer and thief who is an expert at what he does. He's ready to sacrifice all, including the love of his nightclub dancer girlfriend (Reiko Oshida), to gain acceptance in the lofty circle of back-stabbing businessmen. At the conclusion, he's mortified to find that all the top captains of industry are the same. No matter how many times he's raised their stock prices or saved their businesses by his underhanded tactics, no matter how good he is at his dirty job, to them he will always be nothing more than a second-class citizen.

Up On Thirty Charges is a skilful, seamless integration of humor and action. Number seven of the *Viper Brothers* series, Bunta Sugawara and Tamio Kawaji return as the perpetual ex-cons – two amoral, soft-hearted bumpkins who idolize the *yakuza* idyll, yet end up sabotaged by their naiveté and blindness to the betraying ways of their gangster brethren. Of course, the murderous betrayals – in this case the slaying of their tomboy protegé (Michi Azuma) – never fail to result in their homicidally over-the-top payback assaults on bad guy headquarters.

Aftermath Of Battles Without Honor And Humanity was the ninth and final film in the *Battles* series, and was the sole one not made by the original director, Kinji Fukasaku. Hiroki Matsukata is the only main star returning from previous installments with newcomers Jinpachi Nezu, Mieko Harada and Rudo Uzaki pumping new blood into the proceedings as up-and-coming gangbangers. Although a good idea to have Kudo at the helm, a man responsible for what might be termed *jitsuroku* samurai movies as well as several excellent *yakuza* sagas, the end result is somewhat uneven. Kudo elicits good performances from his young stars, but the writing is not quite up to the high standards of the previous *Battles* entries.

Poster for *Japan's Underworld History – Blood Feud*

Kudo finally got to make *Beast Detective* in 1982, a picture that had been put on hold in the late seventies while Toei studios had brought the *Battles* series to conclusion. Ken Ogata plays a maverick cop at odds with his superiors while trying to establish a relationship with his new love, a single mother. Kudo worked mostly in television in the eighties, most notably on the *Sure Death* (*Hissatsu*) series, and *Beast Detective* remains one of his best movies of that decade.

Tale Of A Scarface is the story of a middle-aged gangster (Kiyoshi Nakajo) returning from prison who feels out of place back at home with his gang, a bunch now populated with brash punks and only a few old-timers. He starts an uneasy friendship with one young subordinate, but things take a turn for the worse when he's wounded in a skirmish with a rival gang. He goes to a doctor's office for treatment, falls in love with his nurse, but soon realizes his feelings are in vain as she is married. The picture is a poignant meditation on loss of all kinds, and never resorts to cheap sentiment or manipulation of audience emotion to achieve its effect.

Although in 1998 Kudo directed episodes of a television series about the famous samurai assassins group, the *Shinsengumi*, 1997's *Tale Of A Scarface* was the last feature film he completed before his death in 2000.

EIICHI KUDO – SELECTED FILMOGRAPHY

1960   *BLOODY ACCOUNT OF JIROCHO – DUEL AT AKIBA (JIROCHO KESSHO-KI – AKIBA NO TAIKETSU)*
        BLOODY ACCOUNT OF JIROCHO – MASSACRE JOURNEY (JIROCHO KESSHO-KI – NAGURIKOMI DOCHU)
        BLOODY ACCOUNT OF JIROCHO – DUEL AT FUJIMI PASS (JIROCHO KESSHO-KI –FUJIMI TOGE NO TAIKETSU)
        BLOODY ACCOUNT OF JIROCHO – ATTACK AT KOJIN MOUNTAIN (JIROCHO KESSHO-KI – NAGURIKOMI KOJIN YAMA)

1961   *LADY YAKUZA, FLOWER OF GREAT EDO (HANA NO O EDO NO YAKUZA HIME)*

1963   *THIRTEEN ASSASSINS (JUSAN-NIN NO SHIKAKU)*
        CASTLE OF OWLS (NINJA HICHO – FUKURO NO SHIRO, aka NINJA SECRET SCROLL – OWL'S CASTLE)

1964   *THE GREAT MELEE (DAI SATSUJIN)*

1965   *MEIJI ERA UNDERWORLD – YAKUZA G-MEN (MEIJI ANKOKUGAI – YAKUZA G-MEN)*

1967   *ELEVEN SAMURAI (JUICHI-NIN NO SAMURAI)*
        JAPAN'S UNDERWORLD HISTORY – BLOOD FEUD (NIHON ANKOKUSHI – CHI NO KOSO)

1968   *INDUSTRIAL SPY (SANGYO SUPAI)*
        JAPAN'S UNDERWORLD HISTORY – FUTILE COMPASSION (NIHON ANKOKUSHI – NASAKE MUYO)

1969   *FIVE BOUNTY HUNTERS (GONIN NO SHOKIN KASEGI,* aka *FORT OF DEATH)*

1973   *YAKUZA VS. G-MEN – DECOY (YAKUZA TAI G-MEN – OTORI)*

1974   *THE VIPER BROTHERS – UP ON THIRTY CHARGES (MAMUSHI NO KYODAI – FUTARI AWASETTE SAN-JUPPAN)*

1979   *AFTERMATH OF BATTLES WITHOUT HONOR AND HUMANITY (SONOGONO JINGINAKI TATAKAI)*

1980   *SHADOW WARRIOR – HATTORI HANZO (KAGE NO GUNDAN – HATTORI HANZO)*

1982   *BEAST DETECTIVE (YAJU DEKA)*

1986   *SURE DEATH 3 (HISSATSU 3 – URA KA OMOTE KA,* aka *ASSASSINS 3)*

1992   *PASSION'S RED AND BLACK (AKA TO KURO NO NETSUJO)*

1997   *TALE OF A SCARFACE (GUNRO NO KEIFU,* aka *THE GANG OF WOLVES FAMILY TREE)*

EIICHI KUDO – INTERVIEW

The following interview took place in the offices of Creative Enterprises International in Tokyo in October, 1997. Shoko Ishiyama translated on-site.

CD: *What made you decide to want to become a filmmaker?*

KUDO: I knew Mr Kinji Fukasaku, and he got me to come to work at Toei. That was in 1952. Three or four years later, by the time 1956 had rolled around, Toei studios had grown quite big and successful.

CD: *What made you decide, though, to try to make a career in film?*

KUDO: At the time I went into Toei, the Japanese economy was very bad. It was extremely difficult to get employed. Before that I'd been a stage manager for various theater groups. I also needed to support my wife. Then came the Toei job, but I didn't have any concrete idea at the time about one day becoming a movie director.

CD: *Who were some of the directors that you worked under in the beginning?*

KUDO: Well, I first started in planning and development, coming up with ideas for the movies. It was a starting position, much like you would do at any job in the beginning, and I did that for about the first year. Then something happened. Toei had two studio branches, one in Tokyo that made *gendai* films, and the other in Kyoto that made the *jidai-geki* films. My boss came to me and said that he wanted me to go to work in Kyoto. However, I felt that I was so unfamiliar with *jidai-geki* film it made me really resistant to going. I felt that I would be much better working in Tokyo. He said, 'But you know *chanbara* from when you were a kid, you played *jidai-geki*, being a samurai and swinging an imaginary sword.' However, it's quite different to try to do it as an adult working in film. I kept saying that I didn't want to go, asking my boss for some way out. And every night, after work, he would take me out for drinks, trying to convince me to go. It got to the point where I just kept telling him 'No, I don't want to go,' so he would take me out for drinks every night! (*laughs*) Finally, one of my supervisors put his foot down and ordered me to do it: 'You have to go to Kyoto, and that's it!' So, I ended up in Kyoto. For the first six months I did various production jobs. After that, I was made an assistant director and worked in rotation with probably ten different directors, all doing *jidai-geki*. It's very difficult to just single out one or two.

CD: The first film you directed was The Flute-Playing Warrior, *a shorter movie. Was this a serious, adult* jidai-geki *picture or more like the juvenile* chanbara *serials starring Sentaro Fushimi, movies aimed at children?*

KUDO: At the studio they called that kind of film an SP, I'm not sure why, maybe it stood for 'short program'. When a director was starting out, they always gave you a shorter picture to begin with, something that wouldn't be too overwhelming or risk too much money. Back then all theaters showed double features. The first film would be 90 minutes or so, then the second feature would run anywhere from 50 to 70 minutes. As far as the story, that particular film was aimed at more of a matinee audience.

CD: In 1960, you did the four-film Bloody Account Of Jirocho *series. Were these like the good-natured, somewhat humorous* Jirocho *films that directors like Masahiro Makino made? Or did they have the grim, downbeat quality of your* jidai-geki *in the mid-sixties?*

KUDO: Most of the other *Jirocho* films that had been made were about the character when he was already a full-fledged *yakuza* boss. I was told to make my films about the beginnings of Jirocho's clan, what it was like when he was trying to make a name for himself. Since the idea of portraying the character was fundamentally different, yes, it was also a different approach to the story.

CD: You made a few jidai-geki *pictures with famous singing star Hibari Misora in the early sixties. I haven't seen them, but I have seen several that she did with director Tadashi Sawashima. Were your films with her like that with musical numbers, or were they more serious?*

KUDO: Mr Sawashima was the first to direct her pictures at Toei. Then, yes, I also worked with her, and the films we did were, I'm sure, like the ones you saw – the Japanese-style *jidai-geki* musicals. The producers would always want to make sure she sang musical numbers because it brought more people into the theater. I had seen musicals from America and Europe, but quite often they were much more spectacular. I thought to myself, 'How can I do that? We don't have the budget.' So we needed to make the traditional Japanese-style musical with everyone periodically breaking into song and dance in a regular *jidai-geki* setting.

CD: You made Castle Of Owls *in 1963, and it was a serious ninja story, although it has a more upbeat ending than some of your later movies. How would you compare this to the* Ninja, Band Of Assassins *(*Shinobi No Mono*) series starring Raizo Ichikawa?*

KUDO: The *Ninja, Band Of Assassins* series was based on a novel by Kanoi Murayama, a Communist who belonged to a pretty radical group, and his books were realistic and historically accurate. *Castle Of Owls* was also based on a work of fiction, but a more mainstream, award-winning novel by the popular *jidai-geki* writer Ryotaro Shiba. The original script was fairly different, then the final film ended up even more of a departure. Shiba's novel had had more of a 'found diaries' format, and the original script kept many of the social observations. But my film ended up being an even more fictionalized interpretation of the novel.

CD: Your Thirteen Assassins *was one of the first more realistic, profound jidai-geki movies made at Toei. There were a couple of others at Toei with a similar tone almost simultaneously, Tadashi Imai's* Tale Of Bushido Cruelty *(Bushido Zankoku Monogatari, 1963) and Tai Kato's* Cruelty Of The Shogunate's Downfall *(Bakamatsu Zankoku Monogatari, 1964). Was there any trouble getting those more truthful jidai-geki pictures made at Toei, as opposed to their usual glossy entertainment style?*

KUDO: If I remember correctly, it was from the Toei side, some of the Toei producers who wanted to try that approach. Even though there were some dissenting opinions, I still ended up being more helped than hindered by everyone in creating that more gritty style.

CD: Why do you think that you, Mr Imai and Mr Kato all wanted to make more realistic jidai-geki films right at the same time? Had all of you been talking together or was it just a coincidence?

KUDO: Of course, before I made *Thirteen Assassins* I and other directors at the studio would be communicating with each other about ideas and approaches to style. Just like any studio situation, even now, where you're coming into contact with other filmmakers. At the same time, it was the Toei policy to generally produce pictures that were happy and entertaining. But some people at Toei were starting to have their doubts about moving exclusively in that direction. So, at the top, Toei's attitude about doing the majority of their pictures in that vein was weakening. We decided to try to do this more serious kind of *jidai-geki* picture, and Toei agreed.

CD: The next more realistic jidai-geki film you did, The Great Melee, *was made in 1964 and had a pretty grim resolution. Was the assassin's group and the events in the picture based on real-life historical personalities and events?*

KUDO: It was fiction and not based on any specific historical facts.

CD: The film critic Tadao Sato has compared The Great Melee *to the Japanese student protest movement, the demonstrations happening at the same time the film was made. Is there any truth in that or is that simply Mr Sato's own perception?*

KUDO: Yes, the story itself was based on the student movement of the sixties. But we did it in the style and period of a *jidai-geki* film, so many people are not aware of it. Political scenarios tend to get targeted and criticized when done in a contemporary milieu. When you tell a story about that kind of movement, there are basic things that don't change. You have a system or a movement, and the originator of the movement who expresses ideology, and then other leaders who steer the followers and promote action. They all initially share the same goals, but, as so often happens in protest movements, things collapse for a variety of reasons. And chaos results. We portrayed those political structures, agendas of the day symbolically in *jidai-geki* form, showing the way people get conflicted and betray their ideals, or unexpectedly follow through.

CD: There's some unusual things that happen in The Great Melee. *Shiro Osaka's character kills his family, whom he loves very much, because he knows what's going to happen after he sacrifices himself trying to kill the* daimyo. *Mikijiro Hira's character, though, is basically a hard-drinking, womanizing* ronin *without any political convictions whatsoever. That is, until he sees his comrade, Kotaro Satomi, lying dead and realizes he needs to fulfill his friend's mission. And he's the one who ends up killing the lord. Were you trying to say that most common people won't take any overt, strong political action until someone they know is hurt or killed, or until their own lives are affected in some way? Or am I reading too much into it?*

KUDO: Osaka's character is like many political radicals in that he might have family ties but he's living his life more and more as a fugitive. He has these other people, his wife and children, depending on him. Yet he will soon be in an even worse position. Perhaps it's an Eastern way of thinking, but he takes responsibility for his actions and their lives. He knows there will be no one there to take care of his family after he assassinates the lord. So he, rightly or wrongly, mercifully kills them himself. Kotaro Satomi, whose wife is murdered at the beginning by the lord's men, is similar but his friend, the Mikijiro Hira character, is the exact opposite. He loves to have fun and isn't worried about the future. Then suddenly, when he sees Satomi there dead, he pauses, shocked. Almost without even any conscious thought, he shifts towards commitment, following through with the killing. There's one other character, the priest played by Rinichi Yamamoto, a man working with the rebels but a total animal when it comes to his one weakness, women. Someone with conflicts and weaknesses. And all these characters mixed together with the repressive forces of government – it's anarchy.

CD: In Thirteen Assassins *and* Eleven Samurai *you had music by Akira Ifukube. But in* The Great Melee *there was a total of only a few minutes of music. I was wondering why this was. Even though the other two are also serious* jidai-geki *pictures,* The Great Melee *seems almost like a documentary.*

KUDO: When we were filming *The Great Melee*, there were some days where we had between 200 and 300 people on the set. It could take a whole day just to rehearse each mob scene. So we divided those scenes in the script into three or four parts. In each part, I would put two or three experienced actors who were already in the scenes to help coordinate the extras, to be responsible for the mob movement blocking and the emotional attitude. I would tell them: 'You really have to be on top of this, because if someone you're supervising screws up then we'll have to do the whole thing all over again.' I think that, as well as our approach to the script and shooting style, could have helped to create that documentary-like feeling. Also, I purposely wanted to keep the music to a minimum so it wouldn't seem artificial or detract from the realism.

CD: *The two* Japan's Underworld History *pictures,* Blood Feud *and* Futile Compassion, *were* yakuza *films that anticipated the later* jitsuroku *trend of the seventies, movies like the* Battles Without Honor And Humanity *series. Were these films based on any real-life events or people? Or were they works of fiction? Both of these featured former* yakuza, *Noboru Ando, who had been in films that were either purportedly based on his real-life experiences or written by him.*

KUDO: Those films were fiction. But for certain scenes I would ask Mr Ando for his advice on how someone would act, because the other actors had never had any real contact with the underworld. To help make it credible. I wanted to focus on the forming of the gang, the building of the family. How the individual gangsters meet, form bonds, draw up their daily activities, go to war with other gangs. I'm not really attracted to the *ninkyo-* or *jingi*-slanted stories. So this more realistic, true-to-life approach was natural to me. I'm interested in chronicling what the persons were like before they joined the gang, then how the 'family' life changes them and their comrades.

CD: *Was Ando supposed to be the same character in both films?*

KUDO: (*laughs*)

CD: *Ando's character dies at the end of the second one, but it's not clear if he dies in the first film.*

KUDO: Well, they're supposed to be different stories. The series title, *Japan's Underworld History*, was just Toei's way of marketing the films, linking them together.

CD: *In the first one,* Blood Feud, *the older police detective played by Junzaburo Ban is almost a surrogate father figure to Ando's character. He helps him out of the jam with the US occupation forces in the beginning, monitors his progress as a gangster and, in the end, is so enraged at Ando's unredeemed character he has to be pulled off from beating Ando when he's arrested. This is such a strange relationship to see in a* yakuza *movie.*

KUDO: The original idea was to make two characters meet at the beginning then, by the end, they're trying to kill each other. In the case of most *yakuza,* they're lacking love – family love, brother love, any kind of love. As a result, they act out, perpetrating violent acts, stealing money, whatever. I wanted to make Ban's character a bit like a counsellor, someone who naturally wants to help and steer people right. He develops a fondness for Ando, in spite of himself, and as the picture goes on he gets more and more frustrated with his behavior. That's probably why you felt that Ban was something of a father figure to Ando.

CD: Five Bounty Hunters *was the second in a film series starring Tomisaburo Wakayama as a bounty hunter in the mid-1800s. I know there was a TV series, too, at one point, if I'm not mistaken. Did that come before or after the films?*

KUDO: I'm not too sure about the TV series. But Wakayama not only starred in the film, he also was kind of a producer and was instrumental in getting the cast together.

CD: *What was it like working with him?*

KUDO: (*laughs*) He was a lot of fun to work with, but he was also pretty immature. For certain things, when people didn't agree with him he would get really upset. Then, when he knew he was wrong, he would become very quiet. Much like a big child. He could swing from one extreme to another.

CD: *Your film* The Viper Brothers – Up On Thirty Charges *was a bit of a departure for you as it was a humorous* yakuza *picture. Did you enjoy that or would you rather have been doing a more serious film?*

KUDO: It's a tough question. Personally, I prefer doing the more serious pictures. But I think that it's good to take a break occasionally in between those more serious projects and do a lighter, more comical film. You can approach things in a different way and try new things.

CD: *I've seen several of the others in the* Viper Brothers *series, and your entry is my favorite. There's great stuff you do with the tomboy character played by Michi Azuma when she transforms herself into a beautiful woman because of her infatuation with Bunta Sugawara. Then after she's killed by the villains, Sugawara and Kawaji put her in the coffin filled with flowers. It really is done just right. It's moving without resorting to sentimentality and is quite unusual in some ways for that type of picture.*

KUDO: Well, Azuma's character as the tomboy who suddenly becomes a beautiful woman was, of course, in the scenario for comic effect. The audience would always enjoy seeing that kind of transformation, it's a typical kind of Japanese situation in theatrical plays and films. But I'm glad you appreciated my approach and the death scene with the flowers.

CD: *You directed the last of the* Battles Without Honor *series,* Aftermath Of Battles Without Honor And Humanity. *There were many real-life events in the post-war Japanese underworld that inspired those other films, and I was wondering if this also holds true for* Aftermath... ?

KUDO: When *Battles Without Honor And Humanity* had started, it was based on the exploits of various gangland factions. But this one was fictitious. The point of the film was to look at a gang family tree, the lineage of a *yakuza* group, how leadership was passed down to successors.

CD: *Where does the sub-plot with the pop singer fit in, the young gangster who goes on to become a success in pop music?*

KUDO: There was always a certain look, a certain specific image of a *yakuza* in the *Battles Without Honor* series, as well as other Toei *yakuza* movies from that period. There were actors who would audition for roles in those movies who would study the previous films to get the look and the mannerisms correct. So for this one, we wanted to do something different, something unexpected. That's why we used those kids, Jinpachi Nezu and Rudo Uzaki. They had a different style and energy that still seemed to work in a *yakuza* film. We made the other more established stars who had the usual *yakuza* image, actors like Hiroki Matsukata, into more secondary lead characters.

CD: The ninja film, Shadow Warrior – Hattori Hanzo; *how did you approach that differently from the* Castle Of Owls *ninja story? Obviously,* Shadow Warrior *was made much later and had a different character.*

KUDO: Compared to *Castle Of Owls, Shadow Warrior* was more about struggle in the strictest sense, the fight between opposing forces. Also, the style of acting, the action, everything was more exaggerated and bigger than life than in *Castle Of Owls.* That was very much Toei's approach to movie storytelling at the time.

CD: Ken Ogata plays a police detective who is also a single father in Beast Detective. *That seems like an unusual character for that type of film. How did the idea come about?*

KUDO: He's not the real father. But the woman he becomes involved with, it's her child. She's a single mother.

CD: I see ...

Poster for *Thirteen Assassins*

KUDO: The idea for the film had really taken shape about four or five years before it was actually shot. It was like many other films, too, that were kind of waiting in the wings in the late seventies. Most of Toei's energies were channelled into the *Battles Without Honor* series. It was so incredibly popular, several other scenarios, including *Beast Detective*, had to wait their turn. Once the popularity of *Battles Without Honor* began winding down, I was finally able to get it into pre-production and get ready to film.

CD: I don't know if you've seen it, but Al Pacino's part in the film Heat, *directed by Michael Mann, reminded me of Ken Ogata's character in* Beast Detective.

KUDO: (*laughs*)

CD: You directed the film Sure Death 3 *and you also directed many of the episodes of the* Sure Death *(Hissatsu) TV series. It was an extremely popular show in Japan. How did the films differ from the TV productions?*

KUDO: Makoto Fujita also played the main character in the TV series. And on TV we always went much more into Fujita's family life. He's this upright citizen, a samurai constable, but still a quiet guy who likes to spend time at home. Even though he's sometimes a bit henpecked by his mother-in-law. But then in his secret life, he's just the opposite, the leader of a squad of assassins. Of course, when you get into making a movie you have to create a more involved story, a bigger, more spectacular picture than you could do on television, more action and so forth. You have to make sure to give the audience something more, something they won't get on TV, so they'll come out to the theaters. It was much more difficult doing that film, partly because the series was so popular.

CD: Do you think doing jidai-geki *on television that you get to be more introspective, do more character-driven stories, then, in the movies, you need to paint on a bigger canvas? You can have intimate moments but still the emphasis is more on action and spectacle?*

KUDO: In TV you have to concentrate on the characters, their relationships with each other, how they interact. Also, the violence and depiction of evil is much more simplistic and obvious compared to film. You can't really let down your guard, you always have to have something happening on TV to keep people from changing the channel. Then there's the interruptions to sell something. With film you can build the narrative more subtly, you don't have to make it so obvious who the villain is. You can have more shadings of character, maybe characters who aren't even heroes or villains in the strictest sense. You can take a more subtle approach.

CD: How did Passion's Red And Black *differ from earlier Toei* yakuza *films you made in the sixties and seventies?*

KUDO: The earlier films were usually plot-driven. But the basic idea behind *Passion's Red And Black* is the instability of emotions, the uncertainty of human relationships. How friendships are sometimes fragile, they can be broken and then you can't go back to start over again, no matter how much you might want to. That was the premise.

CD: Do you have any projects that you're working on now?

KUDO: I recently completed a *yakuza* film that I'm editing now. But it's different from the usual gangster picture, a *yakuza* romance. It stars Kyoshi Nakajo, who is also a singer. His character is finally released from prison after 14 years. He rejoins his gang, but he doesn't quite know what's going on because he's been away so long. Now the others in his group are much younger than him. He's starting to get back into the life when he's hurt in a fight and has to go to a clinic. While he's there he falls in love with his nurse, but she's married and has a child. It's a different kind of *yakuza* film.

CD: What's the title?

KUDO: *Gunro No Keifu* or *The Gang Of Wolves' Family Tree* [The festival English release title is *Tale Of A Scarface*].

CD: Is this at Toei?

KUDO: Yes, they've put up some of the production money, but it'll be independently distributed. At the end of the film the main character kills his surrogate kid, this young *yakuza*. He knows that he himself is going to be killed soon, and he sees certain death for this young *yakuza* and his comrades. It'll be interesting because I'm not sure how some people will react, if they'll accept the ending. I have the character doing unusual things for a *yakuza*. Being sensitive and having an emotional life. Some people have objected and said, 'No, you can't do that! (*laughs*) This is a *yakuza* film!'

CD: What kind of films do you see?

KUDO: Well, when I'm making a film, I don't go see anything. When I do go to a theater now, (*laughs*) I don't know, maybe it's because of my age, but if I get bored I just fall right to sleep.

CD: Are there films you've seen recently that you like?

KUDO: I liked *The English Patient*. But it's strange. It won the Academy Award and all this praise, and I kept thinking they sure are making these characters really *nice*. Kind of too good to be true. I mean, the film is a love story, but it is just so unreal. All these beautiful, idealized pictures. You see, the Japanese tend to pickle everything – in other words, give it a sour twist.

3

Shinichi 'Sonny' Chiba

1939–

Despite the glowering expression that Sonny Chiba exhibits in many stills from his films, in person the man is outgoing, friendly and charmingly upbeat. Like a young boy opening up his presents on Christmas morning, Mr Chiba is obviously delighted to be an action-film star. He has always had a great deal of fun doing it, and his gleeful approach to his work is evidence of a man who has found his vocation in life. He has portrayed a number of sadistic heavies, or at least callous anti-heroes, in his time, as well as outright heroes. However, the two roles which seem closest to his own personality are one of his first and one of his latest. He still has the youthful spirit of his barely-out-of-his-teens-rocket-scientist-moonlighting-as-a-superhero role in *Invasion Of The Neptune Men*. And yet he also has the mature, sly humor, the grace of a man who has been under fire more than once, that we see in his sword-master-turned-sushi-chef in director Quentin Tarantino's *Kill Bill*. A martial arts expert in his own right, he does not have any arrogance or unwarranted pride in his skill.

The aforementioned *Neptune Men* and director Hajime Sato's *Terror Beneath The Sea* and *Golden Bat* were the first sightings of the actor on Western shores, though these were accessible only on American television. The late Sato, who also directed the amazing *Goke – Bodysnatcher From Hell*, is one of the most unappreciated genre film-makers from sixties Japan, and his two films with Chiba are unabashed entertainments, oddball live-action *manga* that are as appealing to adults as children.

But probably the most formative pictures Chiba made in his early career were four shorter action features which were slotted into the second halves of double bills. Made up of the pair of *Wandering Detective* and the pair of *Funky Hat* movies respectively, they were also the first efforts of genre master Kinji Fukasaku. All are infectious, knockabout affairs suffused with the charm of seeing two young talents – one an actor, one a director – getting together and discovering the fun of making movies. It was an important convergence of personalities, and cemented a bond between the two men that lasted until Mr Fukasaku's death in early 2003.

Chiba's initial martial arts forays in the movies came not in the early seventies, as one might think, but as early as 1963, with *Judo Life*, and then its sequel in 1964, *Judo Hall Demon*. There were a number of judo films made in the fifties, particularly at Toho and Daiei studios, and both of these, directed by Kiyoshi Saeki for Toei, blended *kodokan* (or judo hall) sagas with the burgeoning *ninkyo yakuza* craze. Chiba made action pictures all through the sixties, with his notable *ninkyo* efforts the *Legendary Lullaby* trilogy and *Tale Of Kawachi Chivalry*, and his most visible modern crime movies, *Kamikaze Man* and *Organized Crime*.

One of Chiba's biggest challenges came in 1969 with a role in Sadao Nakajima's epic *Secrets Of Japanese Assassinations*. Clocking in at over 140 minutes, the anthology film consists of several incidents in the late nineteenth and early twentieth centuries when assassins changed the course of Japanese history. Chiba displays a wide range of emotions, emerging as a vulnerable, tormented young man manipulated by an elder mentor (Chiezo Kataoka) into assassinating a prominent politician. His story takes up a considerable chunk of the running time, and he more than holds his own against such other heavyweights as Ken Takakura, Jiro Tamiya and Koji Tsuruta.

Starting in 1970, Toei studios began featuring Chiba in a string of progressively more violent action movies, more often than not punctuated with humor. Some, like the *Yakuza Cop* and *Bodyguard Kiba* pictures, were enjoyable but forgettable time-wasters. Others, like the *Yakuza Wolf* pair and *Killing Fist And Child*, were savage, outlandish tall tales filled with amazing swordfights, gunplay and bouts of hand-to-hand combat as well as colorful characters. *Yakuza Wolf – I Perform Murder* is especially memorable, filled with surreal *manga* imagery, Suzukiesque color schemes and an out-of-left-field spaghetti western influence that makes it one of Chiba's and director Ryuichi Takemori's best efforts.

Without question, Chiba's most famous movie series took shape in 1974, with Toei assigning top *ninkyo yakuza* director Shigehiro Ozawa to shepherd what would become *The Killing Fist* trilogy. Released in America as *The Streetfighter*, *Return Of The Streetfighter* and *The Streetfighter's Last Revenge*, these go-for-broke, gore-drenched martial arts sagas cemented Chiba's reputation as the only motion picture star who could come remotely close to challenging Bruce Lee's legend. With an X-ray perspective of one villain's skull being crushed, with genitals and throats torn out, all perpetrated by Chiba's anti-hero, Terry Tsurugi, the initial film was rated X for violence. Distributors New Line trimmed it to get an R rating, and for years it was only available in a diluted version until it was finally restored to its uncut, widescreen glory for video in the mid-nineties. The first two *Streetfighter* films retain an astonishing impact, despite the atrocious dubbing, and the first remains nearly as shocking today as when it was originally released. Much of the trilogy's visceral wallop is due as much to expert Ozawa's direction as to Chiba's brutal performance, and Toei attempted to hit pay dirt again when they assigned maverick Teruo Ishii to direct *The Executioner* pair of films the same year. Ishii, often mistakenly credited as director of the last *Streetfighter* film, succeeds admirably with the more serious first *Executioner* entry. However, Ishii didn't particularly want to make the sequel, *The Big Turnabout*, so he turned it into a silly, scatological heist action/comedy more in keeping with Blake Edwards' later *Pink Panther* films.

Chiba did a number of action-packed biography films in the mid-seventies, too, portraying Doshin So, originator of *shorinji kenpo*, in *The Killing Machine* and *kyokushin kenka karate* master Mas Oyama in *Champion Of Death* and *Karate Bearfighter*. But one of Chiba's most obscure, hard-to-see pictures, *Wolfguy – The Burning Wolfman*, directed by Kazuhiko Yamaguchi in 1975, truly beggars any kind

Poster for *Tale Of Kawachi Chivalry*

of classification. Not a typical lycanthrope horror yarn, it concerns a select number of people, including Chiba, who have been cursed with weird, supernatural energy that can rip to pieces or severely burn whomever angers them. Saddled with numerous exploitable elements, it ultimately evolves into a hybrid of David-Cronenberg-style organic/body horror and an action-oriented *yakuza* tale, the kind of movie that Takashi Miike might now make.

Most memorable of Chiba's more serious *yakuza* pictures during this period were Kinji Fukasaku's first sequel in the *Battles Without Honor And Humanity* series, *Hiroshima Death Match* and Sadao Nakajima's blood-soaked *Great Okinawa Yakuza War*. Chiba plays irredeemable psychopaths in both, and emerges as one of his scariest creations in the latter, a disfigured, psychotic karate expert/gangster who owes more than a little to an unrestrained re-imagining of his *Streetfighter* persona.

Nevertheless, vying for first place with *The Streetfighter* pictures as Chiba roles most visible to Western eyes were the handful of characters he portrayed in samurai movies and television in the late seventies and early eighties. Starting with his most conspicuous, *The Shadow Warrior* TV series chronicled various incarnations of famous ninja Hattori Hanzo, and inspired legions of fans, young and old alike. One of Quentin Tarantino's favorites, the director paid tribute to the show and Chiba by casting him as the modern personification of Hanzo in *Kill Bill*. Chiba also shone brightly in all-star *jidai-geki* spectaculars *Shogun's Samurai* and *Samurai Reincarnation*. Both were directed by master and old friend Kinji Fukasaku, and star Chiba as legendary Jubei Yagyu. In the first, based on the popular Japanese TV series *Yagyu Clan Conspiracy*, Fukasaku takes a more historical approach, but the second is delirious fantasy horror *chanbara*, with Chiba's Jubei having to fight famous undead swordsmen conjured by resurrected Christian samurai-turned-satanist Amakusa Shiro Tokisada. Played by Kenji Sawada, the Tokisada character was based on a real-life Christian swordsman who was executed for his beliefs.

Sonny Chiba continues to work at a feverish pace, in demand all over the world in both motion pictures and television, and, as mentioned above, he can be seen most recently on Western screens in Tarantino's *Kill Bill*.

SHINICHI 'SONNY' CHIBA – SELECTED FILMOGRAPHY

(Note: Sonny Chiba's complete filmography is quite lengthy. I have omitted almost all films where his appearances amount to little more than cameos – i.e. several of Etsuko 'Sue' Shiomi's pictures. I've also omitted many of his non-Japanese films and/or films that are of dubious genre significance.)

1961   *INVASION OF THE NEPTUNE MEN (UCHI KAISOKU-SEN)*
       WANDERING DETECTIVE – TRAGEDY IN RED VALLEY (FURAIBO TANTEI – AKAI TANI NO SANGEKI)

*WANDERING DETECTIVE – BLACK WIND IN THE HARBOR (FURAIBO
TANTEI – MISAKI O WATARU KUROI KAZE)*
VIGILANTE'S FUNKY HAT (FUNKY HATTO NO KAIDANJI)
*VIGILANTE'S FUNKY HAT – 200,000 YEN ARM (FUNKY HATTO NO KAIDANJI
– NISANMEN-EN NO UDE)*

1962   *GANG VS. G-MEN (GYANGU TAI G-MEN)*
          CHESS MASTER (OSHO)

1963   *YAKUZA'S SONG (YAKUZA NO UTA)*
          JUDO LIFE (JUDO ICHIDAI)

1964   *JUDO LIFE – JUDO HALL DEMON (JUDO ICHIDAI – KODOKAN NO ONI)*

1966   *TERROR BENEATH THE SEA (KAITEI DAI SENSO)*
          GOLDEN BAT (OGON BATTO)
          *KAMIKAZE MAN – SHOWDOWN AT NOON (KAMIKAZE YARO – MAHIRU NO
          KETTO)*
          LEGENDARY LULLABY (ROKYOKU KOMORI UTA)
          *ABASHIRI PRISON – NORTHERN SEACOAST STORY (ABASHIRI BANGAICHI
          – HOKKAI HEN)*

1967   *LEGENDARY LULLABY 2 (ZOKU ROKYOKU KOMORI UTA)*
          LULLABY FOR MY SON (SHUSSE KOMORI UTA)
          ORGANIZED CRIME (SOSHIKI BORYOKU)
          TALE OF KAWACHI CHIVALRY (KAWACHI YUKYODEN, aka *ROUGHS OF
          KAWACHI)*

1969   *SECRETS OF JAPANESE ASSASSINATIONS (NIPPON ANSATSU HIROKU,* aka
          MEMOIRS OF JAPANESE ASSASSINS)

1970   *THE LAST KAMIKAZE (SAIGO NO TOKKOTAI)*
          YAKUZA COP (YAKUZA DEKA, aka *GAMBLER COP)*
          *YAKUZA COP – MARIJUANA GANG (YAKUZA DEKA – MARIFANA MITSUBAI
          SOSHIKI,* aka *THE ASSASSIN)*

1971   *YAKUZA COP – POISON GAS AFFAIR (YAKUZA DEKA – KYOFU NO DOKU
          GASU,* aka *POISON GAS TERROR)*
          *YAKUZA COP – NO EPITAPHS FOR US (YAKUZA DEKA – ORETACHI NI
          HAKAWANAI)*

1972   *NARCOTICS/PROSTITUTION G-MEN (MAYAKU BAISHUN G-MEN)*
          *NARCOTICS/PROSTITUTION G-MEN – FRIGHTENING FLESH HELL
          (MAYAKU BAISHUN G-MEN – KYOFU NO NIKU JIGOKU)*
          *YAKUZA WOLF – I PERFORM MURDER (OKAMI YAKUZA – KOROSHI WA ORE
          GA YARU)*
          *YAKUZA WOLF – EXTEND MY CONDOLENCES (OKAMI YAKUZA – TOMURA
          IWA ORE GA DESU)*

1973   *BATTLES WITHOUT HONOR AND HUMANITY – HIROSHIMA DEATH
          MATCH (JINGINAKI TATAKAI – HIROSHIMA SHITO HEN)* [no. 2 of the
          series]

BODYGUARD KIBA (BODDEE GADO KIBA, aka THE BODYGUARD, aka KARATE KIBA) [no. 1 of 2]

BODYGUARD KIBA 2 (BODDEE GADO KIBA – HISSATSU SAN KAKUTOBI) [no. 2 of 2]

1974   *THE STREETFIGHTER (GEKI TOTSU! SATSUJINKEN, aka SUDDEN ATTACK! THE KILLING FIST)* [no.1 of 3]

RETURN OF THE STREETFIGHTER (SATSUJINKEN 2, aka KILLING FIST 2) [no. 2 of 3]

STREETFIGHTER'S LAST REVENGE (GYAKUSHU! SATSUJINKEN, aka COUNTERATTACK! THE KILLING FIST) [no. 3 of 3]

THE EXECUTIONER (CHOKU GEKI! JIGOKU HEN, aka DIRECT HIT! – HELL FIST) [no. 1 of 2]

THE EXECUTIONER – THE BIG TURNABOUT (CHOKU GEKI! JIGOKU HEN – DAI GYAKUTEN, aka DIRECT HIT! HELL FIST – THE BIG COUNTERATTACK) [no. 2 of 2]

SISTER STREETFIGHTER (ONNA HISSATSU KEN)

1975   *DETONATION! VIOLENT TRIBE (BAKUHATSU! BOSOZOKU)*

KILLING MACHINE (SHORINJI KENPO)

BULLET TRAIN (SHINKANSEN DAIBAKUHA)

WOLFGUY – BURNING WOLFMAN (WOLFGUY – MOERO OKAMI OTOKO)

CHAMPION OF DEATH (KENKA KARATE KYOKU SHINKEN)

GREAT OKINAWA YAKUZA WAR (OKINAWA YAKUZA DAI SENSO)

1976   *KILLING FIST AND CHILD (KOZURE SATSUJINKEN, aka KARATE WARRIORS)*

YOKOHAMA UNDERWORLD – DRAGON'S MACHINE GUN (YOKOHAMA ANKOKUGAI – MASHIN GAN NO RYU)

1977   *KARATE BEARFIGHTER (KYOKUSHIN KENKA KARATE BURAI KEN)*

HOKURIKU PROXY WAR (HOKURIKU DAIRI SENSO, aka AGENT OF WAR OF THE NORTH)

DOBERMAN DETECTIVE (DOOBERUMAN DEKA)

GAMBLING CODE OF JAPAN (NIHON NO JINGI)

GOLGO 13 – KOWLOON ASSIGNMENT (GORUGO 13 – KURYU NO KUBI, aka GOLGO 13 – HEAD OF NINE DRAGONS)

1978   *OKINAWA TEN YEAR WAR (OKINAWA JUN NEN SENSO)*

MESSAGE FROM SPACE (UCHU KARA NO MESSIJI)

SHOGUN'S SAMURAI (YAGYUIZOKU NO INBO, aka YAGYU CLAN CONSPIRACY)

1979   *HUNTER IN THE DARK (YAMI NO KARIUDO)*

1980   *VIRUS (FUKKATSU NO HI)*

SHOGUN'S NINJA (NINJA BUGEICHO – MOMOCHI SANDA YU)

1981   *SAMURAI REINCARNATION (MAKAI TENSHO)*

1982   *NINJA WARS (IGA NINPO CHO, aka IGA NINJA MAGIC SCROLL, aka BLACK MAGIC WARS)*

ROARING FIRE (HOERO TEKKEN, aka HERO'S IRON FIRST)

1985   *THE LAST GAMBLER (SAIGO NO BAKUTO)*

1987   *SURE DEATH 4 (HISSATSU 4 – URAMI HARASHIMASU*, aka *ASSASSINS #4 – WE WILL AVENGE YOU)*

1989   *SHOGUN'S SHADOW (SHOGUN IEMITSU NO RANSHIN – GEKI TOTSU!*, aka *THE INSANITY OF SHOGUN IEMITSU – SUDDEN ATTACK)*

1992   *TRIPLE CROSS (ITSUKA GIRA GIRA SURU HI*, aka *THE DAY'S TOO BRIGHT)*

2003   *BATTLE ROYALE 2*

         KILL BILL, vol. 1

SHINICHI 'SONNY' CHIBA – INTERVIEW

This interview was conducted in mid-November, 1997, in a suite at an upscale Tokyo hotel. Shoko Ishiyama translated on-site. Dr Akiko Agishi from Creative Enterprises International was also present, along with two of Mr Chiba's assistants. Ai Kennedy also helped on some retranslation and clarification on portions of the interview that were hard to hear because of recording anomalies.

CHIBA: Right now the Japanese film industry is not doing that well. I'm hoping to do more *jidai-geki* because I think it will help movie business in general. I want to do the *Zato Masa* project, which is a spin-off from the *Zatoichi* films. It's a story about Zatoichi's brother. I've talked to Mr Katsu's wife, Tamao Nakamura, and she was very happy about my interest. She told me that Mr Katsu had so much he wanted to do that he didn't get to accomplish. I would like to resurrect Katsu's world. Hopefully, we will be able to do it next year. I prefer *jidai-geki* to contemporary films. What is your interest in *jidai-geki*?

CD: *There's a feeling I get, something intangible. I get a similar sensation from spaghetti westerns. I do think Japan has made some of the best action films, both in-period and modern era. Especially films from the sixties and seventies.*

CHIBA: I like *jidai-geki* not only from the past in Japan but from all over the world, different ideas of historical period film.

CD: *When you started out, you were involved in the New Faces competition at Toei. How did you become involved with that talent search?*

CHIBA: Originally, I had no interest in getting involved in the movie industry. I wanted to be a gymnast, and that's what I was working towards. But unfortunately I was injured and was not able to pursue that professionally. I've loved movies since I was very little, and they've always meant a lot to me. So, I thought as an alternative I'd try to get a job in that area since I had to make a living somehow. I started to study acting, applied for the Toei New Faces program, and I passed the exam. This was when I was about 22 years old.

CD: The first movies of yours that I think got exposure in America were Invasion Of The Neptune Men, Terror Beneath The Sea …

CHIBA: *(laughs)* … Yeah, yeah, yeah …

CD: … and Golden Bat, *the last two directed by Hajime Sato.*

CHIBA: *(laughs heartily)*

CD: I know people who are big fans of Terror Beneath The Sea *and* Golden Bat.

CHIBA: American fans? How do they know them?

CD: They've seen them on video.

CHIBA: Ah, video. There were many American performers in *Terror Beneath The Sea*. Unfortunately, the director, Hajime Sato, died in 1995.

CD: The two Wandering Detective *films –*

CHIBA: – Directed by Kinji Fukasaku! His first films as director. They were also my first really 'leading man' roles in the movies. Those were kind of a rite of passage for both of us. I was really amazed at his skills as a novice director. The films were short but so intense. Mr Fukasaku became more and more famous and successful, going on to work in the top of the Japanese film industry with people like Ken Takakura and Koji Tsuruta. But, because we made those first films together when we were both starting out, we've stayed close. I consider him a master and good friend. He's always been a very important person in my life. Whenever we've worked together, I always end up hoping to work with him again in the future. Mr Fukasaku has a really good heart, I respect him very much.

CD: What were the next two films you did with Mr Fukasaku, the Vigilante In The Funky Hat *pictures ?*

CHIBA: *(laughs)* The *Wandering Detective* films are action movies. But the *Funky Hat* ones are more offbeat, they have almost a beatnik flavor. They're quirky, fast-paced, about a flashy dresser who thinks he's cool, has a girl and gets involved in trouble. Further out than the *Wandering Detective* pictures, almost the opposite. Mr Fukasaku said at the time that, if the *Funky Hat* movies were a type of music, they'd be up-tempo jazz. I really learned so much about acting on those two films. Whereas the *Wandering Detective* films were more conventional, Mr Fukasaku asked me to be light, funky, very physical in the *Funky Hat* movies. I wasn't sure how to do it. Mr Fukasaku had us improvise the rhythms. It was difficult but challenging. In some ways, those four films, the *Wandering Detective* and *Funky Hat* pictures, were the most important of the early years of my career. They were instrumental in creating the skeletal bone structure of my acting in movies. They were two very different types of character, both from each other and from many of the roles I later played. They gave me groundwork for being able to perform as an evil samurai or a *yakuza* in later films.

DR AGISHI: As in *Kage No Gundan* (aka *Shadow Warrior*) …

CD: Oh, the ninja film from the eighties?

CHIBA: It was a television show, too. It ran for many episodes. I played the famous *ninja*, Hattori Hanzo. He was a master of subterfuge and assassinating evil people. The English title was *The Shadow Warrior*, and it was syndicated on TV in the States.

CD: Gang Vs. G-Men, Kamikaze Man, Organized Crime are good, entertaining action pictures, but they're kind of tame when compared to the action and yakuza films that came later in the seventies, movies that were extremely violent. How do you remember those earlier films?

CHIBA: In those early *yakuza* films, the sides of good and evil were made very clear. Much like the films of John Ford. Those films were all influenced by American cinema. But people started to question if there really was that distinction between good and evil in the world of the *yakuza*. Some directors wanted to start taking a more realistic approach to the *yakuza*, in much the way Mr Fukasaku did later in the *Battles Without Honor And Humanity* series. Also, the Japanese release of *The Godfather* was very influential on that concept of realism. Showing the ego and power struggles behind the scenes, the involvement with politics. Those were influences that changed the movies in the early seventies. In the earlier gangster movies you usually had the very clear-cut approach, where good triumphed at the end and the good guys killed the cruel *yakuza*.

CD: The three films in the Legendary Lullaby *series and* Tales Of Kawachi Chivalry, *all directed by Ryuichi Takemori – were these the only* ninkyo yakuza *movies you did?*

CHIBA: (*laughs*) Aahhh, *Legendary Lullaby* ... have you seen those pictures?

CD: Unfortunately, no ...

CHIBA: The *Legendary Lullaby* pictures weren't really hardcore *yakuza* films. They had a kind of *ninkyo* action feel, but there was also a small child who co-starred. This was the film star, Hiroyuki Sanada, when he was very young, only five years old.

CD: The four Yakuza Cop *movies and the two* Bodyguard Kiba *films, it seemed Toei was attempting to groom you into even more of an action star, a character thrown into dangerous situations but often with humor added to the mix. How much influence did you have in creating that persona?*

CHIBA: Your impression of Toei trying to turn me into a fast-paced action hero is correct. As I've mentioned, I had originally wanted to be an Olympic athlete, until I was injured. So I'd been training before my injury, and continued to train after I began my movie career. And, because of my constant training, I was able to do many things other actors were either unable or unwilling to do, such as doing most of my own stunts. The studio and writers were able to tailor my roles more in that direction. And I really stressed that in my performances and in my preparations, because it was necessary for my professional survival. I did not have the kind of acting background of many other film actors. At times, I've wanted to branch out and do other things. I've wanted to develop more diverse stories over the years from my own treatments. But Toei always pushed the extreme action-hero image.

CD: And how did the extreme martial arts, the karate and hand-to-hand fighting enter into the films, which seemed to be your main genre in the seventies? Was that because of the phenomenal success of Bruce Lee? How much of that was your input?

CHIBA: The *Bodyguard Kiba* movies and before didn't have any Bruce Lee influence. After Bruce Lee's pictures started to be distributed in Japan, my later films like *The Streetfighter*, the whole depiction of martial arts, the approach to how it was shown became more serious. Yes, in that way there was an influence. But it was still a very different style of fighting.

CD: How much did you bring to shaping the Terry Tsurugi persona in the Streetfighter *films?*

CHIBA: Most of your typical Japanese action films, your main character is never an evil guy. The whole idea for *The Streetfighter* was to make the main protagonist, while not exactly a whole-hearted villain, still a bit of a bad guy. As far as the blood and the gore, Tsurugi wasn't fazed by it – if he felt he needed to kill someone, he just went ahead and did it. I'd played a real villain in *Battles Without Honor And Humanity 2 – Hiroshima Death Match*. So I thought about approaching Tsurugi from that direction but not going as far with it. With the *Hiroshima Death Match* role, I was probably a little too influenced by Robert DeNiro in his more violent films. Sometimes his character would kill many people, but he somehow managed to remain cool, to maintain some kind of authority, even some kind of morality to his bad side. He had an aesthetic. But I wanted to try to take that cool, that smoothness and go in the opposite direction. Make my *Hiroshima Death Match* character rude, brutish in a way. Straightforward in his brutality and cool by being uncool. I wanted to make myself into an ugly human being. That's the first time I played a real villain, and I broke through to a new level with that role. That's the way I decided to approach Tsurugi in *The Streetfighter*.

CD: However, Tsurugi still has some humanity to him. In Hiroshima Death Match *and especially* Great Okinawa Yakuza War *you are really a* bad *guy!*

Battles Without Honor And Humanity – Hiroshima Death Match

CHIBA: (*laughs heartily*)

CD: In Great Okinawa Yakuza War, *your karate-obsessed character is almost exactly like Tsurugi but with no redeeming qualities.*

CHIBA: But I was more of a supporting character in that film. It was a major part but more of a role supporting the main star, Hiroki Matsukata. I would always get very interested in doing villain roles. It made me able to look at some other things inside of myself, explore other ways of playing a part.

CD: Another film where you were kind of a bad guy hero, or anti-hero, was Golgo 13: Kowloon Assignment. *There had been one* Golgo 13 *film before, in the early seventies with Ken Takakura, then that one with you. But it never became a series of films. Why was that? It seems like it would have been very popular.*

CHIBA: *Golgo 13* was the type of series that, because of the stories, needs to be worldwide. The one I did was in Hong Kong, and Ken Takakura's film was in Iran. The stories from the *manga* virtually never take place in Japan, so it really comes down to a financial question of trying to continually film in exotic locations. I think it's the kind of series that's perfect to be produced in America. The character is brutal and cold in many ways, but he has a tragic background. In some ways he's a modern version of Zatoichi, wandering from place to place dispatching bad guys. That may seem an odd comparison, but the Zatoichi character, though physically blind, also has a tragic past, a background filled with trauma, just as Golgo 13. Golgo 13 has a similar ability to Zatoichi as far as immediately sensing things about his opponents.

CD: You appeared in Shogun's Samurai *and* Fall Of Ako Castle, *both directed by Kinji Fukasaku, and both were two of the biggest films Toei released in the late seventies. You also starred in Toei's more recent* Shogun's Shadow. *Obviously, the productions were more expensive, but how did Toei's approach to those later* jidai-geki *films differ from the earlier period films in the fifties and sixties?*

CHIBA: The main difference is in the more realistic approach to the stories. *Fall Of Ako Castle* is another version of the *Chushingura* (*The Loyal 47 Ronin*) story. For a while, the film industry was doing a remake of the legend every year or two. There have been many versions over the last 30 or 40 years. Everyone in Japan is familiar with that story. But the thing about Kinji Fukasaku, he captures the mood and time of a story quickly and always attempts to do something new and original, whatever it is. He's almost a revolutionary when it comes to creating a film. The *Chushingura* story is a very ordinary tale that the entire Japanese population knows, but he took a different perspective to make it more interesting. He would observe more of the political background, as in *Shogun's Samurai* where the Yagyus were trying to take over the Tokugawa regime. When the Tokugawa character played by Hiroki Matsukata gets his head cut off, something like that is unheard-of in most *jidai-geki*. It comes as a huge surprise, a shock to the audience expecting run-of-the-mill *jidai-geki*. But Fukasaku's attitude is 'you never know, this *might* have happened.' Mr Fukasaku was always going for a different approach. His ideas and style are very different from the *jidai-geki* of the fifties and sixties. And when *Shogun's Shadow* was released in 1989, there was a lot of controversy about there being too much swordplay in the film. That it wasn't true *jidai-geki* or faithful to the historical period. But in any situation where you're showing swordplay, the question always is, if you're showing it, people are fighting to kill and survive. Someone will live, someone will die. How much of that is okay? The question is how to make it as real as possible and not resort to the old fake style of *chanbara*.

CD: In Hunter In The Dark, *directed by Hideo Gosha, you play a villain again. There's the spectacular swordfight at the end between you and Tatsuya Nakadai. How long did that take to shoot and how much rehearsal was involved?*

CHIBA: As you know, there were also hundreds of chickens in that scene. So that complicated things. I don't remember exactly how long just that scene took. It was time-consuming. The whole film took three months to shoot, and I was working for about two months of that. Mr Gosha was very devoted to detail and perfection when doing the swordfights in his films. So it took quite a while because he wanted to make sure it was done just right. The rehearsing was hard. It was a hard job all around. That style of swordfighting in such a fast choreographed style is called *tachimawari*. The person you are fighting in the scene has to be very skilled, too. If they're not, it can end up looking bad. It also can be very dangerous if you're working with someone who doesn't quite know what they're doing. When I do *tachimawari* with someone who is really good, the scene can be amazing. But

it's difficult to find actors willing to spend the time training with a sword. This isn't true of Mr Gosha's films, but quite often the Japanese movie industry will accept performers who haven't trained enough. Then the quality of the productions goes down, and, consequently, the audiences are disappointed.

CD: I wanted to ask you about Etsuko 'Sue' Shiomi and Hiroyuki Sanada, who seemed to, at least early in their careers, appear in your films. I have heard they were your protégés to some extent. Is it true that you helped to develop their careers at Toei and trained them in martial arts?

CHIBA: I had taught them since they were little kids. They were my students off and on as they were

Shogun's Samurai

growing up. I had input with both Etsuko and Hiroyuki when they were in training to become stars. They had quite a bit of talent to begin with. Etsuko and Hiroyuki also had considerable athletic ability, which was important. And, of course, they both became very successful.

CD: Can you talk about the JAC, the Japan Action Club, that you developed and how you got the idea for it?

CHIBA: Well, the word 'action', in proper English, is used in the American film world when someone calls: 'Action!' It's your signal as a performer, you're supposed to start to act. But with other definitions, such as in Japanese film, you hear the word 'action,' you might think of martial arts, or gunplay or bombs going off. But the way I wanted to use the word was as in 'acting,' to convey the idea of 'pure acting' and not just relegated to martial arts, or violent action but overall acting. In some ways, it's really no different than other schools of acting. My philosophy is that you speak as much through the rest of your body as you do through your mouth. Your body is an instrument you use in the language of acting, as much as the way you might interpret the lines from the script. It's a very fundamental thing, in regards to the physical body, for every actor or actress. First, even before you start studying the basics of acting, you need to train physically with stretching and various exercises. It's essential, even in voice training, for your body to be in good physical shape. So, if you're starting from that point, when you go into movement or voice training, you find you can do anything. It's much easier because you've built a good foundation.

CD: What are you working on right now as an actor?

CHIBA: A Hong Kong film called *Storm Riders*. I've also done a couple of films in America recently. I'd like to do more work in the States. And then there's the *Zato Masa* project, the *Zatoichi* spin-off, that I want to try to get off the ground.

4

Meiko Kaji

1947–

I have to admit I was a little shocked when Meiko Kaji walked in the room. I had expected her to be well educated and intelligent, and had had an intuition that she was going to be outspoken. But I had not been quite prepared for her charismatic presence. It had been almost a quarter-century since Ms Kaji's genre film prime, but it seemed as if we had entered some kind of time warp. Clad in a conservative, elegant pants suit, Ms Kaji seemed to have aged only a few years. She was brimming with the youthful exuberance, grace and beauty of her *Lady Snowblood* days. No doubt Ms Kaji's enthusiasm, lack of cynicism and impatience with mediocrity is what has kept her so refreshingly vital.

Meiko Kaji started at Nikkatsu studios as Masako Ota, in 1965. I have seen only a couple of her early appearances in such films as *A Man's Crest – Wanderer's Code* and *Women's Police*, and she has little to do in either one. Yasuharu Hasebe's *Territorial Dispute* from 1968 was a step in the right direction for her, though, with a decent part as *yakuza* Akira Kobayashi's girlfriend. Still in her teens, she has a fearless quality about her that shines through, right up until her death scene, when she perishes in a drive-by meant for her beau.

Her one and only top-billed role as Masako Ota was in the girl gang exploitation programmer, *Mini-Skirt Lynchers*, alongside Annu Mari (the exotic femme fatale fresh from *Branded To Kill*). Another sought-after picture that has remained elusive, from all reports it's a precursor of the girl gang pictures that proliferated on Japanese movie screens in the 1970s.

Her first film under the name Meiko Kaji was a contemporary gangster picture called *The Clean Up* in 1969, an all-star bash featuring not only Nikkatsu top draws like Yujiro Ishihara, Joe Shishido and Tetsuya Watari but also Toho's Mie Hama. Following was the *ninkyo yakuza* film *Chivalrous Flower's Life Story – Gambling Heir* directed by Keiichi Ozawa. Top-billed with Hideki Takahashi, Chieko Matsubara portrays a girl who becomes *oyabun* of her father's gang after his death. But co-stars Kaji and Tatsuya Fuji had by far the more interesting roles with Kaji playing outcast Fuji's tattooed and knife-wielding card-sharp lover.

Tale Of The Last Japanese Yakuza was directed by Kaji's mentor, Masahiro Makino, and it remains one of the veteran filmmaker's best *ninkyo yakuza* pictures, matching his efforts at Toei studios in the *Tales Of The Last Showa Yakuza* series. Unfortunately, Kaji's part is quite small.

Which brings us to Kaji's first top-billed role under her new name. Director Teruo Ishii's *Blind Woman's Curse* from 1970 was meant to be the third and concluding film in star, Hiroko Ogi's *Rising Dragon*, a *ninkyo yakuza* series. But Ogi did not appear on-screen, instead making way for Kaji as a benevolent gang boss tormented by a vengeful woman (Hoki Tokuda) she had blinded in a swordfight. Kaji had also killed her brother, so there's a hefty score to settle. Tokuda, now a knife-thrower in a travelling erotic/grotesque horror carnival and abetted by a demented hunchback (played by wild Tatsumi Hijikata from Ishii's *Horror Of Malformed Men*), hooks up with a villainous gang boss (Toru Abe), a man who has his own reasons for wanting Kaji and her gang out of the way. A bizarre amalgam of both *kaidan* and *ninkyo yakuza* elements, *Blind Woman's Curse* is never less than entertaining, and, at some moments, such as the phantasmagorical final swordfight between Kaji and Tokuda, it transcends into heady heights.

Later that same year a fortuitous chain of events led Kaji to be cast in the first of a new series about delinquent teenagers, the *Stray Cat Rock* films. Initially intended as a promotional vehicle for hugely popular singer Akiko Wada, top-billed in the initial outing, it wasn't long before co-stars Meiko Kaji and Tatsuya Fuji took center stage. In *Girl Boss*, Akiko Wada is a motorcycle-driving rebel who helps buckskin-clad Kaji and her girls in a fight with rival female hoods. The area is also plagued with a fascist *yakuza* bunch, The Black Shirt Corps, and Kaji's beau (Koji Wada) wants admittance. When he bungles a bid to fix a fight near the end he's fatally shot, and Kaji and Akiko Wada go on a revenge binge that leads to Kaji's death, as well as that of the lead villain. Although a bit convoluted and chaotic, the film still vibrates with an infectious energy. Toshiya Fujita directed the following entry, *Wild Jumbo*, a disjointed mix of heist thriller and goofy teen antics with delinquents robbing funds from a religious cult. Director Fujita redeems the picture at the close as the teenagers are cut down by their ruthless pursuers. Especially memorable is Kaji's death in a river at the downbeat climax. The best *Stray Cat Rock* film

Lady Snowblood

came next with *Sex Hunter*, director Hasebe putting Kaji through her paces as the stylish, whip-wielding leader of a girl gang. Kaji has her conscience awakened when her impotent *yakuza* beau, the Baron (Tatsuya Fuji) orders his gang to not only persecute teens of mixed-race parentage but shanghais Kaji's girls as sex slaves for foreign businessmen. A triangle takes shape when Kaji falls for a half-breed stud (Ricky Yasuoka), and the saga builds to a bloody, tragic ending. I haven't seen the fourth film, *Machine Animal*, another directed by Hasebe, but Kaji plays a gang girl who is chased after stealing 500 LSD doses from the bad guys, one of whom is a US army deserter. The concluding *Stray Cat* movie, *Violent Showdown '71*, saw

Detail from poster for *Stray Cat Rock – Wild Jumbo*

Fujita once again at the helm, directing Yoshio Harada as the leader of a gang of hippie hoods trying to get back one of their own who has been kidnapped by his rich father. The boy returns and rejoins his girl (Kaji), but both are killed in the crossfire between his bunch and his dad's hoodlum henchmen.

That same year, 1971, saw the transformation of Kaji's home studio, Nikkatsu, from mainstream movie production to *roman porn* factory. Not to Kaji's taste, she decided to accept an offer from Toei, a studio already churning out plenty of female action pictures. Kaji's first there was 1972's *Ginjo Wanderer*, directed by Kazuhiko Yamaguchi, who also directed the majority of Etsuko 'Sue' Shiomi's *Sister Streetfighter* films. Kaji, an ex-con whose girl gang had killed a mobster, meets a lone wolf dandy (Tsunehiko Watase) at her uncle's billiard parlor and, through him, soon has a job at mama-san Akiko Koyama's hostess bar. The last third of the film has billiard expert Kaji playing against villain boss Koji Nanbara's junkie champion (Matasaburo Tanba) for the deed to Koyama's club. When the villains win by cheating, then murder Kaji's friend (Tatsuo Umemiya) who intervenes, Kaji and Watase head over to Nanbara's HQ with swords to slaughter the mob. Despite meager production values, the picture's an unpretentious, entertaining vehicle, putting a unique spin on its programmer elements. It's too bad the same can't be said for the sequel, *Ginjo Drifter – Cat Girl Gambling*, where, despite co-star Sonny Chiba, the film dissolves too often into silly comedy before its violent finish.

Kaji's outings in her first mega-popular movie series were born later the same year. *The Female Convict Scorpion* films, adapted from the women's prison manga of Toru Shinohara, possess traditional exploitation traits but with a surreal, comic book use of color and mythical, archetypal images. Meiko Kaji as Matsu, nicknamed Sasori (Scorpion), is an unjustly convicted woman and a fanatical avenger, raining down wrath on various evil males. As portrayed by Kaji, Sasori is mysteriously elemental, a virtually silent, deadly force, uttering only a few cryptic sentences in each picture. All four of the films starring Kaji are quite good, but the second, *Jailhouse 41*, and the third, *Department Of Beasts*, are phenomenal. *Jailhouse 41* follows Kaji and even more hardened inmates breaking out of stir. They cross a desolate blasted landscape – a ghost village half buried in volcanic ash, melancholic autumnal woods and barren mountains of stone – all the time retaliating against pursuing guards and bestial, vacationing salarymen. A transcendental, exhilarating masterpiece that is at times reminiscent of John Boorman's *Point Blank* and Donald Cammell/Nicolas Roeg's *Performance* in its sheer audacity. *Department Of Beasts* finds Kaji as Scorpion once again on the lam, nearly captured when handcuffed to a nutcase cop (Mikio Narita), but then eluding him when she jumps off the subway – something which causes Narita's arm to be torn off. Kaji is soon abducted by a perverse gang boss (Koji Nanbara) and his mistress, a grudge-holding foe from prison clad in black feathers who cages our anti-heroine in a cell full of vicious ravens. Needless to say, Kaji escapes, hiding out in underground storm drains until she can return to wreak vengeance on her tormentors. Eventually captured, the film concludes when she strangles gloating cop Narita through the bars on her cell door. The final *Scorpion* picture with Kaji, *Number 701's Song Of Hate*, follows Scorpion as she falls in love with a crippled, henpecked-by-his-mother former student radical (Masakazu Tamura). Briefly Kaji's Scorpion finds happiness. But her dreams of normalcy are dashed when a fascist cop (Toshiyuki Hosokawa) uses the weak-willed boy's mom to pressure him into revealing her whereabouts. Kaji kills betraying Tamura and, at the sunset climax, lynches evil Hosokawa on the very scaffold on which she was to be executed the following morning.

Right after the second Scorpion film, Kaji signed on as the lead in *Lady Snowblood* and its sequel, *Lady Snowblood – Love Song Of Vengeance*, to film at Toho during a hiatus from her Toei obligations. Both were directed by Toshiya Fujita and adapted from *manga* by Kazuo Koike, creator of *Lone Wolf And Cub* and *Razor Hanzo*. Set at the start of the twentieth century, Kaji plays Yuki, an orphan trained by a priest in swordfighting so she can avenge her parents' murder by violent conmen. Aided by a leftist writer (Toshio Kurosawa), Kaji tracks down, then kills, each of the murderers. But the last man (Eiji Okada) has changed his identity and is now a respected right-wing fanatic raising havoc in the government. Kurosawa dies, and severely wounded Kaji stumbles away in the falling snow after both have dispatched Okada at a masked ball at his mansion. The sequel, *Love Song* is even more overtly political, with Kaji caught after killing scores of police, then shanghaied by a nationalist bunch led by Shin Kishida, who coerce her into becoming their assassin. They plant her as a maid in the house of a Communist writer (played by director Juzo Itami), but she grows to like him and refuses to help in his betrayal. When the fanatics kidnap Itami, Kaji manages to escape, but Itami's torture ensues. Kaji finds refuge with Itami's estranged brother (Yoshio Harada), a cynical doctor who now resides in the ghetto. The fascists, in collusion with the police, release the dying writer on the edge of the slum, and he finds his way to Harada. However, the authorities have infected Itami with plague in a grotesque experiment, which they hope will eradicate undesirables from the impoverished area. Once the writer dies, the now infected Harada helps Kaji attack and kill Kishida and his cohorts. Both *Snowblood* films veer between quietly majestic beauty and blood-drenched Grand Guignol, achieving a strangely radiant, nihilistic poetry.

Kaji also appeared in three of director Kinji Fukasaku's films during the seventies, most notably *Yakuza Burial – Jasmine Flower*, as the anguished Korean wife of an imprisoned gang boss, a woman who finally finds love with an alienated, loner cop (Tetsuya Watari). Once more, happiness is not in the cards, as Watari's character is doomed by his innate hatred of hypocrisy on whichever side of the law he finds it.

Kaji's favorite of her films is *Love Suicides At Sonezaki*, a densely written adaptation of a Monzaemon Chikamatsu play that has been filmed several times. Kaji is awe-inspiring in the role of an indentured courtesan who escapes with her young merchant lover for a last few days of freedom. Director Yasuzo Masumura chronicles the pair's final hours together with a simplicity and a surgical skill for unearthing long-buried emotions.

Since the eighties Kaji has worked continually, but mostly in television. She remains an opinionated, fearless champion of women in the entertainment industry. Most recently, Quentin Tarantino used two of her most famous songs, 'Flower of Carnage (*Shura No Hana*)' from *Lady Snowblood* and 'Song Of Hate (*Urami Bushi*)' from the *Female Convict Scorpion* series, in the concluding duel and end credits respectively of *Kill Bill, Vol. 1*.

MEIKO KAJI – SELECTED FILMOGRAPHY

1968   *TERRITORIAL DISPUTE (SHIMA WA MORATTA, aka TURF WAR)* [as Masako Ota]

1969   *MINI-SKIRT LYNCHERS (ZANKOKU ONNA RINCHI, aka CRUEL WOMEN'S LYNCH LAW)* [as Masako Ota]

         THE CLEAN-UP (ARASHI NO YOSHATACHI) [as Meiko Kaji this title and all films below]

         FLOWER OF CHIVALRY'S LIFE STORY – GAMBLING HEIR (KYOKA RETSUDEN – SHUMEI TOBA)

         TALE OF THE LAST JAPANESE YAKUZA (NIHON ZAN KYODEN)

         ONE HUNDRED GAMBLERS – CHIVALROUS PATH (BAKUTO HYAKUNIN – NINKYODO)

1970   *BLIND WOMAN'S CURSE (KAIDAN NOBORI RYU, aka RISING DRAGON GHOST STORY, aka THE TATTOOED SWORDSWOMAN, aka HAUNTED LIFE OF A DRAGON-TATTOOED LASS)*

         STEP ON THE GAS! (SHINJUKU AUTORO – BUTTOBASE)

         GREATEST BOSS OF JAPAN (NIHON SAIDAI NO KAOYAKU)

         GIRL BOSS – STRAY CAT ROCK (ONNA BANCHO – NORA NEKO ROKKU)

         STRAY CAT ROCK – WILD JUMBO (NORA NEKO ROKKU – WAIRUDO JYANBO)

         STRAY CAT ROCK – SEX HUNTER (NORA NEKO ROKKU – SEKKUSU HANTAA)

         STRAY CAT ROCK – MACHINE ANIMAL (NORA NEKO ROKKU – MASHIN ANIMARU)

         MELODY OF REBELLION (HAN GYAKU NO MERODEE)

1971   *STRAY CAT ROCK – VIOLENT SHOWDOWN '71 (NORA NEKO ROKKU – BOSO SHUDAN '71)*

         BLOODY FEUD (RYUKETSU NO KOSO)

1972   *GINJO WANDERER (GINJO WATARIDORI, aka SILVER BUTTERFLY WANDERER)*

         GINJO DRIFTER – CAT GIRL GAMBLING (GINJO NAGAREMONO – MESU NEKO BAKUCHI)

         FEMALE CONVICT NUMBER 701 – SCORPION (JOSHUU GO 701 – SASORI)

FEMALE CONVICT SCORPION – JAILHOUSE 41 (JOSHUU SASORI – DAI 41 ZAKKYOBO)

1973   *MODERN CHIVALRY (GENDAI NINKYOSHI)*
LADY SNOWBLOOD (SHURA YUKIHIME, aka FIGHTING LADY SNOW)
FEMALE CONVICT SCORPION – DEPARTMENT OF BEASTS (JOSHUU SASORI – KEMONO BEYA)
FEMALE CONVICT SCORPION – NUMBER 701'S SONG OF HATE (JOSHUU SASORI –701 GO RAMI BUSHI)
BATTLES WITHOUT HONOR AND HUMANITY – HIROSHIMA DEATH MATCH (JINGINAKI TATAKAI – HIROSHIMA SHITO HEN)

1974   *JEAN'S BLUES – VILLAINS WITHOUT A TOMORROW (JIINZU BURUSU – ASU NAKI BURAI HA)*
LADY SNOWBLOOD – LOVE SONG OF VENGEANCE (SHURA YUKIHIME – URAMI KOI UTA)
HOMELESS VAGABONDS (YADONASHI)

1975   *NEW BATTLES WITHOUT HONOR AND HUMANITY – THE BOSS'S HEAD (SHIN JINGINAKI TATAKAI – KUMICHO NO KUBI)*
PULSATING ISLAND (DOMYAKU RETTO)

1976   *YAKUZA BURIAL – JASMINE FLOWER (YAKUZA NO HAKABA – KUCHINASHI NO HANA, aka YAKUZA GRAVEYARD)*

1977   *RUSTY FLAMES (SABITA HONOO)*

1978   *LOVE SUICIDES AT SONEZAKI (SONEZAKI SHINJU, aka DOUBLE SUICIDE AT SONEZAKI))*

1980   *BAD SORTS (WARUI YATSURA)*

1995   *ONIHEI'S CRIME FILE (ONIHEI HANKA-CHO)*

MEIKO KAJI – INTERVIEW

The following interview took place at the offices of Creative Enterprises International in Tokyo in October, 1997. Shoko Ishiyama translated on-site. Ms Kaneda, Ms Kaji's long-time friend and manager, was also present. Ai Kennedy helped with some clarification and translated small portions not originally translated.

CD: *I have heard that you had a pop music career before you entered film?*

KAJI: Not before the films. It was common back then, especially at Nikkatsu, for performers to sing the theme songs for the films they were in. It doesn't mean that I was really active as a pop singer. I've made about seven or eight albums. When I was at Toei later on a couple of the songs were successful, and one sold a million copies, so some people thought I'd had a pop music career when I was making films at Nikkatsu because I'd done some theme songs.

CD: *The successful song was '*Song Of Hate *(Urami Bushi)' from* Female Convict Scorpion?

KAJI: (*laughs*) Yes.

CD: *Working at Nikkatsu, what was the catalyst for you going from more of a regular supporting actress to an action star?*

KAJI: Of all the movie companies, Nikkatsu had the image of the actress as a young girl, like Sayuri Yoshnaga, who had this 'girlie' kind of character. I was tending to get cast as strong women, and the company steered me to continue with that kind of role. It was a company policy to make an actress into her own image, to aim in the direction each actress seemed to naturally be heading. I was not very confident as a female of being able to do violent action films. But I tried my best to do what was required of me in the role. Back then, too, there was a kind of understood agreement amongst the five major movie companies, Toei, Nikkatsu, Daiei, Shochiku and Toho, about using other company's performers without permission. All the older actors and actresses generally had five-year contracts that were exclusive to that company. I was in a situation in the beginning of having to work only for Nikkatsu. I would have to take whatever role I was offered, fit into whatever mold they put me in. I was well received as an 'outlaw' character, and that was why I appeared again and again in that type of film. It was an unwritten rule at these companies until about 1975 or so. I was in the last generation that really had to go through being pigeon-holed into a certain type of role.

CD: *Was* Flower Of Chivalry's Life Story – Gambling Heir *the first* yakuza *action film you did where you actually did some of the knife – and swordfighting?*

KAJI: That was the year I changed my name from Masako Ota to Meiko Kaji. That was at the behest of the respected director, Masahiro Makino. Mr Makino had been instrumental in developing the *ninkyo yakuza* film at Toei. Before the films in 1969 I was pretty much relegated to playing a high school or college student. These were the first films where I had larger roles, and also often had to do the sword choreography at the same time. It was difficult at first because it was so new to me. Of course, I ended up learning how to do it. But it's very hard work to master the sword forms, you really have to know traditional Japanese dance to master the postures, to work out the balance and choreography. I had to train for a long time.

CD: *How did Masahiro Makino become involved in* Tale Of The Last Japanese Yakuza? *Makino also directed several films at Daiei, a couple with Shintaro Katsu. Since Mr Makino was one of Toei's top directors, how did he end up directing at Nikkatsu and Daiei?*

KAJI: Actors and actresses were the ones who really were subject to the exclusivity policy. Directors didn't have that much trouble making films at other studios. Also, Mr Makino was a respected top director, so he certainly had the ability to go and work where he wanted.

CD: Blind Woman's Curse *was a continuation of the* Rising Dragon *series, starring Hiroko Ogi. Since she didn't appear in* Blind Woman's Curse*, were you supposed to be replacing her?*

KAJI: I wasn't really intended as a replacement. Hiroko Ogi had another *ninkyo yakuza* series of her own, too, at the time. My lead role in *Blind Woman's Curse* was a gift from the company to congratulate me on my new star status, my name change.

CD: Whose idea was it to make Blind Woman's Curse *as a* ninkyo yakuza *ghost story?*

KAJI: I guess it was the first original *ninkyo yakuza* ghost story! But I think the major thrust of the story was the *ninkyo yakuza* side of it, the revenge for the boss. You have to remember that a term like *kaidan* (ghost story) in a movie title is always there to appeal more to the mass audience as a kind of PR gimmick.

CD: There were *many horror elements, maybe not in the form of a ghost story, but there were macabre images. Was that more director Teruo Ishii's input or the studio's?*

KAJI: Probably more the interest of Mr Ishii himself. I don't remember that much of the horror-type imagery. One thing I vividly recall during one of the swordfights, the black cat was supposed to be jumping towards me from behind, and the cat's claws were not trimmed. It scratched me badly, and I still have the scars to this day. So that was sort of a real horror story for me personally. I think it was more of a *ninkyo* picture. One thing that happened a lot with Japanese movies back then was to integrate sensational images or catchphrases into the movie titles to draw people into the theaters. For example, the *Sex Hunter* film in the *Stray Cat Rock* series, you get more of a social consciousness at work dealing with the persecution of the mixed-race teenagers. But then you have the movie called *Sex Hunter!* You used to get that a lot. I'm really convinced that was one of the reasons they used the word *kaidan* in the Japanese title of *Blind Woman's Curse*.

CD: But still, there's a lot of horror movie stuff with the rival boss's sister accidentally blinded by you and then her cat lapping up the blood of your fallen comrades, a lot of kaibyo *(ghost-cat) images. The skinning of the gang girls murdered by the hunchback for their dragon tattoo. To get back to* Stray Cat Rock - Sex Hunter, *you played a strong character like your later* Female Convict Scorpion *persona. There were also some of the outfits, the style and image, for instance the floppy hat, from that film that seemed to reappear later in the* Scorpion *series. Was that your sense of style overlapping in the later films or was it just a coincidence?*

KAJI: Whenever I had a strong role I was always concerned to make it even stronger. But a strength originating as much from kindness and an acceptance of one's elders and of weaker people. To assume the responsibility of being the boss. To maybe go above my elders' heads to help them and be a leader. I was concerned more about a mental strength rather than any physical strength. I had that image of being a strong woman with both the movie industry and with audiences. And once you have that image, and the *look* that goes with it, it is very difficult to get away from it. People ask you again and again to do the same kind of role. I still have the association with that image in people's minds, even now.

CD: In movies like Melody Of Rebellion, Bloody Feud, *both at Nikkatsu, and* Modern Chivalry *at Toei you were one of the main stars, but the stories were dominated by the male characters, Yoshio Harada, Joe Shishido and Ken Takakura respectively. Were you frustrated when you had to take more of a back seat to the men actors?*

KAJI: Not really. It's very typical of that type of Japanese film to have a lead male character who is good-looking and strong or cruel or whatever, then for that character to have a good, strong woman behind him. It's a pattern, and I understand it. So, no, I accepted it, and I wasn't frustrated.

CD: How did your involvement with Toei studios and, in turn, the Female Convict Scorpion *series occur?*

KAJI: I left Nikkatsu after working for them for six years. They were in the midst of severe financial decline and had switched over almost exclusively to the *roman porno* films to stay in business. I didn't agree with that policy and did not wish to participate. Toei expressed their interest, and soon after the *Female Convict Scorpion* series began.

CD: The director of the first three Scorpion *films, Shunya Ito, had been an assistant director for Teruo Ishii and had already been working at Toei for a number of years. His* Scorpion *pictures seem very inspired, with truly incredible imagery. It seems much care and time went into the films, more so than the usual Toei production.*

KAJI: The first one in the series, *Female Convict Number 701 – Scorpion*, was Mr Ito's first film as a director. When he asked me to be in the film, I was totally unfamiliar with the origin of the story, even though the *manga* was extremely popular in Japan at the time. So Mr Ito loaned me the complete set of *Sasori manga*, and I read it. When we met for the second time the script was ready, and I saw that they had kept most of the obscenities the character spoke in the comics. I told him that was unacceptable, that it would end up making the film seem cheap and sleazy, and that taking them out was one of my conditions for accepting the role. He agreed with me, and came to believe it would be more interesting if my character hardly spoke any dialogue, except for a few important sentences. We decided we could convey what Scorpion was thinking, what she was going to do next, by the performance, by the visual instead of the verbal. So we had to work hard on the visuals. What we did was quite radical and a new concept. Since this was Mr Ito's first picture, and we were trying to shoot in sequence, which almost never is done in the Japanese film industry, it took a long time. Also, during that period, the whole industry across the board was slashing budgets on the average feature film. The shooting schedule for Toei films, even the bigger ones with stars like Ken Takakura, was three weeks. But because we were shooting in sequence it took four months, which is extremely long. Fortunately, Mr Ito was head of the union then, so the higher-ups cooperated. Once the movie was released it became a huge hit, both because of the *manga*'s popularity and because of the unique way we approached Scorpion's character. The fact that we had her barely speak at all was quite sensational.

CD: All four of the Scorpion *pictures you appeared in, but especially the second and third ones,* Jailhouse 41 *and* Department Of Beasts, *seemed to be shot under grueling conditions. You were often being sprayed by real fire hoses, tied up and beaten, or nearly drowned in subterranean chambers. What was it like shooting those scenes?*

KAJI: When I did the first film, I was thinking to myself: 'Okay I'm going to do this, and then it'll be over for the *Scorpion* story. She beats the system in the end and then that's it.' But the picture was such a huge hit, Toei obviously wanted to make it into a series. Once you turn a film into a series, it's extremely difficult to maintain the same quality or surpass the quality of the original. Just on a realistic level, the things the main character goes through, it's almost impossible to believe she could survive. So, unfortunately, you have to put these antics, these more fantastic elements, into the film. The whole thrust of each film's scenario would be to abuse and beat the Scorpion character until she once again exacted revenge at the climax, and as a result give the audience what they expected from the series. Consequently, yes, the shooting was very hard. We were working towards a New Year's release date, so we shot the scene that comes at the beginning of *Jailhouse 41*, the scene where I'm sprayed by the fire hoses in the dungeon, at the end of November, when it was extremely cold. We couldn't even use hot water because you would see the steam rising off me and off the set. It became more a test of physical endurance rather than acting skill. I had to be more concerned about not getting sick, not getting hurt on the set. It was, in some ways, very limiting physically and mentally. The shooting was *so* brutal. Then the consciousness of each successive film became more and more grotesque, more radical just to maintain the audience, to make sure the pictures were hits. That

Female Convict Scorpion – Jailhouse 41

was why after the fourth film, *Number 701's Song Of Hate*, I just could not do the role any more.

CD: Lady Snowblood *and* Lady Snowblood – Love Song Of Vengeance, *how did those come about?*

KAJI: I was offered the two films at Toho after the second *Scorpion* film was done. And this series was also based on a popular *manga*.

CD: Were you the one behind Toshiya Fujita being assigned to direct, since he had directed two of the Stray Cat Rock *pictures?*

KAJI: No, that was Toho. I wasn't involved in helping to choose the director.

CD: Both of the films, especially the second, showed sympathy for the radical left-wing characters who were oppressed and persecuted by fascist Japanese authorities. Was that kind of sensibility in the original manga *or was that more from director Fujita?*

KAJI: The films were very faithful to the spirit of the original *manga*. That sympathy towards the radical left was already there. It was one of the things that made the series interesting.

CD: Did Toho have a problem with that at all?

KAJI: No, Toho knew it was in the original *manga* and that the films were close adaptations.

CD: In the first Battles Without Honor And Humanity *sequel,* Hiroshima Death Match, *you played a different type of character, a woman who is dominated by her cruel yakuza boss father, played by Hiroshi Nawa, and has an outcast yakuza lover, played by Kinya Kitaoji. It seems as if this part must have been emotionally quite draining.*

KAJI: That role was different because I was having to subject my emotions to the rest of the cast. I was not necessarily drawing on my feelings as a woman to play the role but more from technique. It was good because I got to show more serious, more typical womanly emotions in the character than I was used to.

CD: I haven't seen Jean's Blues – Villains Without A Tomorrow, *but I recently found the magnificent poster with you holding the shotgun.*

KAJI: (*laughs*) Please don't see it! I stand on being a professional, but I can't say really anything good about it. I suppose the way the picture came about boils down to Toei marketing and studio politics to some extent. The *Scorpion* films had been hits in Tokyo but had not done as well in Kyoto. So Toei's Kyoto branch studio asked for us to shoot the *Jean's Blues* film there to see if they could turn it into a hit in that area. I had this feeling of obligation to Toei Kyoto. But, after reading the script, I didn't like it and didn't really want to do it. I still haven't seen the film. (*laughs*)

CD: What was it like working with Shintaro Katsu and Ken Takakura in Homeless Vagabonds?

KAJI: That was intended to be a kind of Japanese version of *Going Places* with Gerard Depardieu.

CD: Oh, the French film ...

KAJI: It was a fabulous opportunity getting to work with them. I truly think that they are two of the top actors in the history of Japanese film. It was a real pleasure watching those guys work. They are so great.

CD: You made three pictures with director Yasuzo Masumura. Could you talk about working with him, especially on Love Suicides At Sonezaki?

KAJI: It was my dream to work with Mr Masumura from the time I was working at Nikkatsu. When I stopped working at Toei and Toho I met Ms Kaneda, who is my manager now, and she had been working at Daiei, working with Ayako Wakao – who, as you know, did many movies with Mr Masumura. When Ms Kaneda found out how badly I wanted to work with him she thought it was a good idea, and it was really her idea to cast me in *Love Suicides*. It was extremely hard with the fund-raising on that picture, there was no guaranteed salary, and I ended up doing it for basically nothing. We shot it in 19 days, and the last 72 hours of that the whole cast and crew went without sleeping to get it done. Mr Masumura was a complete perfectionist. If he didn't like what you were doing in your performance, he would make you do it over and over again until it conformed to his vision. I'd never worked with a director like that before. But I didn't mind. He had power and strength as a director. I learned so much from him. He had been a first assistant director under Kenji Mizoguchi, and had also studied with many Italian directors at the Centro Sperimentale in Rome. He was so unlike all other Japanese film people. He had both an international sensibility and an international reputation. Whenever I would have trouble later, something would click in my mind, I would think of something he had said when he was shooting the film. I so much wanted to work with him again, but unfortunately he passed away. It's my regret I wasn't able to do one more film with him.

CD: Unfortunately, I am not that familiar with your films after 1980. Are there any of your other films you'd like to talk about? Or anything in general?

KAJI: The latest is *Onihei's Crime File*, this movie version of a *jidai-geki* TV series about a samurai detective played by Kichiemon Nakamura.

(The rest of this below was being spoken predominantly by Meiko Kaji, but her manager, Ms Kaneda, occasionally interjected a comment. For expediency's sake, since quite often it is hard to tell who is saying what, one or two of Ms Kaneda's comments may be credited to Ms Kaji.)

KAJI: Something that really should be said is, and this is even more true since *Love Suicides At Sonezaki*, much of the film industry has been

Jean's Blues – Villains Without A Tomorrow

corrupted by studio politics, the idea of focusing more on the image as well as the performer's age. Once they get a certain image of you, they don't want anything different. As an actress, I can play anything from a young girl to an old woman, or anything in between. As a rule, the industry will not give you the opportunity to show you can do something different. For instance, in America, middle-aged actresses like Meryl Streep can go from movies like *Falling In Love* (1984) to thrillers like *The River Wild* (1994), and it's applauded. But rarely here in Japan. When Japanese men see a strong actress in an American film, a woman who is assertive, many of them will make comments like 'I could never fall in love with a bitch like that!' It makes me very sad. Sometimes Japanese men as a whole can be childish. Anyway, at the time that *Love Suicides* was released, there was an organization called ATG, Art Theater Guild, which funded with grants certain projects that filmmakers couldn't do elsewhere. It was possible to do something experimental or unique and get away from movie company politics. It's almost impossible to make a profit as an independent production, so it's not surprising ATG doesn't exist any more. None of their films ever made any money. The Ministry of Culture also supported films a bit with grants. *Love Suicides* had gotten a grant from them as well as ATG, but it added up to so little money when you factored in all the expenses. For the most part, movie companies are geared for the highest profit margin, and somehow they do make money. That's all they seem to care about, no matter the quality of the output. It's funny, because after *Love Suicides* I received several awards, but it really made no difference in terms of getting jobs. The movie companies see a performer getting an award and suddenly they think: 'Oh, this person got an award,' they won't possibly consider this role because it's too small or it's beneath them. It's hard to survive. It's almost impossible to make a living just from film. Actors and actresses have to do a lot of TV and theater to make a living. There's a very strong hierarchy not only in the film industry but in Japanese business and society in general, and it's quite difficult to make a living if you go outside the system. It's very difficult for me to get involved in movies, the kind of movies I'd like to do. And the kind of stuff I'm offered now, I really don't want to do. But what kind of Japanese films do you like?

CD: All kinds, but what I enjoy most are genre films – samurai chanbara, yakuza films and kaidan. But there are many Japanese directors I like such as Hideo Gosha, Yasuzo Masumura, Kenji Misumi –

KAJI: – Which films by Mr Masumura have you seen?

CD: Manji, Hoodlum Soldier, Blind Beast, The Spider Tattoo, Afraid To Die ...

KANEDA: ... I was there on the set when they were shooting *Afraid To Die*.

KAJI: Do you remember the scene where Mishima dies stretched out on the escalator at the end?

CD: Yes, it's an amazing scene. I've also seen many of Masumura's other films ...

KAJI: (*laughs*) ... You like so many Japanese films. Do you have American films you like?

CD: American films from the fifties, sixties and seventies. Too many to mention. I love American film noir. I'm a fan of Italian cinema, especially genre films. One thing I feel strongly is that the Japanese film industry is the only film industry that has a comparable legacy, as far as quantity and quality, to the United States. Of course, there are fewer films being made in the last 25 years. I think much like the United States, not that many good films have been made since 1980.

KAJI: Yes, it's true. Often in the film business here, if the president of the company has a son, the son takes over when the father steps down whether the son is qualified or not. Then the son invariably repeats the mistakes of the father. Movies are culture, and culture is meant to help the nation, to help the new generation dream.

KANEDA: Is this the first time you've ever interviewed a Japanese actress?

CD: I've interviewed mostly Japanese directors. You're the only actress.

KAJI: Well, I'm very glad to have met you. I've had such a good time. Other actresses are probably different. I probably talk too much. Sometimes I wonder if it's wise for me to be so open about my opinions, that perhaps it would be better if I kept them to myself.

KANEDA: There's a big gap between film and media and the real world in Japan. For example, there are so many words you can't say any more. It's gotten ridiculous.

CD: Politically correct. I know, you can't use words like 'mekura' (blind) and 'oshi' (mute) now. It's absurd. It's even worse than it is in America.

KAJI: Words like '*kojiki*', which means homeless and is often used in *jidai-geki*. Parts of the movie business are at such a childish level, and not childish in a good way. It's immature. How can we get hopes and dreams from it? It makes me sad. But it's not as if I'm saying that I'm so great or superior or that I could do better. It's not about that. The whole industry needs to aspire to higher things. Right now, culturally, we're very poor and we're not growing.

5

Junya Sato

1932–

Junya Sato has always held strong convictions about social injustice, nationalist demagoguery and the economic oppression of the poor. Sentiments that many would label as radically leftist are always presented as background subtext in his movies and are not, despite the inflammatory violence of select films, delivered with any kind of sledgehammer approach. Mr Sato showcases the ills of capitalist excess with a common-sense logic that never gets in the way of his characters or story.

Considering Sato's knack for dealing with sensitive topics, it was perfectly natural he chose *Story Of Military Cruelty* for his first picture, a tale spotlighting the horrors military recruits went through in training for WW2. The film poster, sporting a gory close-up of a suicided recruit (Rentaro Mikuni) with a large bayonet in his throat, remains to this day one of the more shocking movie promotion campaigns.

There had been a leftist tradition in post-war Japanese cinema from the late forties onward, finding voice in films by not only avowed Communists, like Tadashi Imai and Satsuo Yamamoto, but also from less obviously slanted directors, like Akira Kurosawa. So it was not unusual that young filmmakers like Sato and Kinji Fukasaku would follow suit. Perhaps what is unusual is that the Japanese movie companies, many of them with rather conservative men at the top, would allow leftist directors relatively free rein. Sato managed to bring a consciousness of how materialism and hypocritical cultural and economic policies could gradually chip away at society's fabric, almost imperceptibly undermining human values. He was able to do this even in tragic love stories like *Red Light Breed* and *Passion*, cinema that illuminated how overriding economic concerns could insidiously destroy strong personal feelings and attachments.

Sato's initial gangster films, the three *Organized Crime* entries, are pioneering *jitsuroku* documents. All are loosely based on the same gang wars depicted in the seventies in Kinji Fukasaku's *Battles Without Honor* series, though they focus on different details and don't quite reach the identical level of intense realism. In

Organized Crime, a hard-as-nails police inspector (Tetsuro Tanba) foils a right-wing Shinjuku *oyabun*'s gun-running scheme, but is frustrated when the boss's guilty go-between goes free because of his diplomatic status. *Organized Crime 2* is even better, focusing more on Tanba's determined cop, giving him a world-weariness and compassion missing in the first picture. Tanba tracks the exploits of various underbosses and killers as well as the manipulative old men who control the rackets, puppet masters dispassionately dealing out suffering and death to everyone they

Poster for *Organized Crime 2*

touch. It also has one of Masaru Sato's most memorable, identifiable scores. The third, *Loyalty Offering Brothers*, no longer features the Tanba character, instead concentrating on a post-WW2 veteran (Bunta Sugawara) who defends a Japanese woman from raping US occupation soldiers in the first scene. But, although he eventually marries the woman, he joins other fledgling *yakuza* in setting up make-shift brothels, stealing equally unfortunate girls from US occupation whore-houses to pimp themselves. Before long, any values Sugawara's character has crumble from his partnership with a greedy sociopath (Noboru Ando). The two add protection and extortion to their gang's activities and outfit a torture chamber for 'debt collection' from reluctant businessmen. At the end, a gang war erupts because Sugawara and Ando just don't know when to stop. Everyone perishes in all-out annihilation that matches the wildness of the later *Battles Without Honor And Humanity* films.

Drifting Avenger is a hybrid western, with Australian locations standing in for the American west. Ken Takakura lives with his elderly father, an ex-samurai (Takashi Shimura), and his American mother. A gang of stagecoach robbers stop by, Shimura confronts them with his sword and guns ablaze. The villains leave the family for dead, but Takakura survives. Thenceforward he's on a road to vengeance, and he's helped at first, by a surrogate father figure, then later by the ranch-owning widow of the cruellest bandit. Eventually, he dispatches all the villains, several of whom are regarded as the town's most upstanding citizens. Although Sato disliked the ninkyo *yakuza* genre, this plays like a sagebrush variation, right down to Takakura refusing to stay with the smitten widow at the end, even after he's won over the angry son who despised him for killing his father.

Sato took on Japanese militarism again in *The Last Kamikaze*. Filmed in black and white, it was an all-star big-budget spectacular featuring Koji Tsuruta, Ken Takakura, Sonny Chiba and Tomisaburo Wakayama, amongst others. But its thrust was slightly blunted by the studio.

Violent Gang Re-Arms is a rousing tale of friction in *yakuza* and labor interactions, with Koji Tsuruta as a *yakuza* supervising a dockworkers' union. He finds himself between a rock and a hard place, at odds with both the dockworkers' leader (Tomisaburo Wakayama) and sadistic, unprincipled bosses (Fumio Watanabe and Tetsuro Tanba).

Gambler's Counterattack is the tenth of the *Gambler* films. Sato's installment and two by Kinji Fukasaku were the only *jitsuroku*-slanted amongst the largely *ninkyo* dramas. Once more, Koji Tsuruta is an unrepentant, though principled, gangster, and Sato brings his anti-capitalist-excess feelings and downbeat perspective to climax the series with one of its finest entries. Tetsuro Tanba appears as a police inspector, but here his character is the opposite of his role in the first two *Organized Crime* movies, a cold-blooded, politically ambitious fascist out to circumvent the justice system and the laws he's sworn to uphold.

Sato next tackled the *jitsuroku* trilogy, *True Account Of The Ando Gang*, all three pictures starring ex-*yakuza* Noboru Ando and adapted from Ando's memoir,

Yakuza And Feuds. It's a commonly agreed-upon fact in Japan that true-life accounts such as Ando's carry a huge load of embellishments. Legend, not authentic occurrence, is the priority. Indeed, the first installment, *Yakuza And Feuds*, details Ando's sojourn at a poor people's clinic in the slums when a doctor-and-daughter team nurse him back to health after a gang fight. Eventually, the doctor is murdered by Ando's conflicted *yakuza* comrade (Bunta Sugawara), and our anti-hero then goes on a revenge mission to wipe out the neighborhood oppressors, something that leads to his death as well. The second film, *True Account Of The Ando Gang – Yakuza And Feuds*, finds hard-headed student Ando and his rowdy school chums forming their own post-war mob, a racket that evolves into a maze of both legitimate and illegal businesses. Threatened by a more corporate gang bent on swallowing up his enterprise, Ando readies for a bloody showdown. But, the night before, we're shocked to find him at his wife's hospital bedside as she gives birth by candlelight, the power out from a fierce windstorm. This scene brings a welcome dimension of humanity to the chaotic proceedings, and helps to anchor the film in a poignant reality not found in most *yakuza* pictures. The third and last installment, *Story Of Attack*, sticks most closely to the facts of Ando's life, Sato rigorously putting Ando and cronies through their paces, utilizing a nearly hour-by-hour chronology of the shady business antics that culminated in the non-fatal shooting of an arrogant businessman. This was the real-life incident that sent Ando and gang to prison for several years. The prison term was the impetus for Ando's memoirs, which led to his notoriety and subsequent screen stardom. A fascinating, non-sensationalized account of the mundane microcosm that was the late fifties Japanese underworld. *Pink* filmmaker Noboru Tanaka directed a sexed-up remake, *Noboru Ando's Filthy Escape Into Sex*, in 1976, chronicling Ando's amorous exploits on the run before capture.

Sato's strongest film, *True Account Of Ginza's Secret Enforcers*, is a masterpiece. A post-war saga of returning soldiers and their bestial do-anything-to-survive savagery in building a dog-eat-dog capitalist society, it has some of the most searingly potent juxtapositions I've ever seen in a film. At one point, a corrupt businessman kidnapped by the gang is tortured with boiling grease and accidentally killed. The panicking gangsters dump his body in a pigpen, and we witness the hogs dining on his meaty corpse. Later, another gangster (Tatsuo Umemiya) celebrates with his drunken partners, cavorting in a high-priced Ginza whorehouse and throwing ransom money about in the midst of fornicating bodies. An insane veteran (Tsunehiko Watase) the gang has hooked on methedrine and then used as an assassin, retires to the bathroom to shoot up. However, he starts to vomit prodigious amounts of blood before he can fix, geysers of the stuff, until his body is left drained and lifeless on the crimson floor. A devastating, emotionally exhausting experience somewhat similar to the insanity on display in many of James Ellroy's latest novels.

Sato's other genre pictures in the seventies were an odd bunch. He made the first film adaptation from *manga* of *Golgo 13*, starring Ken Takakura as the globetrotting hitman. Due as much to the threadbare source material as location woes in the Middle East, the picture was an awkward misfire.

Probably Sato's biggest film, up until 1988's *The Silk Road*, was *Bullet Train*, a suspense thriller about a desperate machine parts manufacturer (Ken Takakura), driven out of business, who decides to extort money by planting a bomb on the bullet train. He teams up with disillusioned student radicals, who help him implement his scheme. The bulk of the film depicts the over-zealous police trying to find the culprits so they can disarm the bomb, but the authorities' ruthlessness helps to push all concerned to the very brink of destruction. Unfortunately, the original 152-minute running time of the movie was cut everywhere else in the world to under two hours. The English-language version – entertaining but poorly dubbed – is, not surprisingly, lacking a great deal of backstory and most of the political subtext. Presumably, the missing details show what drove decent Takakura to estrange himself from his beloved family and strike back at those who rendered him bankrupt and powerless. Notable as the movie American filmmakers looted for the premise of a bomb triggered when a mass-transit vehicle drops below a certain velocity; however, in the box-office hit *Speed* a bus was used instead of a high-speed train.

Not counting the epic *Silk Road*, Sato's last genre picture to date is *When You Cross A River Of Rage*, a framed-cop-on-the-run tall tale. Ken Takakura stars as the put-upon protagonist, saddled with charges we learn at the end were trumped up by a powerful businessman (Ko Nishimura) Takakura had been investigating for murder. Yoshio Harada is Takakura's former colleague on his trail. The picture at times becomes outlandishly incredible, particularly when, at one point, a man-killing bear helps to save Takakura from his pursuer, Harada. Likewise, Takakura's young, impossibly rich, devoted girlfriend whom he's met while on the lam braves all kinds of obstacles for him, even causing a stampede of her horses through city streets to help him escape. A bizarre, over-long movie that is quite entertaining. But it comes off, unintentionally I think, as a wacky adult version of a *Boy's Life* adventure.

JUNYA SATO – SELECTED FILMOGRAPHY

1963	*STORY OF MILITARY CRUELTY (RIKUGUN ZANGYAKU MONOGATARI)*
	CHESS MASTER RETURNS (ZOKU OSHO)
1964	*RED LIGHT BREED (KURUWA SODACHI)*
1966	*PASSION (AIYOKU)*
1967	*ORGANIZED CRIME (SOSHIKI BORYOKU)*
	ORGANIZED CRIME 2 (ZOKU SOSHIKI BORYOKU)
1968	*THE DRIFTING AVENGER (KOYA NO TOSEININ,* aka *CHIVALROUS MAN IN THE WILDERNESS)*

1969   *THE SCOUNDREL'S RETURN TRIP FROM PRISON (TABI NI DETA GOKUDO)*
        ORGANIZED CRIME – LOYALTY OFFERING BROTHERS (SOSHIKI BORYOKU
        – KYODAI SAKAZUKI, aka *PRIVATE POLICE)*
        JAPAN'S VIOLENT GANGS – THE BOSS AND THE KILLERS (NIHON
        BORYOKUDAN – KUMICHO TO SHIKAKU)

1970   *THE LAST KAMIKAZE (SAIGO NO TOKKOTAI)*

1971   *VIOLENT GANG RE-ARMS (BORYOKUDAN SAI BUSO)*
        GAMBLER'S COUNTERATTACK (BAKUTO KIRIKOMI TAI)

1972   *YAKUZA AND FEUDS (YAKUZA TO KOSO)*
        YAKUZA AND FEUDS – TRUE ACCOUNT OF THE ANDO GANG (YAKUZA TO
        KOSO – JITSUROKU ANDOGUMI)
        GANG VS. GANG – RED AND BLACK BLUES (GYANGU TAI GYANGU – AKA
        TO KURO NO BUURUSU)

1973   *TRUE ACCOUNT OF GINZA'S SECRET ENFORCERS (JITSUROKU SHISETSU*
        GINZA KEISATSU, aka *TRUE ACCOUNT OF GINZA TORTURES)*
        TRUE ACCOUNT OF THE ANDO GANG – STORY OF ATTACK (JITSUROKU
        ANDOGUMI – SHUGEKI HEN)
        GOLGO 13 (GORUGO 13)

1975   *BULLET TRAIN (SHINKANSEN DAIBAKUHA)*

1976   *WHEN YOU CROSS A RIVER OF RAGE (KIMI YO FUNNE NO KAWA O*
        WATARE)

1982   *THE GO MASTERS (MIKAN NO TAIKYOKU)*

1983   *THEATER OF LIFE (JINSEI GEKIJO)*

1988   *THE SILK ROAD (DUN-HUANG)*

1992   *DREAM OF RUSSIA (O-RUSHIYA-KOKU SUIMU-DAN)*

JUNYA SATO – INTERVIEW

The following interview took place in the lobby/coffee bar of an upscale Japanese hotel in Tokyo in October, 1997. Shoko Ishiyama translated on-site.

CD: *You originally graduated from Tokyo University and were a French Literature major. How did you start working at Toei studios?*
    SATO: I was about to transfer, looking for a job after graduation, and I wanted to have a career in the movie industry. Toei actually had some openings for graduates. It was amazing, because Toho and Shochiku also had job offerings at the same time.
CD: *What was the year that you started working at Toei?*
    SATO: It was 1956.
CD: *Which directors did you apprentice under?*
    SATO: Toei had only been established for about five years at the time. They didn't have the same history as Toho or Shochiku, they were quite new. Everyone

had to work in rotation with different directors. You were not assigned to only one or two directors, you had to work with a lot of different people. Some of the directors I worked with were Daisuke Ito, Tadashi Imai, Tsuneo Kobayashi.

CD: What were the Daisuke Ito films that you worked on?

SATO: One of the best known was *Chess Master* (*Osho*, 1962) which was about Japanese chess. Mr Ito was very fond of the story; he had made another version of it in the early fifties.

CD: On your first film as director, Story Of Military Cruelty, *what was your interest in that project? Was it your choice or the studio's?*

SATO: Mr Ito and I were trying to decide what I should make as my first film as a director. Mr Ito was forced to put propaganda in his movies during wartime. And I'd gone to the countryside to get away from the war, just like the people who didn't approve of the government or the military excesses. The whole point of this picture was to show the effects of the first two years of training after entering military service. Their priority was to make ordinary people into killers. My assistant was in the navy during the war, and had been told to kill his humanity so he could become a killing machine. Of course, this wasn't just in the navy. Ultimately, it was about conformity and control throughout the entire nation.

CD: At the time of Story of Military Cruelty*'s release, there was a shocking, full-page black-and-white ad in the film journal* Kinejun. *It showed a close-up of the actor, I believe Rentaro Mikuni, with a large bayonet sticking out of his throat. This seems unusual for the time period. Violence in Japanese films was not that graphic until the late sixties, early seventies. And even then you usually didn't see it depicted so blatantly in a magazine like* Kinejun.

SATO: There wasn't too much of a problem with the image itself. Especially in black-and-white ads. The blood was represented by the black ink. But the poster, of course, was in color, and it was a shocking image to a lot of people. The image of someone committing suicide in such a way. But it was never criticized for the imagery since that was the whole point of the film, to expose the cruelty that led to such things.

CD: There were other films from Toei at the same time, Tale Of Bushido Cruelty *and* Cruelty Of The Shogunate's Downfall. *Was this just a coincidence that there seemed to be so much examination of cruelty in Japanese historical cinema of the period?*

SATO: All three films had the same topic, the handing down of traditions that promote cruel repression and adherence to conformity. I wanted to go against those traditions, to show how following them always leads to tragedy. To some extent, it was also expressing the political situation in Japan at the time.

CD: Of your next few films, Red Light Breed *and* Passion, *I understand they are more or less love stories. These seem a departure considering the subject matter of your first film.*

SATO: Not really. *Red Light Breed* is about a district called Yugaku, a poor area, and it's told from one woman's point of view. She's fallen in love, but her mother tells her that her lover will never accept her because she's from Yugaku.

Again, I had a character struggling against the system and authority. It was set in 1958, when a law was passed banning prostitution, so this woman has to suddenly find a new way to make a living. The affair with her lover ends, but he is still trying to patronize her so she ends up killing him. In *Passion*, the main character has two lovers, and I wanted to show how, because of the pressures of a capitalist society, a decision is made by the protagonist to choose the lover who will be better for business rather than the true love, the lover of the heart. Even though those two pictures might seem different on the surface, they are actually very much in keeping with what I wanted to say about living conditions in Japan at the time.

CD: *Your first* yakuza *films, the* Organized Crime *pictures, seem to be amongst the first* jitsuroku yakuza *pictures. Were the characters and events based in reality?*

SATO: The primary scriptwriter for the pictures also worked on *Battles Without Honor And Humanity* when it was a TV series. These films were based on some of the same incidents.

CD: *This was Yoshihiro Ishimatsu?*

SATO: Yes.

CD: *I just met Mr Ishimatsu the other night. I was asking the person I was with about the* Trail Of Blood *trilogy which Mr Ishimatsu wrote, and my friend introduced me to him.*

SATO: He and I went to the same university!

CD: *Masaru Sato did the music for* Story Of Military Cruelty *as well as the first two* Organized Crime *pictures. I know he hadn't done much at Toei, he worked more on Nikkatsu and Toho productions at the time. How did he become involved?*

SATO: Mr Sato was working a lot with Akira Kurosawa on his films. I had seen them and was really impressed by the music. He has a very distinctive sound, a memorable feeling to his scores. He was often experimental. I wanted him to do the music for *Story Of Military Cruelty* because I felt that it was a new, different kind of film. Mr Sato had never really done that kind of film before. It was great getting to work together, it was a good combination.

CD: Organized Crime – Loyalty Offering Brothers *has a post-WW2 sequence showing a woman raped by US occupation forces, then rescued by a Japanese soldier. I've seen similar scenes in other* yakuza *movies set in the post-war period. Was it really that prevalent, American soldiers raping Japanese women?*

SATO: It actually happened a lot. When the war ended, I was about 13 or 14 years old. Before and during the war the Japanese people were educated to believe that Japan was a nation favored by God. The drastic change that came afterwards, what people were supposed to believe under democracy, was being espoused by the new government. But, as I grew up, it seemed to me that the democracy was only supported by American power, American dominance. To stem the tide of violence, the government tried to go along with it. But the *yakuza* were very much against the idea of American democracy. Also, the corporate entities felt threatened by it, almost the same as the *yakuza* gangs. There was a huge underground black market that supported Japan's economy after the war, and there were many *yakuza* conflicts based around market competition. You also had the American-led democracy forces influencing and manipulating things. The image of Japanese women being raped by American soldiers became symbolic of the influence of the US occupation in Japan.

CD: In the film, the Bunta Sugawara character seems to start out as comparatively decent, but is eventually corrupted by the ruthlessness of his comrade, played by Noboru Ando.

SATO: Sugawara's character begins feeling more and more locked into the *yakuza* system. One of my favorite lines in the film is when he says: 'For my survival, there need to be either changes in society or changes in myself. But society is not changing, I am.'

CD: Can you comment on the almost always downbeat conclusions in the genre, especially the jitsuroku yakuza *pictures? The main characters are almost always killed at the end. There are frequently downbeat endings in American and European gangster films, but not to the degree you see in Japanese cinema. How did Toei and the other studios feel about these constantly bleak endings?*

SATO: As the sixties progressed there were more and more student demonstrations. Many young people thought the *yakuza* film characters were almost like the student leaders, fighting the system against impossible odds. They took them quite seriously – both students on the left *and* the right. And they felt deep empathy for the characters when they would die at the end. There was the aesthetic, too, that saw a terrible beauty in dying this way. In these films, often the only way left to make a change in the system is through violence. Many, many students felt this way trying to fight the universities, fight the government. So they related to the struggle. But the majority of the audience for *yakuza* films were blue-collar workers who felt virtually at war with the faceless, white-collar, corporate bosses. No one felt they had a system they could depend on. Everyone identified with the individual hero or anti-hero going up against the established system. So you had that, too. That's why the films were so popular. Even before the *yakuza* movies, Shintaro Katsu had made some films [*Note: referring to the Zatoichi films*] where a wanderer comes to town, interacts with people, and in the end leaves after making a slight change in the order of things.

CD: Right.

SATO: A wandering hero. And the *yakuza* movie, at first, was almost an extension of this wandering hero genre. Then an even more masculine fighting image was introduced, in the form of stars Koji Tsuruta and Ken Takakura. They're fighting against the established corrupt system, and are usually inside the system themselves, one of the only decent persons in the system. They have to be really pushed to react and fight back. So the films were slowly getting more cynical. You have someone in the system who gets pushed beyond their limit and becomes a reluctant hero fighting against the established order. But after a few years it became apparent that these heroes, too, seemed to be fighting a losing battle. Quite often they would die in the process. During this period, students were heavily protesting, often violently, against the US Security Treaty with Japan. But, as far as the larger picture, the students couldn't really see a clear goal, what they were looking for, as in 'the revolution.' *Yakuza eiga* was simultaneously getting more downbeat.

CD: This leads into my next question. Your films with Koji Tsuruta, Japan's Violent Gangs – The Boss and The Killers, Violent Gang Re-Arms *and* Gambler's Counterattack, *even though these films were becoming more* jitsuroku, *Tsuruta was still playing kind of a* ninkyo *hero. His characters always seem somewhat of a contradiction, and the consequences of his ethical convictions and loyalties are much more drastic than even in the most savage of the* ninkyo *films.*

SATO: Koji Tsuruta was known for that type of hero from the time of his samurai *chanbara* pictures to his first *ninkyo yakuza* films. His character was the stoic, strong *yakuza*, with scruples and loyalty to his comrades. Tsuruta's characters were always striving to be the 'perfect' *yakuza*. Perhaps, too, the reason why Koji Tsuruta had these deep convictions in real life was that he'd been in the war, he flew as a navy pilot and many of his friends perished as kamikaze fighters.

CD: Yes, I always have that in the back of my mind when I see him. Do you think Tsuruta was always trying to bring that 'ninkyo *spirit' to his roles, even when perhaps the writers and directors weren't trying to emphasize it as much in these later* jitsuroku *films?*

SATO: Yes.

CD: I think that makes the films with him very interesting. There's an unusual tension created because of it. You also see it in his films directed by Kinji Fukasaku. To see him with his chivalrous spirit amidst horrible violence and unethical behavior. In Gambler's Counterattack, *Tetsuro Tanba plays a police inspector who is as ambitious and ruthless as the worst of the* yakuza *characters. Is my perception right about his character?*

SATO: Yes, he represents very much an underlying evil of the powers that be, hypocrisy in the justice system.

CD: There was an article about yakuza *films by Paul Schraeder in a mid-seventies issue of the American movie journal* Film Comment, *where he described Koji Tsuruta being upset about the scene at the end of the film where his character shoots Tanba in the back. Was there any discussion about this at the time on the set?*

SATO: As you said before, Koji Tsuruta was enamored of that '*ninkyo* spirit', so, yes, naturally he would not feel comfortable having a character he played shoot another character in the back, no matter how much they might have deserved it.

CD: In Violent Gang Re-Arms, *Tsuruta's character, a* yakuza *underboss, is stoned by the dockworkers after he repels and kills the villainous head bosses. Because of this rejection on their part, Tsuruta then takes out his knife and commits* hari-kiri. *It seemed strange to me that the workers would be unable to see the difference between Tsuruta's character and that of the bosses.*

SATO: But that's probably what would happen in real life. Too often you see cases again and again in the news where the public can't tell what is really evil. The perceptions of the dockworkers in the film are confused. They've always looked at the *yakuza* that are exploiting them as all cut from the same cloth. They're from another world. For all they know, Tsuruta has been motivated by selfish interests in killing Watanabe and Tanba. The only way for Tsuruta to atone in the end is to offer them his life.

CD: The Last Kamikaze *seemed to have a big budget and a huge cast of Toei's big stars. You had Koji Tsuruta as one of the main characters. And perhaps a couple of the other actors might have been a bit conservative, too. Did you have to compromise on how you saw the war, the military?*

SATO: At the end of the film, Koji Tsuruta is shown flying off alone into the sunset. Originally, in the ending I wanted to shoot, Tsuruta's character was supposed to turn the plane around after he took off and dive, crashing back into the airfield command post. But that became very controversial with Toei. Also Koji Tsuruta's personal emotions about the subject were very sensitive. It wasn't acceptable to him, either. So I had to compromise the ending, just show him flying off. It's strange because, years later, he came up to me and apologized. His way of thinking had changed, and he'd finally come around to agree that my ending for the film would have been better!

CD: The True Account Of The Ando Gang *pictures with former* yakuza, *Noboru Ando, are fascinating. They supposedly were based on his exploits. What was it like working with him, and how close to the truth were these films?*

SATO: Regarding the events in the films, there had been agreement that we didn't have to adhere too closely to reality. Ando was not overly concerned about accuracy. As far as Ando as a person, he was very aggressive, very active. I think, perhaps, he wanted to show himself as fighting the evils of society. It's funny because earlier, when I'd been living in Shibuya, Mr Ando was also in the neighborhood, governing Shibuya, so to speak. So I had something in common with him before we ever started shooting the films.

CD: Was there any overlap from the past when Ando went into show business, was he still active as a yakuza *when he was acting in movies?*

SATO: No, Ando was retired from the *yakuza* when he started in films.

CD: There's a sequence near the end of one of the Ando Gang *films where he's in a hospital with his wife as she's about to give birth; the power goes off, then she delivers the baby by candlelight. Was that something that actually happened?*

SATO: I don't know how much of his family material was true.

CD: True Account Of Ginza's Secret Enforcers *is one of the most shocking* yakuza *films I've seen. There's disturbing imagery scattered throughout. Tsunehiko Watase plays the soldier returning from the war who murders his wife and the baby she's had with a black American GI, then is hooked on speed and manipulated by the drug dealer played by Ryoji Hayama. Was this symbolic of the destruction of the public's naive idealism behind Japan's military imperialism, or perhaps of the US occupation's dog-eat-dog influences on the Japanese economy?*

SATO: Watase symbolizes the violence that exists in the absence of an ideology, of justice, of a goal, and that then leads to even more chaos. The older *yakuza* films were different because they would show a system to rebel against. But I wanted to use the violence in a different way, to show the chaos from this aimlessness, the lack of ideals or goals, the characters not knowing what to do in this vacuum. The film becomes really downbeat, and negative and cynical at the same time. The gangs in *this* film actually existed, and there was a well-researched script. Along with the other people involved in the film, I wanted to show what happens when ideals and ideologies are taken away, the violence that too often replaces them. It's quite different from other *yakuza* films, for example many *ninkyo eiga*. In this film, there's no goal to the violence. The situation is created out of hopelessness.

CD: What are your feelings about ninkyo eiga? *I notice that you haven't ever directed any.*

SATO: I never agreed with the style or the ideas behind *ninkyo eiga*, of solving a problem by destructive means, by violence. Also, I had difficulty with the

Poster for *True Account of Ginza's Secret Enforcers*

aesthetic beauty of the violence in the films. Justifying the violence as a means to destroying evil is part of the problem. I just couldn't work on them.

CD: Also around this time you did the first film based on the manga, Golgo 13. *There weren't any sequels, which seems strange since it featured Ken Takakura in the lead and was based on a very popular comic. There wasn't another* Golgo 13 *film until several years later with Shinichi 'Sonny' Chiba. What did you think about the film, since it was from* manga *and also featured a main character that was an amoral assassin?*

SATO: This is a difficult question. The *Golgo 13* character is someone who travels all over the world, he doesn't just stick to Japan. His character is very stoic, and doesn't question his assignments. He's asked to go somewhere and kill someone for money, and he does. It's difficult to begin with to know just how to approach the character.

CD: How did the film do, was it popular?

SATO: It did okay at the box office.

CD: Didn't Toei want to do more films with Takakura playing the character?

SATO: The writer of the original *manga*, Takao Saito, did not really like the way the character was portrayed. So I think that may have been part of it. It's just a guess. Also, this film was shot on location in Iran, and we had had quite a few problems shooting there. It was hard, partly because we didn't have a big enough budget. Toei didn't want to do more location shooting abroad in other countries after those difficulties. But if you were going to do the films like the *manga*, you really needed to show the character in these other locations.

CD: Could you talk about the evolution of the thriller, Bullet Train, *a picture which seems to have influenced the Hollywood-produced* Speed, *and your experience working on it?*

SATO: I had been asked if I could figure out a way of using the bullet train in an action film. After thinking about the security issues, how, if there is an accident or some kind of attack, the train must be stopped to solve the problem, I decided that it would be interesting if the train could not be stopped for some reason. If the train stopping or slowing down would be what would cause the disaster, say, cause a bomb to go off. So, I went about starting to set it up, asking permission to do the picture from the operators of the *shinkansen* because we would need their cooperation. But they initially rejected the proposal. They explained they were already getting at least one call a week from someone making a bomb threat. Each time this would cause them to have to shut all the trains down and search through every car, even if they thought the threat was a hoax. They would still have to search, just to make sure. Making this kind of film would give ideas to even more crazy people. Finally, the *shinkansen* people agreed, but it took a lot of time. It was very chaotic in Japan in 1975, there were over one million unemployed. It was the worst the economy had been since just after the war, and there were many companies that declared bankruptcy. So we made the main character of the film, played by Ken Takakura, an owner of one of the bankrupt companies.

Then there are the ex-members of a radical group, and a young employee devoted to the owner who joins them as a last resort to get justice.

CD: You worked on a big-budget production of Theater Of Life, *a story that had been filmed many times before. But this particular version had three directors. You shared the job with Kinji Fukasaku and Sadao Nakajima. I was curious why Toei wanted three directors?*

SATO: Originally, Kinji Fukasaku was supposed to direct by himself. He had wanted to make the film because of his interest in the Taisho era in turn-of-the-century Japan. However, after he had finished his version of the script, not only was it not long enough, he wasn't happy with it either. Toei couldn't just cancel the film because the release date was already set, all the actors had been cast. Mr Nakajima had been involved in the writing, too, so he and Mr Fukasaku and the producers asked if I would help out. Mr Fukasaku and I had collaborated before, we had even written together. As you probably know, the *Theater Of Life* story is very long. We just did not have enough time to do the film and still make the release date that the studio had set. I ended up writing on the script as well, then all three of us divided up the segments. So we each directed roughly a third of the movie!

CD: The Silk Road – *was that a personal project of yours that you had been working on for some time?*

SATO: That was another film that Kinji Fukasaku was supposed to direct. But, once the script was done, there were some problems. Mr Fukasaku was involved in another project at the same time, then he and Daiei had conflicts on the approach. The story is based on Japan's historical interaction in feudal times with China, and I had already been contacted by Daiei because I had some knowledge of China. When Mr Fukasaku and Daiei parted ways, I was asked to take over.

CD: In the American version of The Silk Road, *there's a sequence at the beginning by Saul and Elaine Bass, and I was wondering if this is also in the Japanese version of the film?*

SATO: That was actually arranged by Akiko Agishi. She was behind Saul Bass's involvement.

CD: That's interesting. Akiko has been a big help in setting up some of my interviews. As a last question, what are you working on now?

SATO: I'm just finishing up a picture called *Peking Man*.

6

Kihachi Okamoto

1923–2005

Judging from late fifties vintage photos, Kihacho Okamoto projected the perfect image of a maverick movie director: rail thin, with a cap of the Union Army from the American Civil War poised rakishly on his head and a perpetual cigarette dangling from his lips. His expression is always intensely engaged, burning eyes shining from gaunt face, his entire frame vibrating with energy. In contrast, Kihachi Okamoto still had the intense eyes but was noticeably more laid-back, conserving his stamina, when he appeared at The American Cinematheque in Los Angeles in the summer of 1997. He was in town for screenings of three of his best films from the sixties, *Age Of Assassins*, *Sword Of Doom* and *Kill!*, despite having suffered a temporarily debilitating stroke several years before. Mr Okamoto is not the type to throw in the towel, and he not only accepted the invitation to appear at the screenings but has directed several projects since, including *Vengeance For Sale* in 2001.

The first films Okamoto worked on as director are a mixed bag, offering intoxicating vigor as well as hackneyed scripts (those he didn't write himself) and dated histrionics. Surprisingly, it's the majority of his early gangster films that are in the just-average category. Although *Underworld Bullets* and *Big Shots Die At Dawn* are consistently engaging, with moments reminiscent of Seijun Suzuki's action staging at Nikkatsu from the same period, the tongue-in-cheek humor is broader and less darkly pungent than Suzuki's. Okamoto's highest-profile gangster opuses, *The Big Boss* and *The Last Gunfight*, both starring top Toho studio stars of the time, Koji Tsuruta and Toshiro Mifune, are the most forgettable. Many late fifties Japanese *yakuza* films such as these were heavily influenced by their American counterparts, and this was generally not to their benefit. Okamoto had little input, if any, on the scripts of these films, and *The Big Boss*, despite a couple of inspired sequences, is the worst offender with a convoluted script of contrived situations.

However, there is one gangster film exception that Okamoto directed, the abrasive, downbeat, shot-in-black-and-white *Procurers Of Hell*. Resonating with the same hard-boiled, noirish edginess as Okamoto's darkest samurai movies, it stars Tatsuya Mihashi as an opportunist photographer who extorts money from an old army comrade who has become a high-powered industrialist. Mihashi's dangerous gambit takes him down a twisted path that leads to not only his own downfall but that of all concerned.

Okamoto's first certified masterpiece was, coincidentally, only his fifth film, and was released the same year as *The Big Boss*, in 1959. An exuberantly irreverent anti-war satire-cum-action movie, *Desperado Outpost* starred Makoto Sato as an AWOL

Makoto Sato in *Desperado Outpost*

soldier in pre-WW2 Manchuria, investigating the death of his brother at a lonely military outpost near the front lines. What he finds is a group of cruel, avaricious Japanese officers (Tadao Nakamaru et al.) using their position for personal gain, reaping financial rewards from exploiting the local populace and smuggling illicit goods. Sato's brother has stumbled onto the truth and has been murdered. Toshiro Mifune is simultaneously scary and funny as a colonel who has gone off his rocker. Through Mifune's brief, cock-eyed appearance, Okamoto perfectly illustrates the lunacy of Japanese imperialism. Part of the reason *Desperado Outpost* is so high-grade is that Okamoto was allowed to make the film from his own script, and he had a hand in writing the sequels he directed, *Westward Desperado* and *Operation: Sewer Rats*, films that are nearly as good.

Okamoto also made several more serious war films, *Japan's Longest Day*, *Fort Graveyard* and *Battle Of Okinawa*, pictures with the gravitas of his grimmest, most downbeat *chanbara*. In particular, *Japan's Longest Day* chronicles events leading up to Japan's surrender at the close of WW2, and is a long but never boring tapestry of military men and politicians hashing out their differences with regard to honor, duty and the true nature of what constitutes Japan's national identity. There are stand-out performances from both Chishu Ryu as the more level-headed Prime Minister and Toshiro Mifune as a shamed general who comes to believe his only recourse is *hara-kiri*. The flip side of *Japan's Longest Day*, as Okamoto himself suggests in the following interview, is his devastating anti-war satire *The Human Bullet*, a story of a lowly soldier (Minoru Tezuka) who comes to realize he's nothing but cannon fodder for the powers that be. His ridiculous adventures as he's trained to become a suicide pilot for a one-man sub, a virtual human torpedo to combat incoming American ships, reaches rarefied heights of Buñuelian surrealism and, in a few spots, approaches the kind of absurdity found in Beckett's *Waiting For Godot*.

Age Of Assassins is another sharp-edged lampoon that works just as well as an action film, and compares favorably with such other brilliant, tongue-in-cheek, mod sixties masterpieces as Elio Petri's *The Tenth Victim* and Seijun Suzuki's *Branded To Kill*. Tatsuya Nakadai is superb as a glasses-wearing nebbish who is magically transformed into a suave secret agent. Saddled with limited resources, including a smog-belching junk heap of an automobile, he must do battle with a maniacal asylum director (Eisei Amamoto) who is dispatching unhinged killers as part of a plot to bring Japan to its knees.

Okamoto's personal taste runs to comedy, usually of the dark variety, and it can be found as much in evidence in a number of his *chanbara* as in his gangster and anti-war films. *Warring Clans*, *Kill!*, *Zatoichi Meets Yojinbo* and *Red Lion* all expertly balance bleak humor with their more serious dramatic elements. All four create a synthesis of lunacy and sobriety worthy of the best spaghetti westerns. As point of reference, Sergio Corbucci's exceptionally fine *Compañeros* comes immediately to mind. *Kill!* especially reflects this, with Masaru Sato's Morricone-inflected theme, its opening sequence in a dust-blown ghost town and its sparring friendly rivals: an ex-samurai-turned-*matatabi* (Tatsuya Nakadai) and a wannabe swordsman (Etsushi Takahashi). Okamoto, though, was comparatively unfamiliar with the Italian genre. One can attribute the similarities in *Kill!* as much to previous *chanbara*, like Kurosawa's *Yojinbo* and Hideo Gosha's *Three Outlaw Samurai*. But there is an astonishing symbiotic synchronicity operating just below the conscious level in Japanese and Italian genre cinema of the period. You can see it most obviously in *Yojinbo*, a film as much influenced by Dashiell Hammett as by John Ford, and the picture Sergio Leone, himself, took as direct inspiration for his *Fistful Of Dollars*. Okamoto's *Zatoichi Meets Yojinbo* employs a similar working-both-sides-of-the-street approach to its rural gang war, and even pays homage to *Treasure Of Sierra Madre* in its greed-as-exercise-in-futility climax.

Which brings us to Okamoto's other samurai films, pictures I referred to earlier as his grimmest and most downbeat.

Samurai Assassin features Toshiro Mifune as an expert swordsman intent on joining anti-shogunate conspirators in killing the local lord. But Mifune is tormented by his bastard origins and plagued by perpetual drunkenness. The rebel leader (Yunosuke Ito) decides he is too unstable, thus must also be murdered. Mifune not only survives but joins the attack in the graphic, fever-pitched final massacre in the snow. Okamoto and screenwriter Shinobu Hashimoto then supply one of the most perverse twist endings in any samurai film – an ending I won't divulge, but suffice it to say it concerns the true nature of his illegitimate status.

Okamoto's period film masterpiece is, without question, *Sword Of Doom*, a picture that had been remade many times since its first incarnation under its original title, *The Great Boddhisatva Pass*. Adapted from a novel by Kaizan Nakazato, the initial outing was directed in 1937 by master Hiroshi Inagaki. Remakes did not appear until the early fifties, and are a mixed bag with Kunio Watanabe directing first in a black-and-white trilogy. Toei remade it again in 1957 as *Souls In The Moonlight*. Despite the involvement of exceptional director Tomu Uchida, even this three-part version had only a few electric moments. With Daiei studios taking up the reins in 1959

Shima Iwashita in *Red Lion*

under the English title *Satan's Sword*, the tide changed for the better. Shot in wide-screen color and employing the sublime Kenji Misumi to helm the first two parts of the saga, and Kazuo Mori the third, Raizo Ichikawa was perfectly cast as Ryunosuke Tsukue, the sociopathic swordsman trying to fight his way out of full-blown psychosis. Though lacking the stark, bloody *frissons* of *Sword Of Doom*, *Satan's Sword* is the most complete version of the novel. Ichikawa's Tsukue is a an almost tragic figure, a lost soul physically blinded since midway through part two, but groping his way in spiritual darkness towards some hint of light.

Nevertheless, Okamoto's version in ashen black-and-white scope captures the nihilistic netherworld of the sociopathic paranoid best. It is a riveting, disturbingly desolate picture, anchored by a mesmerizing portrayal from Tatsuya Nakadai as Tsukue. Masaru Sato's music is at the pinnacle of a multitude of great Japanese motion picture scores from the 1960s. The supporting cast, including Michiyo Aratama and Yuzo Kayama, are all excellent. Screenwriter Shinobu Hashimoto's expert distillation from the novel is a masterwork. Which makes it all the more mystifying that this particular version enjoys such a mediocre reputation in its native country. It was a breakout arthouse hit when it was released in the West, particularly in America.

Okamoto's films since the early seventies have never approached that kind of wild-eyed intensity again. He has continued to make some entertaining movies, particularly the over-long but funny *Noisy Dynamite* with Bunta Sugawara and Frankie Sakai, a knockabout black comedy from 1978 about two post-WW2 *yakuza* gangs deciding to settle their differences with a series of ever more ludicrously violent baseball games. But Okamoto endured a couple of awkward misfires in the ensuing years, most notably *East Meets West* in 1995. The samurai-transplanted-to-the-Old-West-tale was plagued by a number of seemingly untrained American stuntmen masquerading as actors, as well as an obnoxious blonde moppet whom I kept hoping lead actor Hiroyuki Sanada was going to drop-kick across the prairie. But, in 2001, Okamoto returned to expert form with his humorous, bitter-sweet *chanbara*, *Vengeance For Sale*. Starring Hiroyuki Sanada and Tatsuya Nakadai, it was a reworking of his 1975 movie *Battle Cry*, and agreeably reminiscent of such earlier pictures as *Kill!* and *Red Lion*.

KIHACHI OKAMOTO – SELECTED FILMOGRAPHY

1959　　*THE BIG BOSS (ANKOKUGAI NO KAOYAKU, aka UNDERWORLD BOSS)*
　　　　DESPERADO OUTPOST (DOKURITSU GURENTAI)

1960　　*THE LAST GUNFIGHT (ANKOKUGAI NO TAIKETSU, aka UNDERWORLD DUEL)*
　　　　THE SPOOK COTTAGE (DAIGAKU NO SANZOKUTACHI, aka BAD BOYS IN UNIVERSITY)

WESTWARD DESPERADO (DOKURITSU GURENTAI NISHI-HE)

1961 *UNDERWORLD BULLETS (ANKOKUGAI NO DANKON,* aka *BULLETHOLES IN THE UNDERWORLD,* aka *BLUEPRINT FOR MURDER)*

BIG SHOTS DIE AT DAWN (KAOYAKU AKATSUKI NI SHISU, aka *DEATH OF THE BOSS)*

PROCURERS OF HELL (JIGOKU NO KYOEN, aka *BANQUET IN HELL)*

1962 *OPERATION SEWER RATS (DOBU NEZUMI SAKUSEN,* aka *OPERATION X)*

SALARY ROBBER (GEKKYU DOROBO)

1963 *WARRING CLANS (SENGOKU YARO)*

THE ELEGANT LIFE OF MR EVERYMAN (EBURI MANSHI NO YUGA-NA SEIKATSU)

1964 *AH! EXPLOSION (AA BAKUDAN,* aka *OH, BOMB)*

1965 *SAMURAI ASSASSIN (SAMURAI)*

FORT GRAVEYARD (CHI TO SUNA, aka *BLOOD AND SAND)*

1966 *SWORD OF DOOM (DAIBOSATSU TOGE,* aka *THE GREAT BODDHISATVA PASS)*

1967 *AGE OF ASSASSINS (SATSUJIN KYOJIDAI)*

JAPAN'S LONGEST DAY (NIHON NO ICHIBAN NAGAI HI, aka *THE EMPEROR AND THE GENERAL)*

1968 *KILL! (KIRU)*

THE HUMAN BULLET (NIKUDAN, aka *THE HUMAN TORPEDO)*

1969 *RED LION (AKAGE)*

1970 *ZATOICHI MEETS YOJINBO (ZATOICHI TO YOJINBO)*

1971 *BATTLE OF OKINAWA (GEKIDO NO SHOWASHI – OKINAWA KESSEN)*

1972 *THREE JAPANESE FIGHTERS – GOODBYE, TOKYO (NIPPON SANJUSHI – OSARABA TOKYO NO MAKI)*

1973 *THREE JAPANESE FIGHTERS – PART TWO (NIPPPON SANJUSHI – HAKATA SHIME IPPON DOKO NO MAKI)*

1975 *BATTLE CRY (TOKKAN,* aka *GO FOR BROKE)*

1977 *SANSHIRO SUGATA (SUGATA SANSHIRO)*

1978 *NOISY DYNAMITE (DAINAMAITO DONDON,* aka *DYNAMITE BANG, BANG)*

BLUE CHRISTMAS (BUURUU KURISAMASU, aka *BLOOD TYPE: BLUE,* aka *UFO BLUE CHRISTMAS)*

1979 *THE LAST GAME (EIRETACHI NO OENKA – SAIGO NO SOKEISEN)*

1986 *JAZZ DAIMYO (JAZU DAIMYO,* aka *DIXIELAND DAIMYO)*

1995 *EAST MEETS WEST*

2001 *VENGEANCE FOR SALE (SUKEDACHIYA SUKEROKU,* aka *VENGEANCE IS SUCH A GREAT BUSINESS,* aka *SUKEROKU, THE HELPER)*

KIHACHI OKAMOTO – INTERVIEW

The following interview took place at the Hollywood Roosevelt Hotel in Hollywood in the summer of 1997. Kurando Mitsutake translated on-site.

CD: What was your original plan for a career? Was it film or ...?

OKAMOTO: All during my early years, until after junior high school, I didn't watch any movies. Many people considered them to be bad for you. Up until I first started working in films, I hadn't really had any specific interest.

CD: What was your experience during WW2? Were you conscripted or were you lucky enough to avoid the military?

OKAMOTO: When I was 17 I moved to Tokyo and started university. That was when I started going to see a lot of films. I loved American action movies and French comedies. The war had already started at that point, and I was thinking that any day I would get drafted, then die. I thought I would probably end my life by about 21. So I decided I was going to see as many movies as possible in the duration. When I was 19 I graduated from university, but I still had not been drafted. I thought to myself that movies were so much fun to watch they must be even more fun to make. So I went to Toho and got a job as an assistant director. Before I got drafted, I was an assistant director to Mikio Naruse. Since I had just joined the company, I was not one of the higher-ranked assistants. Toho decided they didn't need as many assistant directors because of the production slowdown from the war, so I was assigned to work in a factory that was making fighter planes. I didn't get drafted into the army until 1945, but then the war ended in August. I ended up only being in the military for about eight months. Then I went back to Toho.

CD: Who were the other directors besides Mikio Naruse that you worked under?

OKAMOTO: Well, I worked at Toho for two years before going into the army, then I went back after the war. I was an assistant director for 15 years, so I must have worked with almost every director that was working there during that period. I worked with Akira Kurosawa and then with Naruse again. And also Masahiro Makino.

CD: Did you work on any of the period yakuza matatabi *films, the* Jirocho *series that Masahiro Makino directed in the mid-fifties at Toho?*

OKAMOTO: (*laughs*) Yes. We made nine pictures in two years.

CD: In Kurosawa's autobiography, he talks about the prolonged strike that happened post-war at Toho and how eventually some of the producers, directors and stars split off to form Shintoho studios.

OKAMOTO: Right after the war, which had already caused a significant cutback in productions, there were three and a half years of strikes. They were not making as many movies as before. I remember I worked on a couple of independently produced movies at the time, one directed by Kajiro Yamamoto.

CD: I have not seen your first two films as director, All About Marriage *and* Young Daughters. *But from the titles I would guess they were comedies?*

OKAMOTO: They weren't comedies exactly. *All About Marriage* was more the everyday life of everyday people, married people. The other was an adolescent coming-of-age film.

CD: Your first action film was The Big Boss. *Was that what you hoped to do at the time?*

OKAMOTO: All of those first movies, *All About Marriage, Young Daughters, The Big Boss, Someday I Am ..., The Last Gunfight,* were assigned to me. But when I was glancing through the scenes in *The Big Boss* script, I was excited because I'd always wanted to direct action films. I felt more with those earlier films that I was just doing my job, and I didn't enjoy them quite as much. *Desperado Outpost* was the first time I directed where it was my project, something I really wanted to do. I'd written the script a while before as part of Toho's exam to see if I was qualified to become a full-fledged director. I had actually written two scripts, *Desperado Outpost* and *Ah! Explosion,* which I didn't direct until much later.

CD: In the Japanese film magazine Kinejun, *I've noticed that both* Desperado Outpost *and its sequel,* Westward Desperado, *now seem to be highly regarded. Was this also true when they were initially released? They were popular with audiences, but did they also receive the critical acclaim that they seem to enjoy now?*

OKAMOTO: To tell the truth, they did not originally receive very favorable reviews. I was treating the war in Manchuria in an irreverent, satirical way, almost like a sporting event, which many critics looked down on. They felt it was degrading. Most of the negative criticism of the films had that tone. The positive comments said that the war was frequently like that. Most of the war films at the time were very sad, that kind of approach, while *Desperado Outpost* was laughing at the chaos, the insanity that was war. That's something I'm very proud of. Before my later war film, *The Human Bullet,* I was repeatedly targeted as a director who made fun of war. But, after *The Human Bullet* came out, the same critics finally got what I was driving at, and some of them actually apologized to me.

CD: But The Human Bullet *had a similar sense of humor. In some ways it was more serious, but it had a similar tone to* Desperado Outpost.

OKAMOTO: But, because of that more serious anti-war feeling, they finally understood what I was saying, how I felt about the war. Actually, if you look at *Japan's Longest Day,* it looks more at those who were able to stay above the fighting, those in command, who were even at odds with each other, while *The Human Bullet* shows those who were below who got dragged under, became the cannon fodder. Watching the two films together gives you a complete picture.

CD: Age Of Assassins *was the film you made immediately before* Japan's Longest Day, *and was a film Toho did not understand or initially feel was releasable. They shelved it for a time. Yet, instead of giving you some little project to follow it, they had you direct one of the biggest films of your early career,* Japan's Longest Day.

OKAMOTO: Yes, *Age Of Assassins* wasn't released until eight months after it was finished. In the meantime, a producer who I knew there at Toho called me up. He realized I was having a tough time, that I was just sitting around drinking and playing golf, so he said, 'Why don't you come into my office to talk about your feelings?' So I went to Mr Fujimoto's office, we had a couple of drinks and then he asked me what I was thinking about Toho. I told him I had heard Masaki Kobayashi was supposed to be directing *Japan's Longest Day*, but that he didn't want to do it and had refused the assignment, and consequently the picture was just kind of hanging in limbo. I said that I thought that that was a picture Toho should definitely make. Then he said, 'Why don't you do it?' So, that's how that came about.

CD: Do you know why Mr Kobayashi didn't want to make the picture?

OKAMOTO: I never found out.

CD: Looking at Age Of Assassins, *the film is obviously funny, it also has a lot of action. Yet Toho didn't seem to like it. Do you know what their reasons were?*

OKAMOTO: One of the only criticisms I heard was just that it was 'below average'. Nobody really said anything about it as far as its qualities as a picture. From what little I could gather, I heard it was inner studio politics. The two main Toho producers, Mr Fujimoto and Mr Tanaka, were competing, and I believe *Age Of Assassins* was a casualty of that rivalry.

CD: So I take it you were more in Mr Fujimoto's camp than in Mr Tanaka's?

OKAMOTO: Mr Fujimoto was much more powerful than Mr Tanaka. Mr Tanaka was younger, Mr Fujimoto was older. In some ways, you could actually say I was closer to Mr Tanaka. But our relationship was a lot like Tom and Jerry, the cartoon characters. He was always chasing me around, and I was always running away. At the time, the three biggest Japanese movie companies all had this thing about who was the biggest, most powerful person on the lot. It just so happened that, at Toho, it was the producers who were competing for that. At Shochiku it was the directors, and at Toei it was actors. I'm talking about during the sixties. That was a home-grown thing, one of the reasons why it was a very energetic, interesting time period.

CD: To get back to Desperado Outpost, *which became a series, I have not seen other than the first two. Did the others that were made by Senkichi Taniguchi and Jun Fukuda and the last film,* Fort Graveyard, *also directed by you, have the same tone as the first pictures?*

OKAMOTO: *Operation: Sewer Rats*, which I directed, had a pretty close feeling to the original *Desperado Outpost*. But *Fort Graveyard* was more of a serious drama. It was the story of the Japanese army's marching band that was made up of young boys. In the picture, Toshiro Mifune is the one adult soldier leading them. At the end of the film, the boys are playing their music as they are killed one by one. Finally no one is left, and the music stops.

CD: In some of your gangster pictures of the time, like The Last Gunfight, *there was a tongue-in-cheek quality, humor that became typical of the* James Bond *movies later on.*

OKAMOTO: Yes, all the movies I did in the *Underworld* series had that tone, more or less. After I did the first few, the studio wanted me to continue because they were so successful. But I was not interested in continually repeating the same thing over and over again. That actually holds true for the *Desperado Outpost* series, too. Many of them had that tone. But after the first two ...

CD: ... Was Fort Graveyard *actually considered a part of that series, because I've seen it listed with those films in some Japanese film reference books? Or was that more of a marketing strategy from the studio?*

OKAMOTO: That was probably due more to some critics' perceptions, maybe some promotional ads, too, from the studio. But it was clearly different from that series.

CD: The films of yours that I remember the most vividly are your samurai films. Warring Clans, Kill!, Red Lion *and* Zatoichi Meets Yojinbo *mixed the violent drama with humor at times.* Sword of Doom *and* Samurai Assassin *are both fairly serious all the way through. Which of those films do you feel work best?*

OKAMOTO: I like all the *chanbara* films that I made. The more serious ones, such as *Samurai Assassin*, were films that already had the scripts written. Or, as in *Sword of Doom*, were based on a book that had been filmed several times before. Those samurai are very strong, almost inhuman. In *Warring Clans*, *Kill!* and *Red Lion* I wanted to show samurai that were more human, down-to-earth, more philosophical or whimsical samurai, and how they coped with all the violence and killing. Those samurai in the more humorous pictures were a reaction to the superhuman samurai you commonly saw on the screen.

CD: In both Desperado Outpost, *with Izumi Yukimura, and* Warring Clans, *with Yuriko Hoshi and Kumi Mizuno, you had strong female characters who even did some of the fighting alongside the men. The later sixties saw more Japanese fighting heroines, but it was not that common in Japanese films in the early sixties. How did that come about?*

OKAMOTO: When I was given the first draft of the script for *Warring Clans*, I felt the passions were not real. I added some sequences and characters. It wasn't a 'political' decision, it just felt more natural to me to have these strong female characters. Samurai *chanbara* films by their nature are about people struggling for something or some cause. I felt it was only natural that women were struggling right alongside the men. The executives who'd given me the first draft expressed similar feelings, they felt the characters were not realistic. They wanted me to make them more real. So, it was also the producers' decision to try to make the story come more alive.

CD: All the other versions of Sword Of Doom, *or* Great Boddhisatva Pass, *as it is known in Japan, have almost always been made as trilogies. There were the versions in the fifties by Kunio Watanabe and by Tomu Uchida, and the very early sixties version directed by Kenji Misumi and Kazuo Mori. Did Toho originally plan to do two more films after* Sword Of Doom? *Or was it decided to just tell the first part of the story?*

OKAMOTO: Originally Toho had planned to do it in two parts with a second part to come later. However, shortly before the release, the executives decided it would probably not do that well. So they stopped the second film right before it went into production.

CD: How did it do when it was released?

OKAMOTO: The box office was mediocre. You see, the Daiei version with Raizo Ichikawa, and the two versions from Toei had all been big hits. Toho had originally been expecting to do the same kind of business as the other companies' versions. At the last minute, they had a premonition it wasn't going to do that well. Then it came out and *did do* mediocre business. So in a way, they were right. But it was a very successful film overseas, especially the United States. When it first played in New York, there were lines around the block.

CD: It's too bad. I really liked the Raizo Ichikawa version, but yours is certainly my favorite. Moving on to Kill!, Red Lion *and* Zatoichi Meets Yojinbo, *there's ambience similar to the Italian spaghetti westerns of the time, by directors like Sergio Leone and Sergio Corbucci. I know they were influenced by films such as Kurosawa's* Yojinbo *as well as other samurai pictures. Did you ever see any of those spaghetti westerns, especially those directed by Corbucci? There are several of his, especially* Compañeros *and* The Mercenary, *that have a similar tone to* Kill!, Red Lion, Zatoichi Meets Yojinbo.

OKAMOTO: Actually, the only spaghetti western that I ever saw was Leone's version of *Yojinbo*, *A Fistful Of Dollars*. I have not seen any of Corbucci's.

CD: How did you become involved directing the Zatoichi *film? Since it was a Katsu Production, did Shintaro Katsu approach you?*

OKAMOTO: The basic story line for *Zatoichi Meets Yojinbo* came from a story by Dashiell Hammett. You're familiar with him?

CD: Yes. That was Red Harvest?

OKAMOTO: No, Kurosawa may have gotten the original idea for *Yojinbo* from the novel, *Red Harvest*. But the idea for *Zatoichi Meets Yojinbo* was from another Dashiell Hammett short story. Unfortunately, I can't remember the actual title. Everybody thinks that I was into making a *Zatoichi* film, but that's really not the case. And many people thought Katsu brought me into the project. But it was a friend of mine, Shinobu Hashimoto, who called me up and told me one of his students was writing *Zatoichi Meets Yojinbo*, would I like to direct it?

CD: What was it like working with Katsu and Mifune together?

OKAMOTO: (*laughs*) Katsu was saying Zatoichi should be the stronger one, and Mifune was saying it should be Yojinbo. So that was a conflict before the script was even finished! I felt that, since it was part of the *Zatoichi* series, Zatoichi should win in the end. But Mifune felt otherwise. The only way to settle the dispute was to have them call it even in the end and wound each other in a draw.

CD: In Red Lion, *the film is comic up until the last 20 minutes or so, when it becomes serious, even tragic. After Mifune's character is killed, his wife, played by Shima Iwashita, takes up the sword and then is cut down, too. It's very devastating. Would it be too much to take away from* Red Lion *that everyday people with everyday dreams should be their own leaders and not expect deliverance to come from outside themselves?*

OKAMOTO: Everything you're saying is very true. I think now I made the villains a little too comic at times. I think in some ways it weakened the film a bit. Do you think the villains should have been treated more seriously, that it would have made the film more effective?

CD: Perhaps the lord of the district played by Yunosuke Ito was too foolish at times, it diluted his menace. But the forces who betrayed Mifune and his comrades, who betrayed all the fighting farmers under them, were frightening. You were kept guessing what their true motivations were. Their pronouncements about reducing taxes and making sure everyone had enough to eat seemed too good to be true, that they were taking advantage of the naive country samurai, using them as cannon fodder.

OKAMOTO: Hmm, I actually wish I'd made it a little more serious. I think it could have been more powerful.

CD: In your more comic samurai films, you seem to have a couple of main characters who have a friendly rivalry, switching back and forth to opposite sides. In Warring Clans, *it was Yuzo Kayama and Makoto Sato. In* Kill!, *it was Tatsuya Nakadai and Etsushi Takahashi. In* Red Lion, *it was Toshiro Mifune and Etsushi Takahashi. And in* Zatoichi Meets Yojinbo, *of course, it was Katsu and Mifune. But your serious samurai films such as* Sword Of Doom *and* Samurai Assassin, *the main characters are tormented loners trapped inside their psyches, as if they're trying to figure out who they are. Was that something you were consciously trying to go for, or is it only my interpretation?*

OKAMOTO: The comical films do have that rivalry in there. They are almost like 'buddy' movies. They also show individuals in groups, individuals struggling against larger groups. Whereas the more serious ones are focused on the individuals questioning themselves, what they should be doing, what is driving them, their demons, their madness – the study of what that one individual does.

CD: Let me close by telling you that I saw a friend of mine at the screening of Sword Of Doom *last night, someone who I had not seen in many years. He came all the way from Laramie, Wyoming, because he heard that you were going to appear at the screening.* Sword Of Doom *is one of his favorite films!*

OKAMOTO: Wow, that's far away. Will you tell him 'hello' for me?

7

Kazuo Ikehiro

1929–

When I first attempted to schedule an interview with Kazuo Ikehiro, he turned me down, and it took my friend Yoshiki Hayashi, a fanatical *chanbara* film fan, to persuade him via intermediary and mutual acquaintance Yoshihiro Ishimatsu. Mr Ishimatsu is a veteran screenwriter who has his own incredible catalog of credits, including milestone pictures with master directors such as Yasuzo Masumura, Kinji Fukasaku and Junya Sato, as well as Mr Ikehiro. Mr Ishimatsu, who more than deserves to have his own story told and his own films discussed at some point, graciously consented to do the honors, and the interview was arranged.

Meeting Mr Ikehiro was a bit daunting. At the time, he was relatively fresh from an unpleasant experience with another journalist from America, apparently because the interviewer had been unfamiliar with most of Mr Ikehiro's cinematic track record and had espoused a lack of understanding regarding the *chanbara* (or swordplay) genre of Japanese film. So, on introduction, Mr Ikehiro's demeanor was a bit frosty – but he slowly warmed up as the conversation progressed.

Kazuo Ikehiro is fond of directing *chanbara* pictures, in case you hadn't already guessed. One thing about his movies, whatever the type, is that they are all filled to the brim with a youthful vitality, and, for the most part, even his initial works avoid the sentimental contrivances that were too often still found in early sixties Japanese genre cinema. Yet his later, comparatively modern, edgier pictures have a storybook quality to them that is very much in keeping with old-fashioned films. There is a respect for straightforward narrative, an eye for beautiful frame compositions without resorting to mere pictorialism, all the while keeping close to the pulse of his characters' emotional lives.

The combination of the world-weary wanderer, as personified by actor Raizo Ichikawa, and the pioneering swordfight choreography in Ikehiro's version of the oft-filmed *Tokijiro Kustsukake* provides an unusually satisfying *matatabi* tale at a time when the major Japanese studios were still largely bound up in corn-ball subplots and syrupy digressions. This despite the timeworn story of chivalrous gambler Tokijiro (Ichikawa) taking under his wing the wife and child of a rival gang member he's been forced to kill. There *are* moments when you can see that the studio *did* get its way, particularly in the use of the treacly music score, but Ikehiro managed to virtually circumvent that kind of thing by the time of his next serious *matatabi* opus, *Seven Miles To Nakayama*.

Seven Miles To Nakayama is the tale of a laborer smitten by and married to a young inn waitress who then leaves everything behind, taking to the open road after she's raped and murdered by a corrupt magistrate. It's a deftly handled story of the vagaries of fate, even when the tormented protagonist later rescues a young woman from thieves who proves to be his dead wife's doppelgänger. This is a hoary device, used to varying effect in many samurai films, but it's employment here seems perfectly natural and unforced. It sets up our wandering swordsman for even more grief, because the lady is married and is in trouble due to her weak-willed husband's gambling habits. And this chivalrous loner is not the kind of person to leave an innocent woman in jeopardy, especially when she looks like the deceased love of his life. Once again, those familiar with the *matatabi* subgenre of Japanese period film will realize that none of this is especially original. However, with each successive scene Ikehiro gives strong evidence that he is one of the only directors of the tragic wandering gambler film besides Tai Kato who truly understands the melancholia and existential angst behind the anti-hero's travels.

Ikehiro's comprehension of the wandering swordsman psyche made his involvement in the popular *Zatoichi, Blind Swordsman* series a perfect match. Zatoichi, as played by versatile actor Shintaro Katsu, is a blind masseur who has mastered the sword after becoming sick of the persecution and prejudice meted out to him as he travels the backroads of 1860s Japan. Also an independent *yakuza* gambler, Ichi repeatedly finds himself in life-and-death situations, and, by the end of each story, he has to fight his way out.

Ikehiro's first *Zatoichi* outing, *Zatoichi And The Chest Of Gold*, is a bracing tall tale, with Ichi attempting to retrieve a poor village's stolen tax payment from scoundrels under the employ of the local magistrate. The nerve-shredding final battle between Ichi and a scarred, sadistic, whip-wielding swordsman – played by Katsu's real-life brother, Tomisaburo Wakayama – is one of the exhilarating highlights of the early blind swordsman films.

Ikehiro's next entry in the series, *Zatoichi's Flashing Sword*, with Ichi caught between two opposing gangs fighting over river crossing rights, is a bit more conventional. The master set piece that could have been at the climax, where Ichi battles the villains, bathed in the shifting colored lights of a fireworks display, seems truncated and hampered by an inadequate shooting schedule. However, Ikehiro's next and, as it turns out, final blind swordsman entry, *Zatoichi's Pilgrimage*, emerges as one of the best in the midst of the long-running series, and was indicative of the type of direction the films would take when star Katsu began producing them himself. Though slightly compromised by studio interference, Kaneto Shindo's screenplay gives us a deeper glimpse than ever before into Ichi's persona as Ichi vows to atone for his violent ways by visiting 88 temples, one for each man he has killed. Of course, before we're ten minutes into the film, he has to kill again. When Ichi finds himself in the mountain village the dead assailant has called home, he doesn't lift a finger to protect himself when the irate sister (Michiyo Yasuda) of the man attacks him with a sword. The suddenly contrite woman immediately realizes what she's done and dresses his wounded shoulder, bidding him stay long enough to recover. Unfortunately, her brother belonged to a clan of mountain bandits, and they aren't happy when they discover Ichi's presence. But Ichi bides his time, playing a cat-and-mouse game with them, all the while becoming enamored of his hostess, Yasuda, and plagued by dreams of his sighted childhood. The end sees Ichi having to face the bandits totally on his own, as the village inhabitants, in distant echoes of *High Noon*, lock themselves safely inside their houses.

Ikehiro's next and final *matatabi* picture with Raizo Ichikawa, *The Lone Stalker*, is a masterpiece and ranks as one of the finest for both the director and actor. There's a striking use of exterior atmospherics, with cinematographer Hiroshi Imai documenting the passing of the four seasons. Yet the beautiful evocation of a sometimes benign, sometimes cruel, Mother Nature is not an end in itself but a moving backdrop of contrast to one chivalrous individual's descent from naive young man in love to tragic, vengeance-bent wanderer. A descent precipitated by the subtlest of class barriers and a father and mother steadfast in determining who their daughter's husband will be. There's the structure of flashback vignettes within

Tomisaburo Wakayama, Shintaro Katsu in *Zatoichi And The Chest Of Gold*

flashbacks that is reminiscent of Sergio Leone, and the thematic resonance of a lone wolf gambling for the highest stakes recalls the best of the Randolph Scott westerns directed by Budd Boetticher.

Ikehiro's last *matatabi* work to be released theatrically, the *Trail of Blood* trilogy with Yoshio Harada as a revenge-obsessed drifter moving heaven and earth to exterminate the murderers of his family, does not have quite the same emotional impact. No doubt, part of this was due to the duration of the series being abruptly shortened by the studio to only three films. Much of what Ikehiro wanted to achieve went unrealized. Still, the trilogy is a powerhouse of unsentimental narrative, with Harada gradually becoming as cold-blooded as those he has pursued. When Harada dispatches Isao Natsuyagi's character in the concluding installment, *Jumping At The Flash Of Gold*, we're left somewhat shell-shocked. Not only is Natsuyagi not directly linked to the murder of Harada's family, he's also become a distinctly more sympathetic character than our ruthless anti-hero.

Ikehiro also worked on the *ninkyo yakuza* series *Young Boss* with Raizo Ichikawa, directing the first three and the final, eighth, film. As Ikehiro states in the interview, he is not particularly enamored of the *yakuza* genre, *ninkyo* or otherwise, and seems to have little affection for the multitude of such pictures that rival studio Toei produced in the sixties. The *Young Boss* films, reminiscent of Nikkatsu's

Yoshio Harada in *Trail Of Blood*

ninkyo-flavored *A Man's Crest* series in that Ichikawa's character must also return
home to assume gang leadership when his *yakuza* boss father is murdered, are just
as expertly written. But there is a well-researched background on the pre-WW2
military and political environment that is considerably more detailed than the
ninkyo films made at either Toei or Nikkatsu. Provocative stories relate collusion
between industrialists, right-wing nationalists, fascist *kempeitai* and various pro-
fiteering *yakuza* that you don't see in quite the same sober light anywhere else.
That said, at times Ichikawa's ex-naval-officer persona seems a bit too good and
honorable to be true. Fortunately, Ikehiro's *Young Boss* installments never forget
that, in the end, they're supposed to be action films.

Nevertheless, Ikehiro's best *ninkyo yakuza* picture remains *Prison Break*
starring the rising young star Hiroki Matsukata, an actor loaned out by Toei studios
for at least half a dozen pictures at Daiei after Raizo Ichikawa's untimely death.
Prison Break is a runaway freight train of a movie with a ferocious narrative that
doesn't let up for a minute in its kinetic, 86-minute running time.

That brings us to three remaining pictures that, in addition to *The Lone Stalker*,
are Ikehiro's masterpieces: *Sword Of Seduction*, *Trail of Traps* and *Castle Menagerie*.
All of them are entries in the *Kyoshiro Nemuri – Son Of The Black Mass* (aka *Sleepy
Eyes Of Death*) series. Kyoshiro Nemuri, a half-breed Eurasian samurai conceived
when his Christian mother, a lady-in-waiting, is raped by a defrocked Portuguese
missionary performing a Black Mass, is one of the most original, nihilistic anti-
heroes ever to emerge from world literature. His first cinematic incarnation came in
the late fifties with three decent, not particularly special films from Toho studios
starring Koji Tsuruta. When Daiei studios decided in 1963 to feature the mis-
anthropic anti-hero in a series with Raizo Ichikawa, the results at first stressed
action, leaving the weirder elements in the background. By the time of the third film,
Full Moon Killing (*Nemuri Kyoshiro Engetsu Giri*), the pictures were starting to lean
a bit more towards the macabre. However, none of the first three set fires at the box
office. Daiei was seriously considering pulling the plug on the series when Ikehiro
took the reins on *Sword Of Seduction*. Knowing the score not only for the series but
his own career, he decided to pull out the stops, emphasizing the erotic/grotesque
elements of creator Renzaburo Shibata's tales and incorporating the kind of sexy
violence newly in evidence in scores of spy films and spaghetti westerns. His
inspiration was a tonic, rejuvenating the series and allowing it to run for eight more
features with Ichikawa, then two more with Hiroki Matsukata after Ichikawa
succumbed to cancer.

Though lacking nudity, *Sword Of Seduction* pioneered the erotic/grotesque
aesthetic that would soon blossom in full flower when Teruo Ishii unleashed his
bloodthirsty sextet of in-period cruelty films in the late sixties. But, unlike Ishii's
also worthy films, there is a poisonous poetry to the dialogue and an existential angst
in Ichikawa's performance that lifts the *Nemuri* series into genre-transcending
territory. The last four *Nemuri* films with Ichikawa – *Trail Of Traps*, directed by

Ikehiro; *Woman Hell* (*Nemuri Kyoshiro Onna Jigoku*), directed by Tokuzo Tanaka; *The Human Tarantula* (*Nemuri Kyoshiro Hito Hada Gumo*), directed by Kimiyoshi Yasuda; and *Castle Menagerie*, directed by Ikehiro – form an astounding quartet rivaling the hallucinatory works of sensory derangement by such writers as Lautreamont, J.K. Huysmans, Octave Mirbeau and Charles Baudelaire. Along with *Sword Of Seduction*, they represent an astonishing pinnacle for the samurai film, comparable to director Kenji Misumi's *Lone Wolf And Cub* films and the best of director Hideo Gosha's hard-boiled *chanbara*.

With the sole exception of the non-genre feature film *Make-Up*, in 1984, Ikehiro has been consistently busy directing for Japanese television from the mid-seventies until the present day.

KAZUO IKEHIRO – SELECTED FILMOGRAPHY

1961	*TOKIJIRO KUTSUKAKE (KUTSUKAKE TOKIJIRO,* aka *THE GAMBLER'S CODE)*
	THE PHANTOM SAMURAI (KAGERO SAMURAI, aka *THE EPHEMERAL SAMURAI)*
1962	*SEVEN MILES TO NAKAYAMA (NAKAYAMA SHICHI RI,* aka *THE ONE AND ONLY GIRL I EVER LOVED)*
	CUT THE SHADOW (KAGE O KIRU)
1963	*RABBLE TACTICS (ZOYO MONOGATARI,* aka *TALE OF THE RANK AND FILE)*
	LIFE OF BAD TEMPER (DOKONJO ICHIDAI, aka *NOTHING BUT GUTS)*
1964	*ZATOICHI AND THE CHEST OF GOLD (ZATOICHI SEN-RYO KUBI,* aka *ZATOICHI'S 1000 RYO BOUNTY)*
	ZATOICHI'S FLASHING SWORD (ZATOICHI ABARE DAKO)
	KYOSHIRO NEMURI – SWORD OF SEDUCTION (NEMURI KYOSHIRO JOYO KEN, aka *KYOSHIRO NEMURI AT BAY,* aka *SLEEPY EYES OF DEATH – SWORD OF SEDUCTION)*
	NINJA, BAND OF ASSASSINS – RETURN OF MIST SAIZO (SHINOBI NO MONO – ZOKU KIRAGAKURE SAIZO)
1965	*YOUNG BOSS (WAKA OYABUN)*
	YOUNG BOSS – PRISON RELEASE (WAKA OYABUN SHUTSUGOKU)
1966	*YOUNG BOSS – INVITATION TO FIGHT (WAKA OYABUN KENKAJO,* aka *YOUNG BOSS'S FIGHT CHALLENGE)*
	ZATOICHI'S PILGRIMAGE (ZATOICHI UMI O WATARU, aka *BLIND SWORDSMAN'S PILGRIMAGE,* aka *ZATOICHI'S TRIP ACROSS THE SEA)*
	THE THIEVES' WHO'S WHO (DOROBO BANZUKE)
	A NEW BEGINNING – NINJA, BAND OF ASSASSINS (SHINSHO – SHINOBI NO MONO, aka *THE THREE ENEMIES)*
	THE LONE STALKER (HITORI OKAMI, aka *LONE WOLF)*

1967   *TRAIL OF TRAPS (NEMURI KYOSHIRO BURAI HIKAE – MASHO NO HADA*, aka
        KYOSHIRO NEMURI REFRAINING FROM VILLAINY – DEVILISH FLESH, aka
        SLEEPY EYES OF DEATH – TRAIL OF TRAPS)
        YOUNG BOSS – LEADER'S FLESH (WAKA OYABUN – SEN RYO HADA, aka
        TORPEDO X)

1968   *THE DARING NUN (AMA KUZURE)*
        THE PRIEST AND THE GOLD MINT (ZOKU YAKUZA BOZU, aka *RETURN OF
        THE HOODLUM PRIEST)*

1969   *CASTLE MENAGERIE (NEMURI KYOSHIRO AKUJO GARI*, aka *KYOSHIRO
        NEMURI – HUNTING EVIL WOMEN*, aka *SLEEPY EYES OF DEATH – EVIL
        WOMEN HUNT)*
        PRISON BREAK (MUSHYO YABURI)
        BROKEN SWORDS (HIKEN YABURI)
        FYLFOT SWORDPLAY (NEMURI KYOSHIRO MANJI GIRI)
        KILL THE KILLERS (KOROSHIYA O BARASE)

1970   *EVIL WOMAN'S DIARY (ONNA GOKUAKUCHO)*
        *USELESS CREATURE – FIGHTING MAN'S LIFE (DODE KAI YATSU – KENKA
        YA ICHIDAI*, aka *SOFT-BOILED GORO)*

1972   *TRAIL OF BLOOD (MUSHUKUNIN MIKOGAMI NO JOKICHI – KIBA WA HIKI
        RETSU ITA*, aka *JOKICHI MIKOGAMI, WANDERER – PULLING THE FANGS
        THAT RIP AND TEAR)*
        *TRAIL OF BLOOD 2 (MUSHUKUNIN MIKOGAMI NO JOKICHI – KAWAKAZE
        NI KAKO WA NAGARETA*, aka *JOKICHI MIKOGAMI, WANDERER – DRIFTING
        IN THE RIVER WIND)*

1973   *TRAIL OF BLOOD 3 (MUSHUKUNIN MIKOGAMI NO JOKICHI – KOKAI NI
        SENKO GA HINDA*, aka *JOKICHI MIKOGAMI, WANDERER – JUMPING AT THE
        FLASH OF GOLD)*

1984   *MAKE-UP (KESHO)*

KAZUO IKEHIRO – INTERVIEW

The following interview took place in a coffee shop in a Tokyo suburb in November, 1997. The famous screenwriter, Yoshihiro Ishimatsu and my friend Yoshiki Hayashi (who was instrumental in setting up the interview) were also present. Ai Kennedy did the retranslation.

IKEHIRO: What *yakuza* films did I direct?
CD: *The* Young Boss *series.*
IKEHIRO: I don't really think of the *Young Boss* movies as *yakuza* films. I recently did an interview with someone else from America, and I realized that their conception of *chanbara* was quite different from mine. Your ideas of *yakuza*, *matatabi* and *chanbara* films may be different, too.

CD: I'm interested in asking you as much about chanbara *as about* yakuza *films. But don't you agree that there can be some overlap, some* ninkyo yakuza *films could also be* chanbara *films? Such as the* ninkyo *pictures from Toei with Ken Takakura and Koji Tsuruta. The* Young Boss *films.* Matatabi *films can be* chanbara, *but they are also about wandering* yakuza.

IKEHIRO: I don't know if I could consider the *Young Boss* films as *yakuza* pictures. I think our basic conceptions on *chanbara*, which are sword films, *jidai-geki* and *yakuza* movies differ. You think that if someone is cut with a sword that's *chanbara*. I don't think that that is correct. Even though the genre of *chanbara* film is a huge category, generally here in Japan we think of it as *jidai-geki* films. Maybe that's too simple. *Chanbara* usually takes place in the Edo period. You know, samurais with the topknots? The *Young Boss* movies are not quite *chanbara*. They could perhaps be called *ninkyo yakuza*, but there are many different kinds of *yakuza* pictures. To be honest, I don't really like *yakuza* films, and probably wouldn't have done the *Young Boss* films if I had had the choice. But I needed to do them to keep my job at Daiei. I'm more of a *jidai-geki* or *chanbara* filmmaker. What are the common things that interest you about these movies?

CD: In ninkyo yakuza *films, the torment inside the hero when they're torn between duty and humanity, where the values are at odds. The idea of the lone wolf, the outsider alienated from both villains and the common people. You see this in some* jidai-geki, *too, like the* Kyoshiro Nemuri *series. Nemuri being of illegitimate mixed Euro-Japanese heritage, from a renegade Christian background when that was illegal. How he refers to himself as a villain. There's also the outsider status in* Zatoichi *pictures, with blind Ichi becoming an expert swordsman to counteract the abuse he's felt all his life, but still never managing to quite fit in. This type of character is also in most of your* matatabi *films …*

IKEHIRO: … And what movies …?

CD: Tokijiro Kutsukake, Seven Miles To Nakayama, The Lone Stalker *and the* Trail Of Blood *trilogy. How do you see the* matatabi *characters evolving in these films? In* Tokijiro Kutsukake, *there's still a bit of the sentimental approach much in evidence in late fifties jidai-geki, then as the decade went on there's gradually a more realistic, hard-edged view of what* matatabi *life could have been like, ending with Yoshio Harada in the* Trail Of Blood *films.*

IKEHIRO: Your view of the difference in the *matatabi* films is quite right. During that time there had been a change in attitude and approach within the Japanese film industry. In 1960, the year *Tokijiro Kutsukake* was made, there were a great number of people in the movie audience and a huge audience for that type of film. Daiei was committed to making that genre. I was a fairly new director then and, of course, did not have a lot of power. As time went on, I kept pushing to make a more realistic kind of story. Gradually, I was able to do this. *With Seven Miles To Nakayama*, I was able to change the slant from a traditional *yakuza* tale to more of a story about someone who is betrayed, and how betrayal impacts their life. That was my creative input. Before and during shooting on

The Lone Stalker, I had many long discussions with the star, Raizo Ichikawa, about the character and the story. I wanted to show the solitary loneliness in that kind of outcast situation. But we really had to push it with the studio. Luckily, by that time I had been there longer, I had more power in the company, so I was able to make it more original. When I had made *Tokijiro Kutsukake,* the company was quite different. Over the decade, the newer, younger directors that desired a less old-fashioned approach gradually became powerful.

CD: One thing about Tokijiro Kutsukake *that was revolutionary for the time is that it's the first* chanbara *film I can remember that had more realistic swordfight sound effects. There's the sound of blades ripping through flesh, metal clanging against metal. Those kinds of sound effects did not really become prevalent in most* chanbara *pictures until three or four years later, 1963 or 1964.*

IKEHIRO: I used those special sound effects because I thought it was much more natural. I was trying to combine the music and sound effects with the visual to create the maximum effect. At the time, people were not really paying much attention to sound effects. It's good that you recognized that. Another thing is Raizo Ichikawa was a top star at the time, we wanted to do things to be more striking with him, more physical, to get more acrobatic. Also, as the sixties progressed, I was influenced by the spaghetti westerns. They were more real in some ways, grittier than the American westerns. They had those larger-than-life sound effects. The audiences appreciated them, they noticed the sound effects and the ambience.

CD: Are there any spaghetti westerns in particular that stand out in your memory?

IKEHIRO: *Django.*

CD: Ah, that's one of my favorite spaghetti westerns.

IKEHIRO: *(laughs)*

CD: In one of the Trail Of Blood *films, Chuji Kunisada is a tangential character, but he has always been portrayed as a folk hero, Robin Hood kind of* matatabi yakuza, *rather than the way he's shown here as more of a villain.*

IKEHIRO: The original idea for those films was to show more with Yoshio Harada's wife and children while still alive, before they were murdered. But we only ended up getting to make the three pictures. There was a conviction behind showing Harada's character on his vengeance quest that the men he was killing also had their own wives and children. That Harada, in turn, was becoming no different from them. Also, in the original concept for the series, the boss Kunisada character would have been seen again. We would have seen that Kunisada's guilt from association with the murdering gang had no basis, but we didn't get to show that part of the story.

CD: In Zatoichi And The Chest Of Gold, *Shintaro Katsu performs with his real-life brother* Tomisaburo Wakayama *as the villain. What was it like working with those two together?*

IKEHIRO: My memories are that it was a very wonderful but weird experience, a strange entry in the *Zatoichi* series. Because Katsu was still so young he was a lot like a boy in some ways. He very much wanted to emulate his older brother. The two of them were obsessed with turning out the best possible Japanese action production. To make an unbeatable combination. But, as it turns out, I didn't think that their acting was that good. The rest of it, the fighting and action, was excellent. What I remember most is their final duel sequence, where Wakayama is on the horse and, using his whip, drags Katsu along behind him. Katsu was scared because they hadn't planned the action out. They just decided to go for it. And, since they were brothers, they would push each other to go for the most extreme realism.

CD: *That last sequence is grueling, incredibly intense.*

IKEHIRO: That scene was not in the original script. I really wanted to do something more original with that picture.

CD: *I have to say that the* Zatoichi *films directed by you and Kenji Misumi are the best in the series. Another* Zatoichi *movie you did,* Zatoichi's Pilgrimage, *was written by Kaneto Shindo. It seems quite different from many of the other* Zatoichi *entries.*

IKEHIRO: The *Zatoichi* series was a set thing, with very stable numbers as far as consistent audience attendance. Katsu wanted to do something different so they

Poster for *The Lone Stalker*

went to Shindo for the script. Originally, as it was written, the scenario had more pathos, with Ichi's character in a lot of emotional pain. But when the company president saw the script he came back to us and said, 'This is too much, you can't do it as written. You can use Katsu to convey something to an audience, but you can't do it in the *Zatoichi* series, which is a stable asset of the company. There's nothing wrong with Shindo's script, but for the *Zatoichi* series it's way too ideological.' It was a good script. They had another screenwriter there at the studio who was willing to do the changes, so it was rewritten a little bit. You still get some of what Shindo put in there coming through, but ultimately it was ... um ...

CD: ... Somewhat more conventional. That's one thing about the series you can't help but notice: despite all its qualities, it is sometimes formulaic. When Katsu began producing the Zatoichi *films himself, the stories became more daring, unusual, more character-driven, better written. The production values went up, too. The* Kyoshiro Nemuri *films with Raizo Ichikawa are very original, too. Particularly from the fourth one on,* Sword Of Seduction, *which you directed, they often have a macabre, surreal flavor to them. In* Sword Of Seduction, *you have Nemuri decapitate the old Portuguese priest that may be his long-lost father, as well as the killing of the shogunate informer disguised as a nun. These are not the usual actions of a* jidai-geki *'hero'. I know that there are elements of that already in the original writer Renzaburo Shibata's work. But that picture obviously signaled a change. Did you run into trouble with the company producers when you introduced such unorthodox behavior for a 'hero'?*

IKEHIRO: *Sword Of Seduction* was the first entry in the series that I directed. At the time, the series did not enjoy the same popularity that developed later. The first three had not been very successful, and the company heads told me that, if this fourth one didn't do well, they were going to discontinue the series. There were elements in Shibata's original stories that I wanted to include in the film that hadn't been used yet, things like the secret of Nemuri's illegitimate birth, how he was conceived after his mother was raped by the defrocked missionary at the satanic Mass. I'd also seen those first James Bond pictures where they would have these femme fatales – I wanted to integrate that 'Bond girls' element into the story. The original writer was quite surprised, not only because that hadn't been in the script but because of the resultant popularity of the movie. But I *had* talked with the scriptwriter about the quirks in Nemuri's personality, his ambivalent feelings towards God and women because of the circumstances of his birth. I wanted to make sure to incorporate much more of that.

CD: The disfigured, opium-addicted princess who murders her handmaidens for fun because they are beautiful – did she originate in Shibata's original Nemuri *stories, or was she one of the ideas you brought in?*

IKEHIRO: Her character and the scene where Nemuri cuts off her mask to reveal her hideous face are from the original work. Her character is actually not that important to the story. Why were you interested in her?

CD: She appears in the whole first third of the picture, and she is one of the most horrifying villainesses in Japanese film from that period. The fact that she's insane, disfigured, homicidal and a drug addict plus *daughter of the shogun, well, that seems unusual, if not shocking, for a* jidai-geki *picture made in the early sixties. Perhaps if the picture had been made in 1970 it wouldn't have seemed uncommon, but for 1964 I think it's unique! Not to mention the other shocking moment, where Nemuri kills evil Naoko Kubo in cold blood at the climax.*

IKEHIRO: I used the women characters in the film to symbolize different things. For instance, the princess symbolized authority. And Naoko Kubo's character was a symbol of God. Because Nemuri had intense feelings against those things, I used those two women to undergo these symbolic acts by him; the first one was eliminated through humiliation and public exposure, the second one by killing. To shock the audience was the purpose of entertainment films. I basically directed B movies, program pictures that were different from art films or A films. These B program pictures were made as entertainments. It was exciting to make them. To be honest, the audiences were intrigued and entertained seeing women being murdered.

CD: Hmm ... you directed one of the last two films that starred Raizo Ichikawa before his death, Castle Menagerie.

IKEHIRO: The last one I did with him was *Castle Menagerie*, but his very last film was the next picture he did, *Gambler's Life*, directed by Kimiyoshi Yasuda. Before *Castle Menagerie*, Ichikawa already knew about the cancer. He was not feeling at all well and had a bit of a break from work. On *Castle Menagerie* he wasn't able to do much of the fighting, there had to be a stand-in. After the picture was done he went into production with *Gambler's Life*, but he really was feeling extremely bad. A little bit more than halfway through the picture, he died. The remainder of that film had to be completed by a stand-in.

CD: After Raizo Ichikawa died, Hiroki Matsukata, who had been making many yakuza *and* jidai geki *movies at Toei, was brought in by Daiei to fill the void and do some of the pictures they had lined up for Ichikawa. You directed several: another* Kyoshiro Nemuri *film, called* Fylfot Swordplay; *a* ninkyo yakuza *movie,* Prison Break; *and a* chanbara, Broken Swords, *which was a remake of Ichikawa's earlier film,* Samurai Vendetta *(Haku Oki, 1959). Can you describe what it was like working with Matsukata as a replacement for Ichikawa and the atmosphere with the workers at the studio?*

IKEHIRO: When Matsukata came to Daiei he was 26 years old, and he was brought in to fill the gap. But the attempt wasn't very successful because he had such a different kind of personality. The original idea behind *Prison Break* was to depict an intellectual gangster, but Matsukata didn't really fit that image. In *Broken Swords* he fitted the part much better, but it, too, ended up not that successful.

CD. Did you or Kazuo Mori, who directed the other Matsukata-starring Nemuri film, Full Moon Swordsman *(Nemuri Kyoshiro Engetsu Sappo, 1969), feel it was premature to dive right back into making the* Nemuri *pictures? By then the* Nemuri *character had become so identified with Ichikawa.*

IKEHIRO: The film industry was in such decline at the time, especially at Daiei, the powers that be really had no choice but to continue the tried-and-true pictures – in this case with Hiroki Matsukata – just to survive. We tried to make him into a more professional actor. But there was a complaint from workers in the stockroom after the shoot asking if it was appropriate. People were comparing him to Raizo. Raizo was dead, though, and we couldn't do anything about it. You see, besides the difference from Raizo Ichikawa's personality, Hiroki Matsukata had not developed yet into the good actor he would later become. I had wanted to do something different with him. However, Mr Matsukata relied heavily on his father for guidance, and he was also very much influenced by things said to him by his other actor friends from Toei.

CD: And Hiroki Matsukata's father was an actor?

IKEHIRO: Yes, Jushiro Konoe.

CD: Oh, I should have known that. Moving on to Mist Saizo Returns *and* A New Beginning – Ninja, Band Of Assassins, *did you approach those differently from other* jidai-geki *since they were black-and-white ninja pictures and had an almost film noir feeling to them?*

IKEHIRO: The director, Satsuo Yamamoto, had made the first two original pictures in the series. So, I tried to continue in that style. It was a serious, faithful-to-ninja-tradition-and-historical-accuracy approach.

CD: In the later seventies you worked on various chanbara *television series, such as the* Lone Wolf And Cub *show with Kinnosuke Nakamura. How did that compare, working on* chanbara *TV to working previously on* chanbara *movies?*

IKEHIRO: First of all, on TV cruelty is taboo. Also, because it's television, you cannot have a *yakuza* being the main character. The same held true of *Lone Wolf*; you couldn't have Ogami, a renegade executioner on the run, be the sole main character. Many of the *jidai-geki* shows, such as *Toyama No Kinsan*, are not very interesting because you're always having to show the authority figure as being right and winning in the end. Another taboo as far as television producers are concerned are stories about the common people. Then there's less money and time, as well as those other restrictions for TV. There are certain limits I set for myself on TV work, how far I'll compromise, how far I'll go to toe the line.

CD: What are you working on now?

IKEHIRO: A two-and-a-half-hour TV movie called *Kameido Mofuku* for Asahi Television. Also, I recently did a special two-and-a-half-hour television episode of *Maid Eyewitness (Kaseifu Wa Mita)* series.

(*Yoshihiro Ishimatsu and Yoshiki Hayashi laugh*)

IKEHIRO: (*laughs*) Yes, I know! But next year I've been asked to do more *jidai-geki*, a thing on the *Shinsengumi*.

8

Masahiro Shinoda

1931–

When Shinoda started to direct films he was not particularly optimistic about trying to change the entrenched ways of his parent studio, Shochiku. Like his contemporaries, Nagisa Oshima and Yoshishige Yoshida at Shochiku, Shohei Imamura and Seijun Suzuki at Nikkatsu, Yasuzo Masumura at Daiei, he was trying to change not only the content and themes but the basic language of cinema. And, like Suzuki and Masumura, he enthusiastically embraced the opportunity to work in genre films as well as more 'socially relevant' projects. One of Shinoda's strengths, something he has in common with all the directors in this volume, is that he realized the potential to subvert aesthetics, film construction and conventional audience expectations in not just 'art' cinema but through popular entertainment, too.

Shinoda, though wishing to break from the pattern of past masters such as Ozu, Kinoshita, and Mizoguchi (all filmmakers he respected), was, in some ways, the most traditional of his youthful new wave or 'nouvelle vague' compatriots. Traditional in the sense that he was more interested in how past cultural and aesthetic obsessions had shaped the psychology of the national psyche since the Middle Ages, even though he was steadfastly committed to deconstructing and reinterpreting those same traditions. And the way he believed he could examine those traditions best was through integrating methods and aesthetics from other art forms, specifically theater.

Intuiting a kindred spirit in avant garde poet and playwright Shuji Terayama, Shinoda drafted him as screenwriting collaborator on many of his early films, including *Dry Lake*, *Epitaph To My Love*, *My Face Red In The Sunset*, *Tears On The Lion's Mane* and *The Scandalous Adventures Of Buraikan*. You can also see Shinoda's fascination for *bunraku* (puppet play) and seventeenth-century playwright Monzaemon Chikamatsu in *Double Suicide* and the outlandish, wildly irreverent spirit of kabuki in *Buraikan*. He delved into classic literature, too (*With Beauty And Sorrow* from Yasunari Kawabata's novel, *Silence* by Shusaku Endo and *Demon Pond* from a story by Kyoka Izumi), and tapped contemporary popular writers like Shintaro Ishihara (*Pale Flower* and *Petrified Forest*) and Seishi Yokomozo (*Island Of The Evil Spirit*). All his films as well, from *Pale Flower* through to *Demon Pond*, have a painstaking painter's eye for stark, modern shot compositions. Shinoda has also been able to merge music into a film's whole, bridging the gap between sound and visuals quite unlike anyone else, employing the towering genius of avant garde composer Toru Takemitsu in an overwhelming number of his movies, in a similar way to how Hitchcock worked with composer Bernard Herrmann.

Despite being sympathetic to some of the radical politics of the time, Shinoda was always concerned more with aesthetic revolution and the motivation inside an individual that spurred him to participate in either pro- or anti-government activism. He tackled one particular student radical mindset in *Dry Lake*, exposing the neurotic personality, the uncontrolled, frustrated ego giving way to psychosis while using activism as an excuse, years before Koji Wakamatsu would approach similar themes in films like *Sex Jack* and *Ecstasy Of The Angels*.

Shinoda also attempted a color-coded, absurdist comedy take on the *yakuza* hitman genre in *My Face Red In The Sunset* before most of Seijun Suzuki's more subversive action pictures – although, from all accounts, *My Face* was not as successful at the box office as those of his Nikkatsu colleague.

In addition, Shinoda was prescient in daring to expose organized labor being sabotaged by both management and organized crime in the *yakuza* picture *Tears On The Lion's Mane*. To suggest that idea then was considered politically incorrect because corporations using the *yakuza* to bust unions was not an openly acknowledged problem at the time. Shinoda supplied an ironic twist in making the strike-breaking protagonist, who is obligated to the company president, a tough rock 'n' roller espousing a supposedly rebellious lifestyle.

Pale Flower was Shinoda's next, and so far last, *yakuza* picture, a startling masterpiece in every aspect, a nihilistic film that redefines existential dread as a lived-in experience. It shows those who have potential for the most rigorous morality as those also at risk of a ravenous spiritual hunger that gnaws at the entrails. In Ryo Ikebe's middle-aged ex-con killer Muraki, it is something that subverts human emotions and creates a situational morality, turning murder into the one act that makes him feel most alive, a 'thrill' that is akin to spiritual experience. Muraki is not motivated by self-sacrifice as seen in *ninkyo yakuza* heroes, nor is he spurred by poverty and lifelong abuse, as are hoodlum sociopaths in *jitsuroku* gangster films. Instead, Shinoda calls up in Muraki a despair from some ancient predisposition, a sickness of the soul predicated as much from a desire for solitude as a search for identity. When Muraki meets a kindred spirit in the thrill-seeking girl played by Mariko Kaga, Shinoda reveals them as platonic soulmates who have had any sense of innocence long subverted and destroyed – Muraki with his gambling and nearly sociopathic world-view, and the girl with her hunger for life in the fast lane. Shinoda is non-judgemental as well as perversely ironic as he shows Muraki finding fulfillment most thoroughly in the act of killing.

Shinoda doesn't rub our noses in the gloom, though, infusing the drama with occasional bursts of absurdist humor – whether it's Muraki visiting his boss (Seiji Miyaguchi) at the dentist's or gang bosses (Eijiro Tono and Miyaguchi) conversing about their kids and lunchtime manners simultaneously to how best to crush their enemies. Without this element of dark wit, of the gangster's mundane routine, *Pale Flower* could have well committed the unpardonable sin of pretentiousness.

Unfortunately, *Assassination* is not as well known a movie in the West as *Pale Flower*, which is a shame because it's just as fine a film. It exhibits the same desolate portrait of a personality marginalized by the traditions and culture surrounding him as well as his own ideals. Tetsuro Tanba plays a respected swordsman intent on restoring the Emperor to power amidst the political turmoil of the 1860s. But, after he's jailed for killing a shogunate official, Tanba switches sides. Told in a labyrinth of flashbacks, Tanba's motivations are examined, but no answer is ever found. We're left to wonder if it was the murder of his mistress (Shima Iwashita) by shogunate samurai when she refused to betray him or perhaps something else, that has completely destroyed his beliefs, convincing him that all is futile, that being a lone wolf represents his truest self. Tanba's ability to manipulate his situation depending on which side he's talking to leads his new shogunate allies to distrust him, and a master swordsman is sent to take him by surprise. Cinematographer Masao Kosugi and composer Toru Takemitsu, veterans of *Pale Flower*, again return to deliver their stark, atonal purity to the proceedings.

Shinoda followed up *Assasination* with *Samurai Spy* in 1965, another excellent, sometimes bleakly humorous, existentialist *jidai-geki* film. Koji Takahashi is the relatively enlightened, fatalistic ninja Sasuke Sarutobi, who inadvertently becomes the target of rival Tokugawa and Toyotomi ninja when he's the last person to talk to a murdered double agent (Rokko Toura). A master assassin played by Tetsuro Tanba is simultaneously Takahashi's best ally and most dangerous nemesis. *Samurai Spy* has long been unavailable in Japan as well as Western nations, but it recently surfaced for a rare subtitled TV screening on America's Independent Film Channel, courtesy of Quentin Tarantino, as part of a promotion for *Kill Bill, Vol. 2.*

Double Suicide has become Shinoda's most recognized, most celebrated film here in the West. His treatment of the Chikamatsu play about a married merchant (Kichiemon

Ryo Ikebe in *Pale Flower*

Nakamura) and his courtesan lover (Shima Iwashita) who both commit suicide when they're backed into a circumstantial corner is radically unorthodox, Shinoda taking the conventions of the *bunraku* puppet theater and applying them to live human performers. He depicts strangely warped virtual spaces, sometimes nearly empty, sometimes filled with abstract production design in the form of outsize calligraphy. Shima Iwashita playing a double role as the merchant's wife is another ground-breaking element. But *Double Suicide* is a long movie, static in certain stretches, with an occasional pretentiousness that grates on one's nerves. However, the performances and production design are awe-inspiring, and though, as a whole, Mizoguchi's *Crucified Lovers* and Masumura's *Love Suicides At Sonezaki* are both emotionally more affecting, *Double Suicide* has moments of undeniable power, particularly at the end when the two lovers hang themselves, manipulated by the ethereal, black-clad *kuroko* puppet masters.

Shinoda's next effort, *The Scandalous Adventures Of Buraikan*, was a much more successful experiment with theatrical forms, in this case kabuki. Shinoda, in collaboration with screenwriter Shuji Terayama, vigorously conjures up the intoxicating world of an Edo swarming with thieves, conmen, tricksters, outlandish street performers, whores and cold-blooded killers. Tatsuya Nakadai is a lazy actor in love with a beautiful courtesan (Shima Iwashita), but his busybody mother stands in the way. Fed up with her at one point he gives her a good whack, which he believes has killed her, and, resigned, throws her body into the sea. But she's rescued by a pathetic, pederast child murderer, who then returns her to Nakadai. To Nakadai's chagrin, his mom not only acts as if the whole thing has never happened but becomes best friends with his woman, Iwashita. Meanwhile, an abusive lord has taken an innocent girl as his mistress, and a fake priest (Tetsuro Tanba), Nakadai et al. put a plan in motion to rescue her. They manage to free the girl, but all except for Nakadai are tracked down and slain. Nakadai is left at the end carting off his oblivious mother somewhere to die, while Iwashita waits at home. A truly brilliant, often very droll picture that skillfully blends pop art production design to show the links between kabuki and modern underground theater circa the late 1960s. There's a surfeit of *chanbara* swordplay action as well as some very dark humor. The scene near the end where the despairing pederast purposely sits on a fireworks cannon to commit suicide is extremely funny.

Shinoda weaves a similar phantasmagoric spell with *Under The Cherry Blossoms*, a dreamlike horror fantasy about a murdering twelfth-century bandit (Tomisaburo Wakayama) bewitched by a rich lady (Shima Iwashita) he kidnaps in the woods. Soon she has him murdering for *her*, and, while camping out in his forest lair, he becomes her servant and lover. At her bidding, their lifestyle becomes more debauched, and they move into the city so he can surreptitiously decapitate people for her amusement. Soon the bloodlust begins to sicken even him, and she agrees to return with him to the forest. But once they enter a blossoming cherry grove, a taboo area rumored to be haunted, Wakayama sees Iwashita as her true self, a devil witch trying to strangle him. He casts her down and kills her, but her form disappears amongst swirling cherry blossoms. A wonderfully eerie film that spectacularly captures period ambience as well as the erotic frissons of an adult fairy tale.

Set in the early 1920s, *Banished Orin* is another of Shinoda's masterpieces, with his real-life spouse, Shima Iwashita, returning to give one of her most exquisite performances as Orin, a sightless *shamisen* player who has been exiled from her blind troupe after she's been raped. Orin wanders the countryside, finally encountering a deserting soldier (Yoshio Harada), who becomes her friend. Although attracted to her, he refuses her offered availability, and the pair are happy for a time being platonic. Soon things turn sour when a vulgar huckster (Toru Abe) starts to tag along, and Harada eventually murders the man when he tries to take advantage of Iwashita. Shinoda directs subtly and with just the right tone, utilizing Kazuo Miyagawa's ethereal cinematography of changing seasons. A heartbreaking story that doesn't resort to manipulating audience emotion and manages one of the most haunting movie endings ever.

Demon Pond follows a teacher (Tsutomu Yamazaki) as he backpacks in the rural wilderness of 1910 Japan, searching out legends as well as examining the local flora and fauna. He comes upon a strange village suffering from drought, and, feeling unwelcome, wanders into the forest, only to find a remote cottage inhabited by an unassuming young woman, Yuri (Tamasaburo Bando playing one of his famous female roles). Soon enough, it's revealed her husband (Go Kato) is Yamazaki's long-lost friend, who went missing several years before. The pair of friends go on a walk to the fabled *Demon Pond*, and Yamazaki tries to persuade his old comrade to return with him to the city. But Kato refuses, explaining that not only is he devoted to his wife, he also has vowed to ring the ancient bell beside his home twice a day to keep the pond from overflowing and flooding the surrounding countryside. Meanwhile, back at the village, anxiety has taken hold of the inhabitants because of the drought, and they're whipped into a frenzy by a visiting government official who suggests that they need to sacrifice a woman to bring rain. A buffoonish miscreant suggests Yuri as a perfect candidate, an idea seized upon with glee by the callous villagers. Yamazaki and Go return just in time to intervene as the townspeople prepare Yuri to die, but the pair fight a losing battle. Yuri kills herself to make sure Kato and Yamazaki stop resisting before they also perish. However,

Kyoko Kishida and Takashi Fujiki in *Tears On The Lion's Mane*

Kato refuses to ring the bell at the appointed time, kills himself too, and the pond *does* overflow. Yamazaki straps himself to a pillar on the raised hillock as all around him is swept away. He awakens when the sun is up, only to find himself on a little island at the top of a majestic waterfall. As he looks down into the torrent, he's astonished to see the pond's Dragon Princess (also Bando) ascending into heaven accompanied by several of her ladies-in-waiting. Although some critics had a problem with what they described as an uncertain tone and with Bando playing the female roles, I found Shinoda in firm grasp of his fairy tale, weaving a very convincing, gorgeous storybook, achieving an almost drug-like intoxication with his melding of image, performance and the bizarrely alien beauty of the Beaver-and-Krause-style score by Isao Tomita. Really an unqualified masterpiece.

Owl's Castle, one of Masahiro Shinoda's most recent films, is a respectable, often quite good retelling of Ryotaro Shiba's famous ninja novel previously lensed in 1963 by Eiichi Kudo. But, aside from Shinoda's faithfulness to his own nihilistic themes in terms of the dramatically downbeat, poignant ending, there's not too much to distinguish it from other competent *jidai-geki* epics from Japan in the last ten years. Except for some occasionally more judicious shot compositions than many of his colleagues, there isn't Shinoda's same trademark visual boldness in evidence as there was in earlier pictures.

MASAHIRO SHINODA – SELECTED FILMOGRAPHY

1960   *ONE-WAY TICKET FOR LOVE (KOI NO KATAMICHI KIPPU)*
        DRY LAKE (KAWAITA MIZUUMI, aka YOUTH IN FURY)
1961   *MY FACE RED IN THE SUNSET (YUHI NI, AKAI ORE NO KAO, aka KILLERS ON PARADE)*
        EPITAPH TO MY LOVE (WAGA KOI NO TABIJI)
        SHAMISEN AND MOTORCYCLE (SHAMISEN TO OTOBAI, aka LOVE OLD AND NEW)
1962   *TEARS ON THE LION'S MANE (NAMIDA O SHISHI NO TATEGAMI NI)*
        GLORY ON THE SUMMIT – BURNING YOUTH (YAMA NO SANKA – MOERU WAKAMONO TACHI)
1963   *PALE FLOWER (KAWAITA HANA)*
1964   *ASSASSINATION (ANSATSU, aka THE ASSASSIN)*
1965   *WITH BEAUTY AND SORROW (UTSUKUSHISA TO KANASHIMI TO)*
        SAMURAI SPY (IBUN SARUTOBI SASUKE)
1966   *PUNISHMENT ISLAND (SHOKEI NO SHIMA)*
1967   *CLOUDS AT SUNSET (AKANE-GUMO)*
1969   *DOUBLE SUICIDE (SHINJU TEN NO AMIJIMA)*
1970   *THE SCANDALOUS ADVENTURES OF BURAIKAN (BURAIKAN, aka OUTLAWS)*

1971	*SILENCE (CHINMOKU)*
1974	*HIMIKO*
1975	*UNDER THE CHERRY BLOSSOMS (SAKURA NO MORI NO MANKAI NO SHITA)*
1977	*BANISHED ORIN (HANRE GOZE ORIN,* aka *BALLAD OF ORIN,* aka *MELODY IN GRAY)*
1979	*DEMON POND (YASHA GA IKE,* aka *THE DRAGON PRINCESS)*
1981	*ISLAND OF EVIL SPIRITS (AKURYO-TO)*
1986	*GONZA, THE SPEARMAN (YARI NO GONZA)*
1990	*CHILDHOOD DAYS (SHONEN JIDAI)*
1997	*MOONLIGHT SERENADE (SETOUCHI MUNRAITO SERENADE)*
1999	*OWL'S CASTLE (FUKURO NO SHIRO)*
2003	*SPY SORGE*

MASAHIRO SHINODA – INTERVIEW

The following interview took place in a deserted banquet room at the Century Plaza Hotel in Century City (in West Los Angeles) in 1999. Ai Kennedy did the retranslation. The video of this interview appears in edited form as a supplement on the American DVD release of Pale Flower *from American Cinematheque Presents/Vitagraph/Chimera/ through Home Vision.*

CD: I understand when you were young you originally had concentrated on science, then abruptly changed your focus to literature, theater and more artistic endeavors. Why?

SHINODA: Of course, I had a childhood like normal kids. I was enthusiastic about literature. But I liked science, especially physics. That's why I had been thinking I would pursue physical science for a living. But in 1945, when I was 15 years old, Japan was defeated in the war. That incident made me philosophical and introspective for the first time. Japanese culture and tradition had collapsed. And the gods that were supposed to be protecting us were destroyed. A world impossible to reach with my scientific knowledge appeared, and literature and theater and movies came into my mind again.

CD: Could you talk about what it was like at Shochiku when you started there? Directors like Nagisa Oshima and Yoshishige Yoshida were your contemporary colleagues. I'm curious what made Shochiku start this infusion of new blood.

SHINODA: We all joined the studio when we were around 20 or 23 years old. The stuff we were working on as assistant directors seemed very stupid to us. I made up my mind never to become a director who would film those kinds of screenplays. And I temporarily gave up on the idea of directing. However, Oshima and others were trying to form some kind of 'movement' to break through the situation. At the time, I was slowly becoming like a hermit. Since the sea was very close to where I was working, I would often stare for long periods at the ocean. I swam every day after the shoot. I was close to giving up, thinking: 'What am I doing here?' But Oshima and the other young directors would not give up their idea of a revolution. They wanted very badly for things to change. I think what made me want to make my own movies was the feeling that Yasujiro Ozu and Keisuke Kinoshita had gotten old. We had all looked up to them as great masters, even though we thought their work had become merely routine. However, we'd never find our own world if we didn't look for something different from them. We were trying to figure out what *our* current generation *was*, and how *not* to learn the way of the studio. I think we all conceived those feelings when we were about 27 or 28. We decided to make our own movies with our own screenplays whenever the opportunity presented itself. That's what was called 'the new wave.'

CD: Two of your earliest collaborators on screenplays and music scores were the avant garde writer Shuji Terayama and the composer Toru Takemitsu. How did you become involved with them, and what was Shochiku's reaction?

SHINODA: Shochiku had a few reservations about me, that I was too far from their tradition. But they simultaneously had an expectation as well, that these young directors would lead them to a new adventure that would revitalize the old Shochiku. When Yasujiro Ozu and other famous directors were young, Shochiku had taken a chance and decided to use them, and they ended up making great movies. I think that that history inevitably prompted our debut as directors. It allowed them to listen when I wanted to use other talents from outside Shochiku's mediocre staff. They accepted it and didn't take a stand against my opinion. I got some complaints that Shuji Terayama's screenplays were impossible to understand, and that Toru Takemitsu's music was too complex for the public. We always got many complaints after movies were made. But sometimes it meant they were a success. The company must have experienced complex feelings over this.

CD: You dealt with some controversial issues in several of your earliest pictures – student radicals in Dry Lake, *rock-'n-roll and* yakuza *strike-breaking in* Tears On The Lion's Mane *and nihilistic thrillseeking in* Pale Flower. *Those were the kinds of themes often covered by other, even more radical directors, like Nagisa Oshima and the independent Koji Wakamatsu.*

SHINODA: I belonged to Shochiku when I made *Pale Flower*. Even though the subject matter was too hot for Shochiku to handle, they were scheduled to distribute it. But I had to make it through an independent production company. Then, right after the movie was made, it was banned for a time. Shochiku felt it was not a proper movie to exhibit to their audiences. Nagisa Oshima and Koji Wakamatsu were already on their way. Oshima had left Shochiku by then. Wakamatsu didn't really have any experience making movies with the major companies, and had already established his own independent company. *Pale Flower* proved that it was impossible for me to work together with business-oriented Shochiku. And I felt that I was going to have to start my own independent production company, too. Oshima and Wakamatsu were politically ultra-left-field. In my case, it was my techno-centrism that conflicted with Shochiku's commercialism. My reasons were not political.

CD: Three of your earliest films were yakuza *pictures. I'm sure you're familiar with some of the American-influenced gangster movies Kihachi Okamoto made and the somewhat surreal* yakuza *films Seijun Suzuki did around the same time. From what I understand,* My Face Red In The Sunset *was a bit humorous, but* Tears On The Lion's Mane *and* Pale Flower *are quite different. Where did you get your viewpoint?*

SHINODA: I think I had a similar political view to Shintaro Ishihara, who wrote the original story for *Pale Flower*. *Yakuza* are supposed to have this desperate loyalty. We call it *giri to ninjo* in Japanese. It means obligation and human compassion. That's supposed to be the *yakuza*'s principal motivation for living, and I felt that that was total nonsense. Actually, to me it was more like when the United States had their Cold War against the Soviet Union. Which side was Japan going to take? Here, in a conflict between *yakuza*, which side would the lone wolf take? I wanted to do a Cold War situation in a *yakuza* film. If there's a choice of solitude, not to have a boss, and to choose that solitude, it breaks apart your daily life. That was my main *yakuza* character. There might be the obligation and human compassion, even though it never touches this *yakuza*'s true nature. Nihilism was my primary theme. Outlaws go through the motions in some fighting scenes, but that particular kind of spectacle wasn't the object of my films. 'All you need is a light action scene where you're not sure if someone is killed or not,' or 'killing people in movies isn't supposed to be realistic.' Those are descriptions of the style of Toho's *yakuza* films. It was stupid to me. I didn't really care how someone dies or kills someone.

CD: I understand that Tears On The Lion's Mane *was the first picture you did you were really happy with. What did you get to do in that film that you weren't able to do before?*

SHINODA: That movie was actually a commercial hit. Takashi Fujiki, the person who played the main character, was not a professional actor yet, he was a rock singer. And we were trying to make a pop music film, although it seemed like an American-style pop musical was going to be difficult to do in the environment of Japan. But I felt the need to try it. I felt that, if a rock musical picture could succeed in Japan, we would be able to contribute to the modernization of the Japanese film industry. My own internal modernization inspired the making of that movie. The film was very kitsch. I don't think I could make a film like that very often.

CD: But the character is also involved with the yakuza *and union strike-breaking, correct?*

SHINODA: He does the dirty business of disassembling the unions. There was a union in Japan very much involved with poverty/class conflict, and it was a part of a Communist structure. It was bandied about that 'unions' equalled 'justice,' and, because of this, the main character who performs the dirty task of union busting is the villain. Shuji Terayama and I constructed a plot where the villain's outlook was filled with our society's nonsense about that.

CD: So it's somewhat ironic that the rock singer character, someone espousing a rebellious lifestyle, is actually the representative of the forces of repression.

SHINODA: Yes, that's true. And unions have now, in this day and age, actually become the corporate establishment for a whole new generation. I predicted that, too. Back then, unions still had a basic philosophy, an ideal to get out from under poverty through a class war. However, I felt there was a place in Japan that didn't belong to either the unions or the corporations. This was just before I was going to form my own production company, so I was very conscious of these feelings within me, too. A person who makes movies doesn't belong anywhere, either. There were people who lost their place and refused to go back. I was looking for that place between them. You can get a sense of that in the movie, that process of searching. Right before that I had become a freelance. I had not seen Elia Kazan's *On The Waterfront*, and I don't think *West Side Story* had been made yet. When I finally saw those two movies, I felt very strongly that they had scenes similar to what I tried to represent in *Tears On The Lion's Mane*.

CD: People have compared Pale Flower *to the films of French director Jean-Pierre Melville.*

SHINODA: I often watch film noir. Isn't *Le Samourai* by Jean-Pierre Melville? I felt we had a similar atmosphere, but when I made *Pale Flower* I had not seen any of his movies yet. I wanted to show scenes of the assassin passing his time rather than his killing. The daily life of an assassin interests me more than the assassination, The routine of coming home and daydreaming or sitting still and thinking about what you'll do next is what I wanted to capture in *Pale Flower*. The American movie *Odds Against Tomorrow*, by Robert Wise, has a scene with gangsters gathered before their big heist. They have to kill time until the appointed hour, and they're doing nothing but hanging out at a place by the riverside. I was very moved by that scene. I think maybe that feeling was one of the big motivations for creating *Pale Flower*.

CD: Watching Pale Flower, *I get the feeling Ryo Ikebe's character has a deep spiritual hunger that he can only express through gambling or killing, and Mariko Kaga's character has a similar hunger, and with her it's gambling and drag racing and then drugs.*

SHINODA: What you're saying is very true and expresses perfectly how I felt. Muraki, Ikebe's character, doesn't have a daily life. He just gambles. I think the writer of the original story, Shintaro Ishihara, had that same feeling of hunger. Japan's identity struggled during the US and Soviet Cold War. It was impossible for our generation to find our spirit and purpose in life. We were trapped. That feeling matched the hunger of the two characters in the movie, of the writer and of myself. We tried to find our identity, our nationality after making this movie.

The writer Ishihara started a political movement, going into politics rather than continuing as a writer, and I personally wanted to rediscover Japan. We had different ways to grasp our identities, and we didn't even have the word for 'identity' in Japan back then. I can only describe our existences evaporating out of hunger. It was an aspect of that time, just before the word 'identity' was born in Japan.

CD: *The spiritual hunger comes through in the risk of gambling, also the ritual of the* hana fuda *card game itself. Then Ikebe meeting Kaga outside the church, the religious music playing over the final killing. I thought all that brought coherence to the idea of a quest for spiritual meaning.*

SHINODA: I don't think I calculated it, it was a coincidence. It's just by chance that we shot those scenes that way. I was actually amazed how well it came together in the end and worked in the context. I could have created many scenes that explain the hunger, but it would have just been repeating the same thing and wouldn't have moved forward. Muraki, Ikebe's character, was going to kill a person, and the reality of killing makes him see who he is for the very first time. If he doesn't do anything, he won't see. Killing makes him see something. Now, what is 'killing' in this case? For example, Raskolnikov was presented as a murderer of mankind in Dostoyevsky's *Crime And Punishment*. Humanity's existence makes it possible to commit homicide. Just as Raskolnikov bore the universal sin of mankind, I wanted the main character of my movie to do so as well.

CD: *I find it fascinating that, though Ikebe's character himself is a killer, he's frightened of the junkie assassin played by Takashi Fujiki, what Fujiki represents, leading Mariko Kaga's character into addiction. Someone who symbolizes disorder and chaos to Ikebe's world.*

SHINODA: Ikebe's character, Muraki, *does* have morals. Morals stabilize and uphold society's structure. And the junkie character, someone with no hope, no morals, would lead us to ruin. Showing that definite self-destruction to Japanese movie audiences was forbidden for a long time. However, I aggressively wanted to show that often people around you can die or perish and sometimes there just isn't the power to rescue them. The sense of reality inside Ikebe's character was just enough to uphold the morals of our society. It gave me a strong feeling of pathos in the movie.

CD: *I've seen* Pale Flower *several times, and I've always come away with the feeling that Ikebe brings Kaga to witness the final killing in the hope it will somehow satiate her and keep her from going further with the drugs and with Fujiki's character. At the end, when Ikebe's once more in prison and receives the letter from his friend saying that Kaga's character is dead, he realizes the futility.*

SHINODA: I believe that the two characters remained platonic, that there never was a physical relationship. I tried to show that Muraki, Ikebe's character, had the potential for a rigorous morality, even if just barely. He ends up in jail again, and this signifies that the true moralist can't exist in a secular world.

Everyone is very irresponsible in a secular society, and they live with an earthy morality. But the person who has real morals often has to accept the dirtiest, most sinful job. I don't think pure morality can survive in the real world. Therefore, the main character was required to not have a physical relationship with this particular worldly woman, nor was he able to lead a pragmatic way of life. I refused both those things in the movie.

CD: The other woman, played by Chisako Hara, Ikebe's former lover, lives in a small apartment behind her father's cramped clock shop. Could you talk about the clock imagery?

SHINODA: It symbolizes the time when nostalgia for the past is repeatedly broken. It's an affair he can't go back to, it's a love that cannot be recovered. When he visits the place again, only a sense of futility remains. 'Time' is broken, and the clocks represent this.

CD: The other writer who worked with you on the film was reportedly unhappy with the final picture and helped to hold up the release. Why was he dissatisfied?

SHINODA: The screenwriter who wrote with me was Ataru Baba, a good storyteller who could write witty dialogue. We collaborated on the script. He used one line of description for a gambling scene as a writer would usually do. However, I piled up 100 shots for that one line of description. The story flows if you read the screenplay, but there are many detailed gambling sequences in the final picture that he felt hid the story. He said, 'It's impossible to see the story I created!' Right after the first screening, he spat words of hatred at me. But he wasn't the reason the movie's release was postponed. It had too many gambling scenes to make it through the censor. Shochiku was far too 'moral' a company to feature this type of behavior. It's my fault that we couldn't release the movie right away.

CD: Your film Double Suicide *was adventurous as far as blending live action drama with* bunraku *puppet play. I was wondering how you feel your picture fits in with other film adaptations of the writer Chikamatsu, such pictures as Mizoguchi's* Crucified Lovers *(Chikamatsu Monogatari, 1954) and Masumura's* Love Suicides Of Sonezaki *(Sonezaki Shinju, 1978)?*

SHINODA: Kenji Mizoguchi tried to direct Chikamatsu's puppet play in a realistic way. Yasuzo Masumura saw my movie, and he wanted to make his own. He was very cynical about people and his approach to satire. Both of their films are very well made, and I think my movie was located between those two great directors. If I think about my puppet play, the proportionate size of puppets to the stage is very large. That's why the dialogue was very important as the characters cross the stage. I wanted to shoot the dialogue in close-up, inside an abstract space, to represent the experimental space which words can create. I did this by focusing on space that wasn't real. I decided to use *kuroko* (prompters in black hooded costumes) on the set, who connect us from the real world to the fictional world. That concept was different from the other two movies. The prompters served almost as agents for the writer, Monzaemon

Chikamatsu. They moved the story along by dispersing and integrating. The words of dialogue support the whole drama amongst the real live actors as one world, almost as if there weren't any backgrounds. It's a similar effect to what you get with real puppet theater.

CD: One of your latest films, Owl's Castle – *is this a remake of the film by Eiichi Kudo from 1963 that was also based on the same Ryotaro Shiba novel?*

SHINODA: It's a remake as far as being from the same source material by Shiba. But I have never seen the Kudo version, so I can't comment on it. From what I understand by its reputation, Kudo decided to do it as an intimate ninja story. If he had faithfully followed the original novel on its huge scale, he would have driven Toei studios into bankruptcy. But mine is quite a spectacle on a big scale and concerns the rule of Hideyoshi Toyotomi, who ruled Japan in the sixteenth century. Of course, there's a castle, a mansion, a garden, beautiful art objects, plus huge open spaces for the ninja to break into. We created a lot of things digitally, recreating old castles with computer graphics and even using CGI to do some of the ninja action. The movie has 820 shots, 100 of which are special effects.

CD: Are you familiar with the Ninja, Band Of Assassins *(*Shinobi No Mono*) series that Daiei studios made in the sixties with Raizo Ichikawa?*

SHINODA: That movie's original writer was a Communist, and the male ninja character played by Raizo Ichikawa was aggrieved and lower class. He tried to gain revenge on Hideyoshi, but was never able to and eventually was killed. That's the story he wrote, a tragic drama. The movie made an emotional appeal for justice in the class war. My movie's original writer is Ryotaro Shiba. I got some ideas for character development from an old American film, *The Young Lions*, written by Irwin Shaw. Marlon Brando played a Nazi lieutenant and Montgomery Clift played a Jew. The fateful meeting and parting of these two people gave me a clue as to how to approach a key relationship in *Owl's Castle*. It was very similar to that.

9

Yasuharu Hasebe

1932–

Black Tight Killers, Yasuharu Hasebe's first film as a director, is one of those amazing action movies that perfectly synthesizes a number of elements, seemingly without effort, and blends them all into a cohesive whole. There's a versatile score by Naozumi Yamamoto integrating several styles of Japanese pop, a magnificent, lushly colored production design, a terrific ensemble cast headed by Akira Kobayashi, and, of course, Hasebe's guidance. His direction is deceptively invisible, but it deserves praise precisely because it is so unobtrusive. Any director knows how hard it is to keep the right balance of humor, action and pathos in a tongue-in-cheek movie without falling off the high wire. Just ask Seijun Suzuki or Kihachi Okamoto, two directors who were lucky enough to hit pay dirt 95% of the time. Anyone familiar with world cinema, particularly from the sixties, knows there were plenty of poorly realized action pictures, many of them of the secret agent variety, that became top-heavy and fell under the weight of their labored self-consciousness. *Black Tight Killers*, a light film without any heavy message, is *not* one of those ostentatious failures. Star Kobayashi oozes a casual, Elvis-like cool as the combat photographer back from Nam who falls for a stewardess (Chieko Matsubara) whose father secreted a cache of gold somewhere on a remote island post-WW2. She's kidnapped by an alliance of Japanese *yakuza* and American mobsters, and Kobayashi must get her back. But, to do so, he's framed for murder, has potshots taken at him and is attacked by a band of go-go girl assassins who use mod accessories, including razor-sharp 45 rpm records as weapons and wads of bubble gum to blind pursuers. Before long, he realizes the girls are on his side, and he bands together with the female hit squad. Probably one of the funniest running gags in the film is the exquisitely timed, schmaltzy death scene each of the girls enjoys in Kobayashi's arms as the gangsters decimate their ranks one by one. Composer Yamamoto has a specific musical theme that kicks in in each instance, which is deliciously funny and poignant at the same time.

What is so thoroughly rewarding about Hasebe's filmography is that he could do serious, brutally hard-boiled stories as well. And he did a number of them in the late sixties, all contemporary *yakuza* films, all caught in that gradually more hard-edged swing towards realism as the decade ended. *Yakuza* films were slowly transforming, going from the set-in-pre-WW2 period *ninkyo* swordfighting to the more contemporary *jitsuroku* style. Nikkatsu studios never quite reached the most extreme *jitsuroku* territory, which peaked in the mid-seventies, because they nearly went bankrupt in 1971 and had to revamp their production strategy to survive. The studio sidestepped almost exclusively into the *pink* film, and any *yakuza* picture made at Nikkatsu after 1971 would generally have a claustrophobic, misogynistic air and plenty of violent sex. But in the late sixties, most *yakuza* pictures made at Nikkatsu were *ninkyo/jitsuroku* hybrids. They featured gangster anti-heroes but ones who were possessed of some redeemable quality such as honor and loyalty, and were, alas, distressingly outnumbered by legions of corporate *yakuza*. It was from the committed efforts of directors like Hasebe, a director who actually expressed more interest in hard-boiled noir than *yakuza* dramas, that that edgy realism slowly crept into Nikkatsu's gangster films.

Hasebe did *Massacre Gun* in 1967, the same year that Seijun Suzuki filmed his masterpiece, *Branded To Kill*, and Takashi Nomura directed the almost as good *My Gun Is My Passport*. All three starred Joe Shishido, all three were in black and white, and they formed a loosely linked trio, at least as far as Nikkatsu marketing was concerned. Saloon-owning brothers, tough guy Shishido and a womanizing Tatsuya Fuji become ticked off at the local *yakuza* when the mobsters humiliate their younger sibling, a sensitive musician (Jiro Okazaki) in training as a boxer. Shishido and Fuji subsequently start to muscle in on the protection rackets in the neighborhood, violence escalates, and Fuji is assassinated. This spurs Shishido to take on the whole gang. He manages to mow them down, but is then challenged by an old pal from the mob (Hideaki Nitani) on a deserted stretch of unfinished highway. The pair fatally blaze away at each other while Okazaki runs hysterically to the scene.

Territorial Dispute is a decent programmer that Hasebe shoots as if eaves-dropping on many scenes. Some of this staging is effective, but occasionally it results in cluttered compositions that contribute to narrative confusion. Thankfully Hasebe takes his story seriously, because the performances and realistically downbeat situations save the picture. Akira Kobayashi is convincing as an ex-con trying to keep his gang afloat even though his elderly boss has been murdered. He takes over a restaurant, hangs with his friendly-sometime-mortal-enemy played by Joe Shishido and courts a very young Meiko Kaji (still pka Masako Ota). When Kaji gets cut down in a drive-by meant for Kobayashi, our anti-hero goes on the rampage with his comrades in tow. Obliterating the gang, they succumb, too, in a crimson-drenched blaze of glory. When Kobayashi expires after fatally attacking the bad boss, the scene is overexposed and shot in slow motion, and everything dissolves in blood-sprayed chaos against a bright white background.

Coarse Violence starts with boisterous humor as Akira Kobayashi and pals knock over a gambling den and escape, but then Kobayashi is arrested for not having subway fare. Kobayashi's band of foolhardy outlaws continue to harass the more ruthless gang, and the dangers they court become a kind of thrill ride. Kobayashi falls for the decent sister (Masako Izumi) of a womanizing loser comrade (Tatsuya Fuji), but Izumi despises them all. The young hellions misstep, and all are brutally slaughtered except for Kobayashi. An older friend (Ryoji Hayama) from an 'honorable' gang drafts him, and the two go on a vendetta to destroy the villains. The end sees a comparatively conservative, self-satisfied Kobayashi comfortably settling into the established, 'well-respected' mob.

Bloody Territories again stars Kobayashi as an underboss trying to hold his gang together after his elderly *oyabun* (Yoshi Kato) opts out of a corporate mob squeeze play. Before long, Kobayashi's blood brothers are cut down. His fellow underboss (Tadao Nakamaru) is killed by a trusted friend (Ryoji Hayama) from the opposition simultaneously with their head boss, Kato, being assassinated. Repeated skirmishes escalate until Kobayashi enlists the help of a friendly enemy (Hiroshi Nawa), and the two stage a suicide raid which results in the massacre of all concerned.

Hasebe took his first steps into the *bosozoku* subgenre with *Exterminate The Wild Beasts*. Star Tetsuya Watari challenges a wolf pack of delinquent, black marketeers who gang-raped his sister, causing her suicide on the outskirts of the US airbase. Watari has to use all his wits to defeat the gang, led by an especially callous Tatsuya Fuji and Tamio Kawaji.

What came next are some of Hasebe's best pictures: his entries in the *Stray Cat Rock* youth gang series, starring Meiko Kaji and Tatsuya Fuji. The third, *Sex Hunter*, is the finest, a counter-culture masterpiece. There's a great subversive subtext running throughout the whole film, partly due, no doubt, to co-writer Atsushi Yamatoya (co-writer of *Branded To Kill*). [*For more on the* Stray Cat Rock *films, see Meiko Kaji's chapter.*]

One of the last *yakuza* action movies Hasebe directed at Nikkatsu before they switched over to *roman porn*, was another of his gems. *Bloody Feud* is relentlessly back to basics, a straightforward, hard-boiled noir following an ex-con (Joe Shishido) as he gets out of prison. Things have changed while he was inside, and the rival gang boss (Jotaro Togami) first targets Shishido's younger, inexperienced married pal (Tsuneya Oki), then their boss. Shishido joins with lone wolf buddies (Makoto Sato, Tatsuya Fuji) to stage yet another of those prerequisite kamikaze raids on the evil gang's HQ. The writing here really helps to distinguish this from its programmer status, with excellent characterizations and a harrowingly downward spiral charting Shishido and Fuji's last hours together before and after the doomed revenge binge. *Bloody Feud* also has one of underrated composer Hajime Kaburagi's most memorable scores, a testament to just how much music can add to a movie's already exhilarating momentum.

After *Bloody Feud*, Hasebe found himself in the same boat as everyone else at Nikkatsu, given the option of staying to work in the *pink* film arena. Unsure at first, he kept his options open with plenty of television work. Finally, his reservations swept aside, Hasebe dove into the violent sex subgenre, reportedly turning out some of the most disturbing of the lot. I haven't seen any of them, so I must reserve judgement. From all accounts, *Rape!*, about a young woman attacked in an elevator who consequently becomes addicted to violent sex, and *Assault! Jack The Ripper*, about a jaded couple who accidentally kill a hitch-hiker and find themselves turned on by the bloody disposal of the body, are his most disturbing. The latter picture has the most extreme reputation, as the male of the pair becomes so obsessed with sex in the course of murder that he becomes a deranged serial killer. Predictably, it's a path that leads not only to terror in the city but to the character's own despair.

Hasebe did *Leather John's Rebellious Tribe* at Toei in 1978, an offbeat chronicle of a loner mechanic (Hiroshi Tate) who dresses in black leather and tools around on his motorcycle while he's not aping John Travolta on the disco dance floor. Ultimately, Tate's flash-point sexuality proves too much for those around him, including a neighbor boy who mistakenly thinks he's been bedding his mother, a supermarket check-out girl (Aiko Morishita) with whom Tate is smitten and a trashy one-night stand who manipulates her violent boyfriend into killing our anti-hero. As Tate expires, he reaches out to the camera with the white rose he was taking to Morishita, and we see it's covered in blood. The film is a strange melange: delinquents, disco and a teen girl's wet dream, all swimming in Tate's vulnerably romantic hooliganism.

Several action films followed in the eighties, including *Dangerous Detectives*, the first in a successful series adapted from the hit TV show for the big screen. Hasebe also did several straight-to-video films in the early nineties, the best of which was

Joe Shishido, Tatsuya Fuji in *Bloody Feud*

Danger Point, an unpretentious noirish action piece about two hitmen – one younger (Sho Aikawa), one older (Joe Shishido) – who decide to take down a former employer (Hideo Murota). Though differing in the details, the picture is obviously inspired by one of Hasebe's favorite American films, Don Siegel's *The Killers*, and is an effective homage with a suitably nihilistic finale.

YASUHARU HASEBE – SELECTED FILMOGRAPHY

1966   *BLACK TIGHT KILLERS (ORE NI SAWARU TO ABUNAIZE)*

1967   *MASSACRE GUN (MINAGOROSHI NO KENJU)*

1968   *TERRITORIAL DISPUTE (SHIMA WA MORATTA*, aka *TURF WAR)*

1969   *COARSE VIOLENCE (ARAKURE)*
        BLOODY TERRITORIES (KOIKI BORYOKU – RYUKETSU NO SHIMA, aka *DISTRICT OF VIOLENCE, TERRITORY OF BLOODSHED)*
        EXTERMINATE THE WILD BEASTS (YAJU O KESE, aka *SAVAGE WOLF-PACK)*

1970   *PLEASURE RESORT GAMBLING CODE (SAKARIBA JINGI*, aka *A GANGSTER'S MORALS)*
        GIRL BOSS – STRAY CAT ROCK (ONNA BANCHO – NORA NEKO ROKKU)
        STRAY CAT ROCK – SEX HUNTER (NORA NEKO ROKKU – SEKKUSU HANTAA)
        STRAY CAT ROCK – MACHINE ANIMAL (NORA NEKO ROKKU – MASHIN ANIMARU)

1971   *A MAN'S WORLD (OTOKO NO SEKAI)*
        BLOODY FEUD (RYUKETSU NO KOSO)

1973   *FEMALE CONVICT SCORPION – NUMBER 701'S SONG OF HATE (JOSHUU SASORI – 701 GO URAMI BUSHI)*

1974   *GIRL BOSS DETECTIVE – DIRTY MARY (SUKEBAN DEKA – DAATI MARII)*
        NAKED SEVEN (SENGOKU ROKKU HAYATE NO ONNATACHI)

1976   *RAPE! (OKASU!*, aka *VIOLATE!)*
        ASSAULT! JACK THE RIPPER (BOKO! KIRISAKI JACK)

1977   *SECRET HONEYMOON – ASSAULT TRAIN (MARUHI HONI MOONU – BOKO RESSHA)*

1978   *RAMPAGE! (YARU!*, aka *OUTRAGE!)*
        LEATHER JOHN'S REBELLIOUS TRIBE (KAWA JAN HANKO ZOKU)

1982   *PETRIFIED WILDERNESS (KASEKI NO KOYA)*

1987   *DANGEROUS DETECTIVES (ABUNAI DEKA)*

1991   *DANGER POINT (JIGOKU E NO MICHI*, aka *ROAD TO HELL)*

YASUHARU HASEBE – INTERVIEW

The following interview was conducted by Christian Storms (from questions supplied by me) after-hours at a Tokyo video store in 1999. Christian also translated. The video of this interview appears in slightly different form as a supplement on the American DVD release of Black Tight Killers *from American Cinematheque Presents/Vitagraph/Image Entertainment.*

CS: What made you go into film?

HASEBE: I became interested in film when I was a student. At the time, there was virtually no television and only the big screen. I got motivated and started working as an apprentice to a screenwriter, doing rewrites. Then I realized that film was really more of a director's medium and decided to try to get a job at Nikkatsu as an assistant director. My first assignment at Nikkatsu was in 1958. There were quite a few films being made at the time, and, in the beginning as an AD, I was working on about ten pictures a year.

CS: And who were some of the directors you worked under?

HASEBE: Let's see, I was an AD for six or seven years, so that means I worked on maybe 50 or 60 films in that period, give or take a few. I worked mostly with directors Seijun Suzuki, Takashi Nomura and Tan [Motomu] Iida.

CS: How many films did you do a year once you graduated to director?

HASEBE: As a director, I did about four or five films a year. But the work schedule is a little different from what it is in America. How can I best put it? Let's just say that the films were a bit more impromptu. It was never like a big-budget American movie, where you have a year or a year and a half from conception to end of post-production. We usually worked on a 30-day cycle.

CS: Your first film was Black Tight Killers. *It was unusual, what with the all-female hit squad. It also has a sense of humor similar to Seijun Suzuki's movies. What were your influences?*

HASEBE: The motivation behind *Black Tight Killers* was that we were looking for a new kind of action film. At the time, the James Bond pictures were interesting. With that in mind, we found a story we thought had a fairly unusual plot. As you said, it had unusual elements, not like most other action films of that period. I had worked on some of Seijun Suzuki's films so, yes, you're right, I think there was some influence, especially with the humor. I was also influenced by Kihachi Okamoto's films, pictures that often had a satirical quality. As far as non-Japanese influences for that film, there really weren't any. However, I really love John Huston and Don Siegel, and still feel that way today.

CS: Which films by them?

HASEBE: Huston's *The Maltese Falcon* is probably my favorite film from that era. And Don Siegel? That's a tough one. I guess I would have to say *The Killers*.

CS: Akira Kobayashi was a huge star at Nikkatsu. You did several other pictures with him besides Black Tight Killers. *Yakuza pictures like* Bloody Territories. *Can you talk about him?*

HASEBE: I'd worked on a number of features with Akira Kobayashi while I was still an AD. I kept the same impression both before and after directing him, that is of working with a good friend. He had told me, 'Hey, I'll act in your first film,' when I was still an AD.

CS: What was the reaction of the Nikkatsu bosses to Black Tight Killers?

HASEBE: They were very pleased with it. It turned out to be something quite original. For me personally, it was a triumph, because I'd been out of work for a year and a half.

CS: How did the idea for the female hit squad come about? The way that most of them get their own tongue-in-cheek, sentimental death scene in Kobayashi's arms is very funny.

HASEBE: Well, they were sexy and 'bad,' but – how do I put it? I guess the best description of their motif would be go-go girls. That fashion was popular at the time. The deaths of the girls had been in the original novel, but we handled their death scenes differently from the book. The composer of the 'Bad Girl Bites The Dust' theme was Naozumi Yamamoto. I'd worked with him before, and he was a true genius. The feeling in those scenes was part of his own unique contribution.

CS: One thing that is striking about Nikkatsu films is the excellence of the cinematographers and production designers.

HASEBE: Yes, you're right. The cinematographers and production designers really were top-notch. Akiyoshi Satani was the production designer on *Black Tight Killers*. He had an accomplished, interesting sensibility on just about everything. The DP was Kazue Nagatsuka, a mentor who had worked on pictures since the silent era. I'd also worked with him when I was an AD. He was a real master at what he did and greatly assisted me. Technically, he was one of the best.

CS: Many of your yakuza *films are particularly well written, especially* Bloody Territories, Massacre Gun *and* Bloody Feud. *How did you collaborate with writers on your* yakuza *projects of the late sixties?*

HASEBE: It was really on a case-by-case basis. Sometimes I would get together with one or two other writers, and we would check into a hotel to get away from the rest of the world, so we could work without distraction. Other times, I would only become involved after the script was finished.

CS: Nikkatsu was the biggest maker of yakuza *films after Toei studios. Did you ever sense any kind of rivalry between the studios, the philosophy behind each studio's interpretation of the genre?*

HASEBE: Rivalry? I don't think there was any real consciousness of rivalry between Nikkatsu and Toei with their *yakuza* films and the respective styles. At Nikkatsu, the actors were somewhat younger. So, with that in mind, I think the age difference of the performers made some difference. That changed the look, the style of the cinematography. It wasn't a rivalry. More of a difference in colors. The Nikkatsu colors, the Toei colors. Each studio painted with a different palette. Toei, along with Daiei, also had a tradition of making samurai films. Nikkatsu made mostly contemporary films during the sixties and had little experience with period pieces. The films that Daiei were making at the time were of extremely high quality, and I have to say we filmmakers at Nikkatsu learned a lot from watching their pictures.

CS: Bloody Territories *and* Bloody Feud *are two of my favorite Nikkatsu* yakuza *movies. Are there any of your films that stand out for you more than others from that period?*

HASEBE: I'm glad to hear that they're two of your favorites. When I look at them now, I have certain feelings and memories. Trying to think of which one is best, it's difficult, because I would like to remake them all! Two of my favorite pictures by other directors from that time are Yukihiro Sawada's *Attack* (*Kirikomi*, 1970) and Takashi Nomura's *My Gun Is My Passport* (*Korutto Wa Ore No Pasuupotto*, 1967). I think those are two of the Nikkatsu *yakuza* action masterpieces from the period. As far as Toei films, I'm very fond of Kosaku Yamashita's *Gambling Boss* (*Bakuchiuchi – Socho Tobaku*, 1968).

CS: Some of your films that are developing cult status in America are your pictures for the Stray Cat Rock *series:* Girl Boss, Sex Hunter *and* Machine Animal. *How did those films originate?*

HASEBE: The series began as a direct result of singer Akiko Wada, who was just starting her career. She still enjoys popularity, but she was extremely popular then, right from the beginning. I was told that she'd be starring in the films, and that was the plan. Akiko Wada was under the management of an outside production company, so I guess you could call it an outsource production even though Nikkatsu released it. They handled the planning of the film rather than Nikkatsu. I think Nikkatsu was starting to have problems being able to finance the production of full-scale *yakuza* and action pictures.

CS: The films seemed to change a bit after the first one, which had Akiko Wada as the top star over Meiko Kaji and Tatsuya Fuji. By the time of the second one, Wild Jumbo, *all Wada does is just one song. I don't even recall seeing her in the last three movies. Was that Nikkatsu's doing? Did they also rule out any subject matter as taboo?*

HASEBE: No, that wasn't really Nikkatsu. The plan had been to use Akiko Wada and target young audiences, then in the background make use of the social issues and controversy over public morals. When you ask if there were any special orders from Nikkatsu about things we shouldn't touch on, I would have to say 'no.' At the time, Joe Shishido and Akira Kobayashi were the really big stars at Nikkatsu. But Nikkatsu knew that, if they were to continue, they needed to create stars for the next generation; that's why Meiko Kaji and Tatsuya Fuji were selected as the main stars in the *Stray Cat Rock* series. And those two worked very hard because they wanted to be big stars themselves.

CS: Many of the Stray Cat Rock *films, as well as featuring pop music and action, also dealt with social problems of the time. Of course, there was juvenile delinquency and youthful alienation in the films, but there was also the persecution of mixed-race teenagers and the abuse of women in* Sex Hunter, *and the heist of an illicit LSD shipment in* Machine Animal. *Did you ever talk with the cast about the approach to the social issues?*

HASEBE: I don't remember ever talking with Meiko Kaji and Tatsuya Fuji about the social message of *Sex Hunter*. Japan, especially during the sixties and early seventies, had a lot of problems with student demonstrations and protests. America had many similar difficulties. So, going for the most interesting social message at the time, the feeling of strife in the air as the seventies began, that's what we captured on film. We weren't trying to hit people over the head with messages but rather to show what was going on in the background in the lives of many young people in Japan during that period.

CS: Could you describe what it was like when Nikkatsu made the transition to roman porn *film production? Did you feel more restricted on those films? Or that you had more freedom?*

HASEBE: In 1971, when Nikkatsu marched into the *pink* film market, I was uncertain if I was going to be able to participate. Nikkatsu wasn't too sure what it was doing and was not expecting much. I didn't think of leaving them because in Japan there's no real tradition of changing companies. So, I tried to concentrate on films made for television, and I got a lot of work in TV. I have always loved and wanted to direct action films, so for me the *roman porn* films didn't offer too much. Were there more limits? Or more freedom? Well, a lot of creativity was actually left up to the director, and there were things that could be done in the genre. But, with this being said, there were many changes that had to be made.

CS: How did you come on board directing the fourth film in Toei's Female Convict Scorpion *series,* Number 701's Song Of Hate?

HASEBE: Even though I was a contract director still at Nikkatsu, they came to me. The reason for the offer was that the film starred Meiko Kaji, and I believe she wanted to work with me again. I guess that was the reason, and they let me direct the film. Shunya Ito had already directed the first three *Scorpion* pictures and had said that the series was over, that there would be no more films. But Toei wanted to continue making the movies. Since Ito was no longer going to be directing them, I signed on. Also, I'm sure Toei had their reasons for selecting me rather than Ito.

Detail from poster for *Female Convict Scorpion – Number 701's Song Of Hate*

CS: I've heard rumors that director Ito complained that there were progressive budget cuts as the series went along. Were you conscious of that?

HASEBE: Since I hadn't been involved in the first three, I wasn't aware of any of the cuts Ito might have been talking about. The film itself was slated for a New Year's release, and the shooting took place in December. At the time, the end of the year meant labor union negotiations between production company personnel and Toei management. So, both production people and management people were focused on those issues. The film was shot in the midst of those tensions. With that situation in mind, something unique happened. Nobody was allowed to work overtime. A lot was going on. Shooting at the end of the year amidst labor negotiations is probably the worst time of the year to make a movie. (*laughs*) I really don't know all the details about what happened, since it involves Toei and their management, but I do know that director Shunya Ito, was very active in the labor movement. (laughs)

CS: You've made a number of yakuza *and action pictures shot for straight-to-video release in the 1980s and 1990s. What's it like doing those, pictures like* Danger Point *and* First Down And Ten?

HASEBE: During the eighties and nineties I directed a lot of movies for television and none for theatrical release. Essentially, I just wanted to direct action films, and many projects never got beyond the development stage. Many *yakuza* films over the last 15 years have been direct-to-video. The two pictures you've mentioned are examples of the direct-to-video action film. The difference between these movies and the movies of the sixties and seventies is ... well, I've always just wanted to make action films. Films are like living beings. They represent a certain place in time. There are bound to be differences. As far as what I'm working on now, I'm trying to break the mold and create a truly original action picture.

10

Seijun Suzuki

1923–

Seijun Suzuki had what many in mainstream society in the sixties would have probably called a sick sense of humor. Today, his dark comic sense seems most akin to that of David Lynch. And the mainstream success of Quentin Tarantino's latest, *Kill Bill*, a violently over-the-top tall tale spiced with black comedy, is a sure indicator that things have changed since the sixties with regard to pushing the envelope with the movie-going public.

Many of Suzuki's most penetrating influences came during his adolescence and right afterwards as a Japanese soldier in WW2. Suzuki was never held prisoner in a camp, as was director Tomu Uchida, but he still had a rougher wartime experience than many of his filmmaking colleagues, reportedly shipwrecked twice while in the Japanese navy. There were things he saw that darkened his vision, things absurd in their stupidity and irony that colored what would strike him as funny. When violent death comes in a Suzuki film, it isn't necessarily tragic. Often images are juxtaposed in such a fashion that their ridiculousness takes precedence. Ultimately, Suzuki's films, even his early, mostly-by-the-numbers programmers, are about a way of looking at the world. They are instinctive, inspired and – thankfully – bereft of intellectual and aesthetic pretensions. This intuition of how best to approach any given scene, what to emphasize or minimize, applies as much to his use of color as it does to his frame composition or action choreography. Colors may represent certain emotions or character traits, or may be integral in establishing mood, but Suzuki lays no ground rules for himself, no strict aesthetic he cannot go ahead and break in the very next scene if he feels like it.

Suzuki has remarked that his first truly original picture was *Youth Of The Beast* in 1963, and most film journalists, at least in the West, have been content to agree with him. Admittedly, 1963 was the beginning of Suzuki throwing off restraints and truly finding his own voice. But his foremost aim has also always been to deliver what the audience has come to see. So, if that's a genre film, he's done his best to deliver a *superior* genre film, albeit with ground-breaking visuals, editing and production design. Perhaps it's no surprise to discover that many of his pre-1963 efforts are very good movies. Despite the similarities in stories and the hack rush jobs that sometimes plagued the Nikkatsu script department, there were many entertaining action and crime films made at the studio in the late fifties and early sixties, and not just by Suzuki.

Suzuki's third film and first crack at the *yakuza* genre was *Satan's Town*, with Seizaburo Kawazu portraying an ambivalent undercover cop on the track of a sadistic gang kingpin, played by Ichiro Sugai. There are bravura tour de force images, usually involving violent death, and the picture is extremely fierce in its second half, displaying a brutality quotient rare for the time period.

Deliriously romantic, *Inn Of Floating Weeds* stars Hideaki Nitani as a gangster who kills an adversary in a rain-drenched fight on a Yokohama wharf, then, nearly dead himself, disappears for five years. When he returns, he finds his girl is now the mistress of a gang boss saloon owner (Toru Abe). Nitani then becomes smitten with the kid sister of a roving minstrel, and their scenes together are poignantly sweet, more evocative of fifties French cinema than Japanese. Things come to a head when boss Abe and his gang run amok, and again the climactic gunfight is shockingly violent for the period.

The *Nude And The Gun*'s title is a bit of a misnomer, although situations are contrived to have the lead gang moll (Mari Shiraki) parading around in her underwear for at least half the movie. A fun time-waster, with a news photographer (Michitaro Mizushima) drawn into a web of death and deception when he's enamored of Shiraki, and her ruthless heroin smuggler beau (Ichiro Sugai) fails to approve.

Underworld Beauty was Suzuki's first widescreen film, utilizing both real Tokyo locations as well as the studio backlot to full advantage. Lead Michitaro Mizushima is a black-clad lone wolf helping the kid sister of his dead partner retrieve diamonds from a mob operating out of a Turkish bath, and Mari Shiraki is indelibly charismatic as the feisty sibling. A rip-roaring noir action thriller tackling Anthony Mann/Sam Fuller territory with ease, and showing as early as 1958 that Suzuki was already operating on all cylinders.

Passport To Darkness tracks a trombone-playing bandleader (Ryoji Hayama) as he descends into an urban inferno while searching for the strangler of his murdered girlfriend. Trailed by the cops, Hayama falls into classic noir paranoia as he unravels the mystery, learning his lover had been involved with a heroin ring. Suzuki mesmerizes the viewer through the slow patches, meticulously orchestrating Hayama's hellish pilgrimage amongst hitmen, junkies, transvestites, whores and corrupt diplomats.

Age Of Nudity is a short programmer that delivers in spades, observing the antics of a scooter-driving delinquent gang led by Keiichiro Akagi in a coastal resort town. Akagi challenges his rival to a motorcycle race down a mountain road – what amounts to a game of chicken, resulting in Akagi's demise as he plummets over a cliff. Akagi was one of Nikkatsu's up-and-coming young matinee idols, and the ending pre-echoed his own death by car accident in 1961.

A cop (Michitaro Mizushima) has two of his handcuffed mobster passengers assassinated by a sharpshooter when his prison transport bus is waylaid in *Take Aim At The Police Van*. His superiors give him the task of finding the killers, and Suzuki creates a nightmarish gauntlet for Mizushima of foot-chases, red herrings, merciless beatings and near-miss shootings.

Fast-moving noir action also punctuates *Clandestine Zero Line*, with a cynical reporter (Hiroyuki Nagato) and his principled rival (Yuji Kodaka) in opposition while they follow a crime beat. Events spiral out of control when Nagato crosses a sexy, dragon lady boss (Sanae Nakahara), and both are captured. The boys have to fight tooth and nail to escape a foreign freighter that is really a den of drugs and prostitution. Nagato remains shamelessly unrepentant at the hard-boiled finish.

Everything Goes Wrong is an exhilarating, restless-youth-gone-wild saga with Tamio Kawaji as a teenager with a chip on his shoulder and electrifying Yoshiko Nezu as the spitfire tomboy in love with him. Suzuki has cinematographer Izumi Hagiwara's camera prowling and slithering through Tokyo back streets, following Kawaji and his footloose friends. In many ways this reflects the fifties *taiyozoku* (sun tribe) films *Crazed Fruit* and *Seasons In The Sun*, as well as Kon Ichikawa's volcanic *Punishment Room*. It also has elements in common with Nagisa Oshima's great *Cruel Story Of Youth*, though it is noticeably less pretentious. The downbeat ending is a real shocker. A find, and highly recommended.

The Guys Who Bet On Me features Koji Wada as a truck-driving youth with boxing ambitions. Hooking up with a trainer (Ryoji Hayama), he's soon not only in hot water with gangsters harassing Hayama's gym but also in dutch with his ex-girl (Mayumi Shimizu), his new nightclub singer squeeze (Yoko Minamida) as well as Hayama's nymphomaniac wife (Mari Shiraki)! Suzuki delivers ridiculously surreal comic-book delirium with a palette of primary colors that sear the eyes, all the while employing editing rhythms that would make later pioneers like Godard look tame. Despite the happy ending, it's obvious that Wada's ego-driven youth, living in such a chaotic universe, will not be happy for long.

The bizarre nuttiness of *Detective Office 23 – Go To Hell, Bastards!* spotlights a sportscar-driving cool cat (Joe Shishido) who works for a detective bureau trying to break up a band of hoods who have stolen weapons from a US army base. A little more conventional than Suzuki's other 1963 thriller, *Youth Of The Beast*, one can still glimpse his irreverent humor, especially in some hilarious nightclub scenes, a great rock/R&B/ Dixieland hybrid score and a flaming gas jet finale in the villain's cellar.

One of Suzuki's absolutely wildest, *Youth Of The Beast* melds influences from both Kurosawa's *Yojinbo* and Fritz Lang's *Big Heat* in the tall tale of a maniacal tough guy (Joe Shishido) swaggering through squalid streets, surreal nightclubs and apartments, beating-the-hell out of anyone giving him lip. He infiltrates two gangs, playing one bunch off against the other, until midway through it's discovered he's an undercover cop, and thugs start tying him upside down to chandeliers and sticking sharp things under his fingernails. A masterwork, with a deliciously ambiguous, downbeat ending.

Kanto Wanderer chronicles gambler Akira Kobayashi's yen for a crooked, married card dealer (Hiroko Ito) as well as the romantic indiscretions of his hot-headed brother (Daisaburo Hirata), who falls for a rival gangster's daughter. Much of the humor, pathos and violence stems directly from these complications, examining what men are willing to do (or *not* do) to attract a woman.

Turn-of-the-century *ninkyo* saga *Flower And The Angry Waves* finds Akira Kobayashi as a young anti-hero in a coal carters' union up against a rival *yakuza* clan. He's also caught between the virginal Chieko Matsubara and the more worldly Naoko Kubo. Midway through Kobayashi's face gets slightly disfigured, something which must have played havoc with the sensibilities of his teen girl fan base. There are well-choreographed swordfights, but Suzuki subverts audience expectations at the climax, showing Kobayashi acting in somewhat cowardly fashion in the snowbound last act, an unheard-of trait in a *ninkyo yakuza* hero.

Gate Of Flesh is the nihilistic tale of an innocent orphan (Yumiko Nogawa) from the countryside forced to go into prostitution in Tokyo's post-war ruins. Joining up with three whores living in a bombed-out building, she gets a crash course on survival in the dog-eat-dog world of a conquered nation. Joe Shishido immolates the screen in one if his best roles as a veteran-turned-thief who likes to ambush American GIs. Wounded and on the run after stealing a cache of penicillin from the US base, he's given refuge by the women, and soon all are lusting after him, on the verge of breaking their cardinal taboo: having sex without getting paid for it. There are some disturbing scenes, including the whiplash punishment of the girls who violate the sex-for-money-only rule. Because Shishido falls in love with Nogawa, and vice versa, Nogawa ends up brutally thrashed. The three jealous whores then betray Shishido to a gang in cahoots with the US occupation, something that gets him killed before he can rendezvous with Nogawa. Devastating, with Nogawa giving one of the most blistering performances you'll ever see.

Contemporary *yakuza* drama *Our Blood Won't Allow It* relates the anguish of a mob boss's son (Akira Kobayashi) conflicted because of his promise to his dying father that he won't pursue vengeance and will abandon the underworld. However, he continues to lead the mob in secret while trying to put up a straight front for his brash younger brother (Hideki Takahashi). There are phantasmagorical moments, building to a nocturnal shoot-out climax. The final sequence is riveting, as fatally wounded Kobayashi stumbles through the lush countryside, then Takahashi, hampered by darkness, searches in vain for his older sibling. His disembodied, anguished cries echo as the sun rises on an empty horizon.

Adapted from another novel by Taijuro Tamura, who also wrote *Gate Of Flesh*, *Story Of A Prostitute* tells of a woman (Yumiko Nogawa), disillusioned in love, who obliterates herself as a volunteer prostitute for troops in 1937 Manchuria. But she and a soldier (Tamio Kawaji) fall in love, and after making a futile escape into the desert wasteland they eventually die in a ferocious sandstorm. Nogawa gives probably the best performance of her career, a heartbreaking portrayal of a strong woman in spiritual torment being crushed by the animalistic world around her.

Tattooed Life is another *ninkyo* saga set in Taisho-era Japan, with Tetsu (Hideki Takahashi) coerced to kill a rival *yakuza* boss, then compelled to flee with his artistic younger brother when his own gang turns on him. The pair find refuge in a construction company camp in the mountains, and things get complicated not only by a rival gang but by police searching for Tetsu. Just when things couldn't seem to get any worse, Tetsu's brother develops an obsessive love for the boss's wife (Hiroko Ito). Things culminate when Tetsu single-handedly assaults the bad-guy stronghold in a violent thunderstorm. Suzuki pulls out the stops in a theatricalized use of lighting, color and swordfight choreography that once more had the Nikkatsu bosses wagging their fingers when production wrapped. At the close, Tetsu has avenged his brother's death and saved the boss, the wife and their business by wiping out the gang, but he's led off to prison while his love (Masako Izumi) looks on.

Tetsuya Watari stars in *Tokyo Drifter*, an honorable *yakuza* determined to prove that his boss (Ryuji Kita) really has broken up their gang and gone straight. But events transpire to pull both men back into crime, namely a squabble over property

Poster for *Everything Goes Wrong*

rights and unpaid debts. Before you know it, Watari has to go wandering in the hinterlands because hitmen are on his trail. Suzuki had been warned again to curtail his wild visual antics, so, in an attempt to appease the bosses, he slashed *Tokyo Drifter*'s budget. Conversely, this caused him and production designer Takeo Kimura to use even stranger, more imaginative lighting effects, sparsely dressed sets and weird juxtapositions to tell their story. The outcome was an outlandish deconstruction of the genre, a fast-moving piece of cinema made up of flamboyantly eccentric tableaux that is by turns funny, thrilling and romantic.

Working from a perceptive script by Kaneto Shindo, Suzuki's *Fighting Elegy* examines how the sexual energy of naive male students can be channeled by older

Tetsuya Watari, Chieko Matsubara in *Tokyo Drifter*

'mentors' into the controlled violence of the military – specifically, the disparate nationalist factions that merged into one ultra-right-wing conglomerate in pre-WW2 Japan. Where many sixties new wave directors might have taken an overly serious, dry approach, Suzuki juggles serious ideas, visceral displays of barbaric fight choreography and subversive humor. Suzuki puts us right in the thick of it as we follow the tribulations of an impetuous, likeable young man (Hideki Takahashi) on his evolution into budding fascist.

Branded To Kill was unquestionably Suzuki's tour-de-force masterpiece at Nikkatsu, an exhilarating deconstruction of both gangster films and, more specifically, the studio's own hitman subgenre. Excessive violence as well as dreamlike surrealism envelopes an assassin (Joe Shishido) known as Number Three Killer. Having botched a job when a butterfly settled on his rifle sight, both his mercenary wife (Mariko Ogawa) and a stoic hitwoman (Annu Mari) he's become obsessed with try to kill him. Shishido attempts to elude his killers, and the viewer can only deduce from the peculiar events unfolding that he is losing his mind. When Number One Killer (Koji Nanbara) steps in, the mind games escalate to a terrifyingly absurd level. Suzuki had been warned repeatedly about his maverick visual flourishes and 'incoherent' narratives, and this was the picture that broke the Nikkatsu president's proverbial back. Suzuki was fired, but – fortunately – the film *was* still released. Already undergoing financial woes, Nikkatsu's bottom line was apparently so tenuous that they needed every bit of product for release. In America, it undoubtedly would have been shelved, or, at the very least, drastically recut.

Surprisingly, there was a vocal outcry from students, film buffs and intellectuals at Suzuki's dismissal. But the public protests could not get Suzuki reinstated, and he ended up suing the studio in a case that dragged on for years. He finally won, but was blacklisted by all the major studios until 1977, when he made *Tale Of Sorrow And Sadness*. He had subsisted on television commercial production and writing in the interim.

Suzuki's three films known as the *Taisho Trilogy*, set in the 1912–1926 era, are regarded as his finest pictures by many Japanese critics. Starting in 1979 with *Zigeunerweisen*, going through *Heat Haze Theater* in 1981 and concluding with *Yumeji* in 1991, they follow the exploits of various male teachers, playwrights and artists plagued with a sudden rift in their ability to distinguish the real from the unreal, specifically the realm of the living and the dead. As a result, there are ambiguous hauntings by dead lovers from the past. Notwithstanding the critical acclaim heaped on these films, especially in Japan, I find none of the three amongst my favorite Suzuki pictures. Suzuki seems to revel too much in static, mysterious imagery at the expense of narrative coherence. Not that coherence is mandatory, especially in films about the nature of personal mysteries. But, without previously imposed restrictions, such as the ones in the Nikkatsu era, the results are snail-like pacing and a lack of dynamic tension, all producing an aimless sensation conducive to boredom.

Pistol Opera, though certainly as incoherent and non-linear as any of the *Taisho* films, makes up for it in an ongoing flood of provocative, beautiful imagery that doesn't let up till the last frame. Especially when viewed on the big screen, this amazing film, ostensibly about a lone wolf hitwoman marked for death (in a 'plot' reminiscent of *Branded To Kill*), plays more like a kabuki cavalcade of live-action paintings. There's plenty of violence, but virtually no blood is drawn, and the disordered visual commotion on display is so meticulously, instinctively color-coordinated that the viewer is left mesmerized, transported into a weird state of overtly theatrical, erotic/grotesque rapture. Suzuki's last picture to date, it's an appropriate endpiece and an impressive melding of his two visions: the superior action genre film and the literary, dream-nonsense 'art' movie.

SEIJUN SUZUKI – COMPLETE FILMOGRAPHY

1956   *HARBOR TOAST – VICTORY IS IN OUR GRASP (MINATO NO KANPEI – SHORI O WAGATE NI)*
PURE EMOTIONS OF THE SEA (HOZUNA WA UTA-U – UMI NO JUNJO)
SATAN'S TOWN (AKUMA NO MACHI)

1957   *INN OF FLOATING WEEDS (UKIGUSA NO YADO)*
EIGHT HOURS OF TERROR (HACHIJIKAN NO KYOFU)
THE NUDE AND THE GUN (RAJO TO KENJU)

1958   *UNDERWORLD BEAUTY (ANKOKUGAI NO BIJO)*
SPRING NEVER CAME (FUMIHAZUSHITA HARU)
BLUE BREASTS (AOI CHIBUSA, aka YOUNG BREASTS)
VOICE WITHOUT A SHADOW (KAGENAKI OE)

1959   *LOVE LETTER (RABU RETAA)*
PASSPORT TO DARKNESS (ANKOKU NO RYOKEN)
AGE OF NUDITY (SUPPADAKA NO NENREI)

1960   *TAKE AIM AT THE POLICE VAN (SONO GOSOSHA O NERAE)*
SLEEP OF THE BEAST (KEMONO NO NEMURI)
CLANDESTINE ZERO LINE (MIKKO ZERO RAIN)
EVERYTHING GOES WRONG (SUBETE GA KURUTTERU)
FIGHTING DELINQUENTS (KUTABARE GURENTAI)

1961   *TOKYO KNIGHTS (TOKYO NAITSU)*
THE BIG BOSS WHO NEEDS NO GUN (MUTEPPO TAISHO)
MAN WITH A SHOTGUN (SHOTTOGAN NO OTOKO, aka SANDANJU NO OTOKO)
THE WIND OF YOUTH GROUP CROSSES THE MOUNTAIN PASS (TOGE O WATARU WAKAI KAZE)
BLOOD RED WATER IN THE CHANNEL (KAIKYO CHI NI SOMETE)
ONE MILLION DOLLAR SMASH AND GRAB (HYAKUMAN DORU O TATAKIDASE)

1962   HIGH TEEN YAKUZA (HAI TEIN YAKUZA)
         THE GUYS WHO BET ON ME (ORE NI KAKETA YATSURA)
1963   DETECTIVE OFFICE NUMBER 23 – GO TO HELL, BASTARDS! (TANTEI
         JIMUSHO NIJUSAN – KUTABARE AKUTODOMO, aka DETECTIVE OFFICE
         NUMBER 23 – DESTROY THE VILLAINS)
         YOUTH OF THE BEAST (YAJU NO SEISHUN)
         THE BASTARD (AKUTARO)
         KANTO WANDERER (KANTO MUSHUKU)
1964   FLOWER AND THE ANGRY WAVES (HANA TO DOTO)
         GATE OF FLESH (NIKUTAI NO MON)
         OUR BLOOD WON'T ALLOW IT (ORETACHI NO CHI GA YURUSANAI)
1965   STORY OF A PROSTITUTE (SHUNPU DEN, aka JOY GIRLS)
         STORY OF A BASTARD – BORN UNDER A BAD STAR (AKUTARO DEN – WARUI
         HOSHI NO SHITA DEMO)
         TATTOOED LIFE (IREZUMI ICHIDAI, aka ONE GENERATION OF
         TATTOOS)
1966   CARMEN OF KAWACHI (KAWACHI KARUMEN)
         TOKYO DRIFTER (TOKYO NAGAREMONO)
         FIGHTING ELEGY (KENKA EREJI, aka ELEGY TO VIOLENCE)
1967   BRANDED TO KILL (KOROSHI NO RAKUIN)
1977   TALE OF SORROW AND SADNESS (HISHU MONOGATARI)
1980   ZIGEUNERWEISEN
1981   HEAT HAZE THEATER (KAGEROZA)
1985   CAPONE'S FLOOD OF TEARS (KAPONE OI NI NAKU, aka CAPONE CRIES A
         LOT)
1991   YUMEJI
2001   PISTOL OPERA

SEIJUN SUZUKI – INTERVIEW

This interview took place at a Japanese restaurant on Santa Monica Boulevard in West Los Angeles in the spring of 1997. Kurando Mitsutake did the on-site translation. Mark Rance from Film Forum was also present.

CD: First of all, where were you born and raised?
    SUZUKI: I was born and grew up in Tokyo. I went to Hirosaki High School in downtown Tokyo, a very famous and prestigious high school, and, if you went to this high school, you were basically guaranteed to get into the most famous and prestigious university in Tokyo. When I was about to move on to university, Japanese society was going through a lot of change. This was the whole period before WW2. Before I could complete high school, I got drafted.

CD: Now, did you want to go into the movie business from the very beginning?

SUZUKI: No, I'd never dreamed of becoming a movie director. I just hoped to become a successful businessman. At that time, right after the war, if you passed this exam you would get into the very prestigious Tokyo University. But then suddenly they changed things and the exam became much more difficult. I ended up failing the exam to get in as an economy major. Coincidentally, they were holding an exam to become an assistant director at Shochiku studios. I took that, and I passed. That was the beginning of my movie career, and it was kind of by accident.

CD: When did you take this exam at Shochiku?

SUZUKI: 1947. Right after the war.

CD: Did you find that there were any kindred spirits at Shochiku?

SUZUKI: Eight of us passed this exam to be assistant director, and we all were good friends. The interesting thing about Shochiku was that you could choose which director you wanted to work with. If you wanted to work with Ozu, you could pick Ozu. If you wanted to work with Kinoshita, you could pick him. The team I picked to work with was a drinking team. (*laughs*) The director was Tsuruo Iwama. When we went out after work, we were forbidden to talk about movies. The only thing we were allowed to do was drink. I did the drinking thing for about seven years. During that whole period, I was very unfamiliar with what was going on in movies. I had never even heard of the director John Huston.

CD: Why did you stop working at Shochiku and move over to Nikkatsu? I've read that you weren't moving up the ladder and felt there would be a better chance of advancement at Nikkatsu, which had just started up business again after a long interruption.

SUZUKI: There were 16 assistant directors ahead of me at Shochiku. I felt frustrated at ever becoming a director there. Plus, Nikkatsu was offering me three times the money I was currently getting. And, as you've said, Nikkatsu was just starting up again, so I thought I'd have a better chance of moving up.

CD: Nikkatsu virtually stopped making jidai-geki *films by the sixties, but they still were making them in the fifties. After you became a director in the mid-fifties, you never directed any period samurai films. Was this by your choice or did production management make that decision?*

SUZUKI: I worked on some as an assistant director, but, by the time I actually started directing, Nikkatsu had all but stopped making any *jidai-geki* sword films. There were still a few, but the contemporary films far outnumbered them.

CD: What was behind Nikkatsu's decision to stop that kind of film? All the other Japanese studios continued making samurai films through the early seventies.

SUZUKI: Well, the problem was that they were having trouble making good films in that genre. They just didn't have any truly great *jidai-geki* swordplay stars to appear in them. Unlike the other studios. So they decided it would be better to concentrate exclusively on contemporary pictures.

CD: How did you feel about doing the earlier gangster and mystery films in the late fifties, lesser-known movies that I think are quite good?

SUZUKI: My mentor at Nikkatsu, the director I worked with most while I was still an assistant director, was Hiroshi Noguchi. He was really the first to do that kind of picture at Nikkatsu. So, when I began making my own films, Nikkatsu producers felt that I was already familiar with that type of action film. Those are the kind of scripts they started to send my way. As far as my feelings about them, my thoughts, I didn't and don't really think about them. I don't have any regrets. They're nothing special. I think they were okay, but there were many other movies being made like that at Nikkatsu during the same period. What you might call program pictures. I feel really the first film that I could call a signature film would be *Youth Of The Beast*.

CD: You'd also made Detective Office 23 – Go To Hell, Bastards! *and the two very anarchic youth films,* Everything Goes Wrong *and* Age Of Nudity, *all three of which are stylish and seemingly unique to your personality.*

SUZUKI: I suppose I'm not really aware as much of my style as people watching my movies, of how it was different from other directors. It's a difficult question.

RANCE: Do you think a lot of other directors were doing the same kind of editing, the same playing with surfaces by using lighting and actor blocking?

SUZUKI: As a kind of B movie director who would direct features that were usually a second feature to the A feature, the main feature, I was very aware of those other directors' stylistic decisions. My style at the time may have been slightly unusual, but I don't think it was enough to really make a difference.

CD: Could you tell me about the clown/hobo, played by Bokuzen Hidari, who pops up during the exploits of the delinquents in Age Of Nudity? *He's almost like the character that appeared later in Arthur Penn's* Mickey One *(1965) with Warren Beatty, the mute played by Kamatari Fujiwara who would follow Beatty around sometimes. I'm digressing a bit.*

SUZUKI: Hidari's character was already in the film script. His bum drifter character was originally supposed to have a dog. However, the studio thought the dog we had was too expensive for a drifter to have. They were changing all kinds of things. And the edit they did of the film was very different from my final cut. So, he appears at different times from those I had intended. It's very difficult to talk about.

CD: You worked on three films with actress Yumiko Nogawa: Gate Of Flesh, Carmen Of Kawachi *and* Story Of A Prostitute. *She made several* yakuza *films at Nikkatsu, including the* Cat Girl Gambling *(Mesu Neko Bakuchi, 1965–1966) trilogy that Hiroshi Noguchi directed. Were you ever asked to team with her on a* yakuza *scenario?*

SUZUKI: Nikkatsu didn't really make too many female *yakuza* pictures until after I had already left the studio in 1967.

CD: Although Yumiko Nogawa predominantly did films at Nikkatsu, she also appeared in films at Toei and Daiei during the sixties. She's such a unique actress, I was wondering how you became aware of her?

SUZUKI: She was a contract player, but I'm not sure how she worked it out to be in movies at the other studios. She did have a manager, so maybe he contacted them and arranged it.

CD: There were many sequences in your later Nikkatsu films that had offbeat or incongruous imagery; for example, in Youth Of The Beast, *the gang boss beating up his addict mistress with a raging sandstorm outside the window. Was there any meaning behind those images or did you just do it because it looked good on film?*

SUZUKI: There wasn't anything like a symbolic meaning behind those artistic decisions. It was, in that case, how best to emphasize, to reinforce, that something horrible was happening. In my moviemaking philosophy, there are three ways, all using natural elements, to make a film interesting: one is wind, two is rain, three is snow. For that particular scene, it seemed right to use the wind. These are practical reasons.

CD: In Gate Of Flesh, *you had Joe Shishido as a veteran who is anti-American. Since it was the sixties, when there was sensitivity about the Security Treaty with the US and about student demonstrations, was Nikkatsu worried having a character so violently anti-American?*

SUZUKI: No, they didn't feel that it was a problem.

Joe Shishido, Annu Mari in *Branded To Kill*

CD: There were many shocking images in the film, including the scene where Shishido and the girls slaughter the cow. Was that actually filmed on the set?

> SUZUKI: The actual shots of the cow being killed were shot at a slaughterhouse and the shot was lit and composed in such a way that it would match, so we could integrate it easily into the rest of the sequence. The slaughter-house was in the suburbs. We just packed up our trucks, went there without permits, told them we were making a film and they let us shoot it.

CD: There were unusual approaches to color, such as the individual prostitutes shown with their color-coded dresses and coordinated lighting schemes, the superimpositions when Nogawa is tortured, etc. Visual ideas more daring than what you were warned for in the later Tattooed Life. *Did these images in* Gate Of Flesh *pass unnoticed by Nikkatsu, or did you in fact receive warnings?*

> SUZUKI: Yes, I got warned about *Gate Of Flesh*, too. (*laughs*) By that time, I was getting warned every time I made a picture!

CD: Have you seen any of the other later versions of Gate Of Flesh – *the 1977 Nikkatsu version by Shugoro Nishimura, or the 1985 Toei one directed by Hideo Gosha?*

> SUZUKI: My version, too, was actually a remake of the original film that Masahiro Makino did in 1949. To do a remake is a very courageous thing, so I don't look down or feel negatively toward the other versions you mentioned. But I don't really have any feelings about them.

CD: In Flower And The Angry Waves, *Akira Kobayashi gets slightly disfigured. Was that in the script or did you come up with that to subvert the rabid Kobayashi fan base, who revered him as a matinee idol?*

> SUZUKI: To tell you the truth, I don't remember Kobayashi getting scarred in *Flower And The Angry Waves*. But in *Kanto Wanderer*, the first day of shooting, Mr Kobayashi had an idea for the way his character should look and came out of make-up with these huge eyebrows. The producer said, 'That's just ridiculous. We can't have that.' But I said to Kobayashi, 'Let's do it since he doesn't like it.'

CD: Why did the bosses have a problem with Tattooed Life? *There didn't seem to be overt stylistic differences from other Nikkatsu ninkyo yakuza pictures at the time. Aside from a stylized swordfight at the end, there weren't really the radical approaches to action and composition you used in* Tokyo Drifter *and* Branded To Kill.

> SUZUKI: As I've said, by that time I was getting warned on every picture I did. There was this one particular producer at Nikkatsu who used to come up to me every time after I'd just finished a film and say, 'Okay, this it. You can't do anything more. You've gone too far.' I don't think, at that point, it was anything in particular that I was doing. If I hadn't been at Nikkatsu, I don't know if I would have been having the same problems. There were many other people involved in my films, too (for instance, the writer and the production designer), so I can't take credit for every idea that appears up on the screen. Frequently, those were ideas suggested by someone I was working with, and I decided to implement them. I often was merely emphasizing certain elements that already existed in

the script or production design or performer's mind. It's the director's job to make a picture either serious or comic or genuinely tragic. That, in my opinion, is where the idea of a good director or a bad director comes in. How you choose to interpret your material. A director is someone who makes decisions. Say, there's a particular scene in a film showing a technique of killing someone. It's the director's job to decide to make it serious or funny. Those are the kind of decisions that got me into trouble later in *Tokyo Drifter* and especially *Branded To Kill*. The decisions I made went against the grain.

11

Teruo Ishii

1924–

My friend Yoshiki Hayashi, who helped set up the following interview, told me that he and his friends called Teruo Ishii's home the 'spy action house.' Once you entered, you understood the reference. The furnishings and interior combine a hybrid art deco/Aubrey Beardsley sense of style with the spartan functionality of a dyed-in-the-wool filmmaker. Accompanied by his lovely young assistant, who aided in translating the interview, Ishii made his appearance from a corridor lined with videotapes. Although in his mid-seventies, he was clad in black turtleneck and black trousers and crowned with a black mop-top of hair. There was the enigmatic aura of the trickster about him, and his eyes sparkled mischievously as he welcomed us. Enjoying himself, his answers were glib and precise, often no more than a few sentences and missing backstory, perhaps because he instinctively realized I was intent on covering too much ground. The size of his film output is enormous, exceeded in this volume only by Koji Wakamatsu.

Like Wakamatsu, Ishii is a bad boy, someone who has never liked being told what to do by studio higher-ups and is intent on going his own way, no matter the costs. Unlike Wakamatsu, however, Ishii charted a successful career at major Japanese studios that circumnavigated interference, at least for a couple of decades from 1957 through to 1979. He was at least partially responsible for transforming quiet, heroic heart-throb Ken Takakura from a journeyman actor into a huge box-office draw in the mid-sixties, something he accomplished directing the first ten *Abashiri Prison* films with Takakura – entertaining potboilers mixing violent action and romance with the trappings of the burgeoning *yakuza* movie boom.

The English translation of Ishii's autobiography, written with Kenji Fukuma, is *Teruo Ishii, Movie Devil*, and when you've seen a smattering of his wildest pictures you realize why. Ishii's initial cinematic forays at struggling Shintoho studios, the *Super Giant* serial (released straight to television in America as the four *Starman* movies), are his most famous in the West, and are designed primarily for children.

But these superhero-from-space sagas already displayed a macabre visual dementia that would have scared the pants off me had I seen them in a movie theater as a child. Most of Ishii's late fifties Shintoho films were produced by Mitsugu Okura, an instinctive, bigger-than-life showman recruited to rejuvenate Shintoho's stagnant box office. In retrospect, Okura's carnival huckster sensibility seemed tailor-made for filtering Ishii's eccentric world-view, perceptions shaped by everything from quirky *manga* to the erotic/grotesque stories of Japanese mystery writer Edogawa Rampo.

Perhaps Ishii's most significant pictures at Shintoho were for the *Line* series, *Black Line Zone* emerging as the most noirish and relentlessly gutsy, and the *Queen Bee* series, all prophetic in charting a style that would soon become commonplace in contemporary *yakuza* films of the following decade. In particular, the *Queen Bee* movies are trailblazing examples of the female action crime films that later proliferated at most Japanese studios in the late sixties and seventies. The third entry, the superior *Queen Bee And The School For Dragons*, is still astonishing today in its exhilarating vitality and display of virtually non-stop action.

In 1961 Ishii left the nearly bankrupt Shintoho for Toei, a studio reaping financial rewards from its successful samurai and contemporary action pictures. Ishii's first movie there, *The Flower, The Storm And The Gang*, combined swinging rat pack imagery with gangster and heist/caper motifs and proved successful enough to spawn the *Gang* series, the best of which were probably Ishii's *Underworld Boss – Eleven Gangsters* and Kinji Fukasaku's *League Of Gangsters*. Ishii directed one of Toei's first *ninkyo yakuza* pictures, too, the excellent Koji-Tsuruta-starring *Tale Of Showa Era Chivalry* in 1963. He also made one of John Woo's favorite *yakuza* pictures, *The Rogues*, in 1964, a film shot on location in Macao that, along with Jean-Pierre Melville's *Le Samourai*, was enormously influential in the development of Woo's *The Killer*. Ishii helmed *Tattooed Sudden Attack* with Ken Takakura the same year, a nihilistic tale of *yakuza* drafted as shock troops into Japan's late 1930s conflict in Manchuria.

However, *Abashiri Prison* in 1965 was the watershed moment in Ishii's – and Takakura's – career, catapulting them into the front ranks of box-office success stories. Toei, happy with the dividends, convinced Ishii to direct nine more *Abashiri* films in the course of the next two years. All featured Takakura as a hard-headed, soft-hearted ex-con drifter who couldn't keep from falling into doomed love or crossing the path of unscrupulous *yakuza*. But Ishii had had enough by 1967 and turned the reins over to other directors, who continued the series for another eight films.

As a reaction to what had become a monotonous chore Ishii wanted to do something different, and he got the green light from Toei brass for a series of in-period, low-budget Grand Guignol epics detailing horrible, unorthodox 'criminal' punishments throughout Japanese history. Four of the six pictures were constructed as anthologies, but the first, *Shogun And Three Thousand Women*, was one of two that eschewed the multi-story format. It has its moments, with the jaded

Shogun (oft-used Ishii veteran Teruo Yoshida) rejecting the libidinous dictates of his main ladies-in-waiting for the love of his favorite mistress, but unable to follow through when the shy woman goes blind and becomes a Buddhist nun. He is then murdered by one of his other jealous paramours. It's pretty anemic compared to what followed, and gives little hint of the aesthetically beautiful cinema of cruelty Ishii had up his sleeve. *Joys Of Torture* came next, establishing the framing device of a humane doctor of the samurai class (Teruo Yoshida) recalling three horror stories of sadistic oppression by people in power. The doctor (still played by Yoshida) returns in *Orgies of Edo*, another trilogy of erotic/grotesque madness. *Hell's Tattooers* is a feature-length tale of two rival tattoo artists – one decent, one depraved – in love with the same girl, against the backdrop of an illicit trade in tattooed women sold to corrupt Western merchants. *Love And Crime* chronicles four stories of murder motivated by love and lust spanning the 1880s through to the 1960s. Likewise, *Yakuza Punishment – Lynch Law!* spins three yarns of sadistic gangland justice, one from the early 1800s, another from the start of the twentieth century and the last from the swinging sixties. All display Ishii's enthrallingly gruesome, weird brand of showmanship, earmarked by outstanding performances and production design, and sometimes gorily convincing effects.

In 1969 the intoxicating head of creative steam Ishii was building blew its stack. The result, a startling adaptation of several tales by Edogawa Rampo, was the unqualified masterpiece *Horror Of Malformed Men*. Unfortunately, because of its depiction of scientifically altered freaks à la *Island Of Dr Moreau*, it enjoys a politically incorrect reputation in Japan and has never been available on video. Hopefully, this will change in the near future, because it is an exhilarating, mesmerizing horror film that deserves to be seen. The dreamlike journey, which begins in an insane asylum and ends on an island of phantasmagorical terror compares favorably to such other macabre Japanese masterworks as Nobuo Nakagawa's *Hell* (*Jigoku*, 1960).

Throughout the seventies Ishii churned out superior genre films, starting the decade with the gleefully grotesque, occasionally humorous, female *yakuza* film *Blind Woman's Curse*, starring Meiko Kaji. Two more simultaneously beautiful and shocking female *ninkyo yakuza* pictures followed: *The Silk Gambler*, with the late Eiko Nakamura, based on a book by the notorious Oniriku Dan; and *Story Of A Wild Elder Sister – Widespread Lynch Law*, the latter the last of a gonzo pair starring the phenomenal Reiko Ike. In 1973 Ishii helmed the movie adaptation of *manga Bohachi Bushido*, originally penned by *Lone Wolf And Cub* creator Kazuo Koike. A lone wolf *ronin* (Tetsuro Tanba) co-opted by a gang of samurai-controlled pimps and whores comes to brutal, vivid life in the nocturnal wonderland of ancient Edo. Mid-decade, Ishii returned to Japan's snowy northern island of Hokkaido, the home of Abashiri Prison, to direct the atmospheric prison escape/revenge/heist picture *The Big Escape*, starring Ken Takakura and Bunta Sugawara. The years 1975 and 1976 also saw him churning out three of the very entertaining delinquent *Detonation!* series: *Violent Tribe*, *Violent Games* and *Season Of Violence*.

Due to the downturn in Japanese movie production Ishii worked mostly in television in the eighties, finally directing a *yakuza* picture again in 1991. But *The Hit Man* was a straight-to-video release. Ishii at last returned to the big screen in 1993 with an independently produced adaptation from his favorite *manga* writer, Yoshiharu Tsuge. *Master Of Gensan-Kan Inn* is a haunting series of shaggy dog tales, all featuring Shiro Sano as the Tsuge-like protagonist, an itinerant *manga* artist wandering through strange backwoods villages. Alternately funny and creepy, the film is an unassuming little masterwork, balancing dark humor, dreamlike images, erotica and a spooky loneliness that sticks with you long after you've finished watching.

Two more Tsuge adaptations followed, with the early twentieth-century *yakuza* yarn *Villain Field* and the bizarrely humorous *Wind-Up Type*. Ishii closed out the nineties with an ultra-low-budget remake of *Hell*, a gory slice of Grand Guignol theatre that hilariously skewers the Aum Shinkryo sect, amongst others. In 2001 Ishii ventured into digital video production with *Blind Beast Vs. The Dwarf*, another adaptation of Edogawa Rampo tales, this time starring nineties *enfant terrible* film-maker Shinya Tsukamoto, as well as Ishii veteran, Tetsuro Tanba.

TERUO ISHII – SELECTED FILMOGRAPHY

1957   *SUPER GIANT (SUPA JAIANTSU,* aka *KOTETSU NO KYOJIN)*
       RETURN OF SUPER GIANT (ZOKU SUPA JAIANTSU, aka *ZOKU KOTETSU NO KYOJIN)*
       SUPER GIANT – INVADERS FROM SPACE (SUPA JAIANTSU – KAISEIJIN NO MAJO)
       SUPER GIANT – THE EARTH IN DANGER (SUPA JAIANTSU – CHIKYU METSUBO SUNZEN)
       NUDE ACTRESS MURDER CASE – FIVE CRIMINALS (NIKUTAI JOYU GOROSHI – GONIN HANZAISHA)
       SUPER GIANT – SPACESHIP OF HUMAN DESTRUCTION (SUPA JAIANTSU – JINKO EISEI TO JINRUI HAMETSU)
       SUPER GIANT – DESTRUCTION OF THE SPACE FLEET (SUPA JAIANTSU – UCHUTEI TO JINKO EISEI GEKI TOTSU)
1958   *AMAGI LOVE SUICIDES – LOVE THAT BINDS IN HEAVEN (AMAGI SHINJU – TENGOKU NI MUSUBU KOI)*
       A WOMAN'S BODY AND THE WHARF (NYOTAI SAMBASHI)
       SECRET WHITE LINE ZONE (SHIROSEN HIMITSU CHITAI, aka *CALL GIRL TERRITORY)*
       QUEEN BEE'S ANGER (JO BACHI NO IKARI)
1959   *PINK BATTLEFIELD (SENJO NO NADESHI)*
1960   *BLACK LINE ZONE (KUROSEN CHITAI,* aka *INVISIBLE BLACK HANDS)*

GIRLS WITHOUT RETURN TICKETS (JOTAI UZUMAKI-TO, aka *THE ISLAND'S WHIRLPOOL OF WOMEN'S BODIES)*

YELLOW LINE ZONE (IERO RAIN, aka *OSEN CHITAI*, aka *TIGER TRACK ZONE)*

QUEEN BEE AND THE SCHOOL FOR DRAGONS (JO BACHI TO DAIGAKU NO RYU)

1961   *SEXY ZONE (SEKKUSHI – RAIN*, aka *SEKKUSHI CHITAI*, aka *GIRLS OF THE SECRET CLUB)*

THE FLOWER, THE STORM AND THE GANG (HANA TO ARASHI TO GYANGU)

MIST AND SHADOWS (KIRI TO KAGE)

1962   *LOVE AND THE SUN AND THE GANG (KOI TO TAIYO TO GYANGU)*

G-MEN OF THE PACIFIC (TAIHEIYO NO G-MEN)

GANG VS. GANG (GYANGU TAI GYANGU)

1963   *UNDERWORLD BOSS – ELEVEN GANGSTERS (ANKOKU GAI NO KAOYAKU – JUICHININ NO GYANGU)*

GANG VS. G-MEN – BREAK-IN OF THE COMPANY SAFE (GYANGU TAI G-MEN – SHUDAN KINKO YABURI)

KILL THE BOSS (BOSU O TOSE, aka *BOSS'S RUIN)*

TALE OF SHOWA ERA CHIVALRY (SHOWA KYOKAKUDEN)

1964   *TOKYO GANG VS. HONG KONG GANG (TOKYO GYANGU TAI HONG KONG GYANGU)*

THE ROGUES (NARAZU MONO, aka *THE RASCALS)*

GOLD WAREHOUSE BREAK-IN (GOKINZO YABURI, aka *ROBBING THE SHOGUN'S GOLD)*

TATTOOED SUDDEN ATTACK (IREZUMI TOTSU GEKI, aka *SHOCK TROOP OF OUTLAWS)*

1965   *THE BOSS (KAOYAKU)*

ABASHIRI PRISON (ABASHIRI BANGAICHI, aka *THE MAN FROM ABASHIRI JAIL*, aka *ABASHIRI NATIVE GROUND)*

RETURN FROM ABASHIRI PRISON (ZOKU ABASHIRI BANGAICHI)

ABASHIRI PRISON – SAGA OF HOMESICKNESS (ABASHIRI BANGAICHI – BOKYO HEN)

ABASHIRI PRISON – NORTHERN SEACOAST STORY (ABASHIRI BANGAICHI – HOKKAI HEN)

1966   *JAPAN'S ZERO ZONE – NIGHTWATCH (NIHON ZERO CHITAI – YORU O NERAE)*

ABASHIRI PRISON – DUEL IN THE WILDERNESS (ABASHIRI BANGAICHI –KOYA NO TAIKETSU, aka *BULLET AND THE HORSE)*

THE GREAT VILLAIN'S STRATEGY (DAI AKUTO SAKUSEN)

ABASHIRI PRISON – DUEL IN THE SOUTH (ABASHIRI BANGAICHI – NANGOKU NO TAIKETSU)

SACRED FIRE 101 – BODYGUARD'S MURDER (SHINKA 101 – KOROSHI NO YOJINBO)

ABASHIRI PRISON – DUEL IN THE SNOW COUNTRY (ABASHIRI BANGAICHI – DAISETSUGEN NO TAIKETSU)

1967   *ABASHIRI PRISON – DUEL AT THIRTY BELOW (ABASHIRI BANGAICHI – KETTO REIKA JANJU DO)*

THE SETTLEMENT (OTOSHIMAE, aka THREE GAMBLERS)

ABASHIRI PRISON – CHALLENGING THE WICKED (ABASHIRI BANGAICHI – AKU E NO CHOSEN)

ABASHIRI PRISON – DUEL IN THE BLIZZARD (ABASHIRI BANGAICHI – FUBUKI NO TOSO, aka SNOWSTORM COMBAT)

1968   *THE SETTLEMENT 2 (ZOKU OTOSHIMAE, aka THE FINAL DECISION)*

SHOGUN AND THREE THOUSAND WOMEN (TOKUGAWA ONNA KEIZU, aka TOKUGAWA WOMEN'S PEDIGREE)

JOYS OF TORTURE (TOKUGAWA ONNA KEIBATSUSHI, aka TOKUGAWA WOMEN'S PUNISHMENT)

1969   *ORGIES OF EDO (ZANKOKU-IJO-GYAKUTAI – GENROKU ONNA KEIZU, aka CRUEL AND STRANGE OPPRESSION – GENROKU ERA WOMEN'S PEDIGREE)*

RISING DRAGON'S IRON FLESH (NOBORI RYU TEKKA HADA, aka THE FRIENDLY KILLER)

HELL'S TATTOOERS (TOKUGAWA IREZUMI SHI – SEME JIGOKU, aka TOKUGAWA TATTOO STORY – HELL TORTURE, aka INFERNO OF TORTURE)

YAKUZA PUNISHMENT – LYNCH LAW! (YAKUZA KEIBATSUSHI – RINCHI!)

LOVE AND CRIME (MEIJI-TAISHO-SHOWA – RYOKI ONNA HANZAISHI, aka MEIJI, TAISHO AND SHOWA ERAS – SEARCH FOR BIZARRE FEMALE CRIMES)

HORROR OF MALFORMED MEN (EDOGAWA RANPO TAIZEN – KYOFU KIKEI NINGEN)

1970   *KILLERS' HIT LIST (KOROSHIYA NINBETSU CHO, aka KILLERS' CENSUS LIST)*

PRISONERS' BLACK LIST (KANGOKU NINBETSU CHO, aka PRISON CENSUS LIST)

BLIND WOMAN'S CURSE (KAIDAN NOBORI RYU, aka RISING DRAGON GHOST STORY, aka TATTOOED SWORDSWOMAN, aka HAUNTED LIFE OF A DRAGON-TATTOOED LASS)

1972   *THE SILK GAMBLER (HIZIRIMEN BAKUTO, aka TIGER LILY)*

1973   *BOHACHI BUSHIDO (PORUNO JIDAI GEKI – BOHACHI BUSHIDO, aka PORNO HISTORICAL STORY – BOHACHI BUSHIDO)*

STORY OF A WILD ELDER SISTER – WIDESPREAD LYNCH LAW (YASAGURE ANEGO DEN – SOKATSU RINCHI, aka FEMALE YAKUZA TALE – INQUISITION AND TORTURE)

MODERN CHIVALRY (GENDAI NINKYOSHI)

THE EXECUTIONER (CHOKU GEKI! JIGOKU KEN, aka DIRECT HIT! – HELL FIST)

THE EXECUTIONER 2 (CHOKU GEKI JIGOKU KEN – DAI GYAKUTEN, aka *DIRECT HIT! HELL FIST – THE BIG TURNABOUT)*

1975   *THE BIG ESCAPE (DAI DATSUGOKU)*
        DETONATION! VIOLENT TRIBE (BAKUHATSU! BOSO ZOKU)
        TRUE ACCOUNT OF THE 300,000,000 YEN CASE – STATUTE OF LIMITATIONS VERIFICATION (JITSUROKU SANOKU-EN – JIKO SEIRITSU)

1976   *DETONATION! VIOLENT GAMES (BAKUHATSU! BOSO YUGI)*
        SEASON OF VIOLENCE (BOSO NO KISESU)

1979   *VIOLENT WARRIOR (BORYOKU SENSHI)*

1991   *THE HIT MAN (ZA HITTOMAN – CHI WA BARA NO NIOI* , aka *THE HIT MAN – BLOOD SMELLS LIKE ROSES)*

1993   *MASTER OF GENSAN-KAN INN (GENSAN-KAN SHUJIN)*

1995   *VILLAIN FIELD (BURAI HEIYA*, aka *VAGABOND PLAIN)*

1998   *WIND-UP TYPE (NEJI-SHIKI)*

1999   *HELL (JIGOKU)*

2001   *BLIND BEAST VS. THE DWARF (MOJU TAI ISSUN BOSHI)*

TERUO ISHII – INTERVIEW

The following interview was conducted at Teruo Ishii's house in a suburb of Tokyo in early November, 1997. It was translated on-site by Ishii's assistant, Mamiko Itai. My friend who had set up the interview, journalist and writer Yoshiki Hayashi, was also present. Parts of this interview were later retranslated by Ai Kennedy.

CD: *Did you always want to be a film director?*

ISHII: (*laughs*) An accident.

CD: *How did you begin working at Shintoho?*

ISHII: I started working there as a cameraman.

CD: *What would you say was Shintoho's filmmaking philosophy? They were making the kinds of films in the fifties that Toei made in the late sixties.*

ISHII: Shintoho had a philosophy – everything was speed. The first important thing was speed, the second important thing was speed, everything was speed.

CD: *Hmm, because of money?*

ISHII: Yes.

CD: *The subject matter of their films seems shocking for the 1950s compared to other Japanese films at the time.*

ISHII: (*laughs*) I don't know much about that! In the fifties, the eighties or the nineties! The fifties were a long time ago. What titles?

CD: *Let's start at the beginning. You initially worked on the* Supergiant *series (known in the US as* Starman*). What was it like working on those?*

ISHII: Right after my first film, a producer friend said he had an idea. He knew how to make a person look as if they were flying on film through special effects. I asked him, 'Is that really possible?' He was intrigued by this idea that eventually became *Supergiant*.

CD: Shintoho's Queen Bee *series were some of the earliest modern* yakuza *films and went in the same direction Toei did in the sixties. There were visual ideas in the second film's title sequence, where the girls are dancing in the street, then the nightclub scenes, the gambling scenes. I was wondering how much freedom you had, because you can see many similar things in your later films?*

ISHII: I had a lot of freedom to do what I liked. Mainly because I didn't care what the producers said and just went ahead and did what I wanted.

CD: As in the Line *series? How did that series come about?*

ISHII: Before the *Line* series, I had had some trouble with the company. I thought maybe I was going to be fired. Then, after an almost one-year break, it was recommended that I make another kind of film. Which became the *Line* films. [*Note: a series about gangsters, private eyes, cops and hookers in Japan's red-light districts.*]

Poster for *Horror Of Malformed Men*

CD: What kind of trouble?

ISHII: My idea of the kind of film I wanted to make was very different from Shintoho's.

CD: How so?

ISHII: We didn't see eye to eye on the selection of actors, as well as producers and people on the technical side. The company was very strict. They were very specific about subject matter and the selection of actors. I was just bucking them every step of the way. They started to become upset, saying, 'Look, this is the way we do things in this company.' As a result, they gave me the year break. I wasn't too surprised, and thought there was nothing I could do about it. That's another reason I was glad when Toei became interested in me.

CD: How did things change as Shintoho got closer to bankruptcy?

ISHII: At the time I wasn't very surprised that they were going into bankruptcy. And I was on a part-time hiatus starting to work over at Toei, so when it happened I just moved over there.

CD: Why did Shintoho go bankrupt?

ISHII: They had distribution problems. They wanted to be independent of Toho, who distributed their films. And, because of the friction, distribution began getting worse as time went along. If they had stayed under the Toho umbrella, maybe they would have been better off.

CD: One of your first films at Toei was The Flower, The Storm And The Gang. *It seemed there was much more of an American influence on it – as in your Shintoho* Line *films – more of a film noir feel than the* yakuza *films Toei did in the sixties. What kind of freedom did Toei give you in that first* Gang *film?*

ISHII: They didn't give me that much. Which was understandable, since it was my first film there. But I wanted to make it my own, an original film, so I asked them for three days to rewrite the script. Once I got final approval, I just started shooting and followed my instincts. They pretty much left me alone after the script approval. I wanted to be happy with it in case something happened, and I was never able to make another film. But, still, I knew if I didn't succeed at Toei I would have no future in movies. It was a fine line I had to walk: still making sure I gave them what they wanted, but also doing what I thought would make the film work and my own creation.

CD: I know, in many Japanese genre films, studios would sometimes slavishly adhere to certain story elements with little leeway for deviation. Did Toei give you specific guidelines to follow?

ISHII: *(laughs)* They gave me guidelines for the *Gang* movies, but I didn't follow them! So they were surprised by that. But, almost always, after they saw the final cut they were happy with the results.

CD: In Tokyo Gang Vs. Hong Kong Gang, *Koji Tsuruta plays a drug addict. Since he was a star, was he worried about his image, or did Toei have a problem with him playing that kind of role?*

ISHII: No, neither he nor the studio had a problem with it.

CD: So Tokyo Gang Vs. Hong Kong Gang *and* The Rogues *were both shot in Hong Kong?*

ISHII: Yes.

CD: At the same time?

ISHII: No, we went back and forth two or three times during that period.

CD: Tale Of Showa Era Chivalry *was an early* ninkyo yakuza *film set in the pre-WW2 period. What do you think of that genre?*

ISHII: I wasn't interested in making that kind of movie, but the head of Toei forced me to do it.

CD: It's one of my favorite ninkyo yakuza *pictures! I like the ending, where Tsuruta dies on the boat going across the river, with his boss and girl and comrades clustered around him.*

ISHII: Really? *Tale Of Showa Era Chivalry* was one of the first of that type. Later, many other Toei directors did that kind of picture, but it was one of the first.

CD: Did Toei try to get you to direct other ninkyo yakuza *movies?*

ISHII: (*smiles*) No, they didn't try to get me to direct any more of them.

CD: Gold Warehouse Break-in *was one of the only conventional* jidai-geki *films you made. Was that another genre you weren't particularly interested in?*

ISHII: (*laughs*) The head of Toei was interested in the more conventional period *chanbara* film, and he recommended that I direct that picture. He was excited about the story. But I was never really enamored of that genre.

CD: Your most popular pictures from the sixties were from the Abashiri Prison *series. Nikkatsu had made a film adapted from the same* Abashiri Prison *story in 1959.*

ISHII: I hadn't seen the Nikkatsu version, but I'm fairly certain they had been pretty faithful to the original story. I was familiar with the novel, and wasn't interested in following it. I thought I had a good idea for my own version. I asked Toei if I could take a stab at it, and they said yes. So mine is very different from the Nikkatsu one.

CD: Did Toei intend from the start to make it into a series?

ISHII: (*laughs*) No!

CD: It was just going to be the one film?

ISHII: After the first film was so successful, they decided they wanted to continue it as a series. And they wanted me to direct them.

CD: It is obviously a type of yakuza *film. How did you approach it differently from the other Toei* yakuza *pictures?*

ISHII: At the time, I wanted to promote Ken Takakura's stardom. I decided to make his character a kind of everyman, but one who was faithful to a woman and the idea of unconditional love. An unselfish, honest character. I thought he was the perfect match for that romantic kind of role. We didn't always try to focus on the *yakuza* angle.

CD: Where did you get the inspiration for Naoki Sugiura's character, the sunglasses-wearing, tubercular, whistling killer from the third Abashiri Prison *film,* Saga of Homesickness?

ISHII: I had several ideas for his character. I wanted to make him sleazy, but cool at the same time. Sugiura's character was meant to be scary, in contrast to Takakura's character, someone who is almost but not quite square, a helpful and friendly straight arrow.

CD: But Sugiura was still somewhat sympathetic, even though he was a bad guy. You kind of liked him in spite of himself.

ISHII: That's very true.

CD: Duel In The Blizzard, *the tenth in the series, was the last one you directed. What did you think about the series when it continued with other directors?*

ISHII: (*laughs*) I was weary of the series, making almost the same picture time after time. So, I wanted to have Takakura killed in the last one I did. But, of course, that wasn't going to happen. After that I gave up my claim on the series to whichever director wanted to take it over.

CD: How did you think directors Masahiro Makino, Kiyoshi Saeki, Yasuo Furuhata did with the other later films?

ISHII: (*laughs*) I haven't seen any of them!

CD: You then worked on a different kind of film, the erotic/grotesque or zankoku (*cruelty*) *type, such as* Joys Of Torture, Hell's Tattooers, Orgies of Edo, Yakuza Punishment – Lynch Law! *How did that series come about? The films are bloody, full of sex and violence. But also surrealistic, too. Were these films your idea or Toei's?*

ISHII: I was tired of filmmaking after the *Abashiri* series. I wanted to go in a completely different direction. The idea for that kind of film was Toei's. But I wanted to go far out with the sex and the violence, to see as much as would be allowed. I made those films because I really wanted to see how far I could push the limit.

CD: The imagery in the films is distinctive, that erotic/grotesque look. How much of that was you and how much were in the screenplays to begin with?

ISHII: Some were inspired by the tales of Ryunosuke Akutagawa, stories like his *Portrait Of Hell* (*Jigoku Hen*). He also wrote the original stories on which *Rashomon* was based. The actual imagery was mostly mine.

CD: How were those films received by the critics when they were released?

ISHII: (*laughs*) The feedback was horrible. The reviews were all negative!

CD: The films must have been popular, though.

ISHII: Yes, they were popular.

CD: Toei continued to make them, even in the seventies and eighties, with other directors like Yuji Makiguchi.

ISHII: And they got much sicker.

CD: Yakuza Punishment *is the only one out on Japanese video. [Note: this has since changed; – as of spring, 2002, most of these have been released on Japanese video.]*

Are any of the others ever going to be released ? Both Joys Of Torture *and* Orgies of Edo *have been released on German video, dubbed in German.*

ISHII: Really? I didn't know they'd been released on German video. I don't think Toei has any plans to issue them on video here. They're very sensitive about what the critics will say.

CD: Being politically correct. There are many people in America who would like to see all those films. Many have come out as underground bootlegs.

ISHII: *(amazed)* Really?

CD: What about the Horror Of Malformed Men, *which came from Edogawa Rampo stories? How did that originate?*

Ken Takakura in *Abashiri Prison – Duel In The South*

ISHII: I'd liked Edogawa Rampo's stories for a long time. Rampo's stories were not very popular with Toei in the sixties. But, right during that period, Toei needed to get more films into their theaters, they had upcoming open playdates, so they told me to go ahead and make whatever kind of picture I wanted. I took them at their word and made that.

CD: *You then did two films for Nikkatsu,* Rising Dragon's Iron Flesh *and* Blind Woman's Curse.

ISHII: I knew the producer, a man by the name of Hideo Koi. He'd worked for Shintoho. He asked me to come over to Nikkatsu to direct those films.

CD: *Did Toei have a problem with that, that you were going to do some pictures for Nikkatsu?*

ISHII: I didn't have any problem, because I was a freelance director by then.

CD: *How much involvement did you have in the second film in the trilogy,* Rising Dragon's Soft Flesh Exposed *(Nobori Ryu Yawa Hada Kaicho). I saw your name on the movie poster.*

ISHII: I was busy doing a picture over at Toei at the same time so I made my assistant director, Masami Kuzuo, the main director, and I acted as a kind of advisor.

CD: *When I interviewed Meiko Kaji, she felt* Blind Woman's Curse *was basically a* ninkyo yakuza *film. But there were* kaidan *images in the picture, what with the hunchback played by Tatsumi Hijikata (from* Horror Of Malformed Men*), the cat licking up the blood, etc. How did you get the idea to blend the two genres?*

ISHII: *(laughs)* It's supposed to be the third in the *Rising Dragon* series. The company actually wanted me to work the ghost story elements into the film. I was already shooting when they asked me to start blending in the macabre imagery. I never could figure out any specific reason! But they were very insistent.

CD: *I must say it really worked. It's an original film. Very strange.*

ISHII: *(laughs)* The ghost story images? As far as being coherent, I feel the movie was nonsensical.

CD: *But isn't that the idea behind the erotic/grotesque genre? I thought the* yakuza *and horror were well integrated. Speaking of which, did Shintoho ever ask you to direct any* kaidan *while you were working there?*

ISHII: No, they never asked.

CD : *Back at Toei you did a film,* Bohachi Bushido, *that was another adaptation of* manga *by Kazuo Koike, creator of* Lone Wolf And Cub.

ISHII: Tetsuro Tanba and I were good friends. He owned the script and wanted to star with me directing. We went back and forth about it for a while, but he finally convinced me to make it.

CD: *In the sequel, directed by Takashi Harada, co-star Goro Ibuki came back but main star Tetsuro Tanba didn't appear. Do you have any idea why?*

ISHII: I didn't even know there was a second one!

CD: You then did two woman gambler movies: Story Of A Wild Elder Sister – Widespread Lynch Law, *with Reiko Ike, and* The Silk Gambler, *with Eiko Nakamura. Since Junko Fuji, who'd been successful in the* Red Peony Gambler *films, had just retired in 1972, was Toei trying to create another popular female* yakuza *series?*

ISHII: Yes, Toei was looking for a new face, a new personality who was capable of catching on as the next popular female *yakuza*. Sadly, Eiko Nakamura eventually committed suicide, many years later

CD: Did Toei originally intend for The Silk Gambler *to become a series? How did it do along with the* Elder Sister *pair of films?*

Reiko Ike in poster for *Story Of A Wild Elder Sister – Widespread Lynch Law*

ISHII: No, it was always intended to be just that one film. None of those were that successful. Now there are fans who have made those pictures cult films. I hear requests all the time from people who want videotapes of the pictures.

CD: *I'm one of those people. I've actually found posters of all of them.*

ISHII: (*laughs*)

CD: Modern Chivalry *with Ken Takakura was written by Shinobu Hashimoto. He usually did not write* yakuza *films, being more involved in prestigious* jidai-geki *films like* The Seven Samurai *and Hideo Gosha's* Hitokiri. *How did Toei manage to get him to write a* yakuza *film?*

ISHII: It's true, it was very unusual for Hashimoto to work on such a film. I did not really like his scenario. I don't feel that that film was very successful.

CD: *Did you want to change Hashimoto's screenplay?*

ISHII: I changed it some. But Hashimoto didn't like what I did, so he wanted to go back to his original scenario. The whole project seemed compromised.

CD: *After that there were the two* Executioner *films with Shinichi 'Sonny' Chiba.*

ISHII: (*laughs*)

CD: *The first one was more of an action, martial arts film. The second is much more of a comedy. Why was that?*

ISHII: (*laughs*) After I made the first one, which Toei liked a lot, they asked me to do a sequel. I didn't want to do it. So I decided to make it as a comedy!

CD: *At the beginning of the second one,* The Big Turnabout, *there's a sequence of many quick cuts, all violent and gory imagery. But there's not much more like that in the rest of the film. Why?*

ISHII: (*laughs*) I didn't have much of a plan for the film, so I just threw it in there at the beginning to make things more interesting, to hook the viewer.

CD: *The* bosozoku *films for your* Detonation! *series,* Violent Tribe, Violent Games *and* Season of Violence *– why did that genre become so popular? Was there much youth gang activity going on in Japan then?*

ISHII: *Bosozoku* gangs were starting to be in the news, and Toei wanted to take advantage of that, of the topicality, so they asked me to make some films in that vein. To tell you the truth, I didn't much care for the idea.

CD: *In* Violent Games, *there are off-the-wall sequences with choreographed rock 'n'roll numbers, almost modeled on the youth gang numbers in* West Side Story, *the finger-snapping; where did those ideas come from?*

ISHII: (*laughs*) To be frank, I couldn't come up with any other ideas. I decided to go with that because I thought it would be entertaining.

CD: *It really works.*

ISHII: (*laughs*) I don't even like talking about those films!

CD: *You worked in television in the seventies, some* chanbara *shows like* Crimson Bat *and others. What was it like working in Japanese television then, compared to film?*

ISHII: I didn't really see any difference between film and television. Of course, there was less money. Toei asked me to direct some television, so I did.

CD: Was that the Crimson Bat *series?*

ISHII: Yes.

CD: The TV show was Toei, but the films done a little earlier were by Shochiku. Why did Toei do the TV series?

ISHII: The Toei studio producer hadn't work at Toei at the time, he had worked through Shochiku when the movies were made.

CD: You've been enamored of the manga *of Yoshiharu Tsuge, doing films of his:* Master Of Gensan-Kan Inn *and* Villain Field, *and the one you recently completed,* Wind-Up Type. *What is it about Tsuge's* manga *that makes you want to adapt them to film?*

ISHII: He shows the very poor side of society in Japan, that's what interests me.

CD: In Villain Field *there's not only similar imagery from your earlier* yakuza *films but also the bizarre, sadistic imagery of* Horror Of Malformed Men *and* Hell's Tattooers. *I understand this is true of* Wind-Up Type, *also.*

ISHII: I was only using the same kind of imagery I found in the *manga*.

CD: Great minds think alike. When will Wind-Up Type *be released?*

ISHII: It should be out next spring. We've promised one small theater owner to show it in his place. But we haven't contracted with any major distributor as yet.

CD: Do you have any plans to direct any more action or yakuza *films?*

ISHII: (*laughs*) Just last month I was going to start on a *yakuza* movie for Toei but the production ran into – shall we say – some trouble. I ended up having to pull out of the project. They wanted to film a real true-life *yakuza* story, but I wanted to make some changes to the scenario. They rejected my ideas. So that was that.

CD: You've made many profitable films over the years. Can't you now pretty much do what you want?

ISHII: (*laughs*) Not really. I'm a veteran crank.

CD: All the successful films you've made, you'd think producers would just let you do what you want.

ISHII: (*laughs*) It's the same thing that happened with *Wind-Up Type*. No one wanted to adapt it from the *manga* because it is a very unusual story. That's what made me want to do it. I felt it would be an adventure trying to bring it to the screen. You can expect a funny, strange, adventurous film.

12

Koji Wakamatsu

1936–

If we are, indeed, to define outlaw filmmaking as transgression of one sort or another, Koji Wakamatsu would certainly have to receive honors as head transgressor. Even in this book full of wild cards, Wakamatsu sticks out as the wildest in the deck. Although he has managed to escape the kind of serious legal problems that colleagues like Masao Adachi have suffered for their political activism, he has, in some ways, gone much further, creating a body of work that is astounding in its scope. Even judging from the comparatively small number of his films available for viewing, his achievement as an outspoken artist faithful to his uncompromising vision is unquestionable. He is one of those rare catalytic filmmakers who, much like Kinji Fukasaku, Seijun Suzuki – and more recently – Takashi Miike, act as a lightning rod for attracting repressed talents in the fields of acting, writing, cinematography and production design. Talents that Wakamatsu molds, shapes, focuses. And what the unsuspecting viewer is left with is a startling glimpse through the microscope at a substrata of human existence most never even knew existed. His subject matter is dredged up from the primal scream realms of the superego, and he has acknowledged, since all of it is taking place in the make-believe world of film, that matters of morality, of right and wrong do not concern him. More than any other filmmaker I can think of, he approximates a kind of celluloid equivalent to the transgressive literary world-view of writers like Jean Genet and Isidore Ducasse (Lautreamont). A few years ago I wrote the following paragraph in description of Wakamatsu's movies, and I truthfully can't think of any way to better it:

'No matter how horrifying the subject matter, no matter how unflinching the camera eye that refuses to look away… He has the ability to depict disturbed mental states with a gritty visual eloquence, supplying an unobtrusive psychological subtext that coaxes a mysterious compassion for even the most unsympathetic monsters. Wakamatsu's poetic irony of juxtaposition combined with a surface detachment creates an atmosphere of clinical study gone gonzo, beyond all limits, establishing links with nether regions and tapping directly into the sexual libido and the subconscious – unconscious states of being beyond morality shaped in the womb, then molded by our families or lack thereof, and, by extrapolation, society-at-large.'

Wakamatsu goes into detail on his background in the following interview, so I won't repeat that here. Born in 1936, he found himself the youngest in a large family who made their meager living as farmers. Starting early on in school, Wakamatsu seemed to cultivate his smart aleck persona, never walking away from a fight and relishing the resulting reputation as a troublemaker. Finally, having had enough of life in the boondocks, he migrated to Tokyo, where he found a succession of jobs. Fueled by anger at condescending authority, he motivated himself into climbing slowly up the ranks, first in the television industry, then, in desperation, in the threadbare world of early sixties independent adult films.

Contrary to what has appeared previously in print, Wakamatsu was not ever a journeyman director at Nikkatsu studios. He made virtually all his initial films for fledgling adult film production companies, outfits that barely registered on the Japanese film industry's radar, let alone that of the West. He made his first film, the erotic *Sweet Trap*, in 1963.

Wakamatsu already showed promise as a perversely intuitive visual stylist and natural born storyteller from his earliest efforts. *Lead Tombstone* tracks the progress of a young sociopathic rake who had, immediately post-WW2, rescued his country farmer mother from rape by stabbing the offending American soldier in the back with a pitchfork. Once grown, the boy continues his violent life as a hoodlum on the run, repaying an outlaw couple who have sheltered him by raping the wife, then, at his boss's behest, murdering the husband. He's also not above strangling a girl in her bathtub for kicks. The one spot of normalcy in his life is his shop girl girlfriend, an innocent who, once she discovers his other life, confronts his boss. It's something that proves fatal, as the boss then orders the boy to kill her. Shooting her on a rocky cliff overlooking the beach, he's immediately remorseful, but when he bends over to caress her face another shot rings out, and he drops dead at her side.

Career Of Lust finds police investigating a whore who has been discovered with a strangled man in her bed. She gives them the low-down on her many tricks, including an amusing anecdote about the pick-up of a student demonstrator who'd been running from the cops and had taken refuge in her car. Throughout her narrative, she paints herself as a sympathetic victim. But, finally, her main trick gives evidence, admitting he's the murderer. He had been dismayed at finding the man, her pimp, sleeping in his lover's bed. Exonerated, the whore lets loose with a torrent of verbal abuse at the man, and the police have to restrain him from committing further mayhem

In 1964 Wakamatsu briefly worked for Nikkatsu, using the bare bones of a project he had pitched to them, but turning in a picture that his producers were less than happy with. *Secret Acts Within Four Walls* observes a student living at home with his family while he is cramming for exams. No matter how hard he studies, the boy knows he's going to fail, so he distracts himself with pornography and by spying through his telescope at various women who live in the apartment house across the street. One day when his parents are at work, he rapes and strangles his sister, then visits a jaded housewife in the next building. Making what are at first unwanted advances, the woman eventually gives in, having sex with the boy, only for him to suddenly grab a knife from the bedside and stab her to death. Shot in a claustrophobic style, the movie *does* strike a disturbing note, but it seems fairly tame compared to what would come from even major studios later in the decade. Though Nikkatsu was unsure what to do with the picture, a Berlin film festival organizer had seen it and, impressed with its stark, matter-of-fact approach, wanted to feature it in competition. This created a bit of a scandal, as Eirin, the film board who submitted Japanese movies to festivals, had not been consulted. When *Secret Acts* was ultimately released in Japan, Nikkatsu gave it low-key distribution with little publicity, afraid they might be targeted for obscenity again after being raked over the coals by the courts for Tetsuji Takechi's politically radical *Black Snow* (*Kuroi Yuki*).

Stung by what he considered ill-treatment, Wakamatsu began his own production company shortly thereafter, but he also continued to make films for the little adult companies. One of these was *Perverse Liaisons*, the tale of a doctor accused of murdering his unfaithful wife. As the cops investigate, we're treated to flashbacks of a sleazy private eye putting the doctor in the know about his spouse's erotic obsession with another man. Before the running time is up, we learn that the doctor's crippled nurse had hated the wife and had seen her infidelity as a way to snare the doctor for her own. But, when things had not gone her way, she had approached a handyman who had once raped her, extorting him to give her some of his sperm so that she could kill the wife then inject the fluid between the corpse's legs, making it appear she had been killed by a man.

Wakamatsu's first high-profile film that he produced himself was *The Embryo Hunts In Secret*, a steel trap of a movie that is set almost entirely in one claustrophobic apartment. A man makes love to his girlfriend, then suddenly decides to tie her up against her will, brutalizing her with a whip and other tortures while flashbacking to his father's treatment of his mother. Wakamatsu embroiders the shots with delicate, classical music, and an agonizing, oneiric delirium is achieved that threatens to drown the female character in mental toxicity. Finally, she manages to turn the tables, grabbing one of the instruments of torture and stabbing her tormentor. At which point, he curls into a fetus position and dies in her lap, murmuring 'mother'.

Based on Richard Speck's murders of student nurses in Chicago, *Violated Angels* was co-written by, and stars, avant garde playwright Juro Kara as the delusional young man who is invited inside an isolated women's seaside dorm, only to hold them prisoner and kill them one by one. Clocking in at just under an hour, *Violated Angels* is one of Wakamatsu's most harrowing pictures, and one of the most convincing studies in paranoid psychosis ever committed to film. The movie's duration is

rendered nearly unbearable as the women each take different approaches in dealing
with their captor, some trying to tempt him with sex, others trying to reason with
him and still others just panicking. But their efforts are futile. At the conclusion,
when there is only one left alive, a girl who talks soothingly to him and seems to
understand his feelings, the film switches from black and white to color in a shot
that positions the girls' bodies in a bloody mandala pattern radiating outwards, the
sick young man – now nude – resting his head in the lap of the last girl, who is also
naked. Then, just as suddenly, she is gone, and the boy is left with his carnage.
There are still frames of the police breaking in from outside as well as shots of

Poster for *Career Of Lust*

police violence at student demonstrations, a juxtaposition that seems to imply that, in a bigger picture, the institutionalized violence of authority is no more acceptable than that perpetrated by a madman.

In contrast, *Womb To Let* is a very different kind of a story, examining the relationships of a wealthy middle-aged man and his young wife and that of the man's daughter, who is the same age as his spouse, and her student boyfriend. Whereas the young wife is obviously motivated by a desire for a comfortable life and betrays her husband by having an affair with her gynecologist, the daughter is genuinely in love with her boyfriend. However, Wakamatsu doesn't paint the picture as black and white as it first appears. The daughter is tormented by her father's primarily sexual relationship with his new wife, but the daughter's own boyfriend wants her to participate in a free-love orgy he and his hippie friends have organized. When the daughter realizes she's pregnant by her beau, her stepmother arranges for an abortion at her gynecologist. But this leads to the discovery of the wife's affair with the doctor, something that threatens her sheltered existence, and, as her husband appears ready to throw her out, the wife snaps and runs him through with his antique sword. Meanwhile, the daughter collapses in the street, still weak from the abortion. Witnessed by her passing boyfriend, their estrangement terminates as he helps her to his place and gently nurses her back to health. Wakamatsu's ability to calmly dissect economic and sexual components endemic to marriage as a class-based institution is succinct and non-judgemental, letting the reality of the situation speak for itself. *Womb To Let* is one of his least-known but most impressive films.

Although Wakamatsu held an aversion for Japan's major studios, he would sometimes give into a directing-for-hire gig to finance his independent company, an example being Shochiku's *The Concubines*, starring Tomoko Mayama as legendary femme fatale Pan Chin Lien, and future director Juzo Itami as a sex-crazed Chinese warlord who raises her up from her common status after she murders her husband. Wakamatsu's ability to coax astounding mileage up on the screen from every yen was undoubtedly the attraction he held for Shochiku, and, notwithstanding occasionally threadbare production values and clumsy action choreography, he achieves a raw period ambience unlike the studio's other directors, except for perhaps Hideo Gosha. Wakamatsu also unpretentiously shows how personal betrayals, sexual or otherwise, have a way of mushrooming into larger-scale breaches of faith, resulting in political turmoil and economic injustice.

Wakamatsu repeatedly drew from a pool of talented, relatively unknown performers, many of whom he used repeatedly. Ken Yoshisawa, an actor who had appeared in *Womb To Let* as the student boyfriend and who bears more than a passing resemblance to *Violated Angels*' Juro Kara, returns in *Crazy Love Suicides*. Many of Wakamatsu's sixties productions had intermittent color sequences, but this film was one of his few all-color pictures from that decade. Yoshisawa plays a student demonstrator returning home after a protest ends in a violent altercation with the police, only to get into a heated argument with his older brother (Rokko

Toura), who is also a cop. Toura's timid wife stands helplessly by, reluctant to intervene. But, when Toura begins thrashing Yoshisawa, she begins to fear for the boy's life. Toura is still wearing his gun, and when he fails to stop the beating after his wife's repeated pleas she draws the weapon and shoots him. Yoshisawa and the stunned spouse believe him dead, and they go on the run, taking a train north, finally reaching the northern point of Japan. At first they intend on going their separate ways, but the wife is so despondent she attempts suicide several times. Yoshisawa realizes he can't leave her alone, and together they start wandering over the snowy countryside. Eventually, they succumb to their natural attraction to each other, and both escape the guilt of their accidental crime by drowning themselves in sex. One day the husband appears out of nowhere on a deserted, snow-covered road, almost like a ghost. Apparently, he had only been wounded. He has only words of derision for his sibling but proceeds to trounce his wife. Powerless, Yoshisawa looks on sheepishly, unable even to make an attempt to stop Toura, as the wife had done for him. After Toura's finished he walks off, and the wife pathetically picks herself up to follow him. Wakamatsu disallows any kind of catharsis that would come from the boy overcoming his tyrannical brother, instead seeming to imply the impotence of all idealistic, naturally non-violent youth in the face of unreasoning brutality.

A man and his lover, the mistress of a sadistic *yakuza* boss, are spirited away into a deserted wasteland and punished for their liaison in *Violent Virgin*. The woman is crucified with rope to a cross while guffawing gangster flunkies set up a tent in front of her, throwing her boyfriend inside *sans* clothes with a succession of sleazy, wisecracking prostitutes. The man is finally able to get the drop on one of the whores, strangles her, takes her slip to wear and sneaks out under the back flap to run unobserved down a gulley. When the hoods realize what he's done he's long gone, collapsed in an unconscious heap several miles away and having the daddy of all nightmares. He eventually wakes, to realize that the reality of his situation is just as bad. Wandering, he comes upon an encampment of some jaded men, who begin to poke fun at him. They have a high-powered rifle fixed to a tripod and force him to pull the trigger, then let him go. He makes his way back to try to rescue his girl but, to his horror upon arriving, realizes the man with the rifle had been the *yakuza* boss who had tricked him into shooting the girl, himself. At this point, he goes berserk, dispatching the remaining thugs with a club. He's left with utter devastation, and Wakamatsu adds to the delirious nightmare resolution by presenting static compositions of the carnage with various color tints, something that transforms the scene into one of surreal beauty.

On his next picture, Wakamatsu again chased his obsessive need to challenge himself by filming virtually his whole scenario on one claustrophobic set. *Go, Go Second Time Virgin* explores the anachronistic quest for redemption by purifying death in the face of bestial humanity. Wakamatsu witnesses the events of one night as a young girl is repeatedly raped by a gang of delinquent boys on a broiling summer rooftop. After it's over and her assailants gone, she is befriended by a nerdy outcast who did not participate. The viewer learns that he, too, is a victim of sexual abuse, having butchered his molesting parents and friends earlier in the day after being forced to participate in an orgy. A blood-soaked catharsis unfolds, as he kills his fellow teen males then has an awkwardly sweet tryst with his new girlfriend. At dawn, they validate their love with a suicidal leap off the roof into oblivion.

Two undercover cops put a student activist (Ken Yoshisawa) under surveillance by camping out in the apartment below his in a *Tale Of Modern Lovers – Season Of Terror*, keeping a bored vigil beside the tape recorder that's hooked to microphones they planted while he was out. However, nothing much transpires. Unemployed Yoshisawa is supported by his two live-in girlfriends, with whom he enjoys a *ménage à trois*, and all the detectives are ever rewarded with is an aural display of erotic lovemaking, something that makes their job doubly frustrating. At one point, they think they've hit pay dirt when Yoshisawa is visited by one of his former compatriots, especially when the girls are asked to leave. But the disillusioned Yoshisawa is unmoved by his firebrand friend, who eventually departs after becoming fed up. The cops realize they're wasting their time, pack up and leave. But, a few days later, Yoshisawa reads about the brutal suppression of a protest demonstration and abruptly decides to act on his own. Once his girlfriends have left for work, he straps a belt of dynamite around his waist and heads to the Haneda airport. Yoshisawa disappears into the main terminal, and a few minutes later there's the sound of a deafening explosion. Perhaps one of the most disturbing tenets of *Season Of Terror* is Wakamatsu's suggestion that, because of the disharmony and disorganization in most political activist groups, the logical, depressing next step for action comes from suicidal individual commitment.

The police are once more after student demonstrators in *Sex Jack*. At the beginning, Wakamatsu includes some amazing footage that he had shot from a rooftop with Masao Adachi of a peace demonstration being brutally put down by the police. Then, later that night, he cuts to a fleeing band of students who are finally cornered by plainclothes detectives. The youths turn the tide, overcoming their pursuers and confiscating a police revolver before disappearing into the darkness. Holed up in a cramped one-room flat, most of the male activists indulge in non-stop consensual sex with the two girl members. There's one timid boy, though, who always been on the fringe, never able to participate in the violence and intimidated by the open sexual intimacy. By the end, when the police are tipped off by the original student leader and track the rebels to a field on the edge of town, the timid boy is now in possession of the gun. He erupts into action, killing the cops as well as the betrayer.

Secret Flower yet again features Wakamatsu's fetish for spare one-set dramaturgy, centering around a decaying wooden boat wreck on a deserted stretch of beach. A repressed, nondescript young woman pines away for an ex-lover (Ken Yoshisawa) who left her for a more vivacious, loud-mouthed extrovert (Rie Yokoyama).

She often sits in the wreck, flashing back on her hot-blooded trysts there with Yoshisawa and hoping to glimpse him, since he still uses the boat to have sex with his new girl. Whenever the couple run into the old flame, Yoshisawa's new lover spews a torrent of verbal abuse. Yoshisawa meets the ex-lover once when he's alone, and he tries to seduce her – only to find she now wears an iron chastity belt under her traditional kimono. A jealous tug-of-war develops between the three when Yoshisawa briefly returns to his former flame, but the new girl at last wins out, pulling Yoshisawa away. The old lover is left weeping on the sand as the boat bursts into flame and burns. Wakamatsu includes flashbacks culled from Yoshisawa's scenes with Rokko Toura in *Crazy Love Suicides*, and it's unclear if *Secret Flower* is a kind of loose sequel and Yoshisawa the same character, or Wakamatsu merely included the scenes because he had access to the footage and felt the need to create backstory.

By the time of *Ecstasy of the Angels*, Wakamatsu had already been more flagrantly integrating his radical, anarchic world-view into his erotic psychodramas. *Ecstasy* was written by Izuru Deguchi, but Deguchi was not a single individual but a pseudonym. Sometimes it would signify Wakamatsu's collaboration with militant filmmaker Masao Adachi, sometimes scripts done with trailblazing screenwriter Atsushi Yamatoya, and sometimes a combination of the two and/or others. In *Ecstasy*, a deeply submerged militant group who are identified only by their code names – the days of the week – discover that they've been betrayed by their own parent organization when a nocturnal weapons raid on a US army base goes terribly wrong. The delicate balance of mutual trust implodes, and the young militants (Ken Yoshisawa, Rie Yokoyama, et al.) find themselves adrift in sexual paranoia and

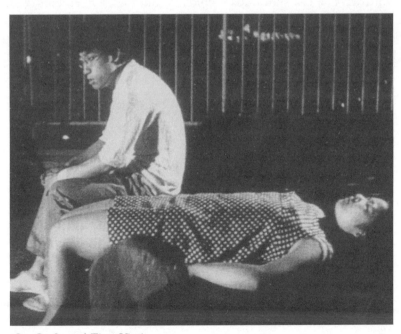

Go, Go Second Time Virgin

fierce recrimination when attacked by a sister group. The outsiders claim to supersede all authority and inflict sadistic torture to enforce their dominance, something that completely destroys Yoshisawa and cohorts' ability to function as a unit. Produced in conjunction with the Art Theater Guild (usually known as ATG), *Ecstasy Of The Angels* is one of Wakamatsu's most bitterly humorous, disturbing and personal dissections of how idealistic fringe groups that could possibly destabilize society become neutralized not only by authority but by their own factional infighting.

Yuya Uchida is a sexually repressed, emotionally numb subway ticketman in *Pool Without Water*. He rescues a girl who is about to be gang-raped in the midst of a driving rainstorm, and, in gratitude, she invites him back to her place for a glass of milk. However, he can't even speak and leaves abruptly. One day, while reading his paper and being harangued by his wife, he notices his little boy using a chemical to render bugs unconscious so he can kill them for his insect collection. Inspired, he researches how to use the toxic chemical, buys a quantity and begins to insert a tube through the windows of various girls he's attracted to, feeding in the knockout gas. Once the girls are unconscious he enters with an air-filtered mask and goes about undressing, photographing and finally molesting them. Often he will clean their house and fix them breakfast before leaving in the morning. The girls become increasingly mystified and unnerved by their unseen stalker. At last, Uchida goes too far, bringing several of his unconscious subjects to another out-cold girl's flat. Overcome with erotic delirium, he removes his mask and promptly passes out, too. The girls awake before he does, and he opens his eyes to find them and nosy neighbors staring down at him with the the police on the way. He hurriedly leaves. The last shot finds Uchida spread eagled in an empty swimming pool he likes to frequent. A bizarre, depressing, sometimes funny examination of what Wakamatsu seems to suggest is the emotionally disconnected psyche of the typical Japanese male.

Ecstasy Of The Angels

Ready To Shoot is one of Wakamatsu's most critically acclaimed recent pictures, a film that strikes a balance between his own tastes and that of the general public without compromising his vision. A former sixties radical (Yoshio Harada) owns a small bar, and, though with little opportunity to show it, he still feels committed to his original ideals. He suddenly gets to put his thoughts into action when a Vietnamese girl forced into prostitution by the *yakuza* hides out in his tiny club. His decision to help her causes friends both to leave him and to die at the hands of the gangsters. By the end he's wiped out her exploiters, but is mortally wounded himself. One of Wakamatsu's most emotionally resonant pictures, *Ready To Shoot* achieves its effect by jettisoning sentimentality and showing real people standing for what they believe in, without any kind of calculated manipulation.

Endless Waltz is essentially the bio of a self-destructive, epileptic Ornette-Coleman-style sax player as seen through the eyes of his independent girlfriend. The viewer is treated to a rare glimpse of Japan's music and arts underground from the bygone era of the 1970s. Reona Hirota is breathtakingly fine as Izumi, the no-nonsense, unconventional woman who eventually bears the disturbed musician a daughter. When he purposely overdoses on pills near the end, she goes heroically on, but ultimately she gives up, hanging herself. As her now six-year-old daughter stares at her mother's body, Wakamatsu cuts to Hirota joining the dead musician on a snow-covered street, ultimately reaching his side permanently in the afterlife. There is no claptrap sentimentalism on display, only the very painful knowledge that their innocent little girl will have to grow up alone under the legacy of suicided parents.

Although uncompromising in concept and execution, pictures like *Ready To Shoot* and *Endless Waltz* may not seem as angry or confrontational on the surface when compared to Wakamatsu's earlier excavations in the dark wilderness of the Japanese psyche. But, like his earlier films, they retain the power to disturb, suck in and mesmerize the viewer with Wakamatsu's ongoing theme: human emotions battling to emerge from desensitized individuals, protagonists poisoned at birth by a cold-hearted, sexually perverse and consumed-by-material-greed society.

KOJI WAKAMATSU – SELECTED FILMOGRAPHY

1963   *SWEET TRAP (AMAI WANA)*
       SAVAGE WOMEN (HAGESHI ONNATACHI)
       EROTIC STRATEGIES (OIROKE SAKUSEN)
1964   *EVIL AGONY (AKU NO MODAE)*
       ILLICIT REWARD (FURIN NO TSUGUNAI)
       GAME OF BITCHES (MESU INU NO KAKE)
       RED CRIME (AKAI HANKO)
       WOMAN IN THE NET (AMI NO NAKA NO ONNA)
       CONTRARY DESIRES (GYAKU JO)

PALE FLESH (KAWAITA HADA)

NAKED SHADOW (HADAKA NO KAGE)

ESCAPE OF WHITE FLESH (SHIROI HADA NO DASSHUTSU)

LEAD TOMBSTONE (NAMARI NO BOHYO), aka *TOMBSTONE DIALECT*

1965   *DIVORCE BUSINESS (RIKONYA KAIGYO CHU)*

CAREER OF LUST (RIREKISHO NO JOJI), aka *HISTORY OF SEXUAL LIAISONS*

THE SUN'S NAVEL (TAIYO NO HESO)

FILTHY TRAP (BODOKU NO WANA)

SECRET ACTS WITHIN FOUR WALLS (KABE NO NAKA NO HIMEGOTO)

PERVERSE LIAISONS (YUGANDA KANKEI), aka *WARPED RELATIONS*

DROPS OF BLOODY PASSION (YOKUBO NO CHI GA SHITATARU), aka
CRAVING IN THE BLOOD

MODEL FOR LOVE (AI NO DEZAIN), aka *THE LOVE ROBOTS*

1966   *BLOOD IS REDDER THAN THE SUN (CHI WA TAIYO YORI AKAI)*

RIPPED-UP DESIRE (HIKISAKARETA JOJI)

THE EMBRYO HUNTS IN SECRET (TAIJI GA MITSURYO SURU TOKI)

WHITE BABY DOLL (SHIRO NO JINZO BIJO)

BLACK FOUNTAIN OF DESIRE (JOYOKU NO KUROZUISEN)

1967   *NET OF VIOLENCE (AMI NO NAKA NO BOKO)*, aka *RAPE TRAP*

A CERTAIN THREE (ARU MITTSU), aka *SECRET STREET*, aka *DARK STREETS*

*UNDERGROUND HISTORY OF JAPANESE VIOLENCE – STRANGER'S BLOOD
(NIHON BOKO ANKOKUSHI – IJOSHA NO CHI)*

SEXUAL VAGABOND (SEI NO HORO), aka *SEX BEAST*

SEX CRIMES (SEI HANZAI)

ORGY (RANKO)

GATE OF LUST (IN MON)

*UNDERGROUND HISTORY OF JAPANESE VIOLENCE NUMBER 2 – RANK
OPPRESSIVE EVIL (NIHON BOKO ANKOKUSHI – BOGYAKU MA)*

VIOLATED ANGELS (OKASARETA BYAKUI), aka *VIOLATED WOMEN IN
WHITE*

1968   *WOMB TO LET (HARAGASHI ONNA)*

DESIRES OF THE FLESH (NIKUTAI NO YOKYU)

*VENGEANCE DEMON – NEW UNDERGROUND HISTORY OF JAPANESE
VIOLENCE (FUKUSHU KI – SHIN NIHON BOKO ANKOKU SHI)*

THE CONCUBINES (KIN PEI BAI), aka *THE NOTORIOUS CONCUBINES*

1969   *CRAZY LOVE SUICIDES (KYOSO JOSHI KO)*, aka *DEATH OF A MADMAN*

VIOLENT VIRGIN (SHOJO GEBA GEBA)

*MAN KILLER, WOMAN KILLER – NAKED BULLET (OTOKO GOROSHI ONNA
GOROSHI-HADAKA NO JUDAN)*

*MODERN UNDERGROUND SEX CRIME STORY – CONFESSIONS OF A DEMON
KILLER (GENDAI SEI HANZAI ANKOKU HEN – ARU TORIMA NO
KOKUHAKU)*

FLESH TARGET ESCAPE (NIKU NO HYOTEKI TOBO), aka *SCREAMING FLESH TARGET*

GO, GO SECOND TIME VIRGIN (YUKE YUKE NIDOME NO SHOJO)

ADULTEROUS LUST (KONGAI JOJI)

TALE OF MODERN LOVERS – SEASON OF TERROR (GENDAI KOSHOKU DEN – TERORU NO KISETSU)

MODERN SEX CRIMES – FIERCE SCREAMS, GRATUITOUS VIOLENCE (GENDAI SEI HANZAI ZEKKYO HEN – RYU NAKI BOKO)

1970   *LOVE TECHNIQUES – THE KAMA SUTRA (AI NO TEKUNIKKU – KAMA SUTORA)*

VIOLENT DRAMAS IN BROAD DAYLIGHT (MAHIRU NO BOKO GEKI), aka *VIOLENT DRAMAS ALL DAY LONG*

MAD SHINJUKU (SHINJUKU MADDO)

SEX JACK (SEIZOKU/SEKKUSU JAKKU)

UNDERGROUND HISTORY OF JAPANESE VIOLENCE – RAGING BEAST (NIHON BOKO ANKOKU SHI – ENJU)

1971   *SEXUAL TRANSMIGRATION – I AM WET – THE WOMAN WHO WANTS TO DIE (SEI RINNE – SEKURA MAGURA – ONNA SHINITAI)*

LOVE TECHNIQUES 2: ACT OF LOVE – I AM WET (ZOKU AI NO TEKUNIKKU: AI NO KOI – WATASHI WA NURETEIRU)

SECRET FLOWER (HIKKA)

RED ARMY – PALESTINE LIBERATION FRONT – DECLARATION OF GLOBAL WAR (SEKIGUN – PFLP – SEKAI SENSO SENGEN) [co-directed by: Masao Adachi]

SEX FAMILY (SEI KAZOKU)

1972   *ECSTASY OF THE ANGELS (TENSHI NO KOKOTSU)*, aka *ANGELIC ORGASM*

MODERN UNDERGROUND HISTORY OF JAPANESE VIOLENCE (GENDAI NIHON BOKO ANKOKU SHI)

YOUNG GIRLS WHO DIE FOR LOVE 1 – ECSTASY APPRENTICE (JOSHI KOKOSEI KOKOTSU NO ARUBAITO 1), aka *ORGASM APPRENTICE*

1973   *YOUNG GIRLS WHO DIE FOR LOVE 2 – CIRCLE OF AGGRESSION (JOSHI KOKOSEI 2 – KAGAI SAKURU)*

BLACK BEAST OF LUST (KUROI JUYOKU)

1974   *THE WET FLOWER'S BUDDING EYE (NURETA SAI NO ME)*

OBSCENE PASSION – BESTIALITY COLLECTIVE (INYOKU RINJU)

1975   *LAW OF THE DELTA (DERUTA NO OKITE)*

MARIA, THE WHORE (BAISHUN MARIA)

ONE HUNDRED YEAR HISTORY OF TORTURE (GOMON HYAKUNEN SHI)

THE BIG ENCYCLOPEDIA OF HONEYMOONS (SHINKON DAI HYAKKU)

DOSSIER ON PORNOGRAPHIC AFFAIRS – THE SEXUAL UNDERGROUND (PORUNO JIKENBO – SEI NO ANKOKU)

TRUE ACCOUNT OF YOUNG SCHOOLGIRL PROSTITUTES (JITSUROKU JOKOSEI SHUDAN BAISHAN)

1976   *UNDERGROUND HISTORY OF SADISTIC WOMEN (ZANNIN ONNA ANKOKU SHI)*

1977   *ONE HUNDRED YEARS OF SEX PROHIBITION AND FEMALE PUNISHMENT (JOKEI GOKINSEI HYAKUNEN)*

         THE EMPEROR'S MOTHER, THE GODDESS OF MERCY AND THE GREAT BODHISATVA – ETERNAL EROS (SEIBO KANNON DAIBOSATSU)

         SEX PROHIBITION IN JAPAN – TRADE IN WOMEN (NIHON GOKINSEI – NYONIN BAIBAI)

1978   *RAGING DEMON'S ATTACK ON THIRTEEN SUCCESSIVE PERSONS (JUSANNIN RENZOKU BOKOMA)*

         THE PREY (EJIKI)

1979   *MODERN SEX CRIMES – VIOLENCE – IMPRISONMENT (GENDAI SEI HANZAI – BOKO – KANKIN)*

         MODERN SEX CRIMES – MURDERING EVERYONE (GENDAI SEI HANZAI – ZENIN SATSUGAI)

1982   *POOL WITHOUT WATER (MIZU NO NAI PUURU)*

1983   *THE KEY (KAGI)*

1984   *SCRAP OF A STORY – STORY OF SECRET LOVE (SUKURAPPU SUTORI – ARU AI NOMONOGATARI)*

1986   *SHOCKING KAZUYO MATSUI (MATSUI KAZUYO NO SHOGEKI)*

1989   *EASILY EMBARRASSED 1 (KISU YORI KANTAN 1)*

1990   *HOLE IN THE PANTS – (PANTSU NO ANA – MUKE SODE MUKE NAI ICHIGOTACHI)*

         READY TO SHOOT (WARE NI UTSU YOI ARI)

1991   *EASILY EMBARRASSED 2 – ADRIFT STORY (KISU YORI KANTAN 2 – HYORYU HEN)*

1992   *LES LIAISONS EROTIQUE (EROTIKKU NO KANKEI)*

         SOSUKE'S STOLEN SLEEP (NETORARE SOSUKE)

1993   *SINGAPORE SLING (SHINGAPORU SURIRINGU)*

1995   *ENDLESS WALTZ (ENDORESU WARUTSU)*

1997   *STREET WITH NO TOMORROW (ASU NAKI MACHIKADO)*

KOJI WAKAMATSU – INTERVIEW

The following interview was conducted by Christian Storms (from questions supplied by me) at a small Tokyo bar in 1999. The video of this interview appears in slightly different form as a supplement on the American DVD releases of Go, Go, Second Time Virgin *and* Ecstasy Of The Angels *from American Cinematheque Presents/Vitagraph Films/Image Entertainment. Christian Storms also translated.*

CS: I know you went through a lot of changes before you became a film director.

WAKAMATSU: It wasn't like I had a dream of becoming a film director. But I did not want to become a farmer. No matter how hard you worked, how much rice you grew, the government would always come in and take it away from you. There was a senior in our judo club who used to pick on me all the time. So, when it came time for me to graduate, I grabbed him, dragged him out in front of the school and kicked the shit out of him. I'd gotten suspended before for smoking and stealing watermelons, but that got me finally kicked out of school. I couldn't stay out in the country any longer and decided to go to Tokyo. My first job was working as a day laborer, 240 yen per day, mostly construction sites. In the morning, the *yakuza* would come and pick us up and take us to the site. Once I got assigned to a candy factory, where we mixed fudge in this big old vat. One day this man fell in, and he died. The company did nothing for him! And it really pissed me off, so I said, 'Fuck it, man!' Afterwards, I had other jobs like bartending, things like that. Then finally, in Shinjuku, I met this gangster boss, and I ended up becoming a gang member.

CS: And how did film enter the picture?

WAKAMATSU: The same isn't true today, but if you wanted to shoot a film in Shinjuku at the time you had to ask the *yakuza*. If you were a gang member assigned to a film crew, all you basically had to do was stand by the camera while they were shooting and watch over things. I would get paid by my boss, who would get paid by the film crew. So, that's how I met my first film people, and that got me started. Later, I got arrested. They called it 'false realization of money,' a robbery misdemeanor. They put me in the joint for six months. The cops beat me and teased me all the time. So, I said to myself, 'Fuck! How can I get these fuckers back?!' 'Express yourself,' I thought; 'what a boring existence you've been living these last 20 years.' But there had to be some kind of authority in the expression, some way to show these guys. So, when I got out of prison, I told my gang boss I wanted out. He said it was okay and let me go. At first I tried becoming a novelist. But, since I never finished school, I could never get beyond ten pages. Then it dawned on me: 'Film! I'll be a producer, make some money.' I went to this producer I knew, got down on my hands and knees in his doorway, saying, 'Please, take me as your understudy!' And so I started a job in production, carrying stuff for the crew. This was in the beginning in television, when I was around 28, and I would get picked on by the assistant director while I was working. You know, it used to be that I would have done something about it. But I was still on probation. No matter how much they picked on me, I couldn't fight because I thought I'd end up back in the joint. A few years earlier, I would have whacked him. So, that made me say to myself, 'I'll become an AD, and I'll make a better AD than you.' So I worked as an AD – you know, assistant director.

CS: How did this lead to your first film, Sweet Trap?

WAKAMATSU: My first job as chief AD, I was in charge of the scheduling, the casting, and one day before the shooting this TV production manager came up to me with a new script and said, 'Everything's changed.' (*laughs*) That was the last straw for me. I wanted to grab my chair and break down the wall, it was fucking inexcusable! I thought I'd give up on TV and films and go back to the country. Beg my parents to take me back, and I would become a farmer. Then I got a call from an actor I knew, this guy Mita. He said, 'Hey, Waka, what's up? What are you doing?' 'I'm thinking of going home,' I said, 'I can't make enough money to eat.' We went out and started drinking together, and he asked me, 'How about directing something?' I said, 'Like what?' He said, 'A film, man!' But I couldn't do it. He said, 'Man, I've been watching you all this time, and you can do it! So, *do* it!' After that I wrote a script and took it to him. He liked it, and that became *Sweet Trap*. I thought to myself, if this film fails, then and only then will I give up. So, I got serious about making films, and when it played in the theaters it was a big hit. I guess that's what you'd call luck. So, now I was a director. I hadn't been to film school or had any other kind of real training, I didn't have any help. I took a notebook and put photos from newspapers and magazines, probably 100 of them, in different cuts – close-ups, long shots, two shots. And when it came time to shoot, I would take the notebook to the cameraman and point, 'This way.' I'd shoot a film, then they'd ask me to do another one, and so on. If you make a film, someone will watch it. The first critics who liked my work were Junji Sato, the editor of *Eiga Hyoron*, then Shuji Terayama, the writer. And Osabe, who is now an award-winning novelist. Their views helped people gather around me. And these people were powerful and irreplaceable. It was a really glorious time, with writers saying, 'Let me write for you!' Producers saying, 'How about this project?' And I knew how to honestly handle it all. If I'd gone to film school, I wouldn't have been able to, I would have lost myself along the way.

CS: *When did you meet your sometime writing collaborator, the filmmaker and activist Masao Adachi?*

WAKAMATSU: That *was* right around the time that I met Adachi. He's now just returned after being held in Lebanon. I started working daily with people like him, and that's how I was able to make interesting films.

CS: *Tell me about the genesis of* Secret Acts Within Four Walls, *the film Nikkatsu distributed and got you your first international recognition.*

WAKAMATSU: A certain distributor contacted me about making a film. I'd been making some successful films and was getting popular. Since they wanted me to make something, I wrote several scripts for them. But they kept refusing them. I thought, 'Fuck these guys, I'll fool them!' I wrote a script with a bunch of naked chicks and people in love, stuff like that, and they were happy. They gave me the initial production money, and I took the money and got going, but also took everyone out, and we got loaded. Of course, I'd had a different shooting script ready. Once you start shooting, the film is yours. We shot the real *Secret Acts Within Four Walls*, then I gave the film to the distributor. When they saw the rough cut, they were so angry. They cried, 'Fraud! This isn't the script, we can't run a film like this in our theaters!' I explained that a lot of crazy things happened, and changes had to be made. This was the film, and there was nothing they could do about it. 'Look,' I said, 'I've made a movie for you under budget, it's not fraud.' Luckily, a German guy named Dolman was looking for films for the Berlin Film Festival, and he saw my picture. He said that he really wanted it for the festival. Would I submit it? I said yes and got the distributor off my back. So, the film was sent to Berlin. Usually, only the Japanese Motion Picture Association decides which films to submit to festivals. And they had a preliminary selection already in Berlin. There were several Japanese pictures already submitted by the JMPA, like *Hunger Straits* (*Kiga Kaikyo*) and some military film. But not all the films made it. Mine was the only one that got accepted.

CS: Are these kinds of experiences what led you to form your own production company?

WAKAMATSU: It wasn't really pressure from the studios. Most people were going, 'What the hell are these films?!' A lot of people were criticizing the shit out of my movies. But, for the most part, five years or so after each release, people would sing praises of those *same* films. At first, they weren't big hits. But people would keep coming, they'd see them. Many critics didn't have their own brains yet. A lot of people *did* support my films and that mindset. Basically, I destroyed all the film grammar there that was conventional. It doesn't really matter how you shoot a movie. If the spirit is there, it will cut together.

CS: Your next movie that attracted attention outside Japan was The Embryo Hunts In Secret.

WAKAMATSU: The inspiration for *The Embryo Hunts In Secret* came from my office apartment. When I wake up in the morning, I have a habit of opening the windows. You know, I want to breathe the air. I love claustrophobic places, and I love being freed from them. Water was coming down in buckets because it was the rainy season. And, while I was watching the rain, I thought about shooting a film in my room. I wouldn't have to worry about the rain, and it'd be cheap. A whole bunch of images were popping in to my mind, and I'm good with images. But I can't write them down, you know, because I didn't go to school, and I'll always miss that part. So, I called Masao Adachi and said, 'Let's meet. I've got a great idea.' He came over in the afternoon, we started drinking some cheap hooch, and I told him my ideas. He was saying, 'Yeah yeah, yeah, but, Waka, I'm not a computer!' So, we bounced ideas off of each other, and he said, 'I'll be back tomorrow night.' And he left. The next night he came with the script written, and I read it. It was incredibly interesting, but it had some parts to it that would cost way too much money, like the walls exploding and birds flying in. And I said, 'I can't just destroy my apartment, man!' And he got the message. Of course, there were no photocopy machines then. He just ripped up the script and threw it in the garbage! And he said, 'I'll be back tomorrow.' And he came back with another version. It hadn't changed that much, but it was good enough, so we said, 'Let's do it.' And that became the film. We painted all the walls in my place white. I got together the crew and the actors. I ordered them not to set foot outside the apartment until we finished shooting. 'You'll sleep here, and I'll cook dinner; I'll feed you until we finish the movie.' We were like these refugees living in there. The only time we went outside was for the rain scene. We shot the whole film in one week. When we finished the picture, we figured we'd get bad reviews, and said, 'Fuck all that.' But we had a screening of the film, and everybody came and loved it. What I'm trying to say is, doing things you love, together with people you really like, no matter how strange the idea or the source, it'll work.

CS: *Probably your most notorious picture, the film with the most shocking reputation, is* Violated Angels.

WAKAMATSU: With *Violated Angels*, I had read a newspaper article about a boy in Chicago who goes into a dormitory where some nurses are living, and he kills five or six of them with a pistol. There's only one female survivor, according to this article, and I wondered what was going on with this boy and the girl who survived. I thought, why didn't he kill her? Maybe she was the only one who understood his feelings. And maybe the others were just screaming and trying to save themselves. Maybe using sex and their bodies to save themselves. When it was done, I figured, 'Hey, it's an underground film, it won't run in a theater.' But the picture had been inspected by Eirin, the motion picture ethics commission. And, when it was being looked at, Mr Tanimuta, who was a film critic, novelist and professor, saw the film. It blew his mind, and he wrote several articles about it, how great it was, and that kind of lit the PR fire. And the film ran and it ran and it ran. It's funny how a queer idea like that story will fascinate you, but if you had tried to take it to a regular film company no one would have given you any money, they'd probably have told you to just forget it. And you never might have done it. Making movies like this – call it 'cheap freedom.'

CS: *You also occasionally have done movies for major Japanese studios, which I believe started with* The Notorious Concubines; *correct?*

WAKAMATSU: Mr Otani, who was pretty much the founder of Shochiku and chairman of the board, liked my films. He used to get prints from other distributors and watch them alone in the Shochiku screening room. He called me. So I go into his office, and we start talking. You know, I wasn't on this guy's payroll, so I spoke my mind about their shit films and let the old man have it. I'm just bitching away, and finally he says, 'How about making something you like at our studio?' (*laughs*)

CS: *What was it like working with Juzo Itami, who at the time was an actor and played one of the lead roles in the film?*

WAKAMATSU: As an actor, Juzo Itami was open to anything. He was a strange guy, and that made him interesting. I cast him in the lead because of this. He was interested in doing it, playing the role of the warlord. He really did everything

I asked, love scenes, you name it, and that was all before he was a director, when he was just a no-name actor.

CS: Could you talk a bit about your association with political activism and student radicals? You see it in many of your movies, such as the beginning of Crazy Love Suicides.

WAKAMATSU: Most of the people who associated with me were student demonstrators. The reason was that no other company would talk to them. So, I would meet with them, and I would feel a sense of resonance with them. We started talking about making a film: 'Let's make an all-color movie!' It was near the end of December. We said, 'Let's make a movie about moving north, going to Hokkaido, and even further.' By chance, Nagisa Oshima was doing a film called *Boy* (*Shonen*, 1969); he and his crew were going to Hokkaido, too. That's how the film got going. The story was this guy commits a crime and moves north.

CS: That same year, 1969, you made one of your most minimalist films, Violent Virgin.

WAKAMATSU: That got started because Masao Adachi was directing a film called *Co-ed Guerrilla*. He was the director and I was the producer. And we went on a location hunt for it, and set off for Gotenba, near Mount Fuji. The writer Atsushi Yamatoya also became a director at my company. He's dead and buried now, but his name lives on. I called him up about going with us, and his wife is in the background, bitching about him leaving. But we got him to go, and on the way back from the location hunt we stopped the car to take a piss, then decided, 'Hey, how about a walk?' There was this little bitty prairie there, and we were walking around, and Adachi and I get this idea. We say, 'Yamatoya, how about making this place a one-shot location?' I had done a lot of films *inside* on one location, but I wanted to try to do the same thing *outside*. He said, 'Ahh, I don't know.' So, we left him in a hotel in Gotenba to write the script, and we drove back to Tokyo. He came back three days later with a script in hand. And it was an exciting script! We went to shoot Adachi's movie, and, with the same staff, shot the other movie, too, four kilometers away. But we still had to name this film. We went out drinking with Oshima, and I said, 'Hey, you got any ideas?' He says, 'How about *Shojo Geba Geba*?' I said, 'I'll take it! Pour that man a drink!' The name didn't matter to me, but much later, it became one of those great titles. It's funny how good films find perfect names.

CS: Another film with not only a great title, but also a one shot location, is Go, Go Second Time Virgin.

WAKAMATSU: I'd gotten kicked out of my apartment after I painted the walls for *The Embryo Hunts in Secret*. So, I had to move. The building I moved into, you could go up on the roof. I liked to go up there and relax and exercise. One day I was up there, and I thought, 'Hey, I can make a movie up here!' I imagined a scene from a poem I was reading, Adachi's *Spring*. I told Adachi to think about the poem, the roof, and that would be the movie. We made *everything* on that picture, the song and the music, *everything*. Yamatoya wrote the lyrics. Yamatoya, the ADs, all of us sang. Yamatoya just happened to know how to play a guitar. We thought it would be a waste to go rent a studio to record it so we did it in the office. It's funny when I look at it today – young girls, for some reason, love this movie. It was another one of those four-day films.

CS: Many of your films seem to have this cathartic emotional impact There's a sensitivity in the characters that has been damaged but somehow retained, an atmosphere of spiritual transcendence by living through these horrible nightmares. Is any of that intentional or is it just coming from your subconscious?

WAKAMATSU: 'Sensitivity retained in my characters, creating an atmosphere of spiritual transcendence by living through those nightmares'? (*smiles*) I don't know, I never planned it that way. I can't make the film unless I become one of the characters. My own feelings guide me. Or maybe I'm just trying to be cool in the end – I don't know, saving myself from it all by doing it on film. I become the main character as much as possible. I often say that making films is like making toys. When you're a kid you make toys, and you work on them, and you get together with the other brats in the neighborhood for a show and tell. And occasionally you take something out, then go, 'That's cool. Now you show me yours.' I still feel those kinds of needs, being childish. People often say to me, 'Waka, you're such a kid!' If you lose your childish nature, you lose your true emotions. You have to be honest and open to create things. Of course, I have made three or four films under a different name to pay some bills. But they were all boring. I made a couple of films like *Les Liaisons Erotique*. That was a fiasco even before Hasebe quit. These films were boring, too.

CS: Why were they boring?

WAKAMATSU: Boring because they weren't me.

CS: Tell me about Mad Shinjuku.

WAKAMATSU: *Mad Shinjuku* is a story about finding someone. There was a lot of madness at the time in Shinjuku, a lot of gangs that are still there today. There's a father who is trying to find the guy who killed his son. But the film is really about me finding myself. The father shows what he's made of and puts up a fight no matter what the circumstances. It's one of my favorite films. *Sex Jack* is another film I made that same year. There were a lot of peace demonstrations going on in Japan then. There was going to be a massive rally in the park. Adachi and I had been tipped off about it by the Emerald Group, and we had heard, too, that the cops were gathering in another part of town, in Harajuku. So, we set up our cameras on my roof and started shooting. I thought, if Japan was ever going to change for the better, it would be now. The protests were finally going to do it. But the protesters got totally wiped out, and none of them helped each other. The cops and the military totally destroyed them. All the protesters were trying to do was protect their own tiny little groups, and I thought, 'It's done. It's the end of the era for the movement.' The only thing left was to fight individually. It seemed individual radicalism was the only hope. That was when

people started hijacking planes to North Korea, the Red Army went to the Middle
East. Anyway, domestically in groups, the movement wouldn't work. They were
some wild times, I guess.

*CS: You mentioned the Red Army in the Middle East. On a similar theme, what was
the genesis of* Red Army – PLO – Declaration Of Global War *in 1971?*

WAKAMATSU: *Violated Angels* and *Sex Jack* had been invited to the
Director's Fortnight at Cannes, and one of Oshima's films, *The Ceremony*
(*Gishiki*, 1971), was also invited. We were supposed to all go, but we thought,
'What the hell are we going to do in Cannes?' So we talked about going somewhere
else. I had just made some cash on a film called *Love Techniques – The Kama
Sutra*, and I dropped a suitcase of money in front of Adachi and said, 'Where
do you want to go?' He said, 'Let's go underground again,' and I said, 'I'm sick
of underground films, I don't want to make any more.' Then he said, 'Let's go
to Palestine.' But I didn't even know where Palestine was! So I asked him. He
tells me that some guys from the Japanese Red Army are there, and they're
helping the Palestinians fight against Israel to get their land back. I thought,
'Now, this is interesting. All the mass media is focused on Vietnam, and there
isn't a word in the press about Palestine.' I knew I could sell a film about it to
Japanese television, and I could make a lot of money out of it. So, we went to
Cannes, then afterwards, on the way to Beirut, we got in touch with the PFLP.
We shot all kinds of interviews with people in Beirut, hijackers, poets and
novelists, Palestinian guerrillas. We went out into the wilds and shot for a week.
There's a triangle between Lebanon, Syria, Jordan and Israel where supposedly
foreigners had never been. We ended up lying to the Jordanian government,

Yoshio Harada (l.) in *Ready To Shoot*

saying we were shooting a travelogue and got permission to enter the area. We stayed there for about three weeks. One interesting thing that happened while we were there, we got in this cab, and we're driving, and the cabbie stops and says, 'I can't drive any further, I've got a wife and kids.' All of a sudden, we got jumped by the guerrillas, they made us get out of the car and put our hands in the air, and then we showed them our invitation from the people in Beirut. So, they took us to the mountain, and their leader asks us, 'If the enemy comes, are you going to grab a gun or grab your camera?' And we thought it would be cool if we said, 'Yeah, we'll grab a gun.' (*laughs*) They took all our cameras away and made us train every day after that for three weeks. On the last day we were there, we got to film everything we wanted. Then they told us they were going to take us down the mountain that night. Before we left, I met this little Palestinian boy. He was only about so high, but he was a guerrilla fighter. He would go out every night with the others. He was mute, and he would talk with sign language. He showed me a pendant that he had around his neck with a picture inside, and he told me, 'Our people can never go home, and someday someone will take my pendant to my home town for me.' Then it hit me: in two days I would be home in my country, but these people are fighting for their home. I suddenly felt I would be wrong to try to make money off of this. My duty was to try to spread the word about their story. That night they took us down the mountain, and we went into Syria and spent the night in Damascus. Then we returned to Beirut the next day. That morning, I saw the newspaper and the front page was full of photos. Those people we'd been with three days earlier, they'd all been either caught or killed. I was in shock. It was a famous battle, I don't remember the name, but they were all wiped out by a cooperative attack from Israel and Jordan. The guerrillas knew it was coming, but let us escape down the mountain. Thanks to them, I'm alive to this day. For I, a guy who originally went there to make *money*, almost lost his life there. I mean, I would have been captured, too. That's how the film came about and how I knew I had to show it when I got back to Japan. Before Palestine I'd been to America many times, but after I went to Palestine the US would no longer give me a visa. I'd given up on it for years, but in 1997 two of my films were going to play in LA [Editor's note: Go, Go Second Time Virgin *and* Ecstasy Of The Angels *were shown in Los Angeles at The American Cinematheque with an affectionate introduction/dissertation on Wakamatsu given by another guest director, Kinji Fukasaku*]. I got invited to go, but I still couldn't get a visa. Kinji Fukasaku was there and apologized for me in my absence. I heard that he said, 'Wakamatsu is not that much of a terrorist.' (*smiles*)

CS: *I understand from all reports that Masao Adachi returned to the Middle East to give his support to the guerrillas, and is now incarcerated in Japan after being deported from Lebanon.*

WAKAMATSU: For a while, I thought about going to do the fight with Adachi. He had said he was going, and I told him that I was going, too. I couldn't just abandon my friend. But Adachi said to me, 'You keep making films in Japan. I'm going to Palestine.' And he was there from 1975 until just recently. I went to Beirut about once a year after 1975. It was one of the only places in the world I could get a visa, and I would visit Adachi and the other surviving guerrillas. In a way, staying here in Japan all the time blackens your heart. Over there, I always got a new sense of myself, like I had to try harder. And that has been a source of my strength over the years.

CS: I was wondering about some of the films you did in the late seventies and through the eighties, many of them purported to be 'true account' murder and sex crime films. What were those all about?

WAKAMATSU: After I got back from Palestine, I didn't get that many jobs. There was the police, the surveillance, the political pressure on my company. I wanted to make a film that would start people talking again, so I started making these 'true account' films. I had to make a living. But then I started doing some major films in the late eighties and nineties.

CS: How would you define the genre of pink *or* roman-porno-*type pictures?*

WAKAMATSU: Movies can't really be called '*pink*' if they're being accepted by the general public. They've always got to be guerrilla. *Pink* films are about putting it out there in the public's face and smashing people's minds! I decided I couldn't make any more *pink* films. I wanted to make higher-quality pictures, movies that would get seen by people. *The Prey* in 1979 was the first of these. It came about because I saw Bob Marley in concert in Japan; and he blew my mind! He would sing like this, like he was holding a machine-gun, singing 'Get up! Stand up! Uprising!' The character in the film is parallel to me or Adachi. The theme of if someone brings a new idea to Japan; no one will listen to them, and, no matter how wonderful the idea is, the outsider will always be the outsider. Ten years after all those demonstrators got killed in Harajuku, these stupid kids who don't know history are listening to idol music and dancing where they died. I just couldn't stand it. Even with the major films I've directed, I always try to insert a bit of myself. The best example is probably *Ready To Shoot*. The character putting his heart into something and getting shot in the end. The idea behind *Ready To Shoot* was that everyone who had been involved in the student movement had sold out, had joined the establishment. The 'realists' had joined the mass media, gone into advertizing or real estate, they'd all forgotten about the revolution. But in the film, the Yoshio Harada character had never even wanted to give in. There are people who haven't given up. I never wanted to give in. These former activists who sold out and sit around and talk about the good old days piss me off. 'So listen up, boy,' I wanted to say, 'there are still some active activists out there.' And I thought it was necessary to say that. What are we going to do if everyone joins the Liberal Democratic Party in Japan? (*laughs*) Because of the revolutionaries in the world and in our country, this is a better place. The minority opinion matters! But nobody gets it. They say, 'These guys are too radical, they stick out.' No! Without them, we'd have nothing but dictators in this world. For example, if the Japanese Communist Party comes into political power for some reason, then I'll join the side that criticizes them! The reason why is that the people who make things, who create in this world, have to remain on the outside, have to look at the world sometimes from a different perspective: saying: 'Hold on!' Somebody taking a different view. People in power always turn into these yes-men. You have to have some kind of resistance to that, or it's all a lie.

13

Takashi Miike

1960–

Probably the single most impressive thing about Takashi Miike is his chameleon-like ability to adapt his filmmaking sensibilities to almost any kind of scenario. There are outrageous, violently over-the-top flights of fancy guaranteed to offend, as well as surprisingly tender, complex dramas of multi-character interaction. Most often, there are traces of both in his movies. There have been critics in both Japan and in the West who have been dying to pigeon-hole him based on his wilder, crazier pictures (*Fudoh*; *Dead Or Alive*; *Ichi, The Killer*), calling him 'flavor of the month' and a 'lowest-common-denominator' director, catering to the sick fantasies of jaded urban fan boys. But these naysayers have failed to see beyond the viscera and bullets. Even Miike's most extreme pictures are distinguished by a balanced spectrum of complex emotions and rare attention to character development.

Miike is a director peculiarly attuned to the realities and rhythms of the street. Born of working-class parents, his main interests were soccer and dirtbike racing in high school. However, he soon realized his racing ambitions were unobtainable and opted for a film school run by director Shohei Imamura. Rarely attending classes, he nevertheless secured internships and freelance jobs, making it finally to assistant TV director. Tiring of the monotonous grind and anonymous quality of the work, Miike decided to switch to film, and eventually worked as assistant to such filmmakers as Shohei Imamura, Hideo Onchi, Toshio Masuda and Kazuo Kuroki, and on such pictures as Imamura's *Black Rain* and Kuroki's *Street Of Masterless Samurai* (*Roningai*).

Miike is one of those rare birds in film, an intelligent, perceptive individual, not damaged from an overabundance of 'arts' education or intellectual baggage, with an unerring eye for the truth. He is unpretentious and creates intuitively from the gut, much like Koji Wakamatsu, with a similar instinct of going for the cinematic jugular. While it took Miike a few years to begin asserting his vision, honing his chops directing for Japan's early nineties movies-released-straight-to-video market, once he got there Japanese genre cinema would never be the same.

Although there were hints of inspiration in *Shinjuku Outlaw* and *The Third Gangster*, Miike's first recognizable masterwork was his thirteenth picture, a movie that was coincidentally the first produced for theatrical release. *Shinjuku Triad Society* is the initial entry in his *Kuroshakai Trilogy*, films that encapsulate the cultural, economic and psychological reverberations from the collision of the Japanese and Chinese underworlds. Heralding the millennial approach of a rootless Asian society, Miike takes a scalpel to the damaged psyches of the dispossessed, examining the plights of even the most monstrous with a combination of objectivity and compassion.

Shinjuku Triad Society follows the travails of Tatsuhito (Kippei Shiina), a ruthless police detective of mixed Japanese–Chinese descent, a man ashamed of his roots and consequently obsessed with destroying the budding crime network of Taiwan native Wang (Tomoro Taguchi), a psychopath gang lord dealing in human organs and haunted by his murder of his father. *Rainy Dog* stars Sho Aikawa as Yuji, a hitman on the run who finds refuge in Taipei working in a slaughterhouse. Living in a one-room flat, Yuji is driven to distraction by the non-stop rainy season, and tenuously maintains his gangster identity by occasionally taking contracts from a local gang lord. One day an ex-girlfriend drops off a young boy, Chen, at his apartment, apparently the offspring from their brief tryst. Finally, on the run from the mob who've marked him for death, Yuji establishes a rapport with a prostitute, Lily. Together with the boy, Chen, they form an ersatz family until the gangsters catch up, killing Lily and holding Chen hostage. Although Yuji wipes the gang out in the rainy streets, he is shot to death by a mystery man. The Taiwanese gang boss has miraculously survived Yuji's bullets thanks to a well-placed cigarette lighter, and, as he leaves, he remarks to Chen he'll be waiting when the boy grows up and comes looking for revenge. *Ley Lines* focuses on two brothers – one a troublemaker, Ryuichi (Kazuki Kitamura), the other a quiet student, Shunrei (Michisuke Kashiwaya) – and their goofball friend Chan (Tomoro Taguchi), all children born in Japan of Chinese immigrants. The three move to Tokyo from their rural Japanese village after a violent encounter with a junkyard owner, but are naively robbed of their money by Chinese whore Anita (Dan Li). Soon they're selling the toxic drug toluene for a fly-by-night dealer, Ikeda (Sho Aikawa). Obsessed with trying to get passports to go to Brazil, the three band together with Anita as kindred spirits, robbing the fake passport business of transplanted Chinese crime lord Wong (Naoto Takenaka). They make their getaway on stolen scooters, but are waylaid by Ikeda and his African henchman with guns blazing. Chan is fatally wounded in the ensuing gunfight, and Shunrei also dies later that night. Having made arrangements to stow themselves away, Ryuichi and Anita reach their rendezvous at a seaside quay, only to find their liaison has sold them out to Wong's gang. Anita fatally shoots Wong, and the couple dive into the ocean as gunfire peppers the surface. Miike cuts to the two adrift in a rowboat, bleeding profusely, rowing doggedly toward the horizon, and poignantly pulls the camera back till the pair are a mere speck on the endless expanse of water.

Fudoh: The New Generation is a perverse, ultra-violent tall tale adapted from a *manga* and starring Shosuke Tanihara as Riki Fudoh, an 18-year-old *yakuza* who controls a gang of grade-school assassins and teenage strippers. Riki's father (Toru Minegishi) had been responsible for killing his older brother to appease gang boss confederates many years before, a murder that Riki had traumatically witnessed. Once Riki is old enough he begins using his young killer associates to whittle away his father's underworld empire. Finally, when his father realizes what's going on, he decides to have him eliminated, utilizing a bastard son who is Riki's Korean half-brother. An all-out war erupts, with Riki and his young minions finally emerging the victors. Miike leaves us hanging in mid-mayhem just as a final confrontation with psycho *yakuza* Daigen (Riki Takeuchi), one of the father's associates, is about to detonate.

As the title suggests, *Full Metal Yakuza* is a tongue-in-cheek take on *Robocop*, a film that already had its own share of satire punctuating the carnage. A nebbish *yakuza*, unable to rise above protegé status, is fatally shot along with his just-released-from-prison mentor, and is shocked to awaken with a superhuman new body. A mad scientist had obtained the two men's corpses from a *yakuza* disposal team and then blended them together, cyborg-style, to make a nearly invulnerable killing machine. Miike strives to bring originality to the proceedings, riddling the melancholy parable with absurd humor – our anti-hero must eat metal for nourishment, and there's an amusing bit with a cereal bowl of nuts and bolts. And for action fans, the movie *does* deliver on the thrills and gore, especially at the end. But, despite the often unorthodox approach, *Full Metal Yakuza* ultimately leaves the impression of a one-note exercise.

Kishiwada Boy Hoodlums – Nostalgia Story is the third in a series, and a prequel to the preceding *Kishiwada* film Miike directed. Riichi grows from child to teenager under the shadow of his drunken, abusive father (Naoto Takenaka). Set in an Osaka working-class neighborhood, Miike imbues the film with an aching nostalgia, the kind that comes from memories mingled more with pain than joy, and there is not a shred of sentiment to pollute the scenario with insincerity. Miike connects emotionally with the material and there are magical moments, such as Riichi and friends building a life-size replica of the Apollo moon capsule, that are a refreshing antidote to the deluge of maudlin coming-of-age sagas made in America in the last 20 years.

Blues Harp is an almost perfect Miike film, blending his affection for rootless outcasts, as seen in *Kishiwada Boy Hoodlums* and *Ley Lines*, with the realistic *yakuza* style he was to engage later in *Graveyard Of Honor* and *The Agitator*. Chuji (Hiroyuki Ikeuchi), the bastard son of a Japanese mother and a homeless, black ex-GI, works as a bartender at a blues rock club in a small town near an American base. One night Chuji shelters a wounded *yakuza*, Kenji (Seiichi Tanabe), and with the help of his soon-to-be girlfriend, Tokiko (Saori Sekino), gives him first aid – a good Samaritan move that will provoke his ultimate downfall. Little does he know that Kenji is homosexual and that, in addition to feeling obligated to Chuji, he has also fallen in love with him. The two begin a strange friendship, which is unaffected by Tokiko moving in with Chuji and eventually becoming pregnant. To complicate matters, stage-shy Chuji is drafted by the departing singer of the bar's resident blues rock group as his replacement. As harmonica-playing frontman he's not only wowed audiences but record company scouts as well. In the meantime, Kenji, having seduced his boss's mistress, plots to take over the gang. But the mistress, suddenly realizing she's being used, and Kenji's loyal sidekick who has his own secret crush on Kenji, throw a monkey wrench into the plan – something that will prove fatal for Chuji as well as Kenji. A truly great picture, *Blues Harp* remains one of Miike's finest, a perfectly realized and emotionally affecting movie.

Dead Or Alive is another of Miike's near-perfect efforts and one of his most popular films. Right off the bat, Miike turns on the mixmaster, launching a nearly ten-minute express ride to hell, an exhilarating montage set to a throbbing rock score that leaves the viewer breathless. Chinese renegade Ryuichi (Riki Takeuchi) and cohorts make hits all over Shinjuku, while Jojima (Sho Aikawa), an overworked, compromised cop, responds to one of the messy murders in a noodle shop. Aoki (Renji Ishibashi), a decadent *yakuza* boss, is attempting to hold onto his turf under Ryuichi's onslaught, an effort which will lead to many deaths, including Ryuichi's stripper girlfriend, who is pumped full of smack then drowned in a wading pool of her own excrement. Before long, not only do Aoki and gang bite the dust but Ryuichi loses his younger brother and Jojima, his partner, in the barrage of firepower. Jojima subsequently manages to sabotage Ryuichi's grandest score, leading to a seizure of heroin in a banana shipment, and thus earns Ryuichi's eternal hatred in the process. As a consequence, Jojima's wife and daughter are blown sky high in a car bomb meant for him. Jojima is left literally with only ashes, and he drives to a remote field to confront Ryuichi in a head-on collision showdown. Miike pulls out the stops, and the film ascends into mythic status. Both Jojima and Ryuichi are left barely alive, Jojima actually tearing off his useless, mangled arm, then producing a rocket launcher from nowhere, upping the ante to such a ridiculous degree you're left speechless. Just as he fires, Ryuichi generates a weird, glowing ball of energy (!), hurling it at the incoming missile. Miike cuts to a view of Earth from space, and we see the impact's tidal wave of devastation engulf the planet, showing that the hatred these two men have for each other is capable of destroying the whole world.

After that, *Dead Or Alive 2* was bound to disappoint many fans of the first picture, viewers expecting another pyrotechnic thrill-ride. Instead, Miike doesn't even try to top it, deciding to tell the comparatively low-key story of two estranged friends, Mizuki (Sho Aikawa) and Shu (Riki Takeuchi), now hitmen who accidentally reunite when both find themselves fugitives on the same ferry bound for their home-town island. Once there, they connect with a third friend (Kenichi Endo) who opted to stay to raise a family. Since all three grew up in the island orphanage, Mizuki and Shu hit on the idea of donating what they earn as hitmen to buy medicine for an orphans' charity. As they continue to ply their trade back in Osaka, the two regress, naively believing – as children would – that they're making a huge difference for millions of kids. But the fact that they are adults killing for money and that Shu has consumption, eventually catches up to them in the form of a trio of killers. Mortally wounded after dispatching their pursuers, they nevertheless return to the island, oblivious to the stares provoked by their blood-soaked appearance, temporarily rejuvenated by their need to fly home like the birds they have often imagined themselves to be.

Following the trend of the first two pictures, *Dead Or Alive: Final* has little in common besides the encore of main stars, Sho Aikawa and Riki Takeuchi. This time set in the future of 2346, Yokohama is a closed-off province ruled by a dictatorial gay mayor (Richard Cheung) enforcing mandatory birth control. The dominant culture is Chinese but a variety of languages are also spoken, including Japanese and English. Aikawa is Ryo, a human-like replicant (à la *Blade Runner*), and Takeuchi is Honda, the mayor's head police enforcer on the hunt for rebel humans. The two cross paths when Ryo rescues the little brother of rebel girl June (Josie Ho). Confrontations ensue and Ryo and the rebels accidentally end up with Honda's son, whom they immediately hold for ransom. June and husband Fong (Terence Yin) hope to exchange the boy for rebel prisoners, but the plan backfires when two of the prisoners turn traitor and blow away their rescuers. Only June, her little brother and Ryo survive. Coincidentally, cop Honda makes the startling discovery that his wife, son and even he, himself, are replicants. This ignites an unusual change of heart in Honda, who gradually grows more sympathetic to the rebel's cause. Pregnant June acknowledges her affection for Ryo, despite knowing he's a replicant, hoping to form a family with him as father to her brother and unborn baby. However, Ryo knows he must still confront Honda. At the climax, the two meet in a fiery martial arts battle, finally coalescing together into one gigantic, black, dildo-headed (!) robot that sprouts wings and takes off. The very twisted, very

Blues Harp

funny last shot of the film is the robot's point of view as it zeroes in on the mayor having sex with one of his rent boys.

Audition is something of an anomaly, a blip on Miike's radar screen. To date it's the only 'serious,' character-driven horror/suspense thriller he's done. Even though *Ichi, The Killer* and *Gozu* have horrific moments, they are also possessed of absurd dark humor, something almost totally missing from *Audition*. Based on a novel by Ryu Murakami, Miike and screenwriter Daisuke Tengan took a great deal of time and care in preparing the film, subversively orchestrating the story structure so the viewer is lulled into a false sense of security and expectation. Loving single father Aoyama (Ryo Ishibashi) reluctantly takes up his friend, Yoshikawa (Jun Kunimura), on the suggestion to hold phoney auditions for their production company, something that will help the lonely man find a suitable marriage candidate. Aoyama is immediately taken with Asami (Eihi Shiina), a self-effacing ex-ballet-dancer with hints of a traumatic past. At first things go well, as love seems to blossom. Hints of Asami's psychotic breakdown almost subliminally sneak into the narrative until we reach the midway point. But, on Aoyama and Asami's first weekend away together, Aoyama is thrown for a loop, and he's not even sure why. Is he having a dream or are his fears about Asami based in reality? We're left to guess, then rudely shown in the end that it's a combination of both, something that makes the glimpses into Asami's past life all the more terrifying. We're shown a disfigured man living in a dirty laundry bag in Asami's empty, run-down apartment. Is he the record company executive who went missing the year before or someone else? Is the sadistic, wheelchair-bound old man (Renji Ishibashi) who played piano for Asami and burned her thighs in her childhood her uncle? What really happened at the boarded-up bar where a gory murder occurred and does it connect with Asami? Miike and Tengan leave the viewer to fill in the blanks, something that makes the chills all the more hackle-raising. When Asami abruptly disappears on their idyllic weekend, Aoyama is racked with guilt at his deceptive ruse in meeting her as much as he is moved by genuine affection. He fixates on locating Asami, and, even though his amateur detective work produces unnerving disclosures, he continues. Once Asami reappears and her true nature is revealed, Aoyama becomes the fly in her web, and Miike suddenly subjects the viewer to Grand Guignol horror as grisly as any Italian thriller from the eighties.

City Of Lost Souls, a lyrical, modern fairy tale, achieves a soulful synthesis, fusing elements from *manga*, Hong Kong action pictures and Japanese *yakuza eiga* as well as playing out an unsentimental love story. Half-caste Japanese–Brazilian Mario (Teah) returns from Sao Paulo to rescue his Chinese girlfriend Kei (Michele Reis) from being deported. Except that their newly acquired passports are ruined by Ko (Mitsuhiro Oikawa), an androgynous Chinese drug lord who is obsessed with Kei. When Mario and Kei sabotage Ko's drug deal with Fushimi (Koji Kikkawa), a ruthless local gangster, it ignites a Chinese mafia versus Japanese *yakuza* war, a development that a bigoted police detective remarks will hopefully destroy all parties concerned.

Miike shows Mario and Kei leaping from a helicopter hundreds of feet high to land unharmed, their Mardi-Gras-style street wedding, a cgi cockfight shot *Matrix*-style and Ko's subterranean cavern hideaway, complete with giant whirling blades of death. Not to mention a tongue-in-cheek flower power sentiment written in blood. In other words, Miike has cooked up a delicious, fractured kaleidoscope of a potboiler that is supremely entertaining, even though he manages significantly less character development than usual. He also provides a heartbreakingly appropriate denouement that is as downbeat as anything in film noir, echoing the doom-laden fate of Jacques Tourneur's *Out Of The Past* or Joseph Lewis's *Gun Crazy*.

An arrogant Japanese businessman, Kohei (Koji Kikkawa), arrested for heroin possession in the Philippines and thrown into Manila's most infernal prison is one of *The Guys From Paradise*, a seemingly sarcastic title for the film until it reaches its unpredictable, not altogether successful climax. Soon after being imprisoned, Kohei meets eccentric Japanese drug dealer Yoshida (Tsutomu Yamazaki), who is hiding out from a *yakuza* gang while in stir and living high on the hog from his illicit shenanigans. When Kohei allows himself to be recruited into Yamazaki's screwball band of cut-throats, he suddenly finds himself receiving privileges, able to periodically leave the prison as courier. But the status quo changes when the *yakuza* discover Yoshida's whereabouts, and his motley gang must make good their escape. Kohei, Yoshida and comrades abscond as fugitives into the jungle, soon finding more happiness in the remote village they pass through than they ever did in their pursuit of money. A diverting fable up until this point, the picture begins to ring a tad false, with the *yakuza* conveniently catching up with our anti-heroes. A shoot-out ensues, and only Kohei and Yoshida are left standing. To make matters more ridiculous, perhaps intentionally mocking the unrealistic turn of events, Miike has Kohei elected Philippine President under his new identity.

Eihi Shiina in *Audition*

Shot on cheap-looking video, *Visitor Q* is a merciless, uncompromising satire on the Japanese family. A washed-up TV reporter (Kenichi Endo) visits his under-age prostitute daughter, pitches hare-brained projects to his former colleague/lover (whom he eventually strangles by accident), then decides to film a *cinéma-vérité* documentary on his teenage son, who is continually bullied by neighborhood ruffians, all the while ignoring his despondent, prodigiously lactating wife (Shungiku Uchida), who clandestinely works as a prostitute to support her drug habit! Visitor Q (Kazushi Watanabe), a mod, zen hipster who had accompanied Endo home (after braining him with a rock!), begins to slowly knit the family unit back together. In his apathetic, freeloading way, he seems to be the metaphor for some cosmic force, or, at the very least, the type of spiritual guru frequently found in martial arts movies. Notwithstanding some of Miike's most outrageous audience-baiting ever, including necrophilia and scatological mishaps, *Visitor Q* emerges as an extraordinarily whimsical, even sensitive, picture.

Adapted from a popular *manga* that was banned outright in numerous Japanese prefectures, *Ichi, The Killer* is a funny, horrific, gore-drenched *yakuza* thriller (and director Miike's most successful film in Japan to date). Nao Omori is Ichi, an immature cry-baby who sports a black rubber superhero outfit and hatchet blade boots to do the bidding of Jiji (Shinya Tsukamoto), a seemingly harmless ex-cop who is really the mastermind behind a plot to shred the fabric of Shinjuku's *yakuza* and destroy bleach-blond mobster Kakihara (Tadanobu Asano). Coincidentally, Kakihara is an S&M freak who gradually becomes more enthralled as Ichi perpetrates each successive gangster massacre. By the end of the story, Ichi has achieved near-legendary status for Kakihara. The perverse mobster masochist has begun to look forward to his encounter with the slice-'em-and-dice-'em killer, hoping for a transcendent pain experience that will be worth dying for. Miraculously, in a mythical, almost metaphysical way, Miike endows his cast of grotesques with a recognizable humanity, making the nightmare and the surreal comedy all the more disturbing. Another of Miike's certified masterworks.

Miike's *Graveyard Of Honor* goes back to the original source novel by Goro Fujita in this remake of the 1976 Kinji-Fukasaku-helmed classic. Goro Kishitani portrays the legendary real-life gangster Rikuo Ishikawa (here called Ishimatsu), a sociopathic loser prey to his own paranoiac delusions. A misunderstanding about his boss's whereabouts causes him to lose his temper, assault his superiors and, soon afterwards, descend into a pit of drug-induced depravity. Eventually the machinations of a cop (Rikiya Yasuoka) and Oshita, the henchman of his best friend, Imamura, start the machinery in motion that will lead to his final destruction. But Ishimatsu's demise had started long beforehand, as he began to give in to every violent impulse and to always assume the worst, even of his friends. Unfortunately, he takes a lot more people down with him, including his adoring girlfriend, Chieko. But little emotional connection is made with the audience, in spite of the excellent performances. The one scene that manages to get under the viewer's skin is when Ishimatsu returns to finish off his friend, Imamura, with the wounded man's spouse holding onto and screaming at the oblivious killer, doing everything she can to save the man she loves – in vain. Miike's version also overstays its welcome in length in a way that just-as-long *Gozu* and even longer *The Agitator* never do. It's an amazing picture, to be sure, but it's a steely cold, grey kind of a movie. Kishitani's convincing performance leeches so much of the humanity out of Ishimatsu that we're left indifferent at the end when he finally jumps to his death. It's quite unlike Fukasaku's earlier version, where Tetsuya Watari delivers a performance that catches the viewers' hearts in their throats all through the last half of the film.

The Agitator is a stunning *jitsuroku yakuza* picture, with Masayo Kato as the street mobster leader of a crew loyal to a hard-boiled boss (Naoto Takenaka), a mentor from Kato's childhood. When a powerful godfather (Hiroki Matsukata) decides to consolidate his power he sets a Machiavellian plot in motion, and the dominoes start to fall. Although the story structure is too complex to relate here, to put it simply Kato manages to uncover evidence that Matsukata is the one orchestrating the mayhem. Soon Takenaka is assassinated, and Kato's young crew goes into hiding. Virtually all his surviving men are killed in his retaliatory assassinations and in a showdown with a vengeful hitman (Hakuryu). We're left with Kato and his one surviving protegé crashing their dump truck through Matsukata's gates before it cuts to the credits. Miike manages to fill up all 152 minutes of the theatrical release (the one I saw), and – reportedly – the 200-minute video version released in two parts, with a mesmerizing epic that never bores the viewer and shows Miike adept at spinning the kind of *jitsuroku* masterpiece that was previously the province of Kinji Fukasaku.

Miike made another left turn the same year with *The Happiness Of The Katakuris*, a musical comedy about a down-on-their-luck family (Kenji Sawada, Keiko Matsuzaka, Tetsro Tanba, et al.) trying to run a mountain inn to renew their fortunes.

Teah, Michele Reis in *City Of Lost Souls*

With highway plans put on hold, it seems that this venture may go bust. But, slowly, guests begin to trickle in. Unfortunately, they all have a habit of dying on the premises, either through suicide, freak accidents or natural causes. Miike integrates seventies-style Japanese karaoke musical numbers into the action, something that only works intermittently and often brings the film, for this viewer anyway, to a screeching halt. Kenji Sawada and Keiko Matsuzaka, in addition to their acting careers, have also enjoyed success with their singing prowess, and that is the obvious exploitation hook for Japanese audiences. Nevertheless, Miike still manages to infuse the film with an off-kilter disposition and even an occasional warmth. *Katakuris* is a remake of the Korean film *The Quiet Family*, and when one considers its source it's a decided improvement. The original is dreadful and all but unwatchable.

Deadly Outlaw: Rekka is a pulpy, slam-bang *yakuza* action picture, comparatively shorter and sweeter at 96 minutes than Miike's other *yakuza* theatrical releases that bookend it. Scripted by the same writer as *Graveyard Of Honor* and *The Agitator*, Shigenori Takechi, *Rekka* is a greatest hits blend of the previous two mega-sagas. But that doesn't negate the enjoyment factor. This time out, Miike offers a tall tale approach, with Riki Takeuchi as Kunisada doing one more variant on his reliably short-fused persona. An enforcer whose boss (Yuya Uchida) has been killed in a plot by an omniscient godfather (this time, Sonny Chiba) bent on fomenting gang war, Kunisada finds he can't sit still for the dishonor, and, with his one remaining ally, Shimatani (Kenichi Endo), goes into battle.

In *Gozu* (or, as it's amusingly called in its full translation from Japanese, *Yakuza Horror Theater – Gozu*), a young *yakuza* thug named Minami (Hideki Sone) is ordered by his boss (Renji Ishibashi) to assassinate best friend Ozaki (Sho Aikawa). The reason? The going-off-his-rocker gangster had labelled a tiny canine as a '*yakuza* attack dog,' then killed it in front of a restaurant of horrified patrons. But, as Minami drives the taciturn Ozaki to the village where the gang has their special body dump, weird things start to happen. When Minami brakes without warning, Ozaki hits his head on the dashboard, something which seems to kill him. The body mysteriously disappears, and Minami goes on an increasingly dreamlike pilgrimage that leads to encounters with riddle-reciting rural mobsters, an elderly but lactating inn proprietress, her idiot savant brother, a cow-headed god called Gozu and, finally, a beautiful girl (Kimika Yoshino) who claims to be Ozaki. By the end, when Minami returns with the girl, he's convinced she really is his long-lost buddy, and bridles at his lecherous boss's advances towards her. This leads to an altercation and a spectacularly gross death for his employer. Later, back at Minami's place, when he finally succumbs to the girl's request for sex, he gets stuck inside her. Any audience expectations are completely thwarted as the girl goes into labor and gives birth – to a full-grown Ozaki! Soon the trio are cohabitating as if it's the most natural thing in the world, and Miike closes the film on a seemingly offhand, happy note. What emerges is a shaggy dog version of *Alice In Wonderland* by route of David Lynch's *Lost Highway* with distant 'triangle' echoes from Truffaut's *Jules*

And Jim and Chabrol's *Les Biches*. But, knowing Miike, this is undoubtedly synchronicity at work rather than any hodgepodge mix of cinematic influences. Poking fun at homophobia as well as other sexual identity issues, *Gozu* is a very funny, offbeat movie, really more of a surreal parable à la Buñuel-on-LSD than any kind of horror film – although there *are* some extremely atmospheric, creepy moments.

Approached by Kadokawa-Daiei productions to add one more supernatural ghost thriller à la *Ring* to the burgeoning legion of current Japanese horror films, Miike responded with *One Missed Call* in 2003. Although hardcore Miike fans might be hard-pressed to spot as many of his out-of-left-field bits of business, *One Missed Call* delivers more than its share of eerie frissons, creating a wealth of dread and atmosphere from a tale of 'bad seed' karma intersecting with omnipresent cellphone technology. Miike also manages to satirically skewer reality participation television in the process.

2004's *Zebraman* grew out of the desire of star Sho Aikawa and director Miike to create a movie that their kids could go and see. I originally had my doubts about this before seeing it, as it's also one of Miike's biggest-budget films to date. Surprisingly, it works as well for adults as children, with Aikawa's alienated married schoolteacher daydreaming in Walter-Mitty-style about his beloved TV superhero from his childhood. His tentative, incompetent steps emulating Zebraman in his free time coincide with the invasion of shape-shifting blob-like aliens. Before long, Aikawa realizes he must somehow tackle his perennial superhero ambitions for real if Earth is to stand a chance against the interlopers..

TAKASHI MIIKE – SELECTED FILMOGRAPHY

(V) *signifies a film shot for direct-to-video release*

1991	*LAST RUN: A HUNDRED MILLION YEN'S WORTH OF LOVE AND BETRAYAL (LAST RUN: AI TO URAGIRI NO HYAKUOKEN EN)* (TV)
1992	*A HUMAN MURDER WEAPON (NINGEN KYOKI)* (V)
1993	*BODYGUARD KIBA* (V)
1994	*SHINJUKU OUTLAW* (V)
	BODYGUARD KIBA: APOCALYPSE GANG (BODYGUARD KIBA: SHURA NO MOKUSHIROKU) (V)
1995	*THE THIRD GANGSTER (DAISAN NO GOKUDO,* aka *THE THIRD SCOUNDREL)* (V)
	BODYGUARD KIBA: APOCALYPSE GANG 2 (BODYGUARD KIBA: SHURA NO MOKUSHIROKU 2) (V)
	OSAKA YAKUZA STORY (NANIWA YUKYODEN) (V)
	SHINJUKU TRIAD SOCIETY (SHINJUKU KUROSHAKAI: CHINESE MAFIA SENSO, aka *SHINJUKU'S UNDERWORLD SOCIETY: CHINESE MAFIA WAR)*[number 1 of Kuroshakai trilogy]

1996   *NEW STORY OF THE THIRD GANGSTER – ERUPTING YAKUZA WAR IN
        KANSAI (SHIN DAISAN NO GOKUDO – BOPPATSU KANSAI GOKUDO SENSO)*
        (V)
        *NEW STORY OF THE THIRD GANGSTER, PART 2 (SHIN DAISAN NO GOKUDO
        2)* (V)
        RUTHLESS AMBITION (JINGINAKI YABO, aka *HEARTLESS AMBITION)*(V)
        *FIGHT ON A FLOWER-COVERED ROAD – LEGEND OF OSAKA'S STRONGEST
        (KENKA NO HANAMICHI – OSAKA SAIKYO DENSETSU)* (V)
        FUDOH: THE NEW GENERATION (GOKUDO SENGOKUSHI: FUDO, aka
        RECORD OF A GANG WAR: FUDOH)

1997   *KISHIWADA BOY HOODLUMS – INNOCENT BLOODSPRAY STORY
        (KISHIWADA SHONEN GURENTAI – CHIKEMURI JUNJO HEN)*
        RUTHLESS AMBITION 2 (JINGINAKI YABO 2, aka *HEARTLESS AMBITION 2)* (V)
        FULL METAL YAKUZA (FULL METAL GOKUDO) (V)
        RAINY DOG (GOKUDO KUROSHAKAI, aka *SCOUNDRELS' UNDERWORLD
        SOCIETY)* [number 2 of Kuroshakai trilogy]

1998   *THE BIRD PEOPLE OF CHINA (CHUGOKU NO CHOJIN)*
        ANDROMEDIA
        *KISHIWADA BOY HOODLUMS – NOSTALGIA STORY (KISHIWADA SHONEN
        GURENTAI – BOKYO HEN)*
        BLUES HARP

1999   *LEY LINES (NIHON KUROSHAKAI,* aka *JAPAN'S UNDERWORLD SOCIETY)*
        [number 3 of Kuroshakai trilogy]
        DEAD OR ALIVE (DEAD OR ALIVE: HANZAISHA)
        AUDITION (ODISHON)

2000   *MPD PSYCHO (TAJU JINKAKU TANTEI SAIKO – AMAMIYA KAZUHIKO NO
        KIKAN,* aka *MULTIPLE PERSONALITY PSYCHO DETECTIVE – KAZUHIKO
        AMAMIYA RETURNS)* (TV mini-series)
        CITY OF LOST SOULS (HYORYU GAI, aka *HAZARD CITY,* aka *CITY OF
        STRANGERS)*
        THE GUYS FROM PARADISE (TENGOKU KARA KITA OTOKO-TACHI)
        DEAD OR ALIVE 2 – BIRDS (DEAD OR ALIVE 2 – TOBOSHA, aka *DEAD OR
        ALIVE – ESCAPE ARTISTS)*
        THE MAKING OF 'GEMINI' (TSUKAMOTO SHINYA GA RAMPO SURU, aka
        *SHINYA TSUKAMOTO DOES RAMPO)(This is a supplement on Shinya Tsukamoto's
        GEMINI DVD in Japan and is a documentary about the making of the film.)* (V)

2001   *VISITOR Q (LOVE CINEMA VOL. 6)* (series title) (V)
        ICHI, THE KILLER (KOROSHIYA ICHI)
        THE AGITATOR (ARABARU TAMASHII-TACHI)
        THE HAPPINESS OF THE KATAKURIS (KATAKURI-KE NO KOFUKU)
        *TONKARARIN DREAM LEGEND (ZUIDO GENSO – TOKARARIN YUME
        DENSETSU)*

KIKUCHI CASTLE STORY – THE SAMURAI GUARD'S SONG (KIKUCHI-JO
MONOGATARI – SAKAMORI–TACHI NO UTA)
2002 DEAD OR ALIVE: FINAL
SABU (TV)
GRAVEYARD OF HONOR (SHIN JINGI NO HAKABA, aka NEW GRAVEYARD OF
HONOR)
SHANGRI-LA (KINYU HAMETSU NIPPON – TOGENKYO NO HITO BITO)
PANDORA (PANDOORA) (V)
DEADLY OUTLAW: REKKA (JITSUROKU ANDO NOBORU KYODO-DEN –
REKKA, aka NOBORU ANDO'S TRUE ACCOUNTS OF YAKUZA LEGENDS –
RAGING FIRE)
2003 THE MAN IN WHITE (YURUSAREZARU MONO)
GOZU (GOKUDO KYOFU DAI-GEKIJO – GOZU, aka YAKUZA HORROR
THEATER – GOZU)
YAKUZA DEMON (KIKOKU)
ONE MISSED CALL (CHAKUSHIN ARI)
2004 ZEBRAMAN
IZO
2005 BIG GHOST WAR (YOKAI DAI SENSO)

TAKASHI MIIKE – INTERVIEW

The following interview was conducted by Dennis Bartok and me on September 10,
2001, at the empty Egyptian Theater (American Cinematheque). The video of this
interview appears as a supplement in slightly different form on the American DVD release
of Audition from American Cinematheque Presents / Vitagraph / Chimera through Ventura
Distribution. Dennis is signified as DB and I am signified as CD.

DB: Was Audition a project that you personally sought out and developed, or was it
more of a work for hire?
    MIIKE: It was originally a story by Ryu Murakami, and the production company
    Omega Projects was developing it. When they got to the point of choosing
    directors, they chose me.
CD: Daisuke Tengan, the son of Shohei Imamura, was the screenwriter. Was he someone
you brought onto the film or was that Omega?
    MIIKE: No, that was me. I thought that he'd be just right for it. I suggested
    Tengan for the job, we had a meeting with him, and, after reading the original,
    he expressed confidence that he could extract a good screenplay from it.
CD: Did you know Mr Tengan from when you worked for his father as an assistant director?
    MIIKE: Daisuke Tengan was originally a salaryman who worked for a company.
    He quit his job about ten years ago, and he's been making movies ever since. He

formed a production company with the director Kaizo Hayashi, and for quite a while they were making films themselves. He's been working as a screenwriter, but I knew him as a director in his own right, not because he's Imamura's son. He was active in film way before me. The fact that he's Imamura's son is really just more of a coincidence.

DB: How similar was the film to the novel? Did you take liberties with the original?

MIIKE: Ryu Murakami, who wrote the original story, is also a film director, too. Before *Audition*, there'd been one other film from his work directed by someone else, and I think he realized there was great potential for another director adapting one of his stories. We, as the filmmakers, have the freedom to adapt the story however we want, and I think he felt that, as long as we kept the spirit of his story intact, he'd allow us to make it how we liked. As far as Daisuke Tengan, he's a strong writer. He can get a bit egotistical at times and could totally destroy the original if he wanted to. But, in the end, I think he delivered a script which is pretty faithful to the source. Except for toward the end of the film, which is more of a visual form of storytelling, Tengan's script is more faithful than the finished film. The story is basically the same, it's just a different form of expressing the same ideas.

DB: For people who have seen some of your other films, like Fudoh: The New Generation *or* Dead Or Alive, *two adrenalin-pumping, high-impact genre films,* Audition *is a different kind of picture. You deal with a middle-aged hero, the trust and betrayal in relations between a man and a woman. It has more of a domestic framework at first, although it evolves into a horror film. Was that part of the challenge, working in this seemingly different area from many of your other movies?*

MIIKE: In this film, as well as in my previous films, even though abbreviated and you may not see it as much, at the heart of these movies is the family unit. Even if on the outside this seemingly normal character goes on a violent rampage, I'm always thinking about this character's background, what life is like at home, things like that. This movie is also a departure, a rebound from my normal filmmaking. And the timing of this project was right for me to spend more time exploring this character's home life. It wasn't more difficult, but rather, an opportunity to more deeply explore the character's background, his domestic life. It was refreshing, a pleasurable challenge.

CD: Something I find interesting is people's reaction to the shocking climax. Before it, although there are sequences open to interpretation, there's nothing that outrageous – and then, at the end, you're blind-sided. People are polarized, either outraged or excited. I've seen Grand Guignol scenes before in Italian horror films, Hong Kong genre pictures, and I'm wondering why this seemed so intolerable to some viewers – if perhaps the film has a larger arthouse audience, people not normally exposed to that imagery.

MIIKE: It's a movie where the story itself kind of self-destructs, it finishes with an incomplete ending. The way the people in the story are incomplete, so the film also has to finish in a kind of broken-down way. That's what I was trying to do. So, to do that, first of all you have to have a normal story to start with. In a total of a 90-minute film, you spend maybe the first hour developing this 'normal' story. And, at that point, the audience on their own develop a sense of how this story is going to end. The film takes them to a different place altogether in the final reel, after they've gotten comfortable. I think it takes about an hour for that comfort to set in. And then the story changes gears, and the characters themselves are affected by this, they start to change, riding along with it. The audience's understanding of the first hour has been undermined. They feel psychologically cheated somehow, betrayed. Especially female viewers, and there were many who came up to me and said: 'You're sick!', then left the theater. (*smiles*) They won't accept this ending, it's as if they've been molested or something. They won't abide by the twists of the story.

DB: Ryo Ishibashi gives a wonderful performance as the lead character with this kind of Average Joe persona. And you like him even though you know he's lying to and manipulating this woman. Was he already involved with the film when you came on board or did you seek him out?

MIIKE: In real life, he's a musician, a rock 'n' roller. He's like a huge rock star. So he's usually seen up on stage. But he also has this personal life, this ideal family life as well. He has these two totally different sides to him. He's a sensitive guy at heart. But the type of movie roles that usually come his way are *yakuza* gangsters. I think he's sick of it, wants to try something different, break out of the mold – that's what I think, anyway. Normally, as a musician who's a big star, I wouldn't think he'd even be interested in a role like this. But in this case, no, he really wanted to try to play a normal guy.

DB: Eihi Shiina is beautifully cast as the psychopathic girlfriend. Did you have to audition a number of actresses for that role or did you already have her in mind?

MIIKE: (*laughs*) It was scary, but I *did* hold auditions. It was a pretty high-level audition. It was not an open casting call. We had short-listed about ten actresses. We weren't looking for a professional actress, so to speak. Eihi, herself, has had some stage experience, but this is only her second film. For the most part, she does modeling. On the set, I like to work with professional actors. But I also like bringing in people with different backgrounds to bring new blood to the project. I like incorporating the different elements that they come up with. What I liked about her in the first place, the same with Ryo Ishibashi, is that they both come from different, high-profile backgrounds. From the first time I met her, saw her first expression, I decided right away.

DB: In a way, Audition *is the perfect revenge fantasy for every performer who ever had to audition and felt they were helpless, powerless and just another face with someone judging them. Did you think about that since you've obviously held many auditions, yourself, as a filmmaker? Did you draw on any of your own experiences with that kind of power dynamic, when you've had people opening themselves up, making themselves vulnerable?*

MIIKE: I guess so. It's something we do all the time, so I suppose we borrowed from that a bit. However, in this case it's really more of a pretext for their meeting. It just so happens that these two meet at an audition. At first they meet and fall in love, at which point the misery sets in. (*smiles*) It's not like we're borrowing directly from our own experience and putting it on film but, rather, something which could possibly come out of that process. As a result, the fallout from these auditions, those who don't make it – who knows? Maybe they all get hurt in the process. But I'm not sure; I think, in this case, this cast aren't the kind of people who get cut and suffer that indignity. Maybe it's not so relevant.

DB: *Can you talk about working with director of photography Hideo Yamamoto. How much freedom do you give him to achieve the visual look of the film?*

MIIKE: I've worked a lot with Hideo Yamamoto. He shot my film *Fudoh* as well. He's also been highly regarded for his work on Takeshi Kitano's film *Fireworks* (*Hana-bi*). Basically, I tell him what I'm after in terms of the content and tone, the shot composition, how I'd like each shot to look, the angle and so forth. I'm not giving over complete control to him as the cameraman, but I don't try to tell him anything about camera work, what's going on inside the camera. He's a very sensitive individual. Sensitive towards death. He might not seem so on the outside. But I think it's an important factor in his work. Both of his parents died very young. He's already older at age 40 than both of his parents who died in their thirties. It's not something that he talks about much. He goes on living with a cool, calm, collected exterior, but underneath I believe he's thinking he might die someday soon. Kind of living in fear. And that feeling, that sensibility, is something that comes through in his work. I think the audience feels it, too. It's something that I want to make the most of. So, in that sense, I give him the freedom that he needs to do things his way. I just give him the basic information, camera angles and so forth.

CD: *In* Audition *as well as your other films, you seem to enjoy a perverse satisfaction in provoking the audience. There are scenes that come out of nowhere that are very shocking. In* Dead Or Alive, *there's the scene with the prostitute drowned in a wading pool of excrement; in* Dead Or Alive 2, *and a couple of other pictures, characters are killed while they're having sex; in* Visitor Q, *there's much taboo imagery. What do you feel it is in yourself, this perverse sense of humor drawing a violent reaction out of the audience?*

MIIKE: First of all, it's not as if I'm trying to elicit a specific response from the audience or manipulate their feelings. When I'm making a film, while we're there working on the set, it's more a question of whether we're having a good time while we're making it. That's what it's about. It's not a matter of whether it's possible for me personally in film but, rather, in terms of visual expression. Like these days in Japan, we make something knowing we're going to be praised for it – it's not *that*. But I think there are more possibilities. You just have to break down that formula or nothing new is going to come out of it. Inside myself, if we're having a good time making the film, the whole thing just kind of escalates.

Then, as a neutralizer to the grotesque, you throw in some humor. And that's not really for the audience's sake but more for my own. As long as that's acknowledged, it gives me the confidence to make films more freely. I'm sick of doing the same things over and over again. To make movies more interesting, I could make them more grotesque if I wanted to. But I like to keep challenging myself in other directions. Others make average films and call them beautiful. Filmmaking is a competitive business. To make something moving, something beautiful, perhaps, or do something praising mankind. But it's not just for the audience, that's not the only purpose of filmmaking.

DB: *How did you create the effect at the end of the film where Eihi Shiina is placing acupuncture needles in Ryo Ishibashi?*

MIIKE: It was all special effects make-up. We have some very talented, very precise, detail-oriented make-up artists in Japan. And they created this mask layer which was laid over his eyes, and the needles were actually placed into that.

DB: *In most countries around the world, if a director makes one movie a year they're very fortunate. You are famous for making four, sometimes five, movies in a year. Where do you get the energy? What is it that drives you to go from one movie to the next without stopping?*

MIIKE: To begin with, in Japan you've got to be very productive. If you don't make a lot of movies it's tough to get by, for one thing. Although I'm not making movies just to survive, that's not my only motivation. There's always this unsatisfied feeling after making a film. Filmmaking requires a lot of physical energy, and the brain is just like the muscles in your body. It *does* wear you down. I think the time that it takes to make a good movie really isn't very long. You want to keep the process moving forward, to get into a groove and just keep it going. And, of course, I'm criticized for this too. Making so many movies, there's no way I could be making them all by myself. 'He doesn't give a damn, he's just cranking them out.' Dismissing me for making so many films. I think naturally people would think that, and I understand. I may even feel that way myself sometimes. But, the more films I make, the more I'm able to streamline, to distil the filmmaking process. And, for me, it's really necessary. It's really the only way I know how to work.

CD: *It's a bit in the tradition of the fifties and sixties in Japan, when the major studios were still cranking out films week after week. There were prominent directors then you remind me of: Suzuki, Fukasaku, Ishii, Wakamatsu, all renowned for pushing the envelope. You've also worked with, what critics would call, 'more serious' directors, like Shohei Imamura, Hideo Onchi and Kazuo Kuroki. Where do your aesthetics come from, your sense of identity as a director?*

MIIKE: I've been influenced by everyone I work with, in some way. Although not how to direct or anything like that. I've worked as an assistant director with many different directors, and I always thought I'm not going to get any more than what that director has in mind. You can't expect any miracles there on the film set. So, even if you spend a year slowly planning a film, there's a limit to that, too. I think the best way is to just go out there and solve your problems as you go, within time limits and within a budget, and make a film that you truly enjoy making. Because it's your one chance to get it right. You have to be right there, driving it along. So, yes, I've been influenced by many other people. But it's not like I've learned this particular *point* in filmmaking. But, rather, the limitations of a director; that's what I feel I've retained from my days working as an assistant to these other directors.

14

Kiyoshi Kurosawa

1955–

Like Takashi Miike, Kiyoshi Kurosawa came to maturity as a filmmaker in the nineties. Also like others in this book who began their careers in the fifties, he is an 'outlaw' master, a filmmaker redefining genre while still delivering the goods.

Although perhaps not immediately recognizable as such, Kiyoshi Kurosawa is one of the most distinctive personalities within these pages. Quiet, unassuming, a great lover of genre film, especially science fiction and horror, but possessed of an aesthetic sense much closer to an independent filmmaker. He can gush enthusiastically one minute over fifties black-and-white science fiction like *Fiend Without A Face*, Robert Aldrich the next, then finally a maverick genius like John Cassavetes.

Kurosawa began making 8mm films as a college student, then worked as an assistant director for a while before directing his first picture, *Kandagawa War*, in 1983 – for lack of a better definition, a *pink* film that was barely an hour long. This was followed in 1985 by yet another *roman porn* movie, *Excitement Of The Do-Re-Mi-Fa Girl*, a stream-of-consciousness piece on a young girl following her pop idol onto a college campus, only to encounter free love orgies and radical political ideas. Reportedly, the film employs stylistic flourishes with color and images that wouldn't be out of place in the early films of Koji Wakamatsu or Jean-Luc Godard. From all accounts, both of these *pink* films were resounding box-office failures.

Director Juzo Itami served as producer on Kurosawa's first horror film, a rather conventional haunted-house piece called *Sweet Home*, which utilized then state-of-the-art-effects. Though more successful, Kurosawa was not entirely satisfied with the result, and he worked at making the no-budget horror opus *Guard From The Underground* happen next. He was able to exert more control, but the lack of money proved a problem. This led to the slyly amusing six-film crime comedy series *Suit Yourself Or Shoot Yourself* starring Sho Aikawa, all direct-to-video productions. More work for hire closed out the year, with the final installment in a gory horror franchise, *Door 3*.

By this time Kurosawa had certainly paid his dues, and the following year, 1997, proved a watershed one, with the release of his subtle, astonishingly creepy serial killer movie *Cure*. Kurosawa achieved something that few directors, even very good directors, get to really do: present an original vision that charts new ground but still manages to deliver the chills promised by the genre film label. Koji Yakusho delivers a devastating portrayal of a homicide detective losing control, a man at the end of his tether from worry about his mentally ill wife and his inability to understand the rash of senseless murders he must investigate. The mystery of the crimes, that it's a different killer each time, people who do not know each other but who all leave a bloody 'X' carved in their victim's throats, pushes him to the brink. When the instigator, an amnesiac savant (Masoto Hagiwara in an unnerving performance), is caught, Yakusho and his psychologist colleague find that he is very dangerous indeed. A fanatical follower of long-dead Franz Mesmer, Hagiwara is able to hypnotize just about anyone after only a few moments of innocuous conversation. Yakusho investigates Hagiwara's background and catalogs enough uncanny backstory details for several nerve-shredding thrillers, let alone one. Once Yakusho is inadvertently hypnotized himself and fully understands Hagiwara's mindset, he takes a giant leap into uncharted Nietzche territory, a mental landscape where total freedom reigns. But the new perception of the human world Yakusho enters is frighteningly beyond good and evil.

Serpent's Path, Kurosawa's next, is also a masterwork, a combination *yakuza/* suspense thriller that is guaranteed to raise the hackles on the back of the neck at its final twist revelation. An icy foray into the heart of darkness, it tails hard-boiled night school trigonometry teacher Nijima (Sho Aikawa) as he helps distraught friend Miyashita (Teruyuki Kagawa) go on the vigilante warpath to find the snuff film gang responsible for his daughter's rape/murder. With each successive gang member they capture and chain in their deserted warehouse, the web becomes more labyrinthine and more chilling. But there's one more shock up Kurosawa's sleeve, as we discover Nijima has been through this before when his own daughter was murdered, and that 'innocent' Miyashita may not be as blameless as he seems.

Sho Aikawa is also called Nijima in *Eye Of The Spider*, and the story, filmed back to back with the preceding picture, is similar. But that's where resemblances end, because Kurosawa takes a different approach, transmuting violent events into an

Cure

absurdist black comedy. Nijima's marriage irrevocably changes when he finds and kills his daughter's murderer, and soon afterwards he is drafted into his friend's clandestine gang of assassins. Subsequently, he's taken under the wing of an elderly, fossil-collecting *yakuza* boss, a relationship that will eventually culminate in its own overflowing body count.

Kurosawa continued his prolific output in 1997 with two more films featuring Sho Aikawa, films that could ultimately be described as variations on the same theme as *Serpent's Path*: vengeance and its consequences. Sho Aikawa is a police detective in *Revenge – A Visit From Fate*, hounded by memories from childhood of his parents' brutal murder. He accidentally discovers the killer's identity while on an unrelated case, but, before he can do anything, the culprit slays his wife. Once again, Kurosawa achieves maximum impact from a minimal budget and cast, delivering a claustrophobic, fast-moving nail-biter that utilizes the one shot/one take method he had begun to perfect in *Cure*. It's a style somewhat similar to that of Takeshi Kitano, many scenes composed as master long or medium shots, long takes occasionally punctuated with robust, emotion-wringing close-ups.

In the sequel, *Revenge – The Scar That Never Fades*, Aikawa is no longer on the police force, employed by a recycling company as he pursues his vendetta against those responsible for the murders that occurred in the previous film. Kurosawa uses more humor here than in *Visit* (which actually had none), placing Aikawa in an awkward between-a-rock-and-a-hard-place situation when a young police detective, Nishi, follows him hoping to prevent further bloodshed. Complicating matters is Aikawa's budding friendship with *yakuza* boss Yoshioka.

Charisma was Kurosawa's return to occult thriller territory, though by an unusually circuitous route. Koji Yakusho stars as a hostage negotiator burnt out after a particularly galling failure. He's forced by his boss to take indefinite leave, and he gravitates to a strange forested area populated by a community of opinionated screwballs. This is Kurosawa at his most dreamlike, a ghostly travelogue where

Eye Of The Spider

everything seems normal on the surface, but things are not quite right. Yakusho wanders, interacting with the inhabitants, from the odd young man who lives in the deserted, overgrown sanitarium, to the grouchy woodsmen to a dedicated female botanist, all of them obsessed with a gigantic tree that they call Charisma. Some believe it's sacred, some believe it has unique properties that can reap huge profits, and the botanist is convinced that its sap is the most virulent toxin on earth. What the viewer never gets to see is the tree actually taking any overt, obvious action of its own, something that might bother the more literal-minded of genre film fans. However, what Kurosawa *does* achieve here, much the same as he does in *Cure* and the later *Pulse*, is exhibit the ultimate impotence of rational thought in the face of the unknown. *Charisma* represents the mysteries of the universe that will be outside man's understanding forever, forces that tap into Jung's collective unconscious and exert their own supernatural will.

Séance, a made-for-television film, is Kurosawa's remake of *Séance On A Wet Afternoon*, complete with a new supernatural twist not found in the original. It works simultaneously as a hackle-raising ghost story and a compassionate, profound meditation on the contradictory plight of exceptional people submerged in mediocrity. Jun Fubuki plays a genuine medium who is as adept at clairvoyance as contacting the spirit world. She's recruited by the police when a young neighborhood girl is kidnapped, but a bizarre coincidence occurs when her foley sound engineer husband (Koji Yakusho) is in the forest recording effects. Unbeknownst to Yakusho the kidnapped girl has escaped into the same woods, and, when she finds his oversized anvil soundcase, she hides inside it. When he returns home and finds her inside, his first instinct is to contact the police. But his wife, Fubuki, stops him, unable to resist seizing an opportunity to cement her notoriety on a national scale. They put off returning the girl until they can engineer a scenario where Fubuki can 'discover' her in the presence of the authorities. But fate disrupts her perfectly laid plans when the girl dies by accident. They're forced to bury her in the forest. From then on, both Fubuki and Yakusho are haunted by her ghost until her body is finally found by the police, and the comparatively relieved and contrite couple surrender, admitting their ruse. A scary little thriller, Kurosawa achieves the frissons by making Yakusho and Fubuki human, identifiable as real people. You sympathize with them and recoil simultaneously as they fall into a trap of their own devising.

Pulse is probably Kurosawa's most perfectly realized horror picture, working on that peculiarly potent Japanese wavelength already charted by *Cure*, as well as by Hideo Nakata's *Ring* and Takashi Miike's *Audition*. But Kurosawa was not entirely happy with *Pulse*, feeling that the end result had been compromised into a more conventional genre picture. The film starts on an ocean liner with the protagonist, Michi, flashing back to the terrors that had led to her running away. It had begun when a missing co-worker had been found as a suicide, hanging in his dreary apartment. She had then discovered a ghostly image appearing with the dead man on one of his computer disks. A plague of ghost sightings on various computers had followed, a mass hysterical trauma inspiring suicides and thus more restless spirits. Kurosawa follows the premise with nightmare precision, which is abetted by his unerring eye for the creepiest 'found' locations imaginable. Notwithstanding an ending that seems a bit hurried, Kurosawa provides more thrills and chills per square inch than in many other recent Japanese ghost films, including the boilerplate gem *Ring*. One can see why the rights to this were quickly snatched up for an American remake.

Kurosawa's latest, *Doppelgänger*, is an absurdly comic variant on alter ego thrillers. Combining elements of such traditional stories as Stevenson's *Dr Jekyll And Mr Hyde* and Poe's *William Wilson*, it's a droll shaggy dog tale of the violently repressed frustrations of an overachieving inventor (Koji Yakusho) suddenly manifesting themselves in the spontaneous appearance of his amoral, wisecracking and unpredictably violent double (also Yakusho).

KIYOSHI KUROSAWA – SELECTED FILMOGRAPHY

1989	*SWEET HOME (SUITO HOMU)*
1992	*GUARD FROM THE UNDERGROUND (JIGOKU NO KEIBIIN,* aka *HELL GUARDIAN)*
1995	*SUIT YOURSELF OR SHOOT YOURSELF (KATTE NI SHIYAGARE)* [six films – two in 1995, four in 1996]
1996	*DOOR 3 (DOA 3)*
1997	*CURE (KYUA)*
	SERPENT'S PATH (HEBI NO MICHI)
	EYE OF THE SPIDER (KUMO NO HITOMI)
	REVENGE – A VISIT FROM FATE (FUKUSHU – UNMEI NO HOMONSHA)
	REVENGE – THE SCAR THAT NEVER FADES (FUKUSHU – KIENAI KIZUATO)
1998	*LICENSE TO LIVE (NINGEN GOKAKU)*
1999	*CHARISMA (KARISUMA)*
	BARREN ILLUSION (OINARU GENEI)
2000	*SÉANCE (KOUREI)*
2001	*PULSE (KAIRO)*
2003	*BRIGHT FUTURE (AKARUI MIRAI)*
2004	*DOPPELGANGER*

KIYOSHI KUROSAWA – INTERVIEW

The following interview is composed of three question-and-answer sessions Kiyoshi Kurosawa had with Dennis Bartok and me following screenings of his films Cure, Charisma *and* Séance *at the American Cinematheque's Egyptian Theatre in Hollywood in July, 2001. Linda Hoaglund did on-site translation on all of them. Dennis is signified as DB and I am signified as CD.*

DB: Did you scare yourself when you were in the process of making Cure?

KUROSAWA: While I was making it, I was so absorbed in the task at hand that it didn't even occur to me. But I'm a super scaredy-cat, so when I saw it with an audience I completely freaked out.

DB: What was the idea for Cure *when you began writing the script? What did you begin with, the mesmerism? The murder of the prostitute with the 'X' carved in the throat?*

KUROSAWA: I had the idea about ten years ago, when there were constant reports from American TV and newspapers about a murderer who had been arrested here. I don't know about in the United States but in Japan the media immediately goes to the neighbor, who invariably says, 'He was just an average guy. I could never imagine he would do such a gruesome deed.' And the news commentators conclude that he was a fiend masquerading as an average person. A conclusion that I could never find myself agreeing with, and I always wondered what if, in fact, it was a genuinely good person who had been tripped by happenstance into committing a murder. And that was the beginning of the film.

DB: The link between the murders, the 'X' carved in the carotid arteries; was that your original idea, or did you have other things that were also unifying links?

KUROSAWA: I was always looking for an appropriate symbol to tie the murders together, and I was tormenting myself with what would be the most appropriate sign to express the rage and hatred deep in the hearts of all of us. My wife suggested that, if she was going to kill someone she hated, she would slash their throats with an 'X'. I said, 'There we go!'

DB: Thank God for your wife! She really helped out with the filmmaking. The character of the mesmerist is unique, almost a shamanic character, an evil priest. How difficult was it to find the right actor for that role?

KUROSAWA: His name is Masoto Hagiwara. He's a young and fine actor, but he's mostly appeared on television. In Japan, there's not so much of a line delineating film actors from television actors. But he's always played an upright, decent young man. And I thought this guy's got a shadow somewhere. So I went ahead, and I think we found a new side of him.

DB: How much did you rehearse with him and the other cast members, like Koji Yakusho, prior to shooting?

KUROSAWA: Generally, I don't rehearse. I guess I may be unique in this, but I find that, through the rehearsal process and then as the take numbers rise, the performers lose their initial hesitation, and they become comfortable in their roles. My ideal understanding of what an actor is on-screen is a unique amalgam of the fictional character I've created on the page and the actor as a living human being, who then enacts it so it's neither the fictional character that I wrote nor the actor as human being but some strange, wonderful, unimaginable combination of the two. So, I'm interested in capturing the actor in the moment before he actually becomes transformed into the fictional character I've created. I'm interested in that point of entry where the human being is trying to become a fictional character and hasn't quite made it yet. Urban dwellers in Japan are always shifting and waffling between their real selves and their social selves that they've created in order to survive in society. So, in that sense, when I capture the actor in the process of trying to become the fictional character, I have, in fact, created the reflection of the typical Japanese urban dweller straddling the two.

DB: You do something very subtle in the film. In Tokyo, one of the key elements of life in the city is that there are so many people everywhere, and yet in Cure *you use a lot of empty space – empty rooms, scenes where there are one or two, maybe three people. It almost creates the sense of a ghost city. Did you do that consciously?*

KUROSAWA: Yes, my films are characterized by rooms that are too large and streets that are too empty. In fact, the rooms are very small and the streets very crowded in Tokyo. I'm not 100 percent sure why I prefer this ghost town effect. I think perhaps it has something to do with my understanding that many of us, although we may live in physically crowded areas, existentially we often find ourselves alone and adrift in empty space. And I think that's why I tend to prefer this style.

DB: You have a beautiful eye for choosing locations. All of the locations in Cure *– the hospital, the kind of abandoned barn building at the end – feel like the desiccated bones of some ancient creature. They're all dilapidated, about to collapse. How hard is it for you to find those locations?*

KUROSAWA: In general, I do have a preference for ruins and abandoned buildings, and, in fact, they are quite hard to find in Tokyo. In the script, it just says innocently 'a house,' 'a hospital.' And then what happens, I'm driving around Tokyo and suddenly I come across a ruined hospital or an empty building and go, 'That's it! We're shooting there!' However, unfortunately in Japan we have a tradition of immediately demolishing buildings as soon as they become defunct and then building new ones over them. So, if I am driving around and happen to find the perfect building, I know I have to shoot it quickly for the film. I'm kind of a one-man landmark commission, recording it in my movie for posterity.

DB: Another remarkable thing about the film is the sound design, the cyclical mechanical noises in the background – how long did you spend designing the soundtrack for Cure?

KUROSAWA: Probably shorter than a typical American film. I would say, with *Cure*, it was about a month. We *do* record the actors' dialogue on location. However, I'm always telling my sound crew to be alert and record *any* available sounds, whether it's a nearby river or a construction site, because I have no idea at the time what sounds I might want to use later in the final mix. My definition of live-action film is that, although we can only peep into the reality that's framed by the four sides of the screen, in fact there's a world that extends far deeper, well into and beyond the screen, and all sides around the frame. That's my understanding. In terms of sound as well, I'm interested in conveying to my audience all the ways that that world beyond the screen sounds. I'm interested in the sounds that emanate from next door, from behind the walls, what's over the mountain, across the street.

Audience member: What are we to make of what happens to the detective at the end? Has he gone crazy because of all the knowledge he's acquired? Are we able to see any hope at the end?

KUROSAWA: My understanding of what has happened to the detective is not that he has gone crazy but that, since he now understands everything, for the first time he is completely and totally sane, realizing that living the complacent average life is what is truly sick. Because of that understanding, he has now finally leaped beyond and outside the morality, justice and conventions that bind people to society. So, of course, in the eyes of society he is now a criminal. The question is: does this leave us with any hope? Certainly, I'm not advocating that people go out and do this in their real lives. But, seeing as how we are in the realm of fiction, if we were to posit a person finding true, unmitigated freedom, I think you would have to agree that that person would find himself outside the confines of the law. What I wanted to suggest is that, for him, this is hope, and that at the end of the film he is definitely walking very clear-eyed towards what is hopeful. Once again, this is in the world of fiction, and I'm not suggesting that people should find hope in this way in their personal lives.

Audience member: I find it interesting that water usually symbolizes something pure, but you have used it as a hypnotic trigger for murder.

KUROSAWA: Well, I think, yes, water can symbolize many things, and the water that is once seen to be pure now has a precipitating effect on murderous feelings. I was mostly just interested in showing it being tasteless and transparent.

Audience member: There seem to be several ambiguous ideas and story elements in Cure *that defy description. Did you do this intentionally?*

KUROSAWA: I never intentionally make ambiguous that which should be clear. Certainly, my understanding of film is that the story is an element of film, but it's very much about portraying a reality, a world that exists beyond the screen. I think you would have to agree that our encounters with reality can sometimes be clear and unambiguous, but more often they are confoundingly complex, and the meaning of events that unfold before us can often elude comprehension forever. So, when I make my films, I am not the all-seeing, omniscient God explaining to you in the audience what has happened and why. You should just think of my movies as a string of scenes of pondering what I would do and how I would face these events unfolding before my eyes. The reality that I find incomprehensible and confounding, I present it exactly to you how I encounter it myself. That's the approach I take to moviemaking.

DB: Moving onto Charisma, *was the story gestating in your mind for a while or did it happen very quickly?*

KUROSAWA: The story first came to my mind about ten years ago, and as soon as it occurred to me I wrote it very quickly. But it actually took many years before I could get it produced, so over the years it went around and around in my head, metamorphosing.

DB: Japanese culture, arts, literature have always seemed to be fascinated with nature. There are even a number of festivals celebrating nature. How much of that worked its way into your subconscious when you were writing Charisma?

KUROSAWA: The film is imbued with my personal ideas of nature, but whether it's really reflective of a larger tradition, I'd have to say that Japan today is composed of a wide range of value systems. Some may hold the traditional values dear, but many young people have abandoned them completely. I, myself, can't say I've felt closely associated with traditional relationships to nature. But I have to say, too, that I've never whole-heartedly embraced the idea of human beings protecting nature, because I feel that that inadvertently – or advertently – places us as being above nature. Which we then condescend to protect. That idea has never been all that appealing to me. If anything, I think of nature as an alarming, terrifying, vast force that, at times, can be beautiful and peaceful, but can just as readily come after you and devour you. So, far from human beings being above it, we're actually below it. I think the thing to do is leave well enough alone and not provoke nature. In that sense, I may be traditionally Japanese.

DB: How long did you search for the locations? The forest and woods are very haunting, but they are not spectacularly beautiful. There are more scenic vistas in Japan. Why did you choose those specific locations?

KUROSAWA: It was difficult to find the right location. When I first came up with the idea ten years ago, I'd just seen an Italian movie with beautiful woods in it, and I thought, 'Oh, gosh, maybe it should be an Italian *Charisma*.' And, once we actually started prepping, I happened to have been invited to the Toronto Film Festival. So, when I was riding the train to Toronto, I thought, 'Oh, maybe a Canadian *Charisma*.' When I confided these thoughts to my producer, he accused me of being completely stupid and said, 'Maybe Taiwan, no farther.' I was about to depart to go location scouting in Taiwan when my producer told me that there were some terrific woods in southern Japan. I realized at this point that destiny was calling me into the woods very near Tokyo. We actually wound up shooting in woods near Mt. Fuji, which is relatively close to Tokyo. And, in order to come under the very low budget, we ended up driving three and a half hours each way because we couldn't even afford a hotel. So, I think this may give you a sense of what it's like to make a movie in Japan – you dream of Italian woods then sort of end up with brush anywhere.

DB: Koji Yakusho stars in both Cure *and* Charisma, *and gives a fantastic performance in both. How did you first meet him?*

KUROSAWA: I first met him when I cast him in *Cure*. By that time, he was already a star. Perhaps some of you have seen *Shall We Dance*, which has been released here too? That movie made him a star in Japan, and my casting condition for the lead in *Cure* was that he had to be a star and be about my age. There's actually only one person who fits that description in Japan, and that's him. By the time I met him, he had played everything from a samurai to a weak-willed salaryman to murderers to cops. I looked forward to meeting someone who I felt must be a very powerful actor. But I found him to be a down-to-earth, everyday man, without even a whiff of stardom about him. In that sense, I very much consider myself, too, an average person. Ever since I've started working with him, it's been my ambition to push him to his very limits of normality, to see just how far I can drive him towards shattering that normality. Which goes even a step farther in my film *Séance*.

DB: You use music sparingly in all of your films. Here, in Charisma, *you use it in only a few places, a kind of bouncy, almost light-hearted theme. Why did you decide to use that type of score?*

KUROSAWA: In *Charisma*, which is very much a jumble of a genre film, I was torn about what kind of music to use. I mostly simply eliminated it. For the one tune to use, my request to my composer was to score folk music that would sound like it was from nowhere exactly on this planet. So I made him listen to folk music from Europe, Asia, the United States, from all over the world. And then told him, 'None of the above.' It nearly drove him out of his mind. Finally, we settled on what we used.

DB: Charisma *is also one of your funniest films, in a perverse kind of way. There are these beautiful little moments, such as when Koji Yakusho is walking through the forest and hears his cellphone ringing, and it's his boss. Or when the sister at the end grabs the 10,000,000 yen and runs off. Did the audiences in Japan respond to the comedy in the movie?*

KUROSAWA: Nobody laughed! I thought it was funny while I was making it, but, unfortunately, without the kind of appropriate musical or other signifying cues that would give the Japanese audience permission to laugh, they were left a little flummoxed. And it made me feel very sad and lonely. (*laughter from audience*)

DB: I was wondering how you see your titles. Cure, Charisma, Séance, Pulse – *they're all enigmatic, one-word titles. Certainly, you have other films with longer titles, like* Serpent's Path. *But movie titles are obviously important to you. How do you go about deciding on a title?*

KUROSAWA: It is very difficult to come up with titles. Ten years ago, when I was writing the screenplay for this one, it never even occurred to me to call it *Charisma*. Then I woke up one day and saw a headline in the newspaper that Von Karajan, the conductor, had died. At the end of the article it said – I guess in English, to make it grammatically correct – 'The last charismatic individual has died.' But in Japanese it more literally translates as 'the last charisma dies.' So, in that moment, I realized the title of my new movie. I decided not only to call the tree in the film Charisma but to make one of the themes a questioning of

what 'charisma' is. I had already written half of the screenplay, which I promptly
threw out and started all over again. For *Cure*, I didn't have the title until we had
finished shooting and editing, until we were almost done with post-production.
The young people in the advertising and publicity department started a rumor
that *Cure* was the right title for the film. That's how that one came about. Naming
a movie is actually a profound source of anxiety for me. I never know when one
will pounce at me.

DB: Do we have any questions from the audience?

*Audience member: Can you explain where you see yourself in the whole of Japanese
cinema?*

KUROSAWA: Of course, you're familiar with classical Japanese film directors
such as Ozu and Akira Kurosawa. The studio system that spawned and nurtured
them came to a halt and died in the 1970s. I belong to the generation that came
of age after the end of the studio system as we used to know it. It's difficult for
me to evaluate my own position in Japanese film now. Of the people who came
along later, who came of age during the eighties, many have gone on to become
quite commercial directors and others remain making very personal films. I guess
I would say that I'm halfway in between – making neither, in a sense. I'm sort
of the eldest of the new generation of filmmakers. Sometimes I think I'm a bit
passé. However, most Japanese films are neither purely commercial nor are they,
except for a few, completely independent or *auteur*-based. Most films being
made fall somewhere in between. Hold onto your seats, but *Charisma* is actually
considered a fairly commercial film in Japan. It was produced by a bona fide but

Jun Fubuki, Koji Yakusho in *Séance*

small studio called Nikkatsu. It had commercial runs in both Japan and France. And, most importantly, it made its money back.

Audience member: What are you planning to film next?

KUROSAWA: I have just finished some treatment and am about to write the screenplay for what I think will be a very low-budget, quiet film. And I don't think it will be a horror film.

Audience member: Can you talk a little about some of your favorite films?

KUROSAWA: I'm not that familiar with recent American films. But I am familiar with many earlier American films, and I think there are many really wonderful ones. Certainly all of John Cassavetes's films. But I don't want you to think I'm only interested in independently made films. I'm also a huge Peckinpah fan. *The Ballad Of Cable Hogue* I can watch over and over again.

CD: Was Séance *a project that was brought to you or something that you developed yourself?*

KUROSAWA: It was a job for hire put together by a Japanese television network.

CD: I don't know if it started with the original Japanese Ring, *but there's been a real resurgence of the Japanese horror film in the nineties. And contemporary Japanese horror pictures differ quite a bit from the majority of nineties American horror films, which seem to consist largely of the 'teens-in-jeopardy-from-a-slasher' genre. What do you think of the difference between the two styles?*

KUROSAWA: As you say, *Ring* did spawn quite the horror boom in Japan, and you could say that *Séance* was part of that boom in that a television network wanted to catch that wave. From many years ago, way before *Ring*, there was the tradition of the *kaidan* or ghost story film, a tradition that really died out in the seventies. And I think we're really seeing a resurrection in contemporary form of that. I think one of the biggest things that distinguishes a Japanese ghost story from an American one is that the Japanese ghosts are usually fairly passive and really don't do too much. So, in an American horror movie, if it's a monster or a slasher who comes after you aggressively, then the human being has the choice of fighting back, running away; if the creature speaks English you can speak to it and try to negotiate an escape... (*audience laughter*) It can be a wonderful way to make a movie. But, trust me, it can be a very expensive way to make a movie. What Japanese ghosts do is they just want to impress upon the living their deadness, so they basically just appear and are there. So, because the ghosts are passive, the human being who sees them doesn't really need to run away or speak to them or even attack them. And, actually, daily life can continue more or less normally even in their presence. I think that's what really distinguishes the Japanese ghost film; suddenly death is very close by, and you have to go on about the business of living. It's the horrifying, awfully close presence of death. And, in that sense, it also has the benefit of being cheap to produce. Basically, you're showing how the daily life, the mundane routine of someone suddenly graced by the presence of a ghost, is affected. And that's where your skill as a writer and director comes in to portray those subtle changes.

CD: There's also a characteristic in some Japanese ghost stories, as well as European and American ones, of the person haunted being somehow complicit in the death of the person that is now a ghost. You see that in The Yotsuya Ghost Story *(Yotsuya Kaidan),* Ghosts Of Kasane Swamp *(Kaidan Kasanegafuchi). There were countless versions of those, as well as various cat ghost tales from the silent movie era through the late seventies. Do you have any favorite Japanese* kaidan *movies from that time?*

KUROSAWA: *The Yotsuya Ghost Story* or *Yotsuya Kaidan* was something that was written well over 100 years ago as a kabuki stage piece during the Edo period. There are many film versions. The basic story is that a woman is done wrong to by a man who murders her, and then later she comes back to avenge her own death. Instead of attacking him in any way, she just makes her presence acutely felt. And, through his guilt, his sanity slowly dissolves. And, in the many versions, the man who kills her is depicted in varying degrees of evil. In some he's evil incarnate, and in others he almost kills her by chance. The most famous movie of the story was directed by a gentleman named Nobuo Nakagawa, and it was called *Tokaido Yotsuya Kaidan* (1959). In that one, the guy is kind of intermediate bad. It's a very well-done movie. But my favorite is one directed by Kenji Misumi in the early sixties titled simply *Yotsuya Kaidan*, and, in it, the man is not really evil at all, he didn't have any murderous intent, and the woman is killed by accident. But, nonetheless, she comes back with a deadly vengeance, and he slowly self-destructs from her presence from guilt. In that sense, the film is much like what happens with characters in *Séance*. They didn't kill the child through murderous intent. It was much more of an accident. But that does not lessen the rage of the deceased.

CD: One of the things most disturbing about your films, even crime films like Serpent's Path *and the* Revenge *movies, is some event out of nowhere will occur that will completely change a person's life, destroying their sense of self. Could you talk about that, the horror of realizing what one has been using to define their 'self', whether it's job, relationship, exceptional talent, really isn't who one is and, once that disappears, chaos can result?*

KUROSAWA: Yes, I would have to agree that that is a common theme in all my films, regardless of genre. To me, the way I define a typical American film is that we have a main character who is readily identified in terms of personality traits. And no matter what happens in the course of the movie, the hero or heroine will overcome all adversity, and these same personality traits will be completely unchanged, no matter what events the person has been subjected to. Those movies can be a lot of fun to watch. But, as a moviemaker making films in contemporary Japan, I cast a wide net for performers who can be strong like that, keeping their fundamental character unchanged no matter what happens to them. However, we don't seem to have many of these people in Japan. (*audience laughter*) My sense of human life and human experience is that who I am today is not identical to who I am going to be tomorrow, and that we are slowly and subtly changed every day by the experiences we have. Especially if we are to encounter the death of someone in our immediate vicinity. We as human beings are affected. I guess, to state it differently, I think that it's more realistic and natural to think of each of our human identities as quite fragile. Instead of finding it tragic that our sense of self and our identities might be changed profoundly by events that happen to us, I find in it hope and a different sense of self. And so, at the end of *Séance*, in one way it might seem tragic with the police discovering all and the couple being found out. But I actually think that, at the end, the couple's bonds have grown much stronger, that they've overcome the presence of the ghost and have found a new way of being together.

CD: Can you once again say a few words about working with Koji Yakusho, who is a truly tremendous actor?

KUROSAWA: As you know, he is a very big star in Japan. But he does not come off that way. He is self-effacing with no star affectations. If anything, because we're exactly the same age, he feels a bit of a doppelgänger of myself. He immediately and implicitly understood when I was talking about people being changed by their circumstances. We work together effortlessly. And this is true not just of him but also of many famous Japanese movie stars. They have something that is different from American stars in that they show up without any problem on television dramas and commercials. Being the kind of precious icons that American movie stars are, you can generally only see them in a movie theater. What's wonderful for us Japanese moviemakers about this phenomenon is, because they really make their bread and butter through the medium of television, Japanese actors don't come to film expecting to make a lot of money. Which is why Koji Yakusho can continue to do well and continue to show up in my movies. If they like a project, they'll just appear in a film for the fun of it and because they love the idea, however idiosyncratic it might be.

CD: You've talked a bit about sound and music. In all your pictures, Séance *included, not only the music but also the ambient sound, a succession of drones, pulses, tones, will come welling up out of nowhere and then disappear into silence. How involved do you get in the sound direction?*

KUROSAWA: I'm heavily involved in designing the sound, and I think, typically, you could say that in my movies there's less music and more effects. The effects are based on sounds from the real world. I almost never turn to synthesizers or electronics or digital media to generate sounds. In *Séance*, as a cue that the ghost is about to appear, you'll hear a staccato, high-pitched sound. What that really is is an insect from Japan. The reason that I rely on these real sounds is that I'm interested in trying to express to you the world that lies beyond what is visible on-screen. What does that world look like, feel like — that's what I'm interested in.

APPENDICES

APPENDIX – FEMALE YAKUZAS

The female *yakuza* phenomenon pops up in a few of the chapters in this book, particularly in the essay and interview with actress Meiko Kaji. Although a plethora of female *yakuza*s started to appear in the mid–1960s through to the 1970s, and off and on until the present day in genre Japanese cinema, real life is another story. It is commonly acknowledged that female *oyabun*s have existed, either as the head of crime families or sub-gangs, but it's generally been the exception rather than the rule. On rare occasions, the widows, mistresses or daughters of deceased gang lords have taken over the reins. However, it's usually been a temporary situation, and one that the vast contingents of macho male underlings do not like to advertise. The real *yakuza* underworld is based on decidedly repressive feudal values from Japan's past, and male superiority is still a given. Women in the world of the *yakuza* are much more commonly relegated to the role of prostitute, porno actress, housewife, mistress and, occasionally, tattoo artist or card dealer.

Contrary to popular perceptions, there were numerous Japanese noblewomen and warriors over the centuries who were proficient in martial arts. Probably the most recent example of women samurai in Japan were female members of the Satsuma clan during the Meiji Restoration in the 1860s, an era which saw the centuries-old Shogunate fall and an opening up of Japan to the West.

Swordswomen appeared several times in early Japanese cinema, dating from the silent era, but once again this was the exception rather than the rule. The first time women began to be seen wielding swords with any regularity was in the late 1950s in some of Shintoho studios' samurai opuses, particularly in the performances of actress Misako Uji.

Toei, Daiei and Shochiku studios saw actresses Hibari Misora, Fujiko Yamamoto and Michiko Saga display a bit of swordplay in the rare one-off film, or, as in Misora's case, various samurai and/or in-period *yakuza* musicals (!) – all with little connection to reality. As already mentioned in Teruo Ishii's chapter, contemporary female *yakuza*s showed up as well in the late 1950s in the form of actresses Naoko Kubo and Yoko Mihara in Shintoho's *Queen Bee* and *Line* series and in various Shintoho one-offs.

The more violent female movie *yakuza*s didn't crop up until the mid–1960s. The first pioneering effort in this regard seems to be Nikkatsu studios' *Cat Girl Gambling* (*Mesu Neko Bakuchi*) trilogy of films (1965–1966), directed by Seijun Suzuki's mentor Hiroshi Noguchi, and starring the excellent Yumiko Nogawa. Daiei studios jumped on the bandwagon in 1966, inaugurating their uneven but long-running

Woman Gambling Expert (*Onna Tobakushi*) series starring the talented, underrated, Kyoko Enami. Unfortunately, most of the films relegated Enami to doing her thing in the card-playing or dice-throwing arena, while leaving the violent altercations to the villains and Enami's male heroic co-stars. Finally, when it was almost too late, Kenji Misumi directed the seventeenth final entry, *Woman Gambler's Iron Rule* (*Shin Onna Tobakushi Tsubo Gure Hada*, 1971), his first effort in the series. For the first and last time, Enami, teaming up with co-star Michyo Yasuda, got to wield a blade against the bad guys. Is it any wonder that it remains one of the best entries in a frequently humdrum collection?

A watershed year for the depiction of women *yakuza*, all of the *ninkyo* variety (and also of female samurai) came in 1968, most prominently with Toei studios' phenomenally successful *Red Peony Gambler* (*Hibotan Bakuto*) pictures starring soon-to-be superstar Junko Fuji. Fuji, daughter of top Toei executive and former *yakuza* Koji Shundo, had fought long and hard at the beginning of the sixties to get her dad to allow her into acting. Although she'd appeared in numerous co-starring roles in the mid-sixties, with the *Red Peony* films her aspirations were finally fully realized. The *Red Peony Gambler* series ran for eight films between 1968 and 1972, helmed by such top *ninkyo* Toei directors as Kosaku Yamashita and Tai Kato, and often co-written by director (and Fuji's uncle) Norifumi Suzuki. Indeed, Tai Kato's efforts in the series are now universally acclaimed as sublime examples of the *ninkyo yakuza* genre.

The success of the *Red Peony Gambler* films caused an outburst of both female *yakuza* and samurai cinema at not only Toei but other studios, such as Daiei, Nikkatsu and Shochiku. Daiei emerged with the enjoyable *Kanto Woman* (1968–1969) quartet of *yakuza* films and the lesser-known female samurai *One-Eyed, One-Armed Swordswoman* (*Onna Sazen*, 1968–1969) duo, all starring the marvellously talented Michiyo Yasuda (now known as Michiyo Okusu). Yasuda also starred in four out of six of the in-period *Secrets Of A Women's Prison* (*Hiroku Onna-Ro*, 1968–1971).

In 1968 Toei also gave Junko Miyazono a chance to shine in a starring role in the Grand Guignol female samurai *Quick Draw Okatsu* (*Yoen Dokufuden*) trio, two of which were helmed by maestro Nobuo Nakagawa.

Shochiku melded elements from both the *Zatoichi* series and the *Red Peony Gambler* sagas with Yoko Matsuyama as blind Oichi, *The Crimson Bat* (*Mekura No Oichi or Blind Oichi*) in four pictures in 1969–1970. In 1969 Nikkatsu studios, too, showcased singer Hiroko Ogi in two *ninkyo*–flavored series, *Rising Dragon* (*Nobori Ryu*) and *Vermillion Sword Scabbard Code* (*Shuzaya Jingi*), both consisting of two movies (although Meiko Kaji headlined in a third, comparatively unrelated *Rising Dragon* film *Blind Woman's Curse*). There were several *ninkyo* one-offs at Nikkatsu from 1968 through to 1970, starring the likes of Chieko Matsubara, Meiko Kaji and Ogi.

Toei branched out Junko Fuji into other *ninkyo* offerings in 1969, including the two-film *Chivalrous Woman* (*Onna Toseinin*, aka *Okoma, Orphan Gambler*) series, and in 1971, the five-picture *Tales Of Japan's Chivalrous Women* (*Nihon Jokyoden*). Junko Fuji effectively signaled an end to the more traditional female *ninkyo* movies in 1972 when she retired from the screen to get married. Her last picture at Toei was the all-star *ninkyo yakuza Cherry Blossom Fire Gang* (*Kanto Hizakura Ikka*). But Toei tried to hit female *ninkyo* pay dirt once more, first with Kyoko Enami in Tai Kato's *Showa Woman Gambler* (*Showa Onna Bakuto*, 1972), then with the late Eiko Nakamura in Teruo Ishii's graphically Grand Guignol, *The Silk Gambler* (*Hichirimen Bakuto*, 1972). Toei's resident delinquent girl, Reiko Ike, gave it a try in 1973 in the even more over-the-top *Elder Sister* (*Anego Den* aka *Ocho*) pair of films directed by Norifumi Suzuki and Teruo Ishii. Despite all being extremely entertaining tall tales, none caught fire at the box office.

Meiko Kaji did a more contemporary take on the *ninkyo yakuza* heroine, mixing elements from Toei's and Nikkatsu's *sukeban* (delinquent girl boss) genre of films, in director Kazuhiko Yamaguchi's two *Ginjo* (*Silver Butterfly*) movies in 1972. The following year, 1973, saw Toho draft Kaji for director Toshiya Fujita's turn-of-the-century duo of *Lady Snowblood* (*Shura Yukihime*) pictures adapted from Kazuo Koike's popular *manga*. The revenge saga, though not specifically *ninkyo yakuza* or samurai, had the feeling of both and employed a true-to-the-period radical anarchist political background as subtext.

Indeed, though no sword-wielding heroines existed in real life during the late nineteenth/early twentieth century, there *were* numerous female activists, some violent anarchists, who lived and died during the era. All female *ninkyo yakuza* films, and especially the *Lady Snowblood* movies, seem to have derived varying degrees of inspiration from these real-life role models. Fascinating anecdotal evidence of these activists' struggles can be found in Mikiso Hane's exemplary book *Reflections On The Way To The Gallows – Rebel Women In Pre-War Japan* (see Bibliography).

Another element of the female *yakuza* phenomenon in Japanese cinema is the *sukeban*, or delinquent girl boss, subgenre. The first example seems to have been Toei's pair of *Bad Angel* (*Zubeko Tenshi*) films starring Mitsue Komiya in 1960. And, although there were a couple more obscure films at Nikkatsu in the mid-sixties with bad girl characters, none caught on in a big way until the five-entry *Stray Cat Rock* (*Nora Neko Rokku*, 1970–1971) bunch starring Meiko Kaji. Now it was Toei's turn to jump on the bandwagon, as *Stray Cat Rock*'s success spurred them to star, first, Reiko Oshida in director Kazuhiko Yamaguchi's four-picture *Delinquent Girl Boss* (*Zubeko Bancho*, 1970–1971) series, then Reiko Ike and Miki Sugimoto in the hellzapoppin, everything-but-the-kitchen-sink girl gang celebration *Girl Boss* (*Sukeban*). The *Girl Boss* sagas started in 1972 and ran for seven exhilaratingly absurd entries until 1974. There was also the pseudo-*Girl-Boss* spin-off, *Terrifying Girls' High School* (*Kyofu Joshi Kokosei*, 1972–1973) which ran for four films, also featuring Ike and Sugimoto. Also deserving of mention was Toho studios' under-the-radar, low-budget, *manga*-derived *sukeban* film trilogy *Half-Breed Rika* (*Konketsuji Rika*, 1972). Starring Rika Aoki with anarchic, tongue-in-cheek, socially conscious screenplays by Kaneto Shindo, the first two were directed by Ko Nakahira and the third by Kozaburo Yoshimura.

A surreal, important footnote to the 1970s female *yakuza* genre came with the four extremely successful, *manga*-inspired *Female Convict Scorpion* (*Joshu Sasori* 1972–1973) pictures starring Meiko Kaji, transcendental examples of violent seventies cinema. Toei continued to stoke box-office fires without Meiko Kaji in two more *Female Convict Scorpion* films in 1976 and 1977, *New Female Convict Scorpion – Number 701* with Yumi Takigawa and *New Female Convict Scorpion – Special Cell Block X* with Yoko Natsuki, respectively. Both were directed by Yu Kohira but, compared to the Kaji entries, the results were lackluster. When director Toshiharu Ikeda (director of *Evil Death Trap*) turned out a one-off installment in 1991, *Female Convict Scorpion – Death Threat*, the pendulum briefly swang back in the right direction. Two or three fairly innocuous released–direct-to-video installments followed in the later 1990s.

Since the late seventies female *yakuza*s have continued to proliferate in Japanese motion pictures, most notably in *Yakuza Wives* (*Gokudo No Onnatachi*), a tremendously lucrative string of ultra-violent soap operas showcasing the unlikely but unusually effective Shima Iwashita as a *yakuza* widow taking over the reins of her deceased husband's gang. Hideo Gosha directed the quite good first effort with Iwashita in 1986. For some reason, numbers two and three featured different actresses in the lead (Yukiyo Toake and Yoshiko Mita, respectively). By number four, undoubtedly due to Toei's financial carrot-dangling, Iwashita returned to the series. And she kept returning, as the hard-boiled gang boss in a kimono (sometimes wielding an inappropriate, decidedly non-*ninkyo* Uzi in at least one installment), until 1998. Reigning female *yakuza* star Reiko Takashima (of the nineties *ninkyo* franchise *Heat Wave*, aka *Kagero*) took over the role from Iwashita for at least three subsequent entries.

APPENDIX – THE STUDIOS

SHINTOHO

Shintoho studios came into being after several years of contentious labor disputes at Toho studios in the turbulent post-WW2 period (the late 1940s). At the time the Communist Party had a huge following amongst many cast and crew at Toho, as well as at other studios, and was instrumental in helping to unionize the industry. Which was a good thing. However, things got so ridiculous in matters of political correctness that there was an enormous backlash, not just from a more right-wing quarter but also from leftist – as well as apolitical – performers and filmmakers, who were devoted to cinema as an art rather than as simply a business or political platform. A great deal of proletariat propaganda force-fed by the infant unions was starting to show up in some Toho productions, as well as in crippling demands that had the unfortunate effect of making the pendulum swing the other way.

A number of big names, mostly star actors such as Denjiro Okochi and Kazuo Hasegawa, split off, along with various producers and crew, to help form a new company, which became known as Shintoho. In its early years Shintoho was owned by Toho. Eventually Shintoho became an independent, although their films were still distributed by Toho, and they were often subjected to unfair economic constraints due to Toho's massive post-war labor problems and consequent mismanagement. Directors working at Toho, such as Akira Kurosawa, would often make films at Shintoho, superior genre efforts such as *Stray Dog* (1949). Kon Ichikawa also made his debut film at Shintoho, and later turned out such hard-to-now-see genre efforts as *Heat And Mud* (1950) and *Nightshade Flower* (1951).

Older, bigger Toho's distribution of Shintoho products would become an increasingly bitter bone of contention as the decade of the fifties progressed. By 1951 many of the big stars who had helped to start Shintoho had left for better deals at Daiei and Shochiku. Since Shintoho never had too many heavyweight directors in their stable – despite the occasional movies by Daisuke Ito, Nobuo Nakagawa and Kunio Watanabe – and often had to scramble to keep their doors open, there was a constant struggle to keep heads above water.

In 1956, former carnival showman and huckster Mitsugu Okura came on board at Shintoho as executive producer. Okura's manner and taste was laid on with a trowel, and was perceived by many as being vulgar and catering to the lowest common denominator. Okura shifted the emphasis, from a selection of quickly produced prestige dramas, as well as genre films, to almost exclusively genre 'outlaw' cinema. He amped up the sex and violence – as much as he could get away with – and began producing scores of ever more lurid melodramas, sexy gangster thrillers, samurai films chock-full of swordfights, period horror and ghost chillers and disturbingly right-wing, nationalist war movies. The formula worked for a while. Indeed, there were films by directors like Teruo Ishii, with his 'sleaze noir' *Line* (aka *Zone*) series, and Nobuo Nakagawa, with his horror and samurai sagas (such as *Hell* (*Jigoku*, 1960), *Ghost Of Yotsuya* (*Tokaido Yotsuya Kaidan*, 1959), *Shadow Priest's Crime Casebook* (1959), *Black Cat Mansion* (*Borei Kaibyo Yashiki*, 1958), *Wicked Woman Oden Takahashi* (1958), *Military Cop And The Ghost* (*Kenpei to Yurei*, 1958), *The Depths* (*Kaidan Kasanegafuchi*, 1957), et al.) that are now looked on as touchstone classics of their respective genres.

Unfortunately, the distribution issue with Toho became so acrimonious that Shintoho attempted to split off from their symbiotic stronger twin as the decade came to a close. Bankruptcy and studio closure resulted in 1961. The mid-nineties finally saw more and more video and DVD releases of long-unavailable old Shintoho titles, particularly their horror titles and films directed by Ishii and Nakagawa.

TOHO

In 1935 Ichizo Kobayashi, a real-estate tycoon and founder of the Takarazuka all-girl opera troupe, bought up control of PCL (Photo Chemical Laboratories) and J. O. (Jenkins–Ozawa), two production companies that had already been churning out both feature and advertising films. This enabled PCL to finally offer enough of a financial incentive to lure away such big directors as Kajiro Yamamoto from Nikkatsu and Mikio Naruse from Shochiku. By the following year boss Kobayashi had also formed a distribution corporation, although his theater holdings were initially deficient compared to industry giants like Shochiku.

Toho subsequently attempted to develop a friendly, mutually beneficial relationship with cash-deficient Nikkatsu, but this served to escalate antagonism toward both companies from the jealous-to-stay-on-top Shochiku. Distribution feuds followed. Financial intimidation, usually from Shochiku in the form of a booking boycott, was aimed at various theater owners who refused to exclusively play one studio's product. Talent raids, at first primarily from Toho, were used as retaliation, and Toho boss Kobayashi managed to lure away such popular actors as Kazuo Hasegawa and Denjiro Okochi and such directors as Sadao Yamanaka and Mansaku Itami. Shortly after jumping the Shochiku ship in 1937, Hasegawa was actually attacked by a razor-wielding *yakuza* hired by a Shochiku labor boss, and received a scar that would stay with him for the rest of his long career (he retired in 1963 with his 300th film, the classic *An Actor's Revenge*, directed by Kon Ichikawa at Daiei). The attack backfired, putting the public on Toho's side. Toho's fortunes only improved in the ensuing years, as they composed more hit films and acquired more talent looking for greener pastures.

As noted in the Shintoho section above, Toho enjoyed more than its share of labor difficulties post-WW2. But they also continued to make exceptional films, many by respected veteran filmmakers such as Mikio Naruse, Kajiro Yamamoto,

Hiroshi Inagaki and Masahiro Makino, as well as such new talent as Akira Kurosawa, Senkichi Taniguchi and Kon Ichikawa. By the mid-fifties they were back on top with such international hits as *Godzilla* (*Gojira*, 1954) directed by Ishiro Honda, and *The Seven Samurai* (*Shichinin No Samurai*, 1956) directed by Kurosawa, and such domestic gold mines as Masahiro Makino's *matatabi* series *Jirocho Of Three Provinces* (*Jirocho San Gokushi*, 1952–1954).

Although Toho churned out a healthy dose of genre pictures between the mid-fifties and the early eighties, concentrating on the lucrative staple of science fiction /*kaiju* (giant monster) films, *jidai-geki chanbara* and American-influenced crime films, they had a well-rounded line-up of comedies, youth romances, dramas and war movies as well. They also produced a decent crop of unclassifiable 'prestige' and 'art' films during the same period, including critically regarded masterworks by Kurosawa and Masaki Kobayashi.

Hit by the same box-office slump that had virtually destroyed Daiei and Nikkatsu in the early seventies, Toho, like Toei and Shochiku, survived not only because of their savvy marketing instincts but also from prudent diversification into real estate, television and other enterprises.

TOEI

Toei was born at the start of the fifties, financed by railroad and trucking magnate Hiroshi Okawa, who also owned many other businesses, including baseball teams. By 1953 Toei had inaugurated an extremely successful policy of double bills – one longer A picture, one shorter B picture that revolutionized film exhibition in Japan. Theaters had shown double bills previously, but the bills would be split between the output of any two studios. When Toei started supplying both features on double bills, the staid, more conservative studios like Toho and Daiei had a hard time matching the competition.

Toei's output through most of the fifties was almost exclusively samurai and crime genre films. Although there were occasionally 'prestige' films by directors such as Tomu Uchida, Tadashi Imai or Daisuke Ito, they were usually in the guise of samurai swordfests or war films. As the sixties progressed, the fare gradually became more violent and gritty.

Toei was the earliest to jump with both feet on the *yakuza* film bandwagon, continuing with their contemporary urban crime movies, and almost single-handedly creating, circa 1963, the *ninkyo* or chivalrous *yakuza* film. *Ninkyo* gangster films were usually set in the 1890–1930 time period, and invariably featured complex webs of obligation and moral quandaries for the conflicted anti-heroes, played by the likes of Koji Tsuruta and Ken Takakura. Swordfighting rather than gunplay was the norm. Gradually, as the sixties came to a close, the contemporary urban *yakuza* films once more came to take precedence.

By the mid-1970s *ninkyo yakuza* pictures had virtually disappeared from not just Toei's line-up but most other studios' as well. The early seventies saw the rise of the *jitsuroku*, or true account, *yakuza* film, as best personified in the films of directors Kinji Fukasaku, Junya Sato and Sadao Nakajima. Toei also struck pay dirt with their *Girl Boss* (*Sukeban*) girl gang series in the mid-seventies.

The late sixties and seventies saw an increasingly sleazy, sometimes shocking proliferation of nudity, softcore sex and violent bloodshed in many of Toei's efforts. Toei, through pandering to the basest of human nature (albeit in an incredibly entertaining, sometimes transcendentally beautiful, anarchic way), were offering what the dwindling numbers of moviegoers seemed to want. In other words, elements too strong to be found on television, the burgeoning boom of which was helping to destroy the Japanese motion picture industry.

NIKKATSU

Japan's oldest film studio, Nikkatsu was founded in 1912 when the heads of several production companies and theater chains consolidated under a trust into Nippon Katsudo Shashin (Japan Cinematograph Company). The name was soon shortened to Nikkatsu. They were fairly successful for a time, with the pioneering Shozo Makino, and then his son Masahiro, amongst the filmmakers working for them. Akira Kurosawa also got his start as an assistant director at Nikkatsu in the 1930s.

However, in 1941, the wartime government wanting to merge the growing number of film companies that had mushroomed during the thirties, ordered the ten existing concerns to devolve into two. Former Nikkatsu employee and founder of Dai-Ichi Eiga (soon to become Daiei – see below) Masaichi Nagata counter-proposed a new plan, by which the companies would form into four rather than two. The government approved. All the companies were happy about this except for Nikkatsu, who were forced to connect up with the two weakest studios, Shinko and Daito. Not taking kindly to dissent, the committee establishing value for each firm retaliated by purposely undervaluing Nikkatsu, making the third piece of the pie previously known as Shinko, the dominant head of production. This effectively put Nikkatsu out of commission as a film production company (although they were allowed to retain their lucrative theater holdings).

Kyusaku Hori, Nikkatsu's owner, noticing from 1951 onward that there was an expanding growth potential for film production, decided to build new studios, and resumed making movies in 1954. Many assistant directors at other studios such as Shochiku and Toho, tired of waiting in long lines for their chance to direct, jumped at the chance to work for the 'new' player, knowing they would be helming their own features within a year or two. A prime example of this phenomenon was *enfant terrible* Seijun Suzuki.

Although Nikkatsu made a handful of samurai films in the ensuing years, by 1960 they had all but curtailed production on historical swordplay films, deciding to concentrate largely on urban youth dramas, comedies and action and gangster films. From the late 1950s through to 1971, Nikkatsu became renowned for their easily identifiable style of action movie, a sleek, colorful and economic visual signature abetted tremendously by the exceptional collaborations between directors, cinematographers and top-notch production designers. Nikkatsu also cultivated a youthful audience with a succession of young superstars, including Yujiro Ishihara, Akira Kobayashi, Joe Shishido, Tetsuya Watari, Hideki Takahashi, Ruriko Asaoka, Chieko Matsubara and, in the studios' waning days, Meiko Kaji and Tatsuya Fuji. Nikkatsu's primary genre action films during the mid- to late sixties were a combination of contemporary gangster and *ninkyo yakuza* pictures, and they produced the second largest number of those films after reigning outlaw cinema king Toei. Nikkatsu also gave birth to the career of pantheon 'prestige' director Shohei Imamura, who directed at least eight features with the studio between 1958 and 1966, amongst them the astonishing *Pigs And Battleships* (1961), *The Insect Woman* (1963) and *The Pornographers* (1966), before migrating to more independent pastures.

By 1971 television had taken its toll in a profound way. Nikkatsu, like all the other studios, was struggling to make ends meet. Although there were still a microscopic number of mainstream productions in the 1970s, Nikkatsu effectively curtailed their conventional output in 1971 and opted for the *roman porn* or *pink* film market, productions that would spotlight softcore, often violent sex blended with S&M *and* romance. A few talented directors, such as Yasuharu Hasebe, Keiichi Ozawa, Shugoro Nishimura and Koreyoshi Kurahara, decided to stay on while also directing for TV and independent productions. The new order also witnessed the emergence of talented assistant directors like Tatsumi Kumashiro, Masaru Konuma and Chusei Sone into credible, full-blown directorhood.

DAIEI

As mentioned above, Daiei founder and head Masaichi Nagata had previously been employed by Nikkatsu. There were varying rumors why he left, ranging from Nagata's alleged dissatisfaction with Nikkatsu for arbitrarily firing scores of employees to Nikkatsu's accusations that Nagata had been bribed by rival Shochiku to sabotage Nikkatsu productions. Whatever the case, there weren't any complaints from Nagata's quarter when Nikkatsu's filmmaking capability was basically subverted when Nagata's 1942 counter-proposal was accepted by the government to merge existing filmmaking concerns into four companies.

In the ensuing post-war years Daiei head Nagata was often vilified as being a philistine, primarily for his failure to recognize the artistic achievement or worldwide success potential of *Rashomon*, one of Akira Kurosawa's rare efforts with the company.

But, to be fair to Nagata, whatever his faults – which were many – he was still the man responsible for green-lighting Kenji Mizoguchi's final great projects and giving groundbreaking directors such as Kon Ichikawa and Yasuzo Masumura a generous amount of artistic freedom.

Nagata also promoted the period samurai and *jidai-geki* film like no other studio, not even Toei. Daiei's period films, although often falling into formulaic scenarios, retained a high degree of intelligence, and an exceptional beauty of form, and drew from an amazing stable of directors that included such talents as veterans Daisuke Ito, Kazuo Mori, Teinosuke Kinugasa and Kimiyoshi Yasuda as well as first-class newcomers Kenji Misumi, Kazuo Ikehiro, Tokuzo Tanaka and Akira Inoue. Nagata was also responsible for helping to promote the careers of a number of great performers, amongst them the legendary Shintaro Katsu, Raizo Ichikawa and Ayako Wakao.

In the early fifties many of Daiei's period films, such as Kurosawa's *Rashomon* (1950), Kozaburo Yoshimura's *Tale Of Genji* (*Genji Monogatari*, 1951), Mizoguchi's *Ugetsu* (1953) and Kinugasa's *Gate Of Hell* (*Jigokumon*, 1953) were huge hits on the international festival circuit.

Daiei's sixties output featured a large percentage of consistently high-quality genre pieces, a parade of brilliant outlaw cinema, frequently set in-period: samurai films (including the *Zatoichi, Blind Swordsman* and *Kyoshiro Nemuri* series), *ninkyo yakuza, kaidans* – amazing pictures that delivered on thrills but possessed a high degree of taste and intelligence.

Starting in the late sixties, Daiei coincidentally fell on hard times much the same as their former rivals, Nikkatsu. In 1971 they, too, were forced to shut down general production. Masaichi Nagata still produced a few high-profile films in the ensuing decade, but, for all intents and purposes, the heyday of Daiei's 'golden age' was over.

SHOCHIKU

Shochiku, founded circa 1920 by two entrepreneurs, Matsujiro Shirai and Takejiro Otani, who had previously held Shochiku has a theatrical company featuring *kabuki, shimpa* and other traditional forms of Japanese stage play, was at first overly swayed by American films and methods. This excessive early reliance on Western influences, and a habit of throwing money at a problem to solve it, caused significant setbacks. But by 1921, with *Souls On The Road* (*Rojo No Reikon*) and *Jirocho Of Shimizu* (*Shimizu No Jirosho*, 1922), Shochiku was starting to find its voice, a style that successfully integrated American styles and narrative forms with Japanese stagecraft and stories.

Despite their highly publicized feuds with rivals Toho and Nikkatsu in the 1930s, Shochiku remained a wealthy company from the outset, and they continued to reap box-office rewards well into Japan's march towards militarism and war.

Post-war, Shochiku seemed to have an easier time of it with the labor unions. Not only did they take a more conciliatory attitude, company head Shiro Kido and his management already held a record of trying to keep their employees comparatively happy. Of course, this was done less out of altruism and more out of just plain good business sense, knowing that less friction in the workplace would keep films in production and that a healthier work attitude would be reflected in the final product.

Shochiku solidified their reputation for the 'home' drama during the fifties with pantheon directors such as Yasujiro Ozu and Keisuke Kinoshita, producing films specializing in the pathos, romance and humor of everyday life in contemporary families. Shochiku also turned out comedies and musicals like clockwork.

But, along with Daiei, Toei and Toho, they created scores and scores of period *jidai-geki*. Many were exceptional. As the sixties began, Shochiku's samurai pictures, largely through the pioneering efforts of directors like Hideo Gosha with *Three Outlaw Samurai* and *Sword Of The Beast*, Masaki Kobayashi with *Hara-Kiri*, Masahiro Shinoda with *Assassination* and *Samurai Spy* and Kazuo Inoue with *Escape from Hell* (*Mushukunin-betsucho*, aka *Wanderer's Black List*, 1963), began to sport a gritty, hard-boiled sensibility that retained sensitivity toward genuine emotion while jettisoning anything that could pass for sentimentality. This welcome development mirrored similar period pictures being made by Eiichi Kudo, Tai Kato and Tadashi Imai at Toei, Kenji Misumi at Daiei and Kihachi Okamoto and Akira Kurosawa at Toho. Shochiku made a small but impressive number of *kaidans*, too, including Kazuo Hase's superior *Curse Of The Blood* (*Kaidan Zankoku Monogatari*, aka *Cruel Ghost Legend*, 1968). Shochiku also composed crime films – mystery as well as *yakuza*. Unfortunately, these crime genre efforts are as a rule harder to see, even on Japanese cable television, than even the rarest of Shintoho's 1950s thrillers. A real shame.

Of course, Shochiku – despite company head Shiro Kido's misgivings – was responsible as well for one of the most prodigious outpourings of daring *nouvelle vague* (or new wave) cinema from Japan in the early sixties, most prominently seen in the work of Nagisa Oshima, Masahiro Shinoda and Yoshishige Yoshida.

Shochiku was another studio that survived the catastrophic box-office downturn in the late sixties and throughout the seventies. Although they had diversified their holdings, which helped immeasurably, it was not to the same extent as Toho and Toei. But Shochiku was also lucky enough to have one particular director churning out very popular films throughout the seventies and eighties. Yoji Yamada brought a constantly reliable source of revenue into the company coffers thanks not only to his incredibly long-running *Tora-san* (*Otoko Wa Tsurai yo*, aka *It's Tough To Be A Man*, 1969–1995) series but to his other occasional one-off wistful comedy-dramas. One of his most recent efforts is the exceptionally fine character study *The Twilight Samurai* (2002).

NOTE: Since the late 1980s, Daiei and Nikkatsu have reinvented themselves, releasing many of their classics from the 'golden age' of the 1950s–1970s on video, laser disk and now DVD. They have also been engaged in various genre film productions again, many of them co-ventures, either with each other or with Toho and/or Toei. Indeed, co-productions seem the norm in today's Japanese film market place, reducing risk while the co-producers split up territories for domestic and international distribution rights, as well as rights to television and video. The majority of most Japanese genre films are still shot on film or on high-definition video, but most are now released straight to video. Only a small fraction receive a limited theatrical distribution.

ADDITIONAL NOTE: Daiei was bought by Kadokawa Productions in 2002, and, for a short time, became known as the Kadokawa-Daiei. In late 2004, the Daiei moniker was sadly dropped from the name to become solely Kadokawa Pictures. However, Kadokawa Pictures still retains all rights to Daiei's classic film library.

APPENDIX – JAPANESE OUTLAW FILMS ON DVD (SUBTITLED IN ENGLISH)

Selected Videography (DVD) (USA)

AUDITION (1999) Dir: Takashi Miike, Distributor: Chimera/Vitagraph/American Cinematheque Presents through Ventura

BLACK ANGEL Vol. 1 (1997) Dir: Takashi Ishii, Distributor: Media Blasters (also available in a two-disk set with below film as *The Black Angel Collection*)

BLACK ANGEL Vol. 2 (1998) Dir: Takashi Ishii, Distributor: Media Blasters

BLACKMAIL IS MY LIFE (1968) Dir: Kinji Fukasaku, Distributor: Vitagraph/American Cinematheque Presents through Home Vision Entertainment

BLACK ROSE MANSION (1969) Dir: Kinji Fukasaku, Distributor: Chimera/Vitagraph/ American Cinematheque Presents through Ventura

BLACK TIGHT KILLERS (1966) Dir: Yasuharu Hasebe, Distributor: Vitagraph/American Cinematheque Presents through Image Entertainment

BLOODY TERRITORIES (1969) Dir: Yasuharu Hasebe, Distributor: Vitagraph/American Cinematheque Presents through Home Vision Entertainment

BOILING POINT (1990) Dir: Takeshi Kitano, Distributor: Fox Lorber

BRANDED TO KILL (1967) Dir: Seijun Suzuki, Distributor: Criterion Collection

BULLET TRAIN (1975) Dir: Junya Sato, Distribution: Crash Cinema (*Be forewarned that this is the dubbed-in-English version that was cut by approximately 38 minutes from the original 152 minutes and is not a very good transfer – but it is the only way to see the film in English*)

CITY OF LOST SOULS (2001) Dir: Takashi Miike, Distributor: Chimera/Vitagraph/ American Cinematheque Presents through Ventura

CURE (1997) Dir: Kiyoshi Kurosawa, Distributor: Home Vision Entertainment

DEAD OR ALIVE (1999) Dir: Takashi Miike, Distributor: Kino International

DEAD OR ALIVE 2 (2000) Dir: Takashi Miike, Distributor: Kino International

DEAD OR ALIVE: FINAL (2002) Dir: Takashi Miike, Distributor: Kino International

DOUBLE SUICIDE (1969) Dir: Masahiro Shinoda, Distributor: Criterion Collection

ECSTASY OF THE ANGELS (1972) Dir: Koji Wakamatsu, Distributor: Vitagraph/American Cinematheque Presents through Image Entertainment

EVIL DEAD TRAP (1988) Dir: Toshiharu Ikeda, Distributor: Synapse Films

FEMALE CONVICT SCORPION – JAILHOUSE 41 (no. 2) (1972) Dir: Shunya Ito, Distributor: Vitagraph/American Cinematheque Presents through Image Entertainment (with Meiko Kaji)

FEMALE PRISONER NUMBER 701 – SCORPION (no. 1) (1972) Dir: Shunya Ito, Distributor: Media Blasters (with Meiko Kaji)

FIGHTING ELEGY (1966) Dir: Seijun Suzuki, Distributor: Criterion Collection

FIREWORKS (HANA-BI) (1997) Dir: Takeshi Kitano, Distributor: New Yorker

FREEZE ME (2000) Dir: Takashi Ishii, Distributor: Media Blasters

FUDOH: THE NEW GENERATION (1996) Dir: Takashi Miike, Distributor: Media Blasters

GATE OF FLESH (1964) Dir: Seijun Suzuki, Distributor: Home Vision Entertainment (*VHS only*)

GO, GO SECOND TIME VIRGIN (1969) Dir: Koji Wakamatsu, Distributor: Vitagraph/ American Cinematheque Presents through Image Entertainment

GONIN Dir: Takashi Ishii, Distributor: Pathfinder

HAPPINESS OF THE KATAKURIS (2001) Dir: Takashi Miike, Distributor: Chimera/ Vitagraph/American Cinematheque Presents through Ventura

ICHI, THE KILLER (2001) Dir: Takashi Miike, Distributor: Media Blasters (*uncut*)

IF YOU WERE YOUNG – RAGE! (1970) Dir: Kinji Fukasaku, Distributor: Vitagraph/American Cinematheque Presents through Home Vision Entertainment

KANTO WANDERER (1963) Dir: Seijun Suzuki, Distributor: Vitagraph/American Cinematheque Presents through Home Vision Entertainment

KWAIDAN (1964) Dir: Masaki Kobayashi, Distributor: Criterion Collection

LADY SNOWBLOOD (1973) Dir: Toshiya Fujita, Distributor: AniMeigo (Samurai Cinema) (with Meiko Kaji)

LADY SNOWBLOOD 2 – LOVE SONG OF VENGEANCE (1974) Dir: Toshiya Fujita, Distributor: AniMeigo (Samurai Cinema) (with Meiko Kaji)

LONE WOLF AND CUB 1 – SWORD OF VENGEANCE (1972) Dir: Kenji Misumi, Distributor: AniMeigo (Samurai Cinema)

LONE WOLF AND CUB 2 – BABY CART AT THE RIVER STYX (1972) Dir: Kenji Misumi, Distributor: AniMeigo (Samurai Cinema) (LONE WOLF AND CUB 3–6 should also be available through AniMeigo by the time of this book's publication)

THE NOTORIOUS CONCUBINES (1969) Dir: Koji Wakamatsu, Distributor: Something Weird/Image Entertainment

PALE FLOWER (1964) Dir: Masahiro Shinoda, Distributor: Vitagraph/American Cinematheque Presents through Home Vision Entertainment

PISTOL OPERA (2001) Dir: Seijun Suzuki, Distributor: Media Blasters

RED LION (1969) Dir: Kihachi Okamoto, Distributor: AniMeigo (Samurai Cinema) (*out-of-print laser disc and VHS only*)

RETURN OF THE STREETFIGHTER (no. 2) (1974) Dir: Shigehiro Ozawa, Distributor: VCI (with Sonny Chiba)

RING (as *RINGU*) (1998) Dir: Hideo Nakata, Distributor: Universal Studios

SAMURAI ASSASSIN (1965) Dir: Kihachi Okamoto, Distributor: AniMeigo (Samurai Cinema)

SAMURAI REINCARNATION (1981) Dir: Kinji Fukasaku, Distributor: Media Blasters

SLEEPY EYES OF DEATH – SWORD OF SEDUCTION (aka *KYOSHIRO NEMURI AT BAY*) (no. 4) (1964) Dir: Kazuo Ihehiro, Distributor: AniMeigo (Samurai Cinema) (*out-of-print laser disk and VHS only*)

STORY OF A PROSTITUTE (1965) Dir: Seijun Suzuki, Distributor: Home Vision Entertainment (*VHS only*)

STRAY CAT ROCK – SEX HUNTER (1970) Dir: Yasuharu Hasebe, Distributor: Vitagraph/ American Cinematheque Presents through Home Vision Entertainment (with Meiko Kaji)

THE STREETFIGHTER (no. 1) (1974) Dir: Shigehiro Ozawa, Distributor: VCI (with Sonny Chiba)

THE STREETFIGHTER'S LAST REVENGE (no. 3) (1974) Dir: Shigehiro Ozawa, Distributor: VCI (with Sonny Chiba)

SUICIDE CLUB (2002) Dir: Sion Sono, Distributor: TLA Entertainment

SURE DEATH – REVENGE (aka *SURE DEATH 4 – WE WILL AVENGE YOU*) (1987) Dir: Kinji Fukasaku, Distributor: Media Blasters

SWORD OF DOOM (1966) Dir: Kihachi Okamoto, Distributor: Criterion Collection

SYMPATHY FOR THE UNDERDOG (aka *GAMBLER – FOREIGN OPPOSITION*) (1971) Dir: Kinji Fukasaku, Distributor: Home Vision Entertainment

TATTOOED LIFE (1965) Dir: Seijun Suzuki, Distributor: Vitagraph/ American Cinematheque Presents through Home Vision Entertainment

TOKYO DRIFTER (1966) Dir: Seijun Suzuki, Distributor: Criterion Collection

TOKYO FIST (1995) Dir: Shinya Tsukamoto, Distributor: Manga Entertainment

UNDERWORLD BEAUTY (1958) Dir: Seijun Suzuki, Distributor: Vitagraph/ American Cinematheque Presents through Home Vision Entertainment

VIOLENT COP (1989) Dir: Takeshi Kitano, Distributor: Fox Lorber

VISITOR Q (2001) Dir: Takashi Miike, Distributor: Media Blasters

THE YAKUZA PAPERS (first 5 of the BATTLES WITHOUT HONOR AND HUMANITY film series 1973–1974) Dir: Kinji Fukasaku, Distributor: Home Vision Entertainment (*available both singly and in a box set; box set also includes a 6th disc with a wealth of supplemental material, including footage of Fukasaku directing on the set in the mid-1970s*)

YOUTH OF THE BEAST (1963) Dir: Seijun Suzuki, Distributor: Criterion Collection

ZATOICHI (1989) Dir: Shintaro Katsu (*last film with Katsu*), Distributor: Media Blasters

ZATOICHI (Films nos 1–13, 15, 17–19) (1962–1968) Directors various (including Kazuo Ikehiro and Kenji Misumi), Distributor: Home Vision Entertainment

ZATOICHI AT LARGE (no. 23) (1972) Dir: Kazuo Mori, Distributor: AniMeigo (Samurai Cinema)

ZATOICHI'S FESTIVAL OF FIRE (no. 21) (1970) Dir: Kenji Misumi, Distributor: AniMeigo (Samurai Cinema)

ZATOICHI MEETS THE ONE-ARMED SWORDSMAN (no. 22) (1971) Dir: Kimiyoshi Yasuda, Distributor: AniMeigo (Samurai Cinema)

ZATOICHI MEETS YOJINBO (no. 20) (1970) Dir: Kihachi Okamoto, Distributor: AniMeigo (Samurai Cinema)

ZATOICHI, THE OUTLAW (no. 16) (1967) Dir: Satsuo Yamamoto, Distributor: AniMeigo (Samurai Cinema)

Selected Videography (DVD) (UK)

AUDITION (1999) Dir: Takashi Miike, Distributor: Metro-Tartan

BATTLE ROYALE (2000) Dir: Kinji Fukasaku, Distributor: Metro-Tartan

BATTLES WITHOUT HONOR AND HUMANITY (aka *THE YAKUZA PAPERS*) (1973) Dir: Kinji Fukasaku, Distributor: Eureka Video

BOILING POINT (1990) Dir: Takeshi Kitano, Distributor: MIA Entertainment Ltd

COPS VS. THUGS (aka *STATE POLICE VS. ORGANIZED CRIME*) (1975) Dir: Kinji Fukasaku, Distributor: Eureka Video

DEAD OR ALIVE (1999) Dir: Takashi Miike, Distributor: Metro-Tartan

DEAD OR ALIVE 2 (2000) Dir: Takashi Miike, Distributor: Metro-Tartan

FREEZE ME (as *FREEZER*) (2000) Dir: Takashi Ishii, Distributor: Metro-Tartan

GATE OF FLESH (1964) Dir: Seijun Suzuki, Distributor: Pagan

GOKE – BODYSNATCHER FROM HELL (1968) Dir: Hajime Sato, Distributor: ArtsMagic

GRAVEYARD OF HONOUR (1975) Dir: Kinji Fukasaku, Distributor: Eureka Video

HELLISH LOVE (1972) Dir: Chusei Sone, Distributor: Pagan

HIRUKO THE GOBLIN (1990) Dir: Shinya Tsukamoto, Distributor: Eastern Cult Cinema

ICHI, THE KILLER (2001) Dir: Takashi Miike, Distributor: Medusa Communications (*this
     UK edition of ICHI was trimmed by approximately 4 minutes to get past the censors*)

JAPAN ORGANIZED CRIME BOSS (1969) Dir: Kinji Fukasaku, Distributor: Eureka Video

LADY SNOWBLOOD (aka *BLIZZARD FROM THE NETHERWORLD*) (1973) Dir: Toshiya
     Fujita, Distributor: Warrior (with Meiko Kaji)

LADY SNOWBLOOD 2 – LOVE SONG OF VENGEANCE (1974) Dir: Toshiya Fujita,
     Distributor: Warrior (with Meiko Kaji)

LEY LINES (1999) Dir: Takashi Miike, Distributor: Metro–Tartan

LONE WOLF AND CUB 1 – SWORD OF VENGEANCE (1972) Dir: Kenji Misumi,
     Distributor: Warrior (*LONE WOLF AND CUB 2–6* also available through Warrior)

PORTRAIT OF HELL (1969) Dir: Shiro Toyoda, Distributor: Warrior

RAINY DOG (1997) Dir: Takashi Miike, Distributor: Metro–Tartan

RED LION (1969) Dir: Kihachi Okamoto, Distributor: Warrior

RING (1998) Dir: Hideo Nakata, Distributor: Metro–Tartan

RING 2 (1998) Dir: Hideo Nakata, Distributor: Metro–Tartan

SAMURAI ASSASSIN (1965) Dir: Kihachi Okamoto, Distributor: Warrior

SAMURAI REBELLION (1967) Dir: Masaki Kobayashi, Distributor: Warrior

SHINJUKU TRIAD SOCIETY (1995) Dir: Takashi Miike, Distributor: Metro–Tartan

SHOGUN'S SAMURAI (1978) Dir: Kinji Fukasaku, Distributor: Eureka Video

SONATINE (1993) Dir: Takeshi Kitano, Distributor: MIA Entertainment Ltd

STREET MOBSTER (1972) Dir: Kinji Fukasaku, Distributor: Eureka Video

SWORD OF DOOM (1966) Dir: Kihachi Okamoto, Distributor: Warrior

TRIPLE CROSS (1992) Dir: Kinji Fukasaku, Distributor: MIA Entertainment Ltd

VIOLENT COP Dir: Takeshi Kitano, Distributor:

VISITOR Q (2001) Dir: Takashi Miike, Distributor: Metro–Tartan

YAKUZA BURIAL (as *YAKUZA GRAVEYARD*) (1976) Dir: Kinji Fukasaku, Distributor:
     Eureka Video

THE WOLVES (1971) Dir: Hideo Gosha, Distributor: Warrior

ZATOICHI AT LARGE (no. 23) (1972) Dir: Kazuo Mori, Distributor: Warrior

ZATOICHI MEETS THE ONE-ARMED SWORDSMAN (no. 22) (1971) Dir: Kimiyoshi
     Yasuda, Distributor: Warrior

ZATOICHI MEETS YOJINBO (no. 20) (1970) Dir: Kihachi Okamoto, Distributor: Warrior

ZATOICHI, THE OUTLAW (no. 16) (1967) Dir: Satsuo Yamamoto, Distributor: Warrior

Selected Videography (DVD) (Imported DVDs from Hong Kong, South Korea, Japan,
Germany or other countries of Japanese outlaw films but with removable or
embedded English subtitles)

BANDITS VS. SAMURAI SQUAD (1978) Dir: Hideo Gosha, Distributor: Panorama
     Entertainment (Hong Kong) (*Be forewarned that this is a wide-screen film in a pan-and-scan,
     full-screen transfer – the only format available with English subtitles*)

BATTLE ROYALE 2 (2004) Dir: Kenta Fukasaku/Kinji Fukasaku, Distributor: Universe (Hong Kong)

BLACK CAT MANSION (as *BOREI KAIBYO YASHIKI* or *MANSION OF THE GHOST CAT*) (1958) Dir: Nobuo Nakagawa, Distributor: Eclipse Films/Beam Entertainment (Japan)

BLUES HARP (1998) Dir: Takashi Miike, Distributor: Asian Film Network (Germany)

BULLET BALLET (1998) Dir: Shinya Tsukamoto, Distributor: Fejui Media Corporation (Taiwan)

CHARISMA (1999) Dir: Kiyoshi Kurosawa, Distributor: King (Japan)

EVIL DEAD TRAP (1988) Dir: Toshiharu Ikeda, Distributor: Japan Shock (Netherlands)

FULL METAL YAKUZA (1997) Dir: Takashi Miike, Distributor: Asian Film Network (Germany)

GEMINI (as *SOSEIJI*) (1999) Dir: Shinya Tsukamoto, Distributor: Warner Brothers (Japan)

GHOST OF YOTSUYA (as *TOKAIDO YOTSUYA KAIDAN*) (1959) Dir: Nobuo Nakagawa, Distributor: Eclipse Films/Beam Entertainment (Japan)

HARA-KIRI (1962) Dir: Masaki Kobayashi, Distributor: Panorama Entertainment (Hong Kong)

HEAT WAVE (*KAGERO*) (1991) Dir: Hideo Gosha, Distributor: Panorama Entertainment (Hong Kong)

HELL (as *JIGOKU*) (1960) Dir: Nobuo Nakagawa, Distributor: Eclipse Films/Beam Entertainment (Japan)

HUNTER IN THE DARK (1979) Dir: Hideo Gosha, Distributor: Panorama Entertainment (Hong Kong) (*Be forewarned that this is a wide-screen film in a pan-and-scan, full-screen transfer – the only format available with English subtitles that is in print; there is an out-of-print VHS letterboxed video from the USA from World Artists that could still possibly be found in large metropolitan US video rental stores with large foreign film sections*)

KAIRO (*PULSE*) (2001) Dir: Kiyoshi Kurosawa, Distributor: Universe (Hong Kong)

KICHIKU (*BEAST BANQUET*) (1997) Dir: Kazuyoshi Kumakiri, Distributor: Japan Shock (Netherlands)

NINJA, BAND OF ASSASSINS (as *SHINOBI NO MONO*) (1963) Dir: Satsuo Yamamoto, Distributor: Mei Ah (Hong Kong)

NINJA, BAND OF ASSASSINS 2 (as *ZOKU SHINOBI NO MONO*) (1963) Dir: Satsuo Yamamoto, Distributor: Mei Ah (Hong Kong)

OWL'S CASTLE (1999) Dir: Masahiro Shinoda, Distributor: Dawoori (South Korea)

TALE OF SORROW AND SADNESS (as *STORY OF SORROW AND SADNESS*) (1977) Dir: Seijun Suzuki, Distributor: Panorama Entertainment (Hong Kong)

THREE OUTLAW SAMURAI (1964) Dir: Hideo Gosha, Distributor: Panorama Entertainment (Hong Kong)

TRACKED (1985) Dir: Hideo Gosha, Distributor: Panorama Entertainment (Hong Kong)

ZATOICHI (2003) Dir: Takeshi Kitano, Distributor: Intro Media (South Korea)

APPENDIX – JAPANESE OUTLAW FILM SERIES

(These film series below are mentioned in passing in the text and may not have received complete listings in the various directors' respective filmographies – due to the participation of numerous other outlaw filmmakers not featured in their own chapters in this book. But I do not list below such series as the BATTLES WITHOUT HONOR AND HUMANITY group because the first eight films are listed in Kinji Fukasaku's filmography and the ninth picture in that of Eiichi Kudo. Likewise, because of matters of space, I do not list even more prominent series, such as Toei's RED PEONY GAMBLER, GAMBLING DEN, TALES OF LAST SHOWA YAKUZA, GIRL BOSS, Nikkatsu's A MAN'S CREST or Daiei's HOODLUM SOLDIER or BAD REPUTATION series, however important they are, because none of the outlaw filmmakers spotlighted with chapters in this book ever directed entries in those series.)

DESPERADO OUTPOST (DOKURITSU GURENTAI)

> *(Toho studios' irreverent war series, usually starring Yuzo Kayama, Makoto Sato and sometimes Tatsuya Nakadai)* [Note: some Japanese reference books do not include OPERATION SEWER RATS in the series, while they do include FORT GRAVEYARD – a title which director Okamoto asserts was most certainly not part of the series in either tone or subject.]

DESPERADO OUTPOST (no. 1) (DOKURITSU GURENTAI) (1959) Dir: Kihachi Okamoto
WESTWARD DESPERADO (no. 2) (DOKURITSU GURENTAI NISHI HE) (1960) Dir: Kihachi Okamoto
OPERATION SEWER RATS (no. 3) (DOBU NEZUMI SAKUSEN) Dir: Kihachi Okamoto
MOUNTAIN LION STRATEGY (no. 4) (YAMA NEKO SAKUSEN) (1962) Dir: Senkichi Taniguchi
OUTPOST OF HELL (no. 5) (DOKURITUI KIKANJUTAI IMADA SHAGE KICHU) (1963) Dir: Senkichi Taniguchi
OPERATION MAD DOG (no. 6) (NORA INU SAKUSEN, aka STRAY DOG TACTICS) (1963) Dir: Jun Fukuda
FIRE ANTS STRATEGY (no. 7) (ARI-JIGOKU SAKUSEN) (1964) Dir: Takashi Tsuboshima
FORT GRAVEYARD [see note above] (CHI TO SUNA, aka BLOOD AND SAND) (1965) Dir: Kihachi Okamoto

GAMBLER (BAKUTO)
(Toei studios' series starring Koji Tsuruta – except for the entry GAMBLER CLAN, which starred Ken Takakura in his place)
GAMBLER (no. 1) (BAKUTO) (1964) Dir: Shigehiro Ozawa
PRISON GAMBLER (no. 2) (KANGOKU BAKUTO) (1964) Dir: Shigehiro Ozawa
GAMBLERS VS. STREET PEDDLERS (no. 3) (BAKUTO TAI TEKIYA) (1964) Dir: Shigehiro Ozawa
SEVEN GAMBLERS (no. 4) (BAKUTO SHICHININ) (1966) Dir: Shigehiro Ozawa
THREE GAMBLERS (no. 5) (SANNIN NO BAKUTO) (1967) Dir: Shigehiro Ozawa
GAMBLER – CEREMONY OF DISBANDING (no. 6) (BAKUTO KAISANSHIKI) (1968) Dir: Kinji Fukasaku

GAMBLER CLAN (no. 7) (*BAKUTO IKKA,* aka *THE TERRITORY*) (1970) Dir: Shigehiro Ozawa

GAMBLER MONEY (no. 8) (*SATSUTABA BAKUTO*) (1970) Dir: Shigehiro Ozawa

GAMBLER – FOREIGN OPPOSITION, aka *SYMPATHY FOR THE UNDERDOG* (no. 9) (*BAKUTO GAIJIN BUTAI,* aka *GAMBLERS IN OKINAWA,* aka *YAKUZA COMBAT FORCES*) (1971) Dir: Kinji Fukasaku

GAMBLER'S COUNTERATTACK (no. 10) (*BAKUTO KIRIKOMI TAI*) (1971) Dir: Junya Sato

JAPAN'S VIOLENT GANGS (*NIHON BORYOKUDAN*)

(*Toei studios' series starring Koji Tsuruta*)

JAPAN'S VIOLENT GANGS – BOSS (no. 1) (*NIHON BORYOKUDAN – KUMICHO,* aka *JAPAN'S ORGANIZED CRIME BOSS*) (1969) Dir: Kinji Fukasaku

JAPAN'S VIOLENT GANGS – THE BOSS AND THE KILLERS (no. 2) (*NIHON BORYOKUDAN – KUMICHO TO SHIKAKU*) (1969) Dir: Junya Sato

JAPAN'S VIOLENT GANGS – DEGENERATE BOSS (no. 3) (*NIHON BORYOKUDAN – KUMICHO KUZURE,* aka *EPITAPH FOR AN UNKNOWN GANGSTER*) (1970) Dir: Shin Takakuwa

JAPAN'S VIOLENT GANGS – LOYALTY OFFERING MURDER (no. 4) (*NIHON BORYOKUDAN – KOROSHI NO SAKAZUKI*) (1972) Dir: Yasuo Furuhata

KYOSHIRO NEMURI – SON OF THE BLACK MASS (*NEMURI KYOSHIRO,* aka *SLEEPY EYES OF DEATH*)

(*Daiei studios' series starring Raizo Ichikawa*)

KYOSHIRO NEMURI – BOOK OF DEATH (no. 1) (*NEMURI KYOSHIRO SAPPOCHO,* aka *ENTER KYOSHIRO NEMURI, SWORDSMAN,* aka *SLEEPY EYES OF DEATH – CHINESE JADE*) (1963) Dir: Tokuzo Tanaka

ADVENTURES OF KYOSHIRO NEMURI (no. 2) (*NEMURI KYOSHIRO SHOBU,* aka *KYOSHIRO NEMURI – SHOWDOWN,* aka *SLEEPY EYES OF DEATH – SWORD OF ADVENTURE*) (1964) Dir: Kenji Misumi

KYOSHIRO NEMURI – FULL CIRCLE KILLING (no. 3) (*NEMURI KYOSHIRO ENGETSU GIRI,* aka *EXPLOITS OF KYOSHIRO NEMURI*) (1964) Dir: Kimiyoshi Yasuda

KYOSHIRO NEMURI – SWORD OF SEDUCTION (no. 4) (*NEMURI KYOSHIRO JOYOKEN,* aka *KYOSHIRO NEMURI AT BAY*) (1964) Dir: Kazuo Ikehiro

KYOSHIRO NEMURI – SWORD OF FIRE (no. 5) (*NEMURI KYOSHIRO ENJO KEN*) (1965) Dir: Kenji Misumi

KYOSHIRO NEMURI – SATAN'S SWORD (no. 6) (*NEMURI KYOSHIRO MASHO KEN*) (1965) Dir: Kimiyoshi Yasuda

KYOSHIRO NEMURI – THE PRINCESS'S MASK (no. 7) (*NEMURI KYOSHIRO TAJO KEN*) (1966) Dir: Akira Inoue

KYOSHIRO NEMURI – VILLAIN SWORD (no. 8) (*NEMURI KYOSHIRO BURAI KEN*) (1966) Dir: Kenji Misumi

KYOSHIRO NEMURI – TRAIL OF TRAPS (no. 9) (*NEMURI KYOSHIRO BURAI HIKAE – MASHO NO HADA,* aka *KYOSHIRO NEMURI REFRAINING FROM VILLAINY – DEVILISH FLESH*) (1967) Dir: Kazuo Ikehiro

KYOSHIRO NEMURI – WOMAN HELL (no. 10) (*NEMURI KYOSHIRO ONNA JIGOKU,*
aka *A RONIN CALLED NEMURI*) (1968) Dir: Tokuzo Tanaka

KYOSHIRO NEMURI – HUMAN TARANTULA (no. 11) (*NEMURI KYOSHIRO HITO
HADA GUMO*) (1968) Dir: Kimiyoshi Yasuda

KYOSHIRO NEMURI – CASTLE MENAGERIE (no. 12) (*NEMURI KYOSHIRO AKUJO
GARI,* aka *SLEEPY EYES OF DEATH – EVIL WOMEN HUNT*) (1969) Dir: Kazuo
Ikehiro (*final Nemuri film starring Raizo Ichikawa who died in July 1969*)

KYOSHIRO NEMURI – FULL MOON SWORDSMAN (no. 13) (*NEMURI KYOSHIRO
ENGETSU SAPPO*) (1969) Dir: Kazuo Mori (*with Hiroki Matsukata as Nemuri*)

KYOSHIRO NEMURI – FYLFOT SWORDPLAY (no. 14) (*NEMURI KYOSHIRO MANJI
GIRI*) (1970) Dir: Kazuo Ikehiro (*with Hiroki Matsukata as Nemuri*)

MODERN YAKUZA (*GENDAI YAKUZA*)

(*Toei studios' series starring Bunta Sugawara*)

MODERN YAKUZA – CODE OF THE OUTLAW (no. 1) (*GENDAI YAKUZA – YOTA
MONO NO OKITE*) (1969) Dir: Yasuo Furuhata

MODERN YAKUZA – OUTLAW'S HONOR AND HUMANITY (no. 2) (*GENDAI
YAKUZA – YOTA MONO JINGI*) (1969) Dir: Yasuo Furuhata

MODERN YAKUZA – OUTLAW OF SHINJUKU (no. 3) (*GENDAI YAKUZA –
SHINJUKU NO YOTA MONO*) (1970) Dir: Shin Takakuwa

MODERN YAKUZA – LOYATY OFFERING CEREMONY (no. 4) (*GENDAI YAKUZA –
SAKAZUKI KAE SHIMASU*) (1971) Dir: Kiyoshi Saeki

MODERN YAKUZA – THREE CHERRY BLOSSOM BLOOD BROTHERS (no. 5)
(*GENDAI YAKUZA – CHI SAKURA SAN KYODAI*) (1971) Dir: Sadao Nakajima

MODERN YAKUZA – OUTLAW KILLER (no. 6) (*GENDAI YAKUZA – HITOKIRI
YOTA,* aka *STREET MOBSTER*) (1972) Dir: Kinji Fukasaku

NINJA, BAND OF ASSASSINS (*SHINOBI NO MONO*)

(*Daiei studios' series starring Raizo Ichikawa*)

NINJA, BAND OF ASSASSINS (no. 1) (*SHINOBI NO MONO*) (1962) Dir: Satsuo Yamamoto

NINJA, BAND OF ASSASSINS 2 (no. 2) (*ZOKU SHINOBI NO MONO*) (1962) Dir:
Satsuo Yamamoto

GOEMON WILL NEVER DIE! (no. 3) (*SHIN SHINOBI NO MONO,* aka *NINJA, BAND
OF ASSASSINS 3*) (1963) Dir: Kazuo Mori

MIST SAIZO, LAST OF THE NINJAS (no. 4) (*SHINOBI NO MONO – KIRIGAKURE
SAIZO,* aka *NINJA – MIST SAIZO*) (1964) Dir: Tokuzo Tanaka

NINJA, BAND OF ASSASSINS – RETURN OF MIST SAIZO (no. 5) (*SHINOBI NO
MONO – ZOKU KIRIGAKURE SAIZO,* aka *MIST SAIZO RETURNS*) (1964) Dir:
Kazuo Ikehiro

THE LAST IGA SPY (no. 6) (*SHINOBI NO MONO – IGA YASHIKI*) (1965) Dir: Kazuo
Mori

MIST SAIZO STRIKES BACK (no. 7) (*SHINOBI NO MONO – SHIN KIRIGAKURE
SAIZO*) (1966) Dir: Kazuo Mori

A NEW BEGINNING – NINJA, BAND OF ASSASSINS (no. 8) (*SHINSHO – SHINOBI
NO MONO,* aka *THE THREE ENEMIES*) (1966) Dir: Kazuo Ikehiro

YOUNG BOSS (WAKA OYABUN)
(*Daiei studios' series starring Raizo Ichikawa*)
YOUNG BOSS (no. 1) (*WAKA OYABUN*) (1965) Dir: Kazuo Ikehiro
YOUNG BOSS – PRISON RELEASE (no. 2) (*WAKA OYABUN SHUTSUGOKU*) (1966)
    Dir: Kazuo Ikehiro
YOUNG BOSS – INVITATION TO FIGHT (no. 3) (*WAKA OYABUN KENKA JO*) (1966)
    Dir: Kazuo Ikehiro
YOUNG BOSS – OVERCOMING ADVERSITY (no. 4) (*WAKA OYABUN NORIKOMU*)
    (1966) Dir: Akira Inoue
YOUNG BOSS – RICKSHAW MAN RAMPAGE (no. 5) (*WAKA OYABUN – ABARE
    HISHA*) (1966) Dir: Shigeo Tanaka
EXTERMINATE THE YOUNG BOSS! (no. 6) (*WAKA OYABUN O KESE*) (1967) Dir:
    Chuzo Nakanishi
YOUNG BOSS, FUGITIVE (no. 7) (*WAKA OYABUN KYOJOTABI*) (1967) Dir: Kazuo Mori
YOUNG BOSS – A LEADER'S FLESH (no. 8) (*WAKA OYABUN – SEN RYO HADA*, aka
    TORPEDO X) (1967) Dir: Kazuo Ikehiro

ZATOICHI, THE BLIND SWORDSMAN
(*Daiei studios' series starring Shintaro Katsu*)
LIFE AND OPINION OF MASSEUR ICHI (no. 1) (*ZATOICHI MONOGATARI*, aka
    TALE OF ZATOICHI) (1962) Dir: Kenji Misumi
RETURN OF MASSEUR ICHI (no. 2) (*ZOKU ZATOICHI MONOGATARI*, aka *TALE
    OF ZATOICHI CONTINUES*) (1962) Dir: Kazuo Mori
NEW TALE OF ZATOICHI (no. 3) (*SHIN ZATOICHI MONOGATARI*) (1963) Dir: Tokuzo
    Tanaka
ZATOICHI, THE FUGITIVE (no. 4) (*ZATOICHI KYOJOTABI*) (1963) Dir: Tokuzo Tanaka
ZATOICHI ON THE ROAD (no. 5) (*ZATOICHI KENKA TABI*, aka *ZATOICHI AND THE
    SCOUNDRELS*) (1963) Dir: Kimiyoshi Yasuda
ZATOICHI AND THE CHEST OF GOLD (no. 6) (*ZATOICHI SEN-RYO KUBI*) (1964)
    Dir: Kazuo Ikehiro
ZATOICHI'S FLASHING SWORD (no. 7) (*ZATOICHI ABARE DAKO*) (1964) Dir: Kazuo
    Ikehiro
FIGHT, ZATOICHI, FIGHT (no. 8) (*ZATOICHI KESSHO TABI*) (1964) Dir: Kenji Misumi
ADVENTURES OF A BLIND MAN (no. 9) (*ZATOICHI SEKISHO YABURI*) (1964) Dir:
    Kimiyoshi Yasuda
ZATOICHI'S REVENGE (no. 10) (*ZATOICHI NIDAN GIRI*) (1965) Dir: Akira Inoue
ZATOICHI AND THE DOOMED MAN (no. 11) (*ZATOICHI SAKATE GIRI*) (1965) Dir:
    Kazuo Mori
ZATOICHI AND THE CHESS EXPERT (no. 12) (*ZATOICHI JIGOKU TABI*, aka
    ZATOICHI'S TRIP TO HELL) (1965) Dir: Kenji Misumi
THE BLIND SWORDSMAN'S VENGEANCE (no. 13) (*ZATOICHI NO UTA GA
    KIKOERU*) (1966) Dir: Kimiyoshi Yasuda
ZATOICHI'S PILGRIMAGE (no. 14) (*ZATOICHI UMI O WATARU*) (1966) Dir: Kazuo Ikehiro
THE BLIND SWORDSMAN'S CANE SWORD (no. 15) (*ZATOICHI TEKKA TABI*) (1967)
    Dir: Kimiyoshi Yasuda

ZATOICHI, THE OUTLAW (no. 16) (*ZATOICHI RO YABURI*) (1967) Dir: Satsuo Yamamoto

ZATOICHI CHALLENGED (no. 17) (*ZATOICHI CHI KEMURI KAIDO*) (1967) Dir: Kenji Misumi

THE BLIND SWORDSMAN AND THE FUGITIVES (no. 18) (*ZATOICHI HATASHIJO*) (1968) Dir: Kimiyoshi Yasuda

THE BLIND SWORDSMAN SAMARITAN (no. 19) (*ZATOICHI KENKA DAIKO*) (1968) Dir: Kenji Misumi

ZATOICHI MEETS YOJINBO (no. 20) (*ZATOICHI TO YOJINBO*) (1970) Dir: Kihachi Okamoto

ZATOICHI'S FESTIVAL OF FIRE (no. 21) (*ZATOICHI ABARE HIMATSURI*) (1970) Dir: Kenji Misumi

THE BLIND SWORDSMAN MEETS HIS EQUAL (no. 22) (*SHIN ZATOICHI – YABURE! TOJIN KEN!*, aka *ZATOICHI MEETS THE ONE-ARMED SWORDSMAN*) (1971) Dir: Kimiyoshi Yasuda

ZATOICHI AT LARGE (no. 23) (*ZATOICHI GOYO TABI*) (1972) Dir: Kazuo Mori

ZATOICHI IN DESPERATION (no. 24) (*SHIN ZATOICHI MONOGATARI – ORETA TSUE*, aka *ZATOICHI'S BROKEN CANE*) (1972) Dir: Shintaro Katsu

THE BLIND SWORDSMAN'S CONSPIRACY (no. 25) (*SHIN ZATOICHI MONOGATARI – KASAMA NO CHIMATSURI*, aka *NEW ZATOICHI TALE – BLOODBATH AT KASAMA*) (1973) Dir: Kimiyoshi Yasuda

ZATOICHI (no. 26) (1989) Dir: Shintaro Katsu

(*As everyone reading this book probably knows by now, 'Beat' Takeshi Kitano revived the Zatoichi character in 2003, starring in and directing the film ZATOICHI to near-universal acclaim*)

APPENDIX – SELECTED JAPANESE 'OUTLAW' COLLABORATORS

(Screenwriters, Composers, Cinematographers)

Screenplays for Japanese genre cinema, especially in the 1960s and 1970s, were often a collaboration between a writer and the director or amongst several writers. Almost all Japanese outlaw directors had to start out writing scripts in their transition from assistant directors to full-fledged filmmakers to prove their mettle. Due to matters of space, there are numerous, great outlaw screenwriters not represented here, such as Akira Murao, Koji Takada, Susumu Saji, Fumio Konami, Hiro Matsuda, Hideaki Yamamoto, Isao Matsumoto, Morimasa Owaku, Kinya Naoi, Hajime Takaiwa, Seiji Hoshikawa, Yoshihiro Kakefuda, Tatsuhiko Kamoi, Kaneo Ikegami, Goro Tanada, Hisatoshi Kai, Iwao 'Gan' Yamazaki, Atsushi Yamatoya, Kei Tasaka, Tatsuo Nogami, Minoru Inuzuka, Ichiro Miyagawa, Ei Ogawa, Masahiro Shimura and countless others).

YOSHIHIRO ISHIMATSU (1932–) – Selected Filmography (Screenwriter)

BLACK TEST CAR (KURO NO TESUTO KAA) (1962) (co-written with Kazuo Funabashi) Dir: Yasuzo Masumura

BLACK STATEMENT BOOK (KURO NO HOKOKUSHO) (1963) Dir: Yasuzo Masumura

LIPS OF RUIN (KURO NO CHUSAJO) (1963) (co-written with Seiji Hoshikawa) Dir: Taro Yuge

BLACK CHALLENGER (KURO NO CHOSENSHA) (1964) (co-written with Toshio Matsuura) Dir: Mitsuo Murayama

A CERTAIN KILLER (ARU KOROSHIYA) (1967) (co-written with Yasuzo Masumura) Dir: Kazuo Mori

ORGANIZED CRIME 2 (ZOKU SOSHIKI BORYOKU) (1967) Dir: Junya Sato

THE GREAT VILLAIN (DAI AKURO, aka *THE MOST CORRUPTED,* aka *THE EVIL TRIO)* (1968) Dir: and co-written: Yasuzo Masumura

THE DRIFTING AVENGER (KOYA NO TOSEININ) (1968) Dir: Junya Sato

ORGANIZED CRIME – LOYALTY OFFERING BROTHERS (SOSHIKI BORYOKU – KYODAI SAKAZUKI) (1969) Dir: Junya Sato

WOMAN GAMBLING EXPERT – TAINTED DICE (ONNA TOBAKUSHI – SAIKORO GESHO) (1969) Dir: and co-written: Yoshio Inoue

A CREATURE CALLED MAN (JAGA WA HASHITTA) (1970) (co-written with Hiroshi Nagano) Dir: Kiyoshi Nishimura

THE ELECTRIC JELLYFISH (DENKI KURAGE, aka *PLAY IT COOL,* aka *THE ELECTRIC MEDUSA)* (1970) Dir: and co-written:Yasuzo Masumura

CITY OF BEASTS (YAJU TOSHI) (1970) Dir: Jun Fukuda

THE HOT LITTLE GIRL (SHIBIRE KURAGE, aka *THE NEON JELLYFISH)* (1970) Dir: and co-written: Yasuzo Masumura

ROGUE'S SELF-SACRIFICE (SUTEMI NO NARAZU MONO) (1970) (co-written with Shinichiro Sawai) Dir: Yasuo Furuhata

GAMBLER'S COUNTERATTACK (BAKUTO KIRIKOMI TAI) (1971) Dir: and co-written: Junya Sato

STREET MOBSTER (GENDAI YAKUZA – HITOKIRI YOTA, aka *MODERN YAKUZA – OUTLAW KILLER)* (1972) Dir: and co-written: Kinji Fukasaku

TRAIL OF BLOOD (MUSHUKUNIN MIKOGAMI NO JOKICHI – KIBA WA HIKI RETSU ITA, aka *JOKICHI MIKOGAMI, WANDERER – PULLING THE FANGS THAT RIP AND TEAR)* (1972) Dir: Kazuo Ikehiro

TRAIL OF BLOOD 2 (MUSHUKUNIN MIKOGAMI NO JOKICHI – KAWAKAZE NI KAKO WA NAGARETA, aka *JOKICHI MIKOGAMI, WANDERER – DRIFTING IN THE RIVER WIND)* (1972) Dir: and co-written: Kazuo Ikehiro

YAKUZA AND FEUDS (YAKUZA TO KOSO) (1972) Dir: and co-written: Junya Sato

YAKUZA AND FEUDS – TRUE ACCOUNT OF THE ANDO GANG (YAKUZA TO KOSO – JITSUROKU ANDOGUMI) (1973) Dir: Junya Sato

TRUE ACCOUNT OF GINZA'S SECRET ENFORCERS (JITSUROKU SHISETSU GINZA KEISATSU, aka *TRUE ACCOUNT OF GINZA TORTURES)* (1973) (co-written with Fumio Konami and Hiro Matsuda) Dir: Junya Sato

TRUE ACCOUNT OF THE ANDO GANG – STORY OF ATTACK (JITSUROKU ANDOGUMI – SHUGEKI HEN) (1973) Dir, and co-written: Junya Sato

KAZUO KASAHARA (1927–2002) – Selected Filmography (Screenwriter)

THE BOSS (KAOYAKU) (1965) (co-written with Kinji Fukasaku and Teruo Ishii) Dir: Teruo Ishii

JAPAN'S MOST CHIVALROUS (NIHON DAI KYOKAKU) (1966) Dir: Masahiro Makino

SEVEN GAMBLERS (no. 4 of *GAMBLER* series) *(SHICHININ NO BAKUTO)* (1966) Dir: and co-written: Shigehiro Ozawa

EIGHTEEN-YEAR JAIL TERM (CHOEKI JUNHACHI NEN) (1967) (co-written with Shin Morita) Dir: Tai Kato

PATH OF CHIVALRY (KYOKAKUDO) (1967) (co-written with Ichiro Miyagawa) Dir: Norifumi Suzuki

A BOSS IN JAIL (GOKUCHU NO KAOYAKU) (1968) (co-written with Koji Takada and Motohiro Torii) Dir: Yasuo Furuhata

GAMBLER LIFE STORIES (no. 2 of *LIFE STORIES* series) *(BAKUTO RETSUDEN)* (1968) Dir: Shigehiro Ozawa

GAMBLING DEN – GAMBLING BOSS (no. 4 of *GAMBLING DEN* series) *(BAKUCHIUCHI – SOCHO TOBAKU)* (1968) Dir: Kosaku Yamashita

GAMBLER MONEY (no. 8 of *GAMBLER* series) *(SATSUTABA BAKUTO)* (1970) (co-written with Masahiro Shimura) Dir: Shigehiro Ozawa

TALES OF JAPANESE CHIVALRY 10– RISING DRAGON (NIHON KYOKAKUDEN – NOBORI RYU) (1970) Dir: Kosaku Yamashita

TALES OF JAPAN'S CHIVALROUS WOMEN 2 – BRAVE RED FLOWER (NIHON JOKYODEN – MAKKANA DOKYO BANA) (1970) Dir: Yasuo Furuhata

TALES OF JAPAN'S CHIVALROUS WOMEN 5 – DUEL AT CAPE HIMEYURI (NIHON JOKYODEN – GEKI TO HIMEYURI MISAKI) (1971) Dir: Shigehiro Ozawa

CHIVALROUS WOMAN 2 – I REQUEST SHELTER (ONNA TOSEININ – OTA NO MOSHIMASU) (1971) Dir: Kosaku Yamashita

GAMBLING DEN – A LIFE OF CARDS (no. 9 of *GAMBLING DEN* series) *(BAKUCHIUCHI – INOCHI FUDA)* (1971) Dir: Kosaku Yamashita

CHERRY BLOSSOM FIRE GANG (KANTO HIZAKURA IKKA) (1972) Dir: Masahiro Makino

JAPAN'S VIOLENT GANGS 4 – LOYALTY OFFERING MURDER (NIHON BORYOKUDAN – KOROSHI NO SAKAZUKI) (1972) Dir: Yasuo Furuhata

BATTLES WITHOUT HONOR AND HUMANITY (JINGINAKI TATAKAI) (1973) Dir: Kinji Fukasaku

BATTLES WITHOUT HONOR AND HUMANITY 2 – HIROSHIMA DEATH MATCH (JINGINAKI TATAKAI- HIROSHIMA SHITO HEN) (1973) Dir: Kinji Fukasaku

BATTLES WITHOUT HONOR AND HUMANITY 3 – AGENT OF WAR (JINGINAKI TATAKAI – DAIRI SENSO) (1973) Dir: Kinji Fukasaku

BATTLES WITHOUT HONOR AND HUMANITY 4 – SUMMIT OF OPERATIONS (JINGINAKI TATAKAI –CHOJO SAKUSEN) (1974) Dir: Kinji Fukasaku

BATTLES WITHOUT HONOR AND HUMANITY 5 – SAGA CONCLUSION (JINGINAKI TATAKAI – KANKETSU HEN) (1974) Dir: Kinji Fukasaku

STATE POLICE VS. ORGANISED CRIME (KENKEI TAI SOSHIKI BORYOKU, aka *COPS VS. THUGS)* (1975) Dir: Kinji Fukasaku

YAKUZA BURIAL – JASMINE FLOWER (YAKUZA NO HAKABA – KUCHINASHI NO HANA) (1976) Dir: Kinji Fukasaku

TOKYO BORDELLO (YOSHIWARA ENJO, aka *YOSHIWARA CONFLAGRATION)* (1987) (co-written with Sadao Nakajima) Dir: Hideo Gosha

CARMEN: 1945 (NIKUTAI NO MON, aka *GATE OF FLESH)* (1988) Dir: Hideo Gosha

226 (NI-NI-ROKU, aka *FOUR DAYS OF SNOW AND BLOOD)* (1989) Dir: Hideo Gosha

STREET OF MASTERLESS SAMURAI (RONIN-GAI) (1990) Dir: Kazuo Kuroki

There are scores of music composers not represented here because of matters of space. Other worthy composers who deserve mention are Toru Takemitsu, Hajime Kaburagi, Isao Tomita, Sei Ikeno, Ichiro Saito, Masao Yagi, Chumei Watanabe, Chuji Kinoshita, Toshiaki Tsushima, Shunsuke Kikuchi, Riichiro Manabe, Harumi Ibe, Keitaro Miho, Masayoshi Ikeda, Seitaro Omori, Taiichiro Kosugi and Takeo Watanabe amongst numerous others. (Note: Believe it or not, the filmographies below, especially for Sato and Ifukube, represent only a small fraction of their output.)

MASARU SATO (1928–1999) – Selected Filmography (Composer)

NEW TALES OF THE TAIRA CLAN (SHIN HEIKE MONOGATARI) (1955) Dir: Kenji Mizoguchi

CRAZED FRUIT (KURUTAA KAJITSU) (1956) (collaboration with Toru Takemitsu) Dir: Ko Nakahira

THRONE OF BLOOD (KUMO NO SU JO) (1957) Dir: Akira Kurosawa

THE H-MAN (BIJO TO EKITAI NINGEN) (1958) Dir: Ishiro Honda

THE HIDDEN FORTRESS (KAKUSHI TORIDE NO SAN AKUNIN) (1958) Dir: Akira
Kurosawa

DESPERADO OUTPOST (DOKURITSU GURENTAI) (1959) Dir: Kihachi Okamoto

THE LAST GUNFIGHT (ANKOKUGAI NO TAIKETSU) (1960) Dir: Kihachi Okamoto

THE BAD SLEEP WELL (WARUI YATSU HODO YOKU NEMURU) (1960) Dir: Akira
Kurosawa

WESTWARD DESPERADO (DOKURITSU GURENTAI NISHI HE) (1960) Dir: Kihachi
Okamoto

UNDERWORLD BULLETS (ANKOKUGAI NO DANKON) (1961) Dir: Kihachi Okamoto

YOJINBO (1961) Dir: Akira Kurosawa

SANJURO (1962) Dir: Akira Kurosawa

OPERATION SEWER RATS (DOBUNEZUMI SAKUSEN) (1962) Dir: Kihachi Okamoto

HIGH AND LOW TENGOKU TO JIGOKU) (1963) Dir: Akira Kurosawa

WARRING CLANS (SENGOKU YARO) (1963) Dir: Kihachi Okamoto

STORY OF MILITARY CRUELTY (RIKUGUN ZANGYAKU MONOGATARI) (1963)
Dir: Junya Sato

AH! EXPLOSION (AH! BAKUDAN) (1964) Dir: Kihachi Okamoto

SAMURAI FROM NOWHERE (DOJO YABURI) (1964) Dir: Seiichiro Uchikawa

JAKOMAN AND TETSU (1964) Dir: Kinji Fukasaku

PASSION (KURUWA SODACHI) (1964) Dir: Junya Sato

SAMURAI ASSASSIN (SAMURAI) (1965) Dir: Kihachi Okamoto

THE SPIDER TATTOO (IREZUMI) (1965) Dir: Yasuzo Masumura

RED BEARD (AKAHIGE) (1965) Dir: Akira Kurosawa

FORT GRAVEYARD (CHI TO SUNA) (1965) Dir: Kihachi Okamoto

SWORD OF DOOM (DAIBOSATSU TOGE) (1966) Dir: Kihachi Okamoto

AGE OF ASSASSINS (SATSUJIN KYOJIDAI) (1967) Dir: Kihachi Okamoto

ORGANIZED CRIME (SOSHIKI BORYOKU) (1967) Dir: Junya Sato

JAPAN'S LONGEST DAY (NIHON NO ICHIBAN NAGAI HI) (1967) Dir: Kihachi Okamoto

ORGANIZED CRIME 2 (ZOKU SOSHIKI BORYOKU) (1967) Dir: Junya Sato

KILL! (KIRU) (1968) Dir: Kihachi Okamoto

THE HUMAN BULLET (NIKUDAN) (1968) Dir: Kihachi Okamoto

GOYOKIN (1969) Dir: Hideo Gosha

HITOKIRI (aka TENCHU!) (1969) Dir: Hideo Gosha

RED LION (AKAGE) (1969) Dir: Kihachi Okamoto

THE SCANDALOUS ADVENTURES OF BURAIKAN (BURAIKAN) (1970) Dir: Masahiro
Shinoda

CITY OF BEASTS (YAJU TOSHI) (1970) Dir: Jun Fukuda

INCIDENT AT BLOOD PASS (MACHIBUSE) (1970) Dir: Hiroshi Inagaki

BATTLE OF OKINAWA (GEKIDO NO SHOWASHI – OKINAWA KESSEN) (1970) Dir:
Kihachi Okamoto

THE WOLVES (SHUSHO IWAI) (1971) Dir: Hideo Gosha

GODZILLA VS. MECHAGODZILLA (1974) Dir: Jun Fukuda

BATTLE CRY (TOKKAN) (1975) Dir: Kihachi Okamoto

SANSHIRO SUGATA (SUGATA SANSHIRO) (1977) Dir: Kihachi Okamoto

NOISY DYNAMITE! (DAINOMAITO DONDON) (1978) Dir: Kihachi Okamoto

BLUE CHRISTMAS (BURUU KURISUMASU) (1978) Dir: Kihachi Okamoto

HUNTER IN THE DARK (YAMI NO KARIUDO) (1979) Dir: Hideo Gosha

TRACKED (USUGESHO) (1985) Dir: Hideo Gosha

DEATH SHADOWS (JITTEMAI) (1986) Dir: Hideo Gosha

YAKUZA WIVES (GOKUDO NO ONNATACHI) (1986) Dir: Hideo Gosha

TOKYO BORDELLO (YOSHIWARA ENJO) (1987) Dir: Hideo Gosha

THE SILK ROAD (DUN-HUANG) (1988) Dir: Junya Sato

SHOGUN'S SHADOW (SHOGUN IEMITSU NO RANSHIN – GEKI TOTSU) (1989)
    Dir: Yasuo Furuhata

AKIRA IFUKUBE (1914–) – Selected Filmography (Composer)

SNOW TRAIL (GINREI NO HATE) (1947) Dir: Senkichi Taniguchi

JAKOMAN AND TETSU (1949) Dir: Senkichi Taniguchi

ANATAHAN (1954) Dir: Josef Von Sternberg

GODZILLA (GOJIRA) (1954) Dir: Ishiro Honda

THE HARP OF BURMA (BIRUMA NO TATEGOTO) (1956) Dir: Kon Ichikawa

RODAN (SORA NO DAI KAIJU RADON) (1956) Dir: Ishiro Honda

YAGYU SECRET SCROLLS (YAGYU BUGEICHO) (1957) Dir: Hiroshi Inagaki

THE MYSTERIANS (CHIKYU BOEIGUN) (1957) Dir: Ishiro Honda

YAGYU SECRET SCROLLS 2 – NINJITSU (YAGYU BUGEICHO – NINJITSU) (1958)
    Dir: Hiroshi Inagaki

THE BIG BOSS (ANKOKUGAI NO KAOYAKU) (1959) Dir: Kihachi Okamoto

THRONE OF FLAME (HONOO NO SHIRO) (1960) Dir: Tai Kato

DAREDEVIL IN THE CASTLE (OSAKA-JO MONOGATARI) (1961) Dir: Hiroshi Inagaki

ZEN AND SWORD (MIYAMOTO MUSASHI) (1961) Dir: Tomu Uchida

BUDDHA (SHAKA) (1961) Dir: Kenji Misumi

CONSPIRATOR (HANGYAKUJI) (1961) Dir: Daisuke Ito

BAD REPUTATION (AKUMYO) (1961) Dir: Tokuzo Tanaka

LIFE AND OPINION OF MASSEUR ICHI (ZATOICHI MONOGATARI, aka *TALE OF
    ZATOICHI)* (1962) Dir: Kenji Misumi

KING KONG VS. GODZILLA (KINGUKONGU TAI GOJIRA) (1962) Dir: Ishiro Honda

CHUSHINGURA (1962) Dir: Hiroshi Inagaki

NEW TALE OF ZATOICHI (no. 3) *(SHIN ZATOICHI MONOGATARI)* (1963) Dir: Tokuzo
    Tanaka

ZATOICHI, THE FUGITIVE (no. 4) *(ZATOICHI KYOJOTABI)* (1963) Dir: Tokuzo Tanaka

ZATOICHI ON THE ROAD (no. 5) *(ZATOICHI KENKA TABI)* (1963) Dir: Tokuzo Tanaka

THIRTEEN ASSASSINS (JUSANNIN NO SHIKAKU) (1963) Dir: Eiichi Kudo

GODZILLA VS. MOTHRA (MOSURA TAI GOJIRA) (1964) Dir: Ishiro Honda

FIGHT, ZATOICHI, FIGHT (no. 8) *(ZATOICHI KESSHO TABI)* (1964) Dir: Kenji Misumi

*GHIDRAH, THE THREE-HEADED MONSTER (SAN DAI KAIJU – CHIKYU SAIDAI
    NO KESSEN)* (1964) Dir: Ishiro Honda

NINJA, BAND OF ASSASSINS 4 – MIST SAIZO (SHINOBI NO MONO – KIRAGAKURE SAIZO) (1964) Dir: Tokuzo Tanaka

THE BLIND SWORDSMAN'S REVENGE (no. 10) *(ZATOICHI NIDAN GIRI)* (1965) Dir: Akira Inoue

FRANKENSTEIN CONQUERS THE WORLD (FURANKENSHUTAIN TAI CHITEI KAIJU BARAGON) (1965) Dir: Ishiro Honda

INVASION OF ASTRO MONSTER (KAIJU DAI SENSO, aka *GODZILLA VS. MONSTER ZERO)* (1965) Dir: Ishiro Honda

ZATOICHI AND THE CHESS EXPERT (no. 12) *(ZATOICHI JIGOKU TABI)* (1965) Dir: Kenji Misumi

THE PRINCESS'S MASK (NEMURI KYOSHIRO TAJO KEN, aka *SLEEPY EYES OF DEATH 7)* (1966) Dir: Akira Inoue

MAJIN, MONSTER OF TERROR (DAIMAJIN) (1966) Dir: Kimiyoshi Yasuda

THE BLIND SWORDSMAN'S VENGEANCE (no. 13) *(ZATOICHI NO UTA GA KIKOERU)* (1966) Dir: Tokuzo Tanaka

THE BETRAYAL (DAI SATSUJIN – OROCHI) (1966) Dir: Tokuzo Tanaka

THE WRATH OF GIANT MAJIN (no. 2) *(DAIMAJIN IKARU)* (1966) Dir: Kenji Misumi

KYOSHIRO NEMURI – VILLAIN'S SWORD (no. 8) *(NEMURI KYOSHIRO BURAI KEN)* (1966) Dir: Kenji Misumi

MAJIN STRIKES AGAIN (no. 3) *(DAIMAJIN GYAKUSHU)* (1966) Dir: Kazuo Mori

NINJA, BAND OF ASSASSINS – NEW MIST SAIZO STORY (SHINOBI NO MONO – SHIN KIRIGAKURE SAIZO, aka *NINJA 7)* (1966) Dir: Kazuo Mori

ELEVEN SAMURAI (JUICHININ NO SAMURAI) (1966) Dir: Eiichi Kudo

ZATOICHI CHALLENGED (no. 17) *(ZATOICHI CHIKEMURI KAIDO)* (1967) Dir: Kenji Misumi

GHOST OF THE SNOW WOMAN (KAIDAN YUKIONNA) (1968) Dir: Tokuzo Tanaka

DESTROY ALL MONSTERS (KAIJU SOSHINGEKI) (1968) Dir: Ishiro Honda

THE DEVIL'S TEMPLE (ONI NO SUMU YAKATA) (1969) Dir: Kenji Misumi

ZATOICHI MEETS YOJINBO (no. 20) *(ZATOICHI TO YOJINBO)* (1970) Dir: Kihachi Okamoto

ZATOICHI'S CONSPIRACY (no. 25) *(SHIN ZATOICHI MONOGATARI – KASAMA NO CHIMATSURI)* (1973) Dir: Kimiyoshi Yasuda

THE LAST SAMURAI (OKAMI YO RAKUJITSU O KIRE, aka *WOLF! CUT DOWN THE SETTING SUN)* (1974) Dir: Kenji Misumi

NAOZUMI YAMAMOTO (1932–2002) – Selected Filmograph (Composer)

UNDERWORLD BEAUTY (ANKOKUGAI NO BIJO) (1958) Dir: Seijun Suzuki

BREASTS AND BULLETS (CHIBUSA TO JUDAN) (1958) Dir: Hiroshi Noguchi

MY FACE RED IN THE SUNSET (YUHI NI AKAI ORE NO KAO) (1961) Dir: Masahiro Shinoda

GATE OF FLESH (NIKUTAI NO MON) (1964) Dir: Seijun Suzuki

STORY OF A PROSTITUTE (SHUNPU DEN) (1965) Dir: Seijun Suzuki

HOODLUM SOLDIER (HEITAI YAKUZA) (1965) Dir: Yasuzo Masumura

BLACK TIGHT KILLERS (ORE NI SAWARUTO ABUNAIZE) (1965) Dir: Yasuharu Hasebe
FIGHTING ELEGY (KENKA EREJI) (1966) Dir: Seijun Suzuki
SAMURAI YAKUZA (HATAMOTO YAKUZA) (1966) Dir: Sadao Nakajima
SEVEN WILD BEASTS 2 – PROCLAMATION OF BLOOD (SHICHININ NO YAJU –
    CHI NO SENGEN) (1967) Dir: Mio Ezaki
BRANDED TO KILL (KOROSHI NO RAKUIN) (1967) Dir: Seijun Suzuki
DIAMOND OF THE ANDES (SEKIDO O KAKERU OTOKO) (1968) Dir: Buichi Saito
VILLAINY – LEADING MOBSTERS (BURAI YORI – DAI KANBU, aka *GANGSTER*
    VIP) (1968) Dir: Toshio Masuda

(*Yamamoto wrote music scores almost exclusively for comedies, starting in the mid-sixties,
including the* **Krazy Kats** *series at Toho, then almost every single one of the over 40 films
of director Yoji Yamada's* **TORA SAN** *series, climaxing with the final episode in 1995.*)
    *At the risk of seeming redundant – naming one Japanese cinematographer when there
are dozens and dozens of so many excellent ones is a painful chore. There were legions of
amazing cinematographers at all the studios, especially during the golden age of outlaw
cinema.*

KAZUO MIYAGAWA (1908–1999) – Selected Filmography (Cinematographer)

RASHOMON (1950) Dir: Akira Kurosawa
UGETSU (UGETSU MONOGATARI) (1953) Dir: Kenji Mizoguchi
SANSHO THE BAILIFF (SANJO DAYU) (1954) Dir: Kenji Mizoguchi
CRUCIFIED LOVERS (CHIKAMATSU MONOGATARI) (1954) Dir: Kenji Mizoguchi
NEW TALES OF THE TAIRA CLAN (SHIN HEIKE MONOGATARI) (1955) Dir: Kenji
    Mizoguchi
STREET OF SHAME (AKAI CHITAI) (1956) Dir: Kenji Mizoguchi
ENJO (1958) Dir: Kon Ichikawa
ODD OBSESSION (KAGI) (1959) Dir: Kon Ichikawa
YOJINBO (1961) Dir: Akira Kurosawa
ZATOICHI AND THE CHEST OF GOLD (ZATOICHI SEN-RYO KUBI) (1964) Dir:
    Kazuo Ikehiro
THE SPIDER TATTOO (IREZUMI) (1966) Dir: Yasuzo Masumura
THE BLIND SWORDSMAN'S VENGEANCE (ZATOICHI NO UTA GA KIKOERU)
    (1966) Dir: Tokuzo Tanaka
A CERTAIN KILLER (ARU KOROSHI YA) (1967) Dir: Kazuo Mori
ZATOICHI, THE OUTLAW (ZATOICHI RO YABURI) (1967) Dir: Satsuo Yamamoto
ZATOICHI AND THE FUGITIVES (ZATOICHI HATASHIJO) (1968) Dir: Kimiyoshi
    Yasuda
THE DEVIL'S TEMPLE (ONI NO SUMU YAKATA) (1969) Dir: Kenji Misumi
ZATOICHI MEETS YOJINBO (ZATOICHI TO YOJINBO) (1970) Dir: Kihachi Okamoto
ZATOICHI'S FESTIVAL OF FIRE (no. 21) *(ZATOICHI ABARE HIMATSURI)* (1970)
    Dir: Kenji Misumi

TRAIL OF BLOOD 2 – DRIFTING IN THE RIVER WIND (MUSHUKUNIN MIKOGAMI JOKICHI – KAWA KAZE NI KAKO WA NAGARE TA) (1972) Dir: Kazuo Ikehiro

LONE WOLF AND CUB 4 – BABY CART IN PERIL (KOZURE OKAMI – OYA NO KOKORO KO NO KOKORO) (1972) Dir: Buichi Saito

RAZOR HANZO 2 – THE SNARE (GOYO KIBA – KAMISORI HANZO SEME JIGOKU) (1973) Dir: Yasuzo Masumura

BANISHED ORIN (HANREGOZE ORIN) (1977) Dir: Masahiro Shinoda

LOVE SUICIDES AT SONEZAKI (SONEZAKI SHINJU) (1981) Dir: Yasuzo Masumura (with Meiko Kaji)

APPENDIX – PANTHEON OUTLAW DIRECTORS

[Not represented in book by essays/interviews]:

HIDEO GOSHA (1929–1992) – Selected Filmography

1964	*THREE OUTLAW SAMURAI (SANBIKI NO SAMURAI)*
1965	*SWORD OF THE BEAST (KEDAMONO NO KEN, aka SAMURAI GOLD-SEEKERS)*
1966	*SECRET OF THE URN (TANGE SAZEN – HIEN IAIGIRI)*
	SAMURAI WOLF (KIBA OKAMINOSUKE)
	SAMURAI WOLF – HELL CUT (KIBA OKAMINOSUKE – JIGIKU GIRI)
	CASH CALLS HELL (GOHIKI NO SHINSHI, aka FIVE GENTLEMAN)
1969	*GOYOKIN (aka OFFICIAL GOLD, aka STEEL EDGE OF REVENGE)*
	HITOKIRI (aka TENCHU!, aka HEAVEN'S PUNISHMENT, aka THE KILLER)
1972	*THE WOLVES (SHUSSHO IWAI, aka PRISON RELEASE CELEBRATION)*
1974	*VIOLENT STREET (BORYOKU GAI, aka VIOLENT CITY)*
1978	*BANDITS VS. SAMURAI SQUAD (KUMOKIRI NIZAEMON)*
1979	*HUNTER IN THE DARK (YAMI NO KARIUDO)*
1982	*ONI MASA (aka KIRYUIN HANAKO NO SHOGAI)*
1983	*THE GEISHA (YOKIRO)*
1984	*FIREFLIES OF THE NORTH (KITA NO HOTARU)*
1985	*TRACKED (USUGESHO)*
	THE OAR (KAI)
1986	*YAKUZA WIVES (GOKUDO NO ONNATACHI)*
	DEATH SHADOWS (JITTEMAI)
1987	*TOKYO BORDELLO (YOSHIWARA ENJO, aka YOSHIWARA CONFLAGRATION)*
1988	*CARMEN: 1945 (NIKUTAI NO MON, aka GATE OF FLESH)*
1989	*FOUR DAYS OF SNOW AND BLOOD (NI-NI-ROKU, aka 226)*
1991	*HEAT HAZE (KAGERO)*
1992	*THE OIL-HELL MURDER (ONNA GOROSHI ABURA NO JIGOKU, aka WOMAN MURDER IN A HELL OF OIL)*

TAI KATO (1916–1985) – Selected Filmography

1951	*TROUBLE WITH SWORDS, TROUBLE WITH WOMEN – A WOMAN'S MIND (KENAN JONAN – JOSHIN DENSHIN NO MAKI)*
	TROUBLE WITH SWORDS, TROUBLE WITH WOMEN – SWORD'S LIGHT AND SHOOTING STAR (KENAN JONAN – KENKO RYUSEO NO MAKI)
1958	*WIND, WOMEN AND TRAVELLING RAVENS (KAZE TO ONNATO TABIGARASU, aka WIND, WOMEN AND VAGABONDS)*

1959   *MISSION TO HELL (KOGAN NO MISSHI)*

1960   *THRONE OF FLAME (HONOO NO SHIRO)*

1961   *GHOST OF OIWA (KAIDAN OIWA NO BOREI)*

1962   *TANGE SAZEN – MASTERPIECE SWORD (TANGE SAZEN – KAN'UNKONRYU NO MAKI)*
      LONG-SOUGHT MOTHER (MABUTA NO HAHA)

1963   *SASUKE AND HIS COMEDIANS (SANADA FUUNROKU,* aka *RECORDS OF THE BRAVE SANADA CLAN)*

1964   *FIGHTING TATSU, THE RICKSHAW MAN (SHAFU YUKYODEN – KENKA TATSU)*
      CRUEL STORY OF THE SHOGUNATE'S DOWNFALL (BAKUMATSU ZANKOKU MONOGATARI)

1965   *TALE OF MEIJI ERA CHIVALRY – THE THIRD BOSS (MEIJI KYOKAKUDEN – SANDAIME SHUMEI,* aka *BLOOD OF REVENGE)*

1966   *PICKED CLEAN TO THE BONE AND SUCKED DRY (HOMEMADE SHABURU)*
      TOKIJIRO KUTSUKAKE, LONE YAKUZA (KUTSUKAKE TOKIJIRO – YUKYO IPPIKI)
      HISTORY OF A MAN'S FACE (OTOKO NO KAO WA RIREKISHO, aka *BY A MAN'S FACE YOU SHALL KNOW HIM)*
      OPIUM HILLS – HELL SQUAD CHARGES (AHEN DAICHI – JIGOKU BUTAI TOTSU GEKI SEYO)

1967   *EIGHTEEN-YEAR JAIL TERM (CHOEKI JUHACHINEN)*

1968   *I, THE EXECUTIONER (MINAGOROSHI NO REIKA,* aka *GOSPEL HYMN OF MASSACRE)*

1969   *RED PEONY GAMBLER – FLOWER CARDS MATCH (HIBOTAN BAKUTO – HANA FUDA SHOBU)*

1970   *RED PEONY GAMBLER – ORYU'S VISIT (HIBOTAN BAKUTO – ORYU SANJO,* aka *RED PEONY GAMBLES HER LIFE,* aka *THIS IS ORYU)*

1971   *RED PEONY GAMBLER – DEATH TO THE WICKED (HIBOTAN BAKUTO – O INOCHI ITADAKIMASU)*

1972   *SHOWA WOMAN GAMBLER (SHOWA ONNA BAKUTO)*
      THEATER OF LIFE (JINSEI GEKIJO – SEISHUN – AIYOKU – ZANKYO HEN, aka *THEATER OF LIFE – STORY OF YOUTH, PASSION AND SPIRIT)*

1973   *FLOWER AND DRAGON (HANA TO RYU – SEIUN – AIZO – DOTO HEN,* aka *FLOWER AND DRAGON – STORY OF AMBITION, LOVE AND RAGE)*
      SWORD OF FURY (MIYAMOTO MUSASHI)
      BLOSSOM AND THE SWORD (NIHON KYOKA DEN)

1977   *A SCREAM FROM NOWHERE (EDOGAWA RAMPO NO INJU)*

1981   *FLAMES OF BLOOD (HONOO NO GOTOKU,* aka *LIKE A FIRE)*
      THE ONDEKOZA (ZA ONDEKOZA)

YASUZO MASUMURA (1924–1986) – Selected Filmography

1957	*KISSES (KUCHIZUKE)*
	WARM CURRENT (DANRYU)
1958	*THE PRECIPICE (HYOHEKI)*
	GIANTS AND TOYS (KYOJIN TO GANGU)
	THE FEARLESS MAN (FUTEKI NA OTOKO)
1960	*AFRAID TO DIE (KARAKKAZE YARO,* aka *A MAN BLOWN BY THE WIND)*
1961	*THE MAN WHO LOVED LOVE (KOSHOKU ICHIDAI OTOKO,* aka *A LUSTFUL MAN)*
1962	*BLACK TEST CAR (KURO NO TESUTO KAA)*
1963	*BLACK STATEMENT BOOK (KURO NO HOKOKUSHO,* aka *THE BLACK REPORT)*
	BAND OF PURE-HEARTED HOODLUMS (GURENTAI JUNJO HA)
1964	*MODERN FRAUD STORY – CHEAT (GENDAI INCHIKI MONOGATARI – DAMASHIYA)*
	MANJI (aka ALL MIXED UP)
	BLACK MARK SUPEREXPRESS (KURO NO CHOTOKKYU, aka *SUPEREXPRESS)*
1965	*HOODLUM SOLDIER (HEITAI YAKUZA)*
	SEISAKU'S WIFE (SEISAKU NO TSUMA)
1966	*THE SPIDER TATTOO (IREZUMI)*
	NAKANO SPY SCHOOL (RIKU GUN NAKANO GAKKO)
	RED ANGEL (AKAI TENSHI)
1967	*THE WIFE OF SEISHU HANAOKA (HANAOKA SEISHU NO TSUMA)*
1968	*THE GREAT VILLAIN (DAI AKUTO,* aka *THE EVIL TRIO,* aka *THE MOST CORRUPT)*
1969	*BLIND BEAST (MOJU)*
	VIXEN (JOTAI, aka *A WOMAN'S BODY)*
1970	*THE HOT LITTLE GIRL (SHIBIRE KURAGE,* aka *THE ELECTRIC JELLYFISH)*
	PLAY IT COOL (DENKI KURAGE, aka *THE ELECTRIC MEDUSA,* aka *THE ELECTRIC JELLYFISH 2)*
	THE YAKUZA SONG (YAKUZA ZESSHO, aka *THE FINAL PAYOFF,* aka *A YAKUZA MASTERPIECE)*
1971	*GAMES (ASOBI)*
1972	*NEW HOODLUM SOLDIER – FIRING LINE (SHIN HEITAI YAKUZA – KASEN)*
1973	*THE RAZOR 2 – THE SNARE (GOYO KIBA – KAMISORI HANZO JIGOKU SEME,* aka *FANGS OF PUBLIC OFFICE – RAZOR HANZO'S TORTURE HELL)*
1974	*NOTORIOUS DRAGON (AKUMYO – SHIMA ARASHI,* aka *BAD REPUTATION – TURF WAR)*
1975	*PULSATING ISLAND (DOMYAKU RETTO)*

1976   *LULLABY FOR THE GOOD EARTH (DAICHI NO KOMORI-UTA)*
1978   *LOVE SUICIDES AT SONEZAKI (SONEZAKI SHINJU)*

KENJI MISUMI (1921–1975) – Selected Filmography

1954   *TANGE SAZEN – BASKET OF MOSS (TANGE SAZEN – KOKE ZARU NO TSUBO)*
1956   *FLOWER BROTHERS (HANA NO KYODAI)*
        THE FIERY MAGISTRATE (SHIRANUI BUGYO)
        WOVEN HAT GONPACHI (AMIGASA GONPACHI)
1957   *FREE LANCE SAMURAI (MOMOTARO SAMURAI)*
1958   *GHOST CAT'S CURSED WALL (KAIBYO NOROI NO KABE)*
        SNAKE OF VENGEANCE (SHUNEN NO HEBI)
1959   *HALO OF HEAT HAZE (KAGERO GASA)*
        A THOUSAND FLYING CRANES (SENBAZURU HICHO)
        YOTSUYA GHOST STORY (YOTSUYA KAIDAN)
1960   *SATAN'S SWORD (DAIBOSATSU TOGE,* aka *THE GREAT BODDHISATVA PASS)*
        SATAN'S SWORD – THE DRAGON GOD (DAIBOSATSU TOGE – RYUJIN NO MAKI)
1961   *BUDDHA (SHAKA)*
1962   *LIFE AND OPINION OF MASSEUR ICHI (ZATOICHI MONOGATARI)*
        DESTINY'S SON (KIRU)
1963   *ACCOUNT OF SHINSENGUMI LEADERS (SHINSENGUMI SHIMATSUKI,* aka *I WANT TO DIE A SAMURAI)*
1964   *ADVENTURES OF KYOSHIRO NEMURI, SWORDSMAN (NEMURI KYOSHIRO SHOBU)*
        SWORD (KEN)
        LONE WANDERER (MUSHUKU MONO)
        FIGHT, ZATOICHI, FIGHT (ZATOICHI KESSHO TABI, aka *ZATOICHI'S BLOODY JOURNEY)*
1965   *SWORD OF FIRE (NEMURI KYOSHIRO ENJO KEN,* aka *FLAMING SWORD OF KYOSHIRO NEMURI,* aka *SLEEPY EYES OF DEATH – SWORD OF FIRE)*
        SWORD DEVIL (KEN KI)
        ZATOICHI AND THE CHESS EXPERT (ZATOICHI JIGOKU TABI, aka *ZATOICHI'S HELL TRIP)*
1966   *DYNAMITE DOCTOR (YOIDORE HAKASE,* aka *DRUNKEN DOCTOR)*
        THE RETURN OF GIANT MAJIN (DAIMAJIN IKARU, aka *WRATH OF DAIMAJIN)*
        SWORD OF VILLAINY (NEMURI KYOSHIRO BURAI KEN, aka *KYOSHIRO NEMURI – VILLAIN SWORD)*
1967   *SHROUD OF SNOW (YUKI NO MOSHO)*
        ZATOICHI CHALLENGED (ZATOICHI CHIKEMURI KAIDO, aka *ZATOICHI'S BLOODSTAINED PATH)*

1968   *THE FUNERAL RACKET (TOMURAISHI TACHI)*
THE TWO BODYGUARDS (NIHIKI NO YOJINBO)
THE BLIND SWORDSMAN SAMARITAN (ZATOICHI KENKA DAIKO, aka
ZATOICHI AND THE BATTLE DRUM)

1969   *THE DEVIL'S TEMPLE (ONI NO SUMU YAKATA)*
THE MAGOICHI SAGA (SHIRIKURAE MAGOICHI)

1970   *WANDERING FUGITIVE SWORD (KYOJO NAGARE DOSU,* aka *THE
ANGRY SWORD)*
ZATOICHI'S FIRE FESTIVAL (ZATOICHI ABARE HIMATSURI)

1971   *WOMAN GAMBLER'S IRON RULE (SHIN ONNA TOBAKUSHI – TSUBO
GURE HADA)*

1972   *LONE WOLF AND CUB – SWORD OF VENGEANCE (KOZURE OKAMI –
KOWO KASHI UDEKASHI TSUKAMATSURU,* aka *LONE WOLF AND CUB
– SWORD AND CHILD FOR RENT)*
*LONE WOLF AND CUB – BABY CART AT THE RIVER STYX (KOZURE
OKAMI – SANZU NO KAWA NO UBAGURUMA,* aka *SHOGUN'S
ASSASSIN)*
*LONE WOLF AND CUB – BABY CART ON THE WINDS OF DEATH
(KOZURE OKAMI – SHI NI KAZE NI MUKAU UBAGURUMA,* aka
LIGHTNING SWORDS OF DEATH)
THE RAZOR – SWORD OF JUSTICE (GOYO KIBA, aka *FANGS OF PUBLIC
OFFICE)*

1973   *CHERRY BLOSSOM CREST (SAKURA NO DAIMON)*
*LONE WOLF AND CUB – PATH BETWEEN HEAVEN AND HELL (KOZURE
OKAMI – MEIFUMADO,* aka *BABY CART IN THE LAND OF DEMONS)*

1974   *THE LAST SAMURAI (OKAMI YO RAKUJITSU O KIRE,* aka *WOLF! CUT
DOWN THE SETTING SUN)*

SELECTED BIBLIOGRAPHY

Anderson, Joseph L., and Richie, Donald, *The Japanese Film – Art And Industry* (Expanded edition), Princeton, New Jersey, Princeton University Press, 1982

Bock, Audie, *Japanese Film Directors*, Tokyo/New York, Kodansha International, 1978, 1988

Desser, David, *Eros Plus Massacre – An Introduction To Japanese New Wave Cinema*, Bloomington, Indiana, Indiana University Press, 1988

Fukasaku, Kinji, and Yamane, Sadao, *Eiga Kantoku Fukasaku Kinji*, Tokyo, Waizu Shuppan, 2003

Galbraith IV, Stuart, *The Emperor And The Wolf*, New York, Faber & Faber, 2002

Hirano, Kyoko, *Mr Smith Goes To Tokyo – Japanese Cinema Under The American Occupation 1945–1952*, Washington, Smithsonian Institution Press, 1992

Hunter, Jack, *Eros In Hell – Sex, Blood And Madness In Japanese Cinema* (Creation Cinema Collection, Vol. 9), London, Creation Books International, 1998

Ishii, Teruo, and Fukuma, Kenji, *Ishii Teruo Eiga Oni*, Tokyo, Waizu Shuppan, 1992

Kato, Tai, and Kato, Sakae, *Kato Tai Eiga Bana*, Tokyo, Waizu Shuppan, 1996

Mes, Tom, *The Agitator – The Cinema Of Takashi Miike*, Godalming, United Kingdom, Fab Press, 2003

Nachi, Shiro, and Shigeto, Toshiyuki, *Yokashi Okura Shintoho*, Tokyo, Waizu Shuppan, 2001

Nozawa, Kazuma, *Nikkatsu 1954–1971*, Tokyo, Waizu Shuppan, 2000

Quandt, James (editor), *Kon Ichikawa* (Cinematheque Ontario Monograph no. 4) Waterloo, Ontario/Bloomington, Indiana, Toronto International Film Festival Group/Wilfred Laurier University Press/Indiana University Press, 2001

Quandt, James (editor), *Shohei Imamura* (Cinematheque Ontario Monograph no. 1) , Toronto, Onatario, Canada, Toronto International Film Festival Group, 1997

Sato, Tadao, *Currents In Japanese Cinema* (translated by Barrett, Gregory), New York, Kodansha International (distributed by Harper & Row), 1987

Shindo, Kaneto, and Sato, Tadao, and Miyamoto, Haruo, and Hachimori, Minoru, *Nihon Eiga 100 Nen – Miso No Collection*, Tokyo, Asahi Graph, 1995

Silver, Alain, *The Samurai Film*, Woodstock, New York, Overlook Press, 1977

Sugisaku, Jtaro, and Uechi, Takeshi, *Jinginaki Tatakai*, Tokyo, Tokuma, 1998

Sugisaku, Jtaro, and Uechi, Takeshi, *Pinky Violence – Toei's Bad Girl Films*, Tokyo, Tokuma, 1999

Suzuki, Kensuke, *Jigoku De YoiHai Nakagawa Nobuo – Kaidan-Kyofu Eiga*, Tokyo, Waizu Shuppan, 2000

Tayama, Rikiya, *Gendai Nihon Eiga No Kantokutachi*, Tokyo, Shakai Shisosha, 1991

Ueno, Koshi, *Suzuki Seijun – Zen Eiga*, Tokyo, 1986

Yamada, Seiji, *Legend Of Mitsugi Okura And Japanese Horror Film*, Tokyo, Movie Treasures Collection 3, 1997

Yamane, Sadao, et al., *Kihachi – Fubito No Aru Chizan – Okamoto Kihachi Eiga Kantoku*, Tokyo, Toho, 1992

FICTION

(English–language translations only. Authors or works mentioned in text or works of related genre interest – unfortunately most Japanese fiction and genre fiction writers have not had their works translated into English, so authors such as Goro Fujita, Koichi Iiboshi, Renzaburo Shibata, Ryotaro Shiba, et al. do not appear on this list. Writers Shotaro Ikenami and Edogawa Rampo have a phenomenal number of works to their credit, but next to none have been translated into English.)

Akutagawa, Ryunosuke, *Rashomon And Other Stories*, Rutland, Vermont/Tokyo, Charles E. Tuttle Company, 1989

Ikenami, Shotaro, *Bridge Of Darkness – Return Of The Master Assassin*, New York/Tokyo/London, Kodansha International, 1993

Ikenami, Shotaro, *Master Assassin – Tales Of Murder From The Shogun's City*, New York/Tokyo/London, Kodansha International, 1991

Hearn, Lafcadio, *In Ghostly Japan*, Rutland, Vermont/Tokyo, Charles E. Tuttle Company, 1971

Hearn, Lafcadio, *Kwaidan – Stories and Studies Of Strange Things*, Rutland, Vermont/Tokyo, Charles E. Tuttle Company, 1971

Mitford, A. B. (Lord Redesdale), *Tales Of Old Japan*, Rutland, Vermont/Tokyo, Charles E. Tuttle Company, 1966

Rampo, Edogawa, *Japanese Tales Of Mystery And Imagination*, Rutland, Vermont/Tokyo, Charles E. Tuttle Company, 1988

Ueda, Akinari (translated by Zolbrod, Leon), *Ugetsu Monogatari – Tales Of Moonlight And Rain*, Rutland, Vermont/Tokyo, Charles E. Tuttle Company, 1977

MANGA

Ito, Junji, *Flesh Colored Horror*, USA, Comics One, 2002

Ito, Junji, *Tomie 1*, USA, Comics One, 2002

Ito, Junji, *Tomie 2*, USA, Comics One, 2002

Koike, Kazuo, and Kojima, Goseki, *Lone Wolf And Cub, Vols. 1 – 28*, USA, Dark Horse Comics, 2000–2003

NON-FICTION

(Japanese outlaw subjects unrelated to film study)

Hane, Mikiso, and others (translated, edited and introduction by Hane), *Reflections On The Way To The Gallows – Rebel Women In Pre-War Japan*, Berkeley/Los Angeles, University Of California Press, 1988, 1993

Kaplan, David E., and Dubro, Alec, *Yakuza – The Explosive Account Of Japan's Criminal Underworld*, Reading, Massachusetts, Addison-Wesley, 1986

Seymour, Christopher, *Yakuza Diary*, New York, Atlantic Monthly Press, 1996

Whitehead, Robert, *Tokyo Underworld – The Fast Times And Hard Life Of An American Gangster In Japan*, New York, Random House, 1999

INDEX

258